D0894690

EDUCATION IN RURAL ENGLAND 1800–1914

Pamela Horn

Education in Rural England 1800-1914

ST. MARTIN'S PRESS   NEW YORK

Printed in Great Britain
Library of Congress Catalog Card Number 78–58415
ISBN 0–312–23727–8
First published in the United States of America in 1978

'. . . the reforming of Education . . . be one of the greatest and noblest designs that can be thought on, and for the want whereof this Nation perishes'.

'I call therefore a compleat and generous Education that which fits a man to perform justly, skilfully and magnanimously all the offices both private and publick of Peace and War.'

John Milton's *Tractate on Education*, first published in 1644 (From Cambridge 1883 ed., 1 and 8.)

Contents

List of Illustrations

Acknowledgments

I should like to thank all those who have helped in the preparation of this book, either by providing material or in other ways. In particular, my thanks are due to the Social Science Research Council for help in the initial stages of this project and to the staff at the libraries and record offices in which I have worked. These include the Bodleian Library, Oxford, the British Library, the Library of the Department of Education and Science, the Library of the National Union of Teachers, the Museum of English Rural Life, Reading, the Public Record Office, London, Lincoln reference library, and county record offices for Berkshire, Buckinghamshire, Cambridgeshire, Dorset, Essex, Gloucestershire, Hampshire, Northamptonshire, Oxfordshire and Warwickshire. I am indebted to them for much efficient assistance, as also to the staff at Oxfordshire education office. I am equally indebted to the librarians and staff at the various colleges of education at which I have worked, including Culham College, Oxford, the College of St Matthias, Bristol, King Alfred's College, Winchester, Borough Road College, London, Westminster College, Oxford, and St Paul's College, Cheltenham. All have generously made their records available.

The editors of the *Oxford Times* and the *Western Morning News* have kindly inserted appeals for reminiscences and photographs of Victorian and Edwardian school life and I am grateful to them and to all those who so kindly answered these appeals. Some of the material they sent has been incorporated in the book and is acknowledged in notes to the relevant chapters and in the bibliography. I especially enjoyed my visit to Mrs F. A. Bowkett of Banbury, who, at the age of 102, was able to give a fascinating account of life as a school head at the end of the last century. I am grateful to her for the time she gave to me, and to Mr A. R.

Wise of Abingdon College and Mr Goodway of Banbury for arranging the interview.

Finally, I owe a debt of gratitude to my family for help in the preparation of the book. My mother, indeed, has given much help on village school life in the early years of the present century, while my sister-in-law, Mrs M. Horn, has provided many interesting photographs of school life. But my greatest debt, as always, is to my husband, who has helped in many different ways —not least by his criticisms of my work. Without his assistance neither this nor any of my books could have been written.

PAMELA HORN
December 1977

Schools and Teachers of the Old Type

Attendance in a school enures children to a requisite degree of
restraint, and a division of time; employs their minds, and
prevents idleness, and other vicious habits, from taking root:
thus tending to raise them to the rank of RATIONAL BEINGS.
—While the unfortunate offspring of indigence, that are suffered
to loiter away their early days, on commons, in lanes, and bye
places, acquire habits, of indolence and pilfering; give a loose to
their own wills, and unrestrained tempers; commit acts of MIS-
CHIEF; and add to them the GUILT OF LYING (the seedbud
of FRAUD); to skreen them from correction.
   The discipline of a well governed school impresses, on youthful minds, SUBORDINATION, INDUSTRY, PATIENCE, and
its consequent, PERSEVERENCE; and thus *habituates* them to
RECEIVE INSTRUCTIONS.
   WILLIAM MARSHALL, *The Review and Abstract of the County
Reports to the Board of Agriculture,* vol. 5, York 1818, 575.

I think that the want of adequate qualifications in schoolmasters
is almost a national disgrace; but how can it be otherwise while
we have no system for educating schoolmasters at all adequate
to the wants of the people? . . . I fear that multitudes who are
without occupation are anxious to be employed as teachers, to
get their bread.
   Evidence of the Rev. John Blackburn to the *Select Committee
on Education in England and Wales,* Parliamentary Papers
1835, vol. VII, Q.663–664.

A NECESSARY preliminary to any discussion of the growth of
elementary education in the nineteenth century is some account
of developments in the period that went before. For although
such a survey can do little more than indicate the major
trends involved, it will help to fit the problems of Victorian
England into their historical context. To this end, it is necessary
to turn back to the momentous events of the sixteenth century
—for the great religious upheavals of that era also had their effect
on schooling. At the same time, the importance of education
was clearly recognised by Tudor society. 'Better unborn than

untaught' was a favourite Elizabethan maxim[1]—though this did not prevent the majority of sixteenth-century Englishmen from regarding children as diminutive and troublesome adults who must be trained in the way they should go by strict discipline, reinforced when necessary by beatings.

For the better-off members of society the important business of learning one's letters might be carried on in the home under the care of a tutor or domestic chaplain, who might also prepare his charges for entry to university. The widespread practice among the nobility and gentry of sending their sons and sometimes their daughters to board in other gentle households meant that a tutor could have under his charge a miniature private school.[2] In such cases more than mere booklearning would be absorbed. The social graces—the correct way to behave at table or to ride, fence, dance and play musical instruments—would be carefully inculcated, too, fitting the youngsters for their future position in the world. Later, perhaps like Anthony St Leger, who was born in 1496, the eldest son of a Kentish squire, a boy might be sent abroad for a time in order to complete his education. Antony left England at the age of twelve, travelling 'for his grammar learning with his tutor into France, for his carriage into Italy,' and returning 'for his philosophy to Cambridge, for his law to Gray's Inn; and for that which completed all, the government of himself, to court'.[3]

For those a little lower down the scale there were various endowed schools, including such long-established lay foundations as Winchester and Eton. And although many of the schools based on religious institutions were destroyed or disrupted by the Reformation, secular endowments, like Harrow, Tonbridge and Shrewsbury, flourished in their stead, along with the reformed cathedral schools and the countless smaller foundations which were set up in towns throughout the country. In some places, like Sherborne in Dorset or Abingdon, then in Berkshire, the townspeople themselves helped to salvage schools which had been left without status as the abbeys to which they were attached were dissolved. While at Tavistock, where there had formerly been a school in connection with the abbey, it was decided in 1553 to pay £10 a year to a schoolmaster out of the profits of two yearly fairs which had been granted by letters patent shortly beforehand.[4] 'There are not many corporate towns now under the Queen's dominion', wrote an observer in 1577, 'that have not one grammar school at the least.'[5]

Although some of the more modest of these concentrated on instructing their pupils in the use of English and in giving them a working knowledge of the more practical aspects of mathematics and account-keeping, most had a curriculum confined almost entirely 'to classical linguistics and grammar, together with the usual religious instruction'.[6] By modern standards the school day was cruelly long, beginning at 6 a.m. in summer and 7 a.m. in winter and lasting for eight to ten hours. Holidays, mostly at Christmas and Easter, occupied only four or five weeks in the year. Small wonder that a contemporary complained in 1582 : 'The grammar school is a heavy and tedious school.'

At the universities, too, Latin formed the principal language of study, with dialectic, rhetoric, mathematics and theology the major subjects covered, although Greek and Hebrew played their part to a lesser degree, as did astronomy and music. Specialist courses were prescribed for those studying in the faculties of medicine and civil law. After the religious difficulties and the decline in student numbers during the 1530s, undergraduates began to increase once more at both Oxford and Cambridge during the third quarter of the sixteenth century and again in the early years of the seventeenth, so that by the 1630s there were perhaps 4,000 students at university, out of a total population of just over four million.[7] However, save for those who wished to enter the Church of England as clerics, both universities had become by this date largely the preserve of the well-to-do young man without particular scholastic ambitions who was interested chiefly in personal cultivation and gentlemanly accomplishments.

Nevertheless in the second half of the sixteenth century both grammar schools and universities played their part in advancing the Reformation and English protestantism, as a number of the students began to question the old order and to believe that in the last resort a man must follow the dictates of his own conscience. At St John's College, Cambridge, in the early 1570s it was complained that there was 'almost never a Boye . . . which hathe not in his head a platform of a churche'. By many English protestants, and especially the puritans, education was seen as an essential weapon in the fight against Roman Catholicism and the 'three great evils of Ignorance, Prophaneness and Idleness'. Such men were 'convinced of the need to spread the word of God and expose the shallowness of the aesthetic and emotional attractions of Popery'.[8] As one writer urged in 1635: 'Erection of Grammar Schooles is a worke as farre transcending and surpassing the foundation and building of Almes-houses as the instruction of the minde doth excell in outward relieving and sustentation of the bodie.'

Not surprisingly when seeking masters for their foundations most trustees were anxious to appoint men of religious orthodoxy and suitable moral character. At the Free Grammar School of Wakefield—founded by a family of merchants turned gentlemen, in the 1590s—the master was to be an M.A. and one

> withal well reported of for his knowledge, religion and life, and known to be an enemy to popish superstition, a lover and forward imbracer of God's truth, a man . . . diligent and painful in his own studies, of a sober and amiable carriage towards all men, able to maintain the place of a schoolmaster with dignity and gravity, given to the diligent reading of God's word.[9]

His first aim should be 'to instruct and inform his scholars in the grounds of religion', and to this end he must examine them on Saturdays, accompany them to church on Sundays and ensure that notes of sermons were taken, which would be corrected on Monday. He must also 'in the plainest and most familiar sort teach them grammar, and the Latin and Greek tongues, reading unto them the most classic authors'. The final task required was that of 'informing his youth in good nurture and manners which are of themselves an ornament to religion and good learning'. At Chigwell School, which was founded by Archbishop Harsnett of York in 1629, the master was to be 'of a sound religion, neither papist nor puritan, of a grave behaviour, of a sober and honest conversation, no tippler nor haunter of alehouses, no puffer of tobacco; and above all . . . apt to teach and severe in his government.'[10]

Yet despite these careful academic provisions, for the mass of the population they had little relevance. Relatively few boys from humble backgrounds were able to study at one of the larger endowed schools, let alone at university—despite the opportunities for 'poor scholars' to enter Oxford and Cambridge as 'servitors' and 'sizars', and to perform menial services in return for the charity of the college.[11] The Inns of Court, as centres for the burgeoning legal profession, were even more the preserve of the well-to-do—the 'finishing schools for the gentry', as one writer has put it.[12] It is with the position of that majority of the population living for the most part in villages and country towns that this book is concerned. It is to them that we must now turn.

The education of the children of the poor in rural England had always been a haphazard affair, dependent for its existence upon the ebb and flow of local circumstances and upon the degree of interest taken in school provision by village clergy and squires, or, more rarely, parents themselves.[13] In many cases, even where schools did exist, the limited means of the inhabitants, living at or near subsistence level, made it difficult for families either to afford school fees or to forgo their children's labour and earnings when the opportunity to work offered itself. This was especially true during the periods of sharp price rises in the middle and later years of the sixteenth century. As Robert Crowley pointed out in his *Petition against the Oppressors of the Poor Commons of this Realm*, addressed to Parliament in 1548, many youngsters were compelled to turn to handicrafts and day labour to sustain their parents and so prevented from completing their education. He blamed these problems on higher rents and the 'eviction of poorer tenants, enclosures of all kind', which were set in hand by a new class of avaricious landlords.

At the beginning of the sixteenth century—as in earlier times —the responsibility for education rested primarily upon the Church, despite a growing lay involvement in school provision. Through the parish clergy or their clerks those children free to attend learnt to read in English and to receive religious instruction. Some might cover a wider curriculum, including Latin. Thomas Cranmer, who went to Cambridge in 1503 at the age of fourteen, was one of many who had 'learned his grammar of a rude parish clerk'; in his case from the village of Aslockton in Nottinghamshire.[14] But in other cases the limited education of the instructors precluded any such ambitious plans.

This close association between the clergy and education was reinforced in 1557, during Queen Mary's reign, by the action of

Cardinal Pole in reviving the ancient prerogative of bishops to grant a licence to teach.[15] It was a measure which Elizabeth found it advisable to retain after her own accession, for it presented a ready means of ensuring the spread of uniformity through instruction in the catechism. In addition from 1571 all those clergy who were not preachers were ordered 'to teach the children to read and write', though in practice, especially in the next century, this duty was more likely to devolve upon the humble parish clerk or the curate than upon the incumbent himself. Indeed, under the 78th Canon of 1604, the parish curate, if he were a master of arts or bachelor of arts, was to enjoy the sole right of receiving a licence to teach, 'for the better increase of his living and training up of children in principles of true religion'.[16]

Nor did such regulations eliminate unlicensed masters. As early as 1578 there were complaints in the Durham diocese 'that the injunction . . . requiring that masters obtain a licence to teach was by no means always observed; several schoolmasters, even in established schools, were without one.'[17] And at Reculver in Kent one man, presented at the archdeacon's visitation in 1619 for teaching without a licence, confirmed that not only had he been so engaged but his wife, also unlicensed, 'by the minister's consent, teacheth two or three children their hornbooks'.[18] (These latter were reading sheets mounted on a wooden tablet and protected from the sticky fingers of the children by a thin covering of horn.)

During the second half of the seventeenth century, the licensing system was for a time strengthened, when following the disruptions of the Civil War and interregnum, the restoration of the monarchy in 1660 led to the passage of a series of regulatory Acts, known as the Clarendon Code. These were intended to purge church, government—and education—of dissidents. Their stringency may have stemmed in part from a desire to counteract legislation passed in 1649 under the Commonwealth, whereby funds had been diverted from the Church of England for the support of schoolmasters and ministers and to permit the establishment of sixty free schools in Wales. Although the actual financial aid received by education was limited by the heavy military expenditure of the 1650s, the restoration government after 1660 was clearly anxious to eliminate possible opponents who may have been nurtured by Commonwealth policies. Under the Clarendon Code, therefore, all schoolmasters were required to subscribe to a declaration of conformity to the Church of England's liturgy and to obtain a bishop's licence. The penalty for those who taught unlicensed was imprisonment and fine. In the thirty or forty years that followed, episcopal licensing was enforced more rigidly than hitherto, although the zeal with which it was applied varied from diocese to diocese, according to the attitude of individual bishops. Such protestant nonconformist schools as there were, catering mainly for the children of better-off dissenters, were fugitive institutions, often set up in country parishes, where they could hope to evade the attentions of local justices of the peace. Not until the Toleration Act of 1689, granting freedom of worship to this section of the population, did the position ease, with the penalties against unlicensed teaching, though unrepealed, now becoming largely inoperative. From the end of the seventeenth century, therefore, academies were established by Independents, Presbyterians and Congregationalists in such rural centres as Hungerford in Berkshire, Lyme Regis in Dorset and Newport Pagnell in Buckinghamshire. So, for protestants at least, the bishop's courts were little exercised in the eighteenth century, though action was occasionally taken—perhaps by hearing parents' complaints against a master's brutality towards his charges or his neglect of his duties. In 1729, for example, the York consistory court investigated allegations that the master of Knottingley had neglected his school since taking up work as a part-time exciseman.[19] But cases like this were already rare and became rarer as the century advanced.

For Roman Catholics, however, the position was very different. As one writer has put it : 'from the Elizabethan Religious Settlement of 1558–63 down to the first Relief Act of 1778, the policy of the Government had been to make a Catholic education in England impossible'.[20] Such schools as did exist were, therefore, established clandestinely. Swithin Wells, a member of the household of the Earl of Southampton during the 1570s and a prominent participant in a protective organisation for receiving and helping priests, was one who for a time ran a school in the neighbourhood of his patron's property. In other cases, as at Little Crosby in Lancashire about a century and a quarter later, Robert Aldred, chaplain to Nicholas Blundell, the local landowner, began to give catechism instruction to the village children after Vespers. And at Burstwick, in East Yorkshire, in 1735 there was a mixed school kept in a private house by a Catholic convert and suspected priest named Richard Rand. But in general, 'the hint of a popish school was enough to stir the Anglican authorities to action, and the Catholic gentry was highly sensitive to threats of trouble if they allowed one on their estates; under such pressure, the Fairfaxes removed from Gilling [Yorkshire] a Benedictine who seems to have set up a school there.'[21] Not until 1778 was the threat of perpetual imprisonment lifted from Catholic schoolmasters, provided they took an oath of allegiance, and another thirteen years were to elapse before the final abolition of penal restraint on the exercise of the Catholic religion in England.

Meanwhile, for those Elizabethans who had supported the Reformation there were in some parishes, alongside the grammar and church schools already mentioned, minor charitable endowments under which the incumbent could add a few pounds to his stipend by keeping a school, or could appoint a master to keep it in his place. In other cases there were small, short-lived establishments kept by the sexton or the bell-ringer, who would be remunerated from parish funds and pupils' fees. Or perhaps, as one critic noted, village schooling would depend on 'poor women . . . whose necessities compel them to undertake it, as a meer shelter from beggary'.[22] It is significant that Edmund Coote in his book, *The English Schoolmaster*, published in 1596, addressed it to 'such men and women of trades (as tailors, weavers, shopkeepers, seamsters and such other) as have undertaken the charge of teaching others'. For in the eyes of most Elizabethans, as of their successors, 'grounding the little ones' in their alphabet was an employment to be taken up only as a last resort by the financially desperate. And it was instructors of this calibre who were particularly likely to swell the ranks of the 'unlicensed' teachers.

At best the schooling provided was limited to equipping the youngsters to read the Bible and possibly to write and to cast accounts. The methods by which reading and writing were taught in Tudor times were crude but simple, with the children first learning the alphabet, and then putting together vowels and consonants—*ag, eg, ig, og, ug.* Next they went on to 'diphthongs and longer combinations of letters, gradually picking up the art in the dullest and most mechanical way possible.'[23] For their writing lessons they would be provided with carefully penned 'copies', perhaps produced by the local scrivener, which it was their duty to imitate as best they could.

The variable nature of educational provision in any given area is confirmed by investigation at parish level. In Cambridgeshire only twenty villages had no schoolmaster licensed at any time between 1574 and 1628, but in a number of the remainder the facilities were not continuously available. At Over, to quote but one example, there was a master licensed to teach in 1583. In 1604 another man had taken his place and remained a few years, but then there was a gap until 1616, when the vicar assumed the office of master.[24] Usually these schools would be conducted in a cottage or in part of the church, as at Westport near Malmesbury, where Thomas Hobbes, the philosopher, first attended in 1592, learning to 'read well and number four figures' before he was eight.[25] More than a century later Bishop Nicolson of Carlisle was deploring this practice of using the church, whilst reluctantly acceding to it. Thus at Crosby on Eden : 'the school-master . . . teaches . . . in the choir, where the boys and girls sit on good wainscot benches, and write on the Communion Table'. Or at Westward, where he was glad 'to find the curate . . . surrounded with so good a number of scholars; though I could have wished to have seen them elsewhere than in the chancel, and spoiling Mr Barwis's monument . . . with writing their copies upon it'.[26]

Episcopal visitation returns for the early eighteenth century show that the problem of inadequate school provision was equally characteristic of that period. The visitation articles for the Oxford Diocese in 1738 show, for example, that out of a total of 179 parishes making returns, only fifty-three mentioned a school. And some of these were of little value, like the endowed school at Bladon near Woodstock. Here a salary of £20 per annum was paid to the teacher, although in the opinion of the vicar it was 'little other than a Sine-Cure to the Master Mr Du Bois who, I think, was a French Refugee and has been admitted to degrees and Orders at Oxford.'[27] However, as the appointment was the responsibility of Woodstock corporation, he felt unable to intervene. The position at Standlake in the same county was equally unsatisfactory, with the incumbent reporting an endowment of £6 per annum to teach fifteen children to read and write,

> and I make an addition to have five more, give them all Catechism Books and oblige ye master to teach them. This is too poor a salary yt none of Your Lordship's predecessors ever obliged ye Master to take a Licence and it has been fortunate for me because three behaved so ill yt I was forced to remove them and I have had so many complaints of ye present Master I shall soon remove him, but if he takes a Licence I cannot do it without trouble and expense in Yr. Lordship's Court.

Nor had provision in the county improved very much two decades later. For of 163 parish returns which have survived from the 1759 visitations a mere forty-one mention a school. Some of these were also very limited—like that at Saresden, where the rector noted : 'There are 20 Boys kept at School by Mr Walter, who are taught to read, till they are fit to go to service, or otherways able to earn their living', while from another incumbent came the comment : 'The Dean allows a poor Woman at Little Haseley forty Shillings p. an. with the Liberty of living in a House Rent-free for teaching five Children to read.'[28]

Even in Yorkshire the situation, though more satisfactory than in Oxfordshire, left much to be desired. For of 645 returns made at the time of Archbishop Herring's primary visitation of the York diocese in 1743, only 379 reported a school of any kind, and clearly some of these existed on an intermittent basis only : 'There is no . . . regular school,' noted one cleric. 'The clerk undertakes to teach such as come to him; but he is very oft without any scholars.'[29]

Nevertheless an attempt had already been made to improve this spasmodic educational provision with the establishment in 1698 of the Society for Promoting Christian Knowledge. This sought to encourage, for the first time, the setting up of charity schools on a systematic basis throughout the country. They were to cater for children aged seven to eleven (and occasionally even to fourteen), 'whom nature or failure had determined to the plough, the oar and other handicrafts'.[30] As its name suggests, the principal aim was to encourage religious feeling by instructing poor children 'in reading the Bible and the catechism'. The Bible formed the chief reading book in the schools and was the basis of all exercises, although prayer books and religious tracts were distributed as well. Indeed, for the Society's principal founder, a Church of England clergyman named Dr Thomas Bray, one of the main objectives of the whole enterprise was the propagation of the gospel and of Anglicanism both at home and in the colonies. Bray believed that by the establishment of schools the rising tide of 'Vice and Debauchery' which seemed so apparent, especially in London, could be reversed and the correct moral sentiments instilled into the new generation. In founding the SPCK Bray was assisted by four laymen—his friend, Colonel Colchester, who had earlier set up a charity school on his estate at Westbury-on-Severn, Mr Justice Hook, Lord Guilford, the son of Charles II's Lord Keeper North, and Sir Humphrey Mackworth, MP for Cardiganshire, 'who combined his interest in education for children with company promotion of a questionable character'.[31] From the beginning the Society's operations were decentralised, and its provincial supporters and correspondents were urged to raise money for their own institutions by subscriptions or even, in a few cases, by the proceeds of the sale of lottery tickets. Although the initiative for the setting up of a school normally came from well-disposed local clergy, the subscribers covered a wider spectrum of tradesmen, merchants and landed gentry. In fact, the SPCK organisers advocated the new subscription method precisely 'because it allowed men of moderate means to contribute to the schools', although they did not exclude from membership the managers and trustees of schools supported wholly or principally by endowments.[32]

But if the instruction of poor children in 'the principles of the Christian Religion' was the major plank in the Society's platform, it also carried with it strong overtones of moral discipline and of the social subordination expected from those under its guidance. 'In the hymns they sang, the prayers they recited and the sermons they had to listen to, the charity children were constantly reminded of their low estate and the duty and respect they owed their betters.'[33] As Miss M. G. Jones put it in her book, *The Charity School Movement*: 'The . . . schools came into being chiefly, although by no means exclusively . . . to *condition* the children for their primary duty in life as hewers of wood and drawers of water.' Already, therefore, elementary education was seen as an instrument for social engineering, as a means of disciplining the potentially recalcitrant and of fitting a man or woman for the station in life into which he or she had been born.

Yet despite the energy with which the SPCK pursued its objectives over the next thirty or so years, its achievements, especially in the villages, were limited. In part this was a result of the shortage of funds in country areas to provide even the very modest standard of instruction deemed adequate for the poor; in part it was due to a lack of teachers to provide that instruction. In 1704 the qualifications thought desirable for a master in the new charity schools were listed by the Society. He was to be:

1. A member of the Church of England, of a sober life and conversation, and not under the age of twenty-five years.

2. One that frequents Holy Communion.

3. One that hath a Good Government of himself and his Passions.

4. One of a meek Temper and humble behaviour.

5. One of a good Genius for teaching.

6. One who understands well the Grounds and Principles of the Christian Religion, and is able to give a good Account thereof to the Minister of the Parish or Ordinary on Examination.

7. One that can write a good Hand, and who understands the Grounds of Arithmetic.

8. One who keeps good order in his family.

9. One who is approved by the Minister of the Parish (being a subscriber) before he be presented to be Licensed by the Ordinary.[34]

Women teachers were expected to possess the same moral attributes, although in their case skill with knitting and 'plane needlework' was required rather than an ability to teach writing and arithmetic. Both masters and mistresses were to lead their pupils to service twice on Sunday and on every Holy Day. They were to carry their Bibles with them 'bound up with the Common Prayer', while each morning, afternoon and evening the 'master was to say prayers in the school and teach his pupils to pray at home'.[35]

Yet, despite these guidelines, in most villages it proved difficult to obtain suitably qualified and experienced candidates to fill the vacancies in the new schools. Those well enough equipped preferred the higher salaries available in larger towns or in London itself to the uncertain tenure, low status and poor pay which went with country teaching. So, despite attempts to raise the level of tuition, often the parish clerk, the village dame and the private-venture schoolmaster were retained to teach the catechism, reading and writing in the new schools, as they had been in the old. And, as before, their efforts were hampered by the poor attendance of the scholars and the brevity of their school life, with two years the maximum length to be expected for the majority.

Perhaps the harshest condemnation of charity school teachers came in the 1720s from the bitter pen of Bernard Mandeville, when he claimed that they were recruited from 'the starving Wretches of both Sexes . . . that from a natural antipathy to Working, have a great Dislike to their present Employment, and perceiving within a much stronger Inclination to Command than ever they felt to Obey others, think themselves qualify'd, and wish from their Hearts to be Masters and Mistresses of Charity Schools'.[36]

But if the main success of the charity school movement lay in the towns, rather than in the rural areas, there were some advances in the countryside too. One of the most remarkable to be inspired by the SPCK was the Welsh circulating school system which developed in about 1730 under the influence of Griffith Jones, rector of Llanddowror in Carmarthenshire:

> He raised, trained and organised a missionary band of unpaid itinerant teachers who travelled round the countryside conducting day and night schools in Welsh for young and old in church, chapel and farmhouse during the three or four months of the year when field work was slack. Religious instruction was the primary concern, and reading was simply a means to this. Soon after his death in 1761 there were 279 schools scattered throughout Wales, but the movement petered out after his successor died in 1779.[37]

However, in about 1786 Jones's ideas were revived by another Welsh cleric, Thomas Charles, who had changed from being a Church of England clergyman to a preacher with the Welsh

Calvinistic Methodists shortly beforehand. As he subsequently confided to William Wilberforce, he had been shocked to find 'large Districts lying wholly in darkness, without one Person in them that could read in any Language' and whose children lacked instruction 'in the first principles of Religion'. On his own initiative he decided to employ a teacher—at a salary of £10 per annum—to try to remedy some of these deficiencies and by 1793 had managed to gain sufficient support for fourteen more instructors to be engaged, also at £10 per annum. The teachers remained in a community for about six to nine months until the children had learned to read their Bibles, before moving on. For as Charles proudly proclaimed : 'In these Schools every thing is excluded but what has a direct tendency to promote ye Salvation of the Soul. Children are taught to read their Bibles well; are instructed in ye first principle of Divine Truth, according to a little form which I have drawn up for them; taught ye church Catechism. The Teachers are all men of genuine piety, & of good report for their exemplary lives and devotedness to God. They pray & sing Psalms & Hymns with ye children three or four Times a day, and are to do all in their power to impress their young Minds with a due sense of Divine & eternal things. Every Teacher is hired as a Servant. He and his Time are entirely at my disposal, to send him where I think proper & to remove him at pleasure.'[38] Charles's work continued into the nineteenth century, when it merged with the Sunday school movement, while he was also active in promoting the publication of the Bible in the Welsh language, his efforts being instrumental in bringing about the formation of the British and Foreign Bible Society.

Other successful experiments—at least in the eyes of contemporaries—were the 'working schools' at Finedon and Artleborough in Northamptonshire. At the former, the girls were set to work spinning, as well as being taught to read, and were 'lodged and wholly maintained by their labour'. At Artleborough, too, the children learned to read, knit and spin, this time under the direction of a redoubtable mistress named Mrs Harris. Their working day began at 5 a.m. or 6 a.m. in summer and at 6 a.m. or 7 a.m. in winter and continued until about 9 p.m. in the summer and 8 p.m. in the winter. Much of the scholars' time was spent in manual labour, with the products they made sold to dealers in Northampton and Wellingborough. But their intellectual and spiritual development was not neglected, 'the children learning the catechism and prayer book and collects for the day with other good lessons in such a way that they were no hindrance to their manual work'. After harvest, Mrs Harris took her charges into the beanfields, where they gathered enough stubble to serve as firing through the winter, and on Sundays 'she listened to the "Heavenly music of the children", who sang "handsomely cloathed, the greatest part of their own getting" in the gallery of the parish church, erected specially for them by public subscription'. The townspeople were well able to afford this gift of a gallery, for 'the profits of the school was a benefit estimated at a figure between £500 and £600 per annum to the town'.[39]

Few other rural educational establishments could attain such dizzy financial heights as these. Indeed, it was more usual for the clothing of charity children, when supplied at all, to be financed by public subscription or endowment, in the same way as their education. This was the case at Chelmsford, where in 1790 the boys were provided with a blue uniform and stout buckled shoes, while the girls wore yellow gowns and straw hats.[40] Similarly, the Rev. J. Curtis in his *Topographical History of the County of Leicester*, published in 1831, noted that at Barwell there was 'a Green Coat School' endowed with £26 per annum 'for clothing and educating twenty boys', while at Prestwould in the same county, endowments provided for the education and clothing of sixteen boys—six of whom were to be dressed in blue. There are numerous other examples. For its part, the SPCK recommended that charity children should always wear distinctive bands, caps or clothes so that 'Trustees may know them and watch their conduct abroad'.[41]

Meanwhile at the older parish schools which still survived in many communities there were similar difficulties over staffing and pupils' attendances to those which were experienced by their SPCK-inspired competitors. All too often the private enterprise 'dame schools', run by elderly and impoverished men and women as a means of earning a living when they were unfit for manual labour, provided the only instruction available. The fee they charged of a half-penny or a penny per week was their only protection against destitution. F. A. Wendeborn, a German observer of English life in the 1780s, was one who commented on how many schools were set up by failed tradesmen or 'a woman, who never had a proper education herself, or whose moral character cannot very well bear a strict enquiry'.[42] He confessed himself surprised that while a rich man 'when he has a horse to be broken in, or a dog to be trained, will carefully enquire whether the person he entrusts them with, is properly qualified for the business; but, this is not always the case with parents, when they place their children to be educated.' His doubts about such schools were certainly confirmed by one elderly 'dame' who frankly admitted in 1840 : 'It is but little they pays me, and it is but little I teach them.'[43] And it is worth remembering that as late as 1851 a third of all children attending school in England were private day scholars—many of them doubtless attending institutions of the 'dame school' calibre.[44]

Pupils' reminiscences confirm the weaknesses, with many 'mistresses' doing little more than mind the children of their neighbours, perhaps when they were out at work. William Cobbett, for example, had 'some faint recollection' of attending a school at Farnham during the 1760s, where 'an old woman . . . I believe, did not succeed in teaching me my letters'. In his case the omission was rectified by his father, a farmer, who taught him to read and write 'and gave me a pretty tolerable knowledge of arithmetic'.[45] A similar lack of achievement was recorded by Thomas Hall of Farnborough near Banbury when he attended an establishment kept in the 1820s by 'Old Dame Neal' : 'I was one of the Dame's scholars but I do not remember any [of] the lessons she taught me except to touch my forehead with my finger and say "Sarrvant Dame" when I entered or left the school, the punishment for omitting this was three taps on the head with the Dame's thimble, which she called "thimble pie".'[46]

Then there was the aged Gertrude Aram, known as 'Old Gatty', who kept a school in her small cottage at the market town of Gainsborough in Lincolnshire early in the nineteenth century. One of her pupils, the future Chartist leader Thomas Cooper (1805–92), attended from 1809 and recalled that 'Old Gatty'

> was an expert and laborious teacher of the art of reading and spelling. Her knitting, too—for she taught girls as well as boys—was the wonder of the town. I soon became her favourite scholar, and could read the tenth chapter of Nehemiah, with

all its hard names, "like the parson in the church,"—as she used to say,—and could spell wondrously.[47]

Such accomplishments were characteristic of the dame schools, and it is interesting that when Cooper himself was forced by ill-health to abandon the trade of shoemaker, he also turned to teaching. With the help of friends he opened a school in a large club-room at Gainsborough in 1828, when he was in his early twenties. Initially his working hours were extremely long, commencing at 5 a.m., when he had quill pens to make 'in great number . . . and for a time I had early classes each morning. Then again, in the evenings, although other day-schools broke up at five, I drew the elder scholars around the globe, and described the countries upon it, until a late hour, or talked to them on some part of history, or described the structures of animals'. He even tried to teach Latin to a few of his pupils, supplying them with 'copies of declensions and conjugations written out on sheets of paper, with lists of the prepositions, and so on', and required the boys to learn these off by heart. But his ambitions soon aroused the opposition of parents, who told him firmly : 'I want our Jack to larn to write a good hand. What's the use of his larning Latin? It will nivver be no use to him.'[48] Increasingly discouraged by parental hostility, Cooper eventually left Gainsborough in 1833. But if the broad scope of his curriculum was untypical of the 'dame schools' of his day, the method he adopted—learning by rote—and his own lack of training for the job, were all too characteristic.

Perhaps still more surprising was the career of William Brown, who left the Royal Navy in 1816 after spending 'thirteen years on Board His Majesty's Ships'. Within a month or two of his discharge he arrived in the Yorkshire parish of Middleham where, having run out of funds, he decided to set up a school. He hired a small room and painted a sign bearing the legend 'a Day School by William Brown', which he placed in the window : 'I lay on a chaff bed on the floor having no bedstead; I had a board by the side and another at the bottom to prevent my rolling off. I got some sticks and boring some holes in the boards they served for forms by day, and finding a piece of broken spoon it served as a pencil, one of the form legs supplying the want of a ruler. I soon got scholars to the number of sixteen.' If parents were prepared to pay fees for instruction like this, then the cry of Mr Brown's land-lady must, indeed, have been true : 'if you begin I'll uphold you will get forty scholars, poor people's *baines* can get no *larning*'. In fact, a few months after setting up the school he had to move to larger premises, for as he subsequently noted : 'My number of scholars has often exceeded the predicted number of forty.' Almost twelve years later, when he came to write his auto-biography, he was still in business at Middleham.[49]

Not all dame schools were of this poor quality, however, and as early as 1840 the Rev. John Allen, one of Her Majesty's Inspectors of Schools, could distinguish between the lower-class establishments and 'those kept by persons fond of children, and of cleanly and orderly habits'. He considered that these, no matter how 'scanty may be their means of imparting instruction . . . cannot altogether fail at attaining some of the highest ends of education, as regards the formation of character'. The Rev. James Fraser, writing two decades later, considered that there were so many 'useful and even efficient' dame schools, that 'it would be both unfair and untrue to throw them as a class under any one general term of description'.

Nonetheless, in very many cases the office of elementary school teacher continued to be held in the early nineteenth century by those who for reasons of age, infirmity or other disability were unable to obtain employment elsewhere. In 1847, T. B. Macaulay could castigate a high proportion of schools as consisting of

> nothing more than a dirty room, with a heap of fuel on one side, and a brood of chickens on the other; where the only instruments for instruction are a dog's-eared spelling-book and a broken slate . . . And as for the masters . . . how many of these men are . . . the refuse of other callings—discarded ser-vants, or ruined tradesmen; who cannot do a sum of three; who would not be able to write a common letter; who do not know whether the earth is a cube or a sphere, and cannot tell whether Jerusalem is in Asia or America : whom no gentle-man would trust with the key of his cellar, and no tradesman would send [on] a message?[50]

Another critic, Mr H. K. Seymer, MP for Dorset, contemptuously concluded that men 'were generally made schoolmasters because they were unfit for anything else. If a man lost a leg or an arm, the first thing he did was to look for a turnpike; or, failing an empty turnpike, he next applied for the situation of a village schoolmaster, and very often with success.'[51] Only a 'bad moral character' might prove an effective barrier.

Scholastic achievements certainly appear to have been of minor significance when such appointments were made, and in some cases it is clear that the post of teacher in the village school was handed over to unemployed or elderly persons solely to prevent them from becoming a burden on the poor rates. At one Derbyshire parish, in the early years of the nineteenth century a boy of fifteen was appointed parish schoolmaster, 'with a view to giving his mother and family some means of support'. Almost thirty years later he was still in the job, enjoying an endowment of around £35 per annum, although in the view of one of Her Majesty's Inspectors of Schools he was 'utterly inefficient'.[52]

Begbroke in Oxfordshire provided another variation on the same theme. In July 1818 the villagers decided that a school should be established in the parish, and soon settled on the local poor house as a suitable venue, with the tenant of the house, a widow, to be appointed mistress. Initially she resisted this attempt to saddle her with the instruction of the village children but when she was informed that the only alternative was eviction from her home she finally agreed. She was to be paid 'at 6s. per week all the year round, except for 6 weeks at Hay & Corn Harvest, when she is to go afield' for 'her own profit'. This weekly sum was to be provided by the parishioners, but in addition each of the scholars was to pay her a half-penny per week and in this fashion it was estimated that she would earn an average weekly amount of 7s.[53] The quality of the teaching she provided is only too easy to imagine.

At early nineteenth-century Whittlesford in Cambridgeshire a different method was tried. Here in 1723 an endowment of £15 per annum had been established under the Will of William Westley, a Cambridge grocer, to cover the salary of a 'sober, grave, honest man, not under the age of 25', who was to act as schoolmaster, while the sum of £5 was allowed for a 'grave, sober woman not under the age of 30 years' to act as mistress. The school was to cater for thirty boys and fifteen girls, with the master teaching the boys reading, writing and 'casting accounts', and the mistress giving instruction to the girls in reading, sewing,

B

knitting, or 'other such work' as the trustees and managers of the school thought fit. By 1771 the holders of the posts were the parish clerk and his wife, but though the former seems to have carried out his duties satisfactorily until his retirement in 1805, his wife proved unsuitable even by the lax standards of the eighteenth century.[54] Nine years after her appointment the villagers began to complain that she was a 'poor, indigent, mean, illiterate, proud person, who did not know how to knit or sew, nor scarce could read, therefore to learn the poor children she could not, and though poor she was so eaten up with pride that to try to learn them she would not'. At first the managers ignored the villagers' protests but after an anonymous letter had been placed in the key-hole of the church door, complaining that they would not 'protect and relieve, but prolong the poor illiterate and helpless children in their ignorant condition', action was taken. The mistress was given notice and was replaced by the mother of the village shoemaker. Despite this unpromising background she remained at the school until 1827.

Meanwhile in selecting her male colleague from 1805 the managers decided to appoint a wounded naval veteran, Joshua Macer, who had lost an arm at the battle of Copenhagen and so received a service disablement pension to add to the £25 per annum paid to him as master. According to a report by the Charity Commissioners in 1830, the school was at that time 'well conducted, and the children efficiently instructed'. But a former scholar, Mr G. N. Maynard, who entered the school in the 1830s, took a less sanguine view of the situation. According to him, Macer was an eccentric bachelor who often allowed conditions in the classroom to become chaotic—and then restored them with harsh discipline. The master had a whip which he called 'Old Hagger' and this was his 'instrument of torture'. According to Mr Maynard :

> This *donkey whip* of his had acquired the latter name from its constantly requiring the need of repairs from the hands of *Old Hagger* the Village Harness Maker, and mender.
> [Joshua Macer] had but one arm, and that was his *left*, but of this he made good use. In administering punishment on a boy by the means of 'Old Hagger' he would hold the boys between his legs, by thier [*sic*] head and neck, and operate

most unmercifully upon thier hind quarters. Sometimes the
boys would have thier revenge by biteing his legs, and
repetedly have I seen his old grey or white Stockings saturated
with blood from the wounds thus made from the teeth of his
victim, but the old chap had still some of his marine fighting
quality left in him, and before he let his victim free, he would
generally have his revenge . . . Irrespective of his school he was
a sort of factotum for the village being church clerk, Deputy
Overseer, and collector of rates and taxes, Parish Clerk &c. &c.
Often has he, during the legitimate hours of school been called
away from his school & scholars, to look after some parish
affair, and left the school to take care of itself. Then indeed
would there be confusion, confounded . . . One boy would be
in his seat assuming his position with Hat, glasses, Cane &c.
Others would be at leap-frog round the school, some playing at
horses, some at marbles and buttons, others would be outside,
and upon one of these uproarous occasions the boys had amidst
the confusion got the master's Old Donkey into the school . . .
During the height of all this confusion I have seen the master
return and here I must leave the reader to judge what effect
this had upon the scene, it being beyond my power to describe
it.

I will now relate one of his extraordinary and unparalled
[*sic*] methods of imparting information to the youthful mind,
by 'sounding it into the boy's ears'; to effect this object, his
plan was to select one of the *cleverer* of the boys from his
scholars, who would be put over the others under the name of
"Master of Arts", with the authority of this title he was
instructed to carry out his plan, of hearing the boys read and
those who erred either in reading or spelling had the words
that were wrong, bawled *loudly* into the boy's ear, by the
deputed Master of Arts; who immediately gave his pupil a
bang with his hand upon the opposite ear; and then repeat[ed]
the same *vica verca*; this according to the philosophy of this
excentric pedagogue would have the double effect of knocking
the information into the cranium, and *clenching*, or keeping it
there when they had got it in.

When pupils entered the school each morning they would greet
Mr Macer with the phrase 'Sarvenmaster', which was meant to

indicate 'Your servant, master'. A good deal of their time was then spent in learning the church catechism off by heart. However, 'no attempt was ever made to give to the children any explanation upon any part . . . It was a hard and difficult task for little children to remember the (to them) unmeaning words'. When school was finally dismissed for the day, the master would call 'class after class to his table, situated near the door of exit, here they all stood, with caps in their hands, one end of the rank next to the open door, he would then hold a ruler in his hand, suspended by his finger and thumb, and the signal of dismissal was the fall of this ruler : sometimes he would appear to drop it by giving it a sudden jerk; when such was the case, many of the boys who were foremost in the row would have gone out, but they would all have to return as the ruler had not fallen. The order being that none were to leave until this signal had taken place.'[55]

Despite his eccentricities, Joshua Macer remained at Whittlesford until his retirement in 1840, for, as his former pupil remarked, 'at that time any thing seems to have done for a schoolmaster if it could read and write, *"thrashing"* the boys seems to have constituted one of the prominent qualifications.' In this connection, it is worth recalling William Blackstone's dictum that if a master were 'moderately correcting' his scholar and happened to occasion his death, 'it [was] only misadventure'. Although written in the middle of the eighteenth century, this was still largely applicable a hundred years later.[56]

Nor were these educational problems confined to England. In Wales, too, despite the efforts of the 'circulating schools' there were, in the later 1840s, loud complaints about the poor quality of the teachers and of the instruction they provided. Of North Wales, for example, it was noted gloomily :

The teachers . . . are, in fact, drawn from the lowest class in society which contains individuals competent to read, write, and cipher. In many cases even these conditions are dispensed with, and any person who is supposed to understand the English language better than his neighbours is encouraged to undertake the office of schoolmaster. A catalogue of the previous occupations of teachers throughout North Wales . . . [indicates] that several schoolmasters have been selected from the class of agricultural labourers, quarrymen, miners, or weavers, according to the prevailing occupation of the working classes in the neighbourhood; but . . . the majority of school-masters are persons who were formerly employed in some petty trade or occupation which has afforded opportunities of learn-ing English, as carpenters, joiners, innkeepers, assistants in grocers' or drapers' shops, retired soldiers or excisemen . . . the class of schoolmistresses is composed of persons who have been employed as sempstresses, charwoman, and servants of the most humble description . . .

According to this critic: 'The average income of teachers being lower than the wages of able-bodied labourers, few persons are induced to undertake the employment who are not incapacitated by age or infirmity for manual labour.'[57] The effect on the quality of teaching is easy to envisage, and of the countless examples which could be quoted one must suffice here. (See also Appendix 4.) It relates to the church school at Llandrygarn, Anglesey, where an old man had been appointed teacher. None of his scholars could read even 'simple passages in a spelling-book correctly; none could repeat any portion of the Church Catechism; none had any knowledge of Scripture or of the truths of religion. A boy, who professed to be reading in the New Testament, thought that Jesus Christ was another name for Moses. He could not tell what was meant by the Bible . . . Another boy, examined in Welsh, had heard of God, but did not know who He was, and could state nothing about Him. The master is aged and infirm. He appears to have had no education; and, although professing to teach English only, he understands it so little himself that I was compelled to employ an interpreter in order to communicate with him.'[58] Yet despite such absurdities, officially at least English was the medium of instruction in Welsh schools throughout the nine-teenth century with the use of the Welsh language strongly dis-couraged.

Elsewhere, in areas where cottage industries flourished yet another variant on the educational theme appeared with the craft 'dame' schools. These were solely concerned with training the children in the skills of a particular trade and few of their 'teachers' even pretended to give academic instruction. Their main duty was to keep the children working at full stretch in order to maximise output and improve their manual dexterity. Like most of the dame schools they were usually held in the living rooms of small cottages, where the children worked in overcrowded, poorly ventilated, badly lit and often insanitary surroundings. And since those instructors who extracted the largest output from the children were the ones most favoured by parents, discipline was severe. Lacemaking (particularly in Bedfordshire, Buckinghamshire, Devon and Northamptonshire) and straw plaiting for the hat and bonnet trade (in Bedfordshire, Hertfordshire, Suffolk, Buckinghamshire and Essex) were the cottage industries most affected by these conditions. Thus at a lace school in early nineteenth-century Riseley, Bedfordshire, the girls were 'whacked across the shoulders' as a punishment for laziness or poor workmanship, while the boys were 'hung up to a beam by a cord under their arms'.[59] But very often the work itself was punishment enough—as the evidence of many of the young lacemakers testified. At Newport Pagnell in the early 1840s, one fourteen-year-old who had attended a lace school for four years admitted she 'very often [felt] unwell, pain in my head and agin my heart; think it is from sitting so long'. While her colleague, also aged fourteen, who had attended the lace school for eight years, complained that she was 'very often ill . . . was not so before I began lacemaking'. Neither of these girls could write and each worked a ten-hour day for the meagre wage of about 9d. or 1s. per week. Such reading ability as they possessed had been acquired, in both cases, away from the lace schools.[60]

Some of the 'teachers', especially those concerned with plaiting, were not even able to instruct their charges in the skills of the craft they were supervising. That would be carried out by parents before the children went to the schools at the age of about five or six, and the 'teacher's' sole concern in these cases was to work her pupils as hard as possible. Mrs Watts of Hemel Hempstead was one such. She informed the Children's Employment Commission in 1843 that at her small school the youngsters came at 6 a.m. and left at 5 p.m. :

an hour allowed for dinner. In my judgment I think the mothers task the children too much; the mistress is obliged to make them perform it, otherwise they would put them to other schools . . . I teach my own children sewing and reading . . .

and have offered to teach the scholars who come to my school, but the parents care nothing for it, and plaiting alone is everything with them; grown up girls have no more idea of sewing, or making a shift for themselves, than a baby.[61]

Despite their disadvantages, however, the craft schools and their 'teachers' lingered on into the final years of the nineteenth century. (There were said to be 102 plaiting schools in thirty parishes in the Central and South-Eastern divisions of Buckinghamshire alone as late as 1868.[62]) Then, thanks to the effects of factory and education legislation, plus a decline in the importance of the domestic trades themselves, the schools were at last eliminated. Nevertheless in 1871 one of the factory inspectors was still complaining of the early age at which youngsters were set to work in plait schools, 'children as young as four' being by no means uncommon. According to him, the children were crammed in the small rooms 'in any numbers, from 5 to 10 to 50 of them, sitting on little benches or stools . . . the master or mistress presides over them often with cane in hand to remind the idler of its duty'. In his eyes, though, the worst aspect was not the harsh discipline but the unhealthy, confining atmosphere of the cottage rooms and the accompanying 'intellectual evil', with the children deprived 'of the advantages of schooling of the best quality in well ventilated rooms'.[63]

Local clergy shared his unease. The incumbent of Edlesborough, Buckinghamshire, commented on the 'miserable results of plait schools in keeping up gross ignorance', while his colleague at nearby Linslade saw 'the prevalence of *straw plait*' as the 'greatest hindrance to getting hold of the young . . . They will not leave their plait. I find the plait a tremendous evil.'[64] It was an 'evil' which had, however, probably reached its highest level of importance in the late eighteenth and early nineteenth centuries. Then both the plait and lace trades had flourished as war with France cut off better quality continental imports of these products—and before machine-made lace had seriously undermined its domestic competitor. In 1810, indeed, the Rev. St John Priest, reporting on Buckinghamshire for the Board of Agriculture, had declared: 'The making of lace, and the platting of straw, employ all the women, boys, girls, and children throughout the county: it is impossible to pass a poor-house, without seeing some persons so employed. In towns, are schools of lace-makers and straw-platters; and so advantageous are these employments, that young women can earn from 9d. to 16d. per day readily'— a very different position from that of their mid-century successors for whom low wages were all too often the order of the day.[65]

But if lace and plait schools were the least satisfactory of the early nineteenth-century teaching establishments, the standard of academic instruction elsewhere in elementary education left much to be desired. Partly, as has been seen, this was a result of the low wages and poor working conditions characteristic of village schoolkeeping, which discouraged well-qualified applicants from taking up a teaching post. Partly it was the anxiety of school managers, who were normally also major ratepayers in their parishes, to give teaching positions to persons who might otherwise become chargeable on the poor rates. This latter motive was still being pinpointed in the 1840s by the newly appointed government inspectors of schools. Thus the Rev. Frederick Watkins, HMI, reporting on schools in the north of England in 1846, declared that of 495 teachers whom he had encountered during the preceding year:

> I cannot think that above two-thirds are tolerably qualified for their many and important duties, and I must further express my belief that one-third are insufficient, neither intended by nature nor fitted by art for the situation in which they are placed. At one school in Yorkshire, the master is a poor hunch-backed man, very deaf and ignorant, placed in his situation by the parochial authorities, that he may not be burdensome to them, for his support. His only qualification is that he writes a good hand. At another school, on the borders of Lancashire, the master is a crippled weaver 'put in' as they plainly told me 'by the parish to save expense'. At a school in Westmorland, I found that the master and mistress were each of them small farmers, more skilled, I should conceive, in the cultivation of fields, than of children's intellects.[66]

Similarly in Gloucestershire teachers were regarded as little more than 'a kind of necessary appendage', according to HMI Bellairs. In one school, at Winstone, instruction was given by a shepherd who, 'being too infirm at eighty to look after the sheep, had undertaken instead the education of the children, to whom he taught "very elementary writing" '.[67]

Nevertheless it was in the endowed schools, like Whittlesford, that some of the worst problems arose, with inefficient teachers perhaps appointed initially for economy reasons and then proving impossible to remove decades later when new trustees desired to promote efficient instruction in their village. In one Derbyshire parish, where the master had been appointed in 1814, attempts were made to remove him after he had held office eleven years. But they were unsuccessful, even though it was established that he had 'made a practice of hiring himself as a day labourer during harvest time, and had at other seasons of the year been in the habit of sending the children, *during school hours* to gather sticks for him, or to collect manure for the public roads. A second attempt [at removal] was made by different trustees about seven years after'—once more without success. And in 1842 the master was still at his post, 'although at times publicly seen in a state of drunkenness'.[68] Another black sheep was John Charville of Burrough Green, Cambridgeshire, who was first warned about his conduct by the trustees of the charity school in 1828. Eight years later, they wrote again admonishing him 'in consequence of your gross misconduct and continued neglect of your duties, to amend; and if after this admonition you shall not reform your conduct, we hereby give you notice that we shall cause you, in case of the slightest future negligence, to be removed from your office.'[69] According to information before the Charity Commissioners, Charville was 'a man of irregular habits, and addicted to gambling', and the academic progress of his charges was negligible. Nevertheless, in spite of the trustees' efforts, he refused to resign from office and remained as schoolmaster until his death in 1860, at the age of sixty-seven.[70]

These examples are typical of complaints about the misuse of educational endowments in the second quarter of the nineteenth century. It was the prevalence of such maladministration that caused HMI Allen to demand 'that something should effectively be done [to] remedy . . . the present condition of endowed schools'.[71] In his view the injustice was 'a crying one, its existence adds force to the complaints of demagogues and the seditious writings of the disaffected'.[72] Yet, despite his appeals, as the example of Charville shows, it was only slowly that government pressure, bolstered by the stringent provisions of the 1869 Endowed Schools Act, at last remedied the situation.

But Mr Allen was also unhappy about the attitude of certain well-to-do members of rural society whom he had encountered on his travels and 'who were themselves blessed with every advantage of early training and the soundest education', yet who voiced 'the opinion that schools were but of doubtful good'. As a result 'even where pains were taken towards their maintenance, I found instances of persons speaking as if they chose the establishment of a school as the least of two evils, under the impression that if a teacher were not set to work subject to their influences, others subject to worse would find employment in the district.'[73] Such attitudes inevitably vitiated efforts to raise educational standards or to improve the quality of teaching. Very often, too, the equipment remained poor, with inspectors complaining of schools, 'inadequately supplied and continuing to use only the bible or tattered remains of testaments which had been torn up to enable every child to have a fragment from which to read'.[74]

Yet in spite of the unfavourable comments, by the end of the 1830s perhaps two in three of all adult males in England and Wales had acquired a basic level of literacy—enough to permit them to read a simple text and to sign their name. This compares with a mid-seventeenth-century average male literacy rate of around 30 per cent, varying from 15 to 20 per cent in the rural north and west to up to 40 per cent in the countryside near London. By the mid-eighteenth century the average male rate had climbed to about 50 per cent, though among the poorer classes— such as labourers and small farmers—it was a good deal below that level, standing at perhaps 20 or 25 per cent.

At all times there were considerable regional—and sexual— variations in literacy, so that in some counties, like Dorset and Devon, evidence from the marriage registers indicates that by the 1830s about three-quarters of the men and over half the women could sign their name when they married. But in Wales, the Midlands north of Birmingham, and the belt of counties running diagonally north-east from Wiltshire to Norfolk (including the whole of East Anglia) standards were less satisfactory, with forty per cent or more of the men and around sixty per cent of the women unable to sign.[75]

In fact, despite the despondent tones of HMIs in the 1840s,

the first efforts to combat the chaotic and inefficient state of English and Welsh elementary education had already been made in the opening years of the nineteenth century. For it was then that two national societies had been established to promote the spread of elementary schooling on organised lines and to bring day-time instruction within the grasp of the countless youngsters who were still without it. Prior to their emergence—and despite the work of the SPCK and of the Sunday school movement from the 1780s—it was estimated that 'only the twenty-first part of the population was placed in the way of education, and at that date England might be justly looked on as the worst-educated country of Europe'.[76] Anxiety was felt, in particular, about the newly expanding industrial areas. But by 1820 the number of children in daily attendance had risen to around one in fourteen or one in fifteen of the population (including those at the dame schools) and the trend was upwards thereafter. It is to this growth and to its link with the two new societies, and with the Sunday schools, that we must now turn. At the same time it is worth noting that whereas in the early 1830s the number of week-day schools (including those for infants) in Dorset and Devon numbered about one for every 220 and 260 of their respective inhabitants, in low literacy Norfolk and Wiltshire at the same date there was in each case only one school for around 320 inhabitants—a significantly poorer provision, which seriously hampered the academic prospects of local children. Happily in Wiltshire at least a quarter of a century later this deficiency had been effect-ively tackled. The county now had the highest proportion of public week-day scholars to total population of any in England and Wales; the lowest proportion was in the Welsh county of Brecon.[77]

The Monitorial System

To render simple, easy, pleasant, expeditious, and economical
the acquisition of the rudiments of letters, morality, and religion, are the leading objects of elementary education.

    THE REV. ANDREW BELL, *Mutual Tuition and Moral Disci-
pline*, 7th ed., London 1823, 57.

The grand principle of Dr Bell's system is the division of labour
applied to intellectual purposes. . . . The principle in schools
and manufactories is the same.

    SIR THOMAS BERNARD, *Of the Education of the Poor*, 1809.

Our Country, still slumbering as I think, requires to be raised
to a just sense of the debt due to its noble & ingenuous youth,
as well as to their poor brethren.

    THE REV. ANDREW BELL to William Wilberforce, in a letter
dated 22 January 1819 and preserved at the Bodleian Library,
MS. Wilberforce d.13.

. . . we believe the education of this country to be a miserable
make believe, superficial, illusory system. It is one great quackery
from beginning to end. . . . It is all the same with both parties.
There is only a difference in name between the National 'humbug' and the British and Foreign 'humbug'.

    Quoted in *The Economist*, 3 April 1847.

As WE saw in the last chapter, despite all efforts, school provision
in many country parishes at the beginning of the 1800s was
nearly as haphazard as it had been a century earlier. All too often
Sunday schools (appearing particularly from the 1780s) provided
the only instruction available. For as one contemporary enthusiast,
the curate of Tetney, Lincolnshire, observed, they at least had
the merit of putting 'a stop to young people carrying on diver-
sions on the Lord's day', and of providing a means by which
'many may be taught to read their mother tongue in a decent
manner'.[1]

Initially there was a good deal of cooperation between Church and dissent over the setting up of Sunday schools—especially those established under lay influence, like the group formed around Cheddar in Somerset by Hannah More and her sisters. But to some of the more extreme Anglican churchmen this ecumenical approach was unacceptable. They feared it might lead to a jumbling together of 'the errors, inconsistencies and heresies of all', and their anxieties were intensified in the wave of anti-Jacobin, anti-radical feeling which swept the country following the outbreak of the French revolution. So whereas a number of early critics of Sunday schools had thought them undesirable because they might 'over-educate' or unsettle the poor for their roles as hewers of wood and drawers of water, by certain of their more hysterical late eighteenth-century opponents they were con-demned as dangerous disseminators of heterodox religious and political opinions through their alleged toleration of Methodism. In 1800, for example, the Bishop of Rochester claimed that 'Schools of Jacobinical politics abound in this country'. In his opinion the only antidote to the 'poison of Jacobinical schools . . . was the establishment of schools for the same class of children under the management of the parochial clergy'.[2] Bishop Horne of Norwich was alarmed that one possible outcome of continued cooperation through the Sunday school movement might be to 'bring the people of the Church nearer to the sects; but the present times do not give us any hope that it will bring the sects nearer to the Church'.[3] In Somerset even the respectable Miss More was persistently and virulently attacked for encour-aging Methodism, although she herself, as a convinced Anglican, considered that the Methodists were 'more enflamed' against her 'than the High Church bigots'. Happily, despite the bitterness aroused by these controversies, most clerics took the view of Bishop Randolph of Oxford that 'Christ's love of children com-pelled saving the poor from ignorance and giving them minimal instruction to enter into "a life of daily labour, well fortified with the principles of duty".'[4]

The teaching of reading was always a prime objective in Sunday schools, so that the children might peruse the Bible or prayer book for themselves. Instruction was usually given free of charge, often by members of a clergyman's own family, or by the parish clerk, who might receive a small payment of £3 or £4 a year from charitable funds. In the case of Wesleyan schools instruction was normally organised by local preachers or other volunteers. So for a minimal financial outlay it was possible to 'provide enough instruction to these children to make them aware of the dangers of eternal damnation, and to teach them contentment with their natural station'.[5] The schools also had the further merit, at least in the eyes of employers and parents, that they did not interfere with the children's weekday working plans.

Hardly surprisingly, therefore, the number of Sunday scholars in the early nineteenth century far outstripped those in day school attendance, especially in the industrial areas. In 1818 there were estimated to be 452,000 children attending school on Sundays in England and Wales as compared to 168,000 at charity schools and another 53,000 in local dames' schools.[6]

Yet despite the interest taken in Sabbath-day teaching, it was recognised that the amount of information which could be conveyed by untrained instructors on one day per week was strictly limited, even where the régime was as taxing as that at Sandford in Oxfordshire. There the curate reported in 1808:

> The scholars are taught every Sunday, from 8 in the morning till 4, 5 or 6 in the afternoon, according to the season of the year, to read and spell, and to commit to memory Watts' Hymns, the Catechism broke [*sic*] and the Collects and Gospels for the day, after learning which a second time they proceed to the Epistles for the day, Gastrel's Institutes and Mann's Exposition of the Catechism which last books several of the scholars have gone entirely thro'.[7]

Sometimes, too, especially in later years, emphasis was laid almost entirely on the religious or moral aspects of the curriculum rather than on academic matters. Thus Mary Smith, the daughter of a boot and shoemaker from Cropredy, Oxfordshire, remembered attending the Methodist Sunday school in her village during the 1820s:

> One Sunday morning, I do not know how it occurred, another girl and myself transgressed in something, probably in laughter. I never could resist the infection of that sort of thing; and as the teacher was a strict disciplinarian, we were ordered to remain when the others were dismissed.
>
> All having gone, he called us before him, and in the tenderest

tones asked if we would remember for the future, that the all-seeing eye of God beheld us. With tears of deep contrition, I took his proffered hand, and determinedly answered 'Yes.' Then he knelt down with us, and in deep and fervid utterances, in which tears choked his voice at times, he prayed that we might be kept true to God and our promise, and from ever falling into sin again. I left him, a sadder but a wiser child.[8]

A much darker impression was made on William Edwards, who also attended a Methodist Sunday school, this time in East Anglia during the 1870s.

> I used to be frit to death at the old men who run the chapel when I were a child . . . the leaders in chapel were associated in my mind with the tales they used to tell us littl'uns at Sunday school about hell-fire and the bottomless pit, and the Angel of Death coming to fetch good children to heaven and the Devil coming to fetch bad children to hell, and so on. I used to sweat all over wondering which one on 'em 'ould come to fetch me, for I used to come out o' Sunday school convinced I coul'n't live till the next Sunday. This warn't much to be wondered at come to think on it, 'cos a lot of children did die.[9]

So it was against this uncertain background that early in the nineteenth century two new school societies came into existence. Each strove to combat the ignorance and degradation which seemed to overshadow much of the day-to-day existence of working people, particularly in the growing industrial and urban areas. Instead they sought to prepare the labouring classes for a life of honest, self-dependent toil and an acceptance of the social order as it then existed. The new schools were to discipline 'the infant poor to good and orderly habits, to train them to early piety', so that they would subsequently become 'useful and respectable Members of Society', who would not fall victim to the beguiling propaganda of radicals and subversives.[10]

Nevertheless there was a minority of reformers who advocated schooling—as a right—purely on humanitarian or philanthropic grounds rather than for these more devious motives. Among them might be counted the Radical MP, Samuel Whitbread, who in 1807 unsuccessfully sponsored a Bill to provide two years' free elementary education, financed out of the rates, for children between the ages of seven and fourteen who could not afford the penny or twopence per week normally charged for attendance at day school. It was a measure which was opposed by the Archbishop of Canterbury, among others, as likely to 'subvert the first principles of education in this country, which had hitherto been . . . under the control and auspices' of the Church of England.[11] Other critics, like the MP for Fowey, Mr Pole Carew, objected to the cost involved : 'he could never admit the justice of laying such an impost as two millions a year, the amount of the charge according to his own calculation, upon one class of the community, namely, the landed interest . . . to educate another class'. Another Cornish MP, Mr Davies Giddy, considered that teaching the lower orders reading, writing and arithmetic, far from reducing social problems would be likely to add to them, for being enabled to read, they would waste their time in perusing inflammatory handbills, and other political productions. Nonetheless the Bill was approved by the Commons in weakened form, on 6 August—only to be rejected by the Lords five days later. With this failure the onus for educational provision again fell upon voluntary effort.

For reasons of economy both the new school societies adopted the monitorial system for purposes of instruction, with older pupils teaching the younger under the general direction of the teacher. It was a pyramid-like arrangement in which the teacher guided the monitors and was responsible for overall discipline, while the monitors passed on the information to their younger fellow-pupils. The idea had been developed initially in India by Dr Andrew Bell, an Anglican clergyman serving with the East India Company, and for this reason was sometimes also known as the Madras system. In England it was taken up in about 1801 by Joseph Lancaster, a London Quaker, and later by Dr Bell himself and his friends. In 1810 Lancaster and his supporters formed the Royal Lancasterian Association, to promote schools on Lancaster's principles throughout the country. In 1814 this organisation changed its name to the British and Foreign School Society and, although ostensibly unsectarian, it drew its support mainly from dissenters.

The Anglicans, faced with this competition, responded with the formation in 1811 of the National Society for Promoting the

Education of the Poor in the Principles of the Established Church, usually shortened to the National Society. It enjoyed the backing of Dr Bell and was both a continuation of the work of the SPCK and an indication of the Church of England's continuing determination to keep mass education within its own ambience. For as John Randolph, now Bishop of London, observed after its first meeting in October 1811, 'if the great body of the Nation be educated in other principles than those of the established Church, the natural consequence must be to deviate the minds of the people from it or render them indifferent to it, which may in succeeding generations prove fatal to the Church & to the State itself.'[12] And the *First Annual Report* of the Society itself, issued in 1812, noted that it had been created with

> the sole object . . . to communicate to the poor generally, by the means of a summary mode of education, lately brought into practice, such knowledge and habits, as are sufficient to guide them through life, in their proper stations, especially to teach the doctrines of Religion, according to the principles of the Established Church, and to train them to the performance of their religious duties by early discipline.[13]

In the event, thanks to the energy with which its members pursued their task, schools associated with the Church of England soon outstripped their British and Foreign rivals, outnumbering them in the ratio of about 17 to 1 by the end of the 1850s. (Their dominance in the number of scholars was equally striking, with 1,187,086 pupils claimed by Anglican schools in 1858, as opposed to 151,005 claimed by the British Society.) Other religious denominations, like the Wesleyans and the Roman Catholics, also developed their own schools, but in the country districts these had little significance.[14] Nonetheless the hostility and anxiety with which village clergymen viewed the establishment of a nonconformist school within their parish is well illustrated by the situation at Benson in Oxfordshire during the early 1820s. Here, according to the incumbent, the fee-paying village school had been faced with competition from a private dissenting master who 'succeeded in drawing many of the Children away from the Church. We therefore established a free day School and deprived him of his Scholars. Since which he has taken himself off.'[15] But in order to do this the incumbent had had to persuade ten of his fellow villagers to provide regular weekly subscriptions to the school of between 6d. and 3s., to cover its running costs.

The managers of schools in union with the National Society were required to promise that their pupils would be instructed in accordance with the liturgy and catechism of the Church of England and would attend divine service on the Sabbath, while teachers had normally to be members of the Anglican Church. Needless to say the Bible and the catechism provided a large proportion of the reading material, but a preoccupation with the Bible was equally apparent in the Lancasterian schools, although here no sectarian instruction was given. The keynote of both systems was cheapness, with the annual cost of educating a child in a Lancasterian school put at 7s. 6d. per annum, 'and in a very large school this amount could be still more reduced'. In a National school of, say, five hundred pupils the annual cost per head might be even smaller—at 4s. 2d. Inevitably books and equipment were of the cheapest variety possible.[16]

From an early stage the supporters of both the British and Foreign Society and the National Society recognised that one of their principal problems was to secure efficient teachers to supervise the monitors and scholars and to ensure that schools were run in accordance with 'the system'. So each group sought to provide rudimentary training for would-be teachers and also for those already appointed to a school. In the case of the British and Foreign Society this training was given at the Borough Road School, London, opened by Lancaster, while for the National School the venue was the central school in Baldwin's Gardens, London, and later, from 1832, at new premises in Westminster. In addition, the National Society offered facilities in various district central schools in the provinces—these numbered forty-five by the later 1830s—where the trainee could observe the system under the guidance of an experienced practitioner of it.

But, sadly, any favourable impression these provisions might create was immediately undermined by the brevity of the training period and the mechanical, uninspiring mode of instruction adopted. In 1834, the clerical superintendent of the National Society's central school admitted that five months was 'the average time' during which probationary teachers remained in training, while the secretary of the British and Foreign Society at the same date noted that although three months was fixed as the minimum length of the course at Borough Road 'of late we have found it exceedingly difficult to retain them so long, on account of the number of applications we receive for teachers. We think three years nearer the time they ought to remain than three months, but we do the best we can under the circumstances.'[17] Furthermore, although training at the National Society's school was available free of charge, with the student making his or her own arrangements for board and lodgings, the British and Foreign organisers normally required a weekly fee of 6s. to cover part of the cost of instruction and, in some cases, board. It was recognised that 'very few' trainees could afford to pay this sum even 'for six months, and probably none for twelve'.[18]

The benefits to be derived from the courses were thus strictly limited. According to the secretary of the National Society, the new entrant began his training

> in all departments at the same time; the first thing he does is, to go through the classes as it is called. In the school there are three or four classes set apart for the masters' use, and a newly admitted master has to go to the bottom of the junior class as a boy, and say lessons with the children till he can get to the top, and then he is examined and passed up to the higher set of classes, and when he gets to the top of the class, if he has shown quickness, and that he thoroughly understands the working of the classes and the way in which the boys ought to take places, and to give quick answers and explain things, he does not then go through that sort of discipline any more; otherwise he is liable to go a second or a third time through the classes. After that he has certain charges in the school. . . . In the meantime, while he is doing what I have just stated, other parts of the day are devoted in the first instance to reading, writing and arithmetic, and the study of the manual of instruction for managing the schools; it depends of course how long he is making himself perfect in those things, whether he is carried on to any thing further; if he goes on to any thing further in the way of scripture, history or geography, or any thing of that sort, it would be reported; it is not indispensable that he should acquire knowledge of these subjects.[19] (See also Appendix 2.)

By the mid-1830s the National Society claimed to have trained 2,039 teachers in this fashion; 'in addition . . . 657 schools in the country have been organised and provided with temporary teachers.'[20]

The régime meant, in effect, that trainees were treated as older children within the monitorial system, and the standard they achieved at the end of their 'course' might be little higher than that of their younger colleagues. Thus Ann Cooper, who was sent to the central school in London for a two weeks' course in June 1839 by the managers of the Northampton central school, received a somewhat double-edged reference from the National Society on her return, the clerical superintendent stating : 'I cannot allow her departure without bearing testimony to her orderly & regular deportment during the two weeks she has attended the Central School. Her examination paper, however, I am sorry to say, does not speak much for her previous attainments.'[21] It is a sobering thought that after her return to Northampton, Miss Cooper, as a central school teacher, would be expected to provide guidance on the monitorial system for would-be teachers from villages in the area. But perhaps the most amusing description of the National system in operation was provided by Mr F. Crampton, a product of it, in a paper to the Metropolitan Church Schoolmasters' Association in 1861, when he noted that under its auspices :

A well-behaved footman, or a man with a wooden leg, were sure objects for—I was going to say—promotion to the office of schoolmaster. [This latter] was generally what was called trained at Westminster, where you might see him with a little slate round his neck, going up and down in the class with the little boys with whom he was practising the various dodges of Dr. Bell's system, and at twelve o'clock placed in a row, waiting to be bowed to by the Head Master as a sign of dismissal. For about six months he underwent this ordeal, and then went to practise in a school all that he had observed in training. For the most part he had diligently to instil into his pupils the duty of behaving themselves 'lowly and reverently to all their betters'. The chief point in the examinations was the Church Catechism, in which he was a happy man, if a boy had got through the Belief, and did not break down in the

Desire. His pet boys were well up in the Amonites and Hittites, and knew the exact weight of Goliath's spear. His leisure hours, if any hours could be called his, were supposed to be at the disposal of the powers whom he served. A friend of mine . . . was reminded that it would be necessary for him occasionally to saddle the Rev. Mr. Scrubb's horse, and make himself generally useful in the garden. . . . If the National Society did nothing else, it always upheld the Bible as the sheet anchor of the soul, and many a man has found in his little school that he had little else to call his own.[22]

At Borough Road, training conditions were similar. According to Henry Dunn, the British and Foreign School Society secretary, the students were required to rise every morning at 5 a.m. and to spend at least one hour in private study before breakfast:

> They have access to a good library. At seven they are assembled together in a Bible class and questioned as to their knowledge of the Scriptures; from nine to twelve they are employed as monitors in the school, learning to communicate that which they already know or are supposed to know; from two to five they are employed in a similar way; and from five to seven they are engaged under a master who instructs them in arithmetic and the elements of geometry, geography and the globes, or in any other branches in which they may be deficient. The remainder of the evening is generally occupied in preparing exercises for the subsequent day. Our object is to keep them incessantly employed from five in the morning until nine or ten at night. We have rather exceeded in the time devoted to study the limit we would choose, on account of the very short period we are able to keep them, and we have found in some instances that their health has suffered on account of their having been previously quite unaccustomed to mental occupations.[23]

On entry the students were expected to have a minimum level of education, which was defined as the ability to 'read well, . . . write a tolerable hand, be acquainted with the four first rules of arithmetic, and be generally intelligent and energetic.'[24] However both the National Society and the British and Foreign attached particular importance to the moral and religious character of applicants as well. Non-Anglicans were rejected by the former body, and although the latter had a broader approach than this, great stress was laid on the production of satisfactory testimonials from a clergyman or dissenting minister. One Borough Road applicant who admitted that he had once fallen under the influence of 'the works of Paine the Deist' was rejected by Henry Dunn, even though he had good testimonials and had subsequently returned to the religious fold.[25] Even the clothing to be worn by women trainees under the direction of this society was carefully regulated in 1814. They were to be 'habited in cotton or queen stuffs—plain caps without work or lace—and plain straw bonnets at a low price . . . the cloathes they have at present should be made neat and suitable to appear in the schoolroom . . . no white petticoats should be allowed'.[26] Like Caesar's wife, the aspirant teacher must be above suspicion.

Surviving applications and testimonials at Borough Road give a flavour of the approach expected. Thus Thomas Wall of Haddenham, Buckinghamshire, applied for admission in July 1836, so that he might take up a teaching post in his home area. A testimonial was sent by the local Baptist minister, in which it was noted that Wall was 'a man of integrity—firm in judgment —very kind in spirit—good tempered, & of agreeable manners . . . judging from what I have seen in our Sunday school of 300 children . . . I hope he will make progress & be useful. He is acquainted with gardening—making shoes—Lace trade in part & for a comparatively poor man, is one of those who deserve encouragement'. The Borough Road committee obviously agreed, for his application was endorsed to the effect that he was to attend 'on trial'.[27] This referred to the two weeks' trial period normally required of all applicants before they embarked upon their three months' course.

But not all would-be entrants fared as well as this. A baker from Ringwood, Hampshire, who applied for admission in February 1838 on the grounds that he had 'for a considerable time felt an inclination to be engaged in the instruction of the young', received a discouraging reply. In his case, a referee observed that although he was 'regarded as a moral young man' he had 'given no evidence of decided piety. He is by trade a baker, & has in two different places endeavoured to establish himself in business but has not succeeded : it is thought that he is not clean in his business, & that he has not followed it with much *energy & activity.* His natural talent is not remarkable—his general information scanty. I fear that he would not be found "apt to teach", nor quick in observation—I apprehend that his application to you might have been prompted, more by a desire of obtaining the means of subsistence, than by any particular regard to the duties which such an engagement involves.'[28]

But if the British and Foreign and National Societies had only a very limited impact in raising the standards of teacher training in the early nineteenth century, that was not the sole cause of the criticisms levelled at them. Soon adverse comments were being made regarding the monitorial system itself, i.e. upon the whole *basis* of the work of Lancaster, Bell and their disciples. In 1808, Dr Bell had proudly written of his monitorial method:

> This system rests on the simple principle of tuition by the scholars themselves. It is its distinguishing characteristic that the school, how numerous soever, is taught solely by the pupils of the institution under a single master, who, if able and diligent, could, without difficulty, conduct ten continguous schools, each consisting of a thousand scholars. . . . In a word, the advantages of this system, in its political, moral, and religious tendency; in its economy of labour, time, expense and punishment; in the facilities and satisfaction which it affords to the master and the scholar; can only be ascertained by trial and experience. . . . Like the steam engine, or spinning machinery, it diminishes labour and multiplies work, but in a degree which does not admit of the same limits . . . For unlike the mechanical powers, this intellectual and moral engine, the more work it has to perform, the greater is the facility and expedition with which it is performed, and the greater is the degree of perfection to which it is carried.[29]

Both the National and the British schools were conducted in single large rooms, where the master or mistress could keep the entire school under scrutiny. Under the Lancasterian scheme the central area of the room was filled with rows of benches for writing drill, while the surrounding space, where the greater part of the scholars' time was spent, was occupied by groups of children standing for instruction by their respective monitor, usually with the aid of cards hung on the wall to save the cost of books. Lancaster classified his pupils, according to their attainments, into eight classes for reading and twelve for arithmetic; class one in reading was called the ABC class, while classes two to five were taught words of two letters ranging to five or six letters in the fifth class. Classes six and seven were occupied in reading the Testament and the Bible respectively, and the senior class consisted of the best readers. An elaborate system of rewards and punishments was adopted, with 'badges of merit' for those who were first in their class.

Under the National system the desks for writing occupied the outer space, facing the wall, and the central area was used by classes of children standing in squares for instruction by their monitors—who were called 'teachers' or 'assistants'. Each monitor would normally be responsible for ten children, although as many as twenty might be under one youngster's control in the larger urban schools. 'The role of the monitors was to teach the units of work, to recommend pupils for promotion and to keep order.'[30] Under both systems the sand-tray was used for teaching the beginnings of writing and numbering, although older children used slates. (In some schools, indeed, sand-trays lingered on to the end of the century because of their cheapness, though as one Norfolk scholar recalled, a whole morning's toil could easily be obliterated if the tray were unintentionally shaken.)

In the better schools the monitor would receive instruction out of class hours from the master, who for the remainder of the time was largely confined to a supervisory role. But in the less efficient establishments the youngster would be given little tuition and might, in fact, be only of about the same age and ability as members of his 'class'—a case of the blind leading the blind. Some schools taught the three 'r's', plus religious instruction (and sewing for the girls) to all their scholars, but others adopted a more selective policy. At Bampton National School which was instituted in 1812, every child was 'taught Spelling, Reading, the Church-Catechism, and generally the first principles of Religion', but only those boys who had 'made sufficient progress, and . . . recommended themselves by their good behaviour' were to be 'instructed in Writing and Arithmetic'. The rules then added :

It is further intended occasionally to employ the Boys in some handicraft, for the purpose of training them up in the habits of Industry. Those Girls, who have made sufficient progress and have recommended themselves by their good behaviour, will also be instructed in Writing. Needlework, Knitting &c. will form part of their constant employment for the purposes of training them up in habits of useful Industry, and contributing to the support of the School.[31]

Many other places followed this system of emphasising the importance of 'training . . . in the habits of Industry' and of using the children's labour to provide financial backing for the school. In the case of Bampton a printed list of 'prices for work' was incorporated in the rules, so that men's fine shirts were made by the pupils at 2s. each; night shirts for 1od.; a girl's coarse shift for from 3d. to 6d.; and a pair of pillow cases for from 2d. to 4d. In all, twenty-five different articles could be ordered. (See also Appendix 1.)

Another community which early adopted the monitorial system was the village of Enmore, where in 1812 there were seventy children in attendance, divided into eight classes. Each class was under the care of a 'teacher', who had been recruited from members of the seventh and eighth classes. Most of the children in the seventh class and all except the head child in the eighth then took it in turns for an hour at a time to instruct the other classes. At the expiration of the hour those who had been teaching were called back to their classes, and a new set appointed. The change of teachers was under the direction of the head child of the school who also acted as permanent teacher of the eighth class. In addition, a separate monitor was recruited to watch over discipline procedures, and to note the names of any pupils who broke the regulations. Before the children separated for the luncheon or evening breaks the schoolmistress examined the list of names on the monitor's slate, and punished those who had proved persistent offenders. The role of the mistress in this case was purely supervisory and disciplinary, although she was also responsible for the provision of school materials, such as the copper plate copies which were used by the children in their writing lessons.[32] But in many monitorial schools, especially by the second quarter of the century, the master or mistress would take a more active role by teaching the older scholars at least, though these latter would still be responsible for the instruction of their younger colleagues. The opportunities for error and the mechanical, repetitive nature of the instruction which this system engendered are easy to imagine. One seven-year-old who attended Newport Pagnell National School learnt 'very little'. All the boys who could 'read moderately well were appointed to teach the young or lower classes. I was one of these and I had very little time allowed me for either writing or arithmetic, and none for grammar or geography'. The schoolmaster in this case was also the parish clerk, and 'he had to see to the bells being chimed for prayers on Wednesdays and Fridays; he sent the biggest boys to perform the chiming business, I being amongst them'.[33]

Although it could be said in defence of the monitorial schools that they provided a modicum of instruction at a time when trained teachers were in short supply, the *quality* of the education they supplied clearly left a great deal to be desired. After Dr Bell's death in 1832 even the National Society itself began to display dissatisfaction with the method, as in 1842, when the Rev. Henry Hopwood, the Society's inspector, visited schools in the Oxford diocese. On this occasion he condemned the way arithmetic was taught as 'inappropriate and unsuccessful, especially in girls' schools, where the tedious and unintelligent processes recommended in Bell's Manual of the Madras System are still employed'. Similarly in reading lessons:

> Much time is wasted over spelling-cards. Such spelling lessons as 'bla, ble, bli, blo, blu,' are worse than useless. . . . In one girls' school, one of the middle classes is called the 'bla class' from the circumstance that one of the cards . . . beginning with this combination of letters, is the reading lesson for that class; and the Mistress informed me that this card occupied them, an hour daily, for three months. I need hardly say that the minds of the children were quite stagnant.[34]

The monitors, too, were criticised: 'In large monitorial schools, these little deputy rulers—who have sometimes, and not always undeservedly, been called "tyrants in rags"—are very apt to become petulant, conceited and capricious'.[35] Another observer, appearing before the 1835 Select Committee on Education in England and Wales, drew attention to the *noise* in monitorial schools. 'Mr. Lancaster had a notion', he declared, '[that] if he could allow boys to make a noise they would never consider it a drudgery to be taught . . . there is in the school perpetual noise; strangers think it confusion, but it is perfect order; the boys get the power of abstraction so as to go along with ease, notwithstanding there is noise from the process going on.'[36] Whether the teacher was equally able to withstand the babble of voices he did not say.

However, sterner condemnation of the system was given by the government inspectors. J. D. Morell, HMI for nonconformist schools from 1848 to the 1870s, wrote of the disorder in many places : 'I was frequently in despair as to the possibility of doing anything or hearing anything in the classroom'. While in the view of the Rev. Frederick Watkins, HMI, it would be 'difficult to say whether . . . monitors more injure the school *internally* by their insufficient and frequently erroneous teaching, or *externally* by removing from the parents' minds all hope of the improvement of their children in a school taught on such a method.' Mr Watkins then went on to describe the weaknesses he had in mind, and which applied to both town and country :

> In nine-tenths of the schools under my inspection, the monitors are children of the first, second, and sometimes third and fourth classes, taken in turn, 'as they come', without any preparation for their work . . . The only reason is, that it is their turn; and it must be confessed that they often show the unreasonableness of this reason by staying at home when their turn of teaching arrives. It is well to remark, that the parents, in most cases, encourage their child in thus absenting himself from the school. They have often expressed to me their feelings. 'They didn't wish theirs to teach t'others; they want them to larn.' Nor, on the other hand, do they wish their children to learn from others. For, as they say, 'What's master for?' . . .
>
> To return to the Monitors themselves. They are in general very young—rarely 13 years of age. I have found a boy of 9 teaching children of his own age. But their average age in boys' schools is 11. In girls' schools it is rather higher and may reach 12 years. . . . They are ignorant of the subjects taught. They go heavily and unlovingly to it. A card in one hand, the other in their pockets, they go singly or in pairs to their work. What is it? a reading lesson, seldom with any

questions, but with spelling afterwards. I have often stood by in silence and heard the grossest blunders made in both—words miscalled—left out—half said—others substituted for them.—The monitor takes no notice. He frequently does not recognise the blunder if he hears it. In general he does not hear it. His thoughts are elsewhere. . . .

Nor is it, as I am informed, an infrequent occurrence in the intercourse between the monitor and his pupils, that he should receive bribes from them, either that he may advance them in the class, or screen them from punishment. Marbles, apples, oranges, nuts, and sometimes a penknife have been mentioned to me as the price of the monitor's favour! trifles they may seem, yet heavy enough to weigh down all the truthfulness and honesty of the character of childhood, and to impress upon it the first deep marks of hypocrisy and falsehood. On the other hand, also, if the boys in the class are bigger and stronger than the monitor, they are not less prodigal of their threats to him when out of school, than the more timid are of their promises. In a school in which I was interested for some years, the monitors made several complaints that the bigger boys 'bullied them for putting them down.' . . . Again, in another school: 'The monitors took no notice of the children working and knitting during prayers. None of the girl-teachers could do a sum in compound multiplication which they professed . . .' . . .

Under such teaching it would be useless to expect much intelligent progress in our schools.[37]

Other critics condemned the system because of its effect in depreciating still further the *teacher's* social position 'by requiring little else of him than an aptitude for enforcing discipline, an acquaintance with mechanical details for the preservation of order, and that sort of ascendancy in his school which a sergeant-major is required to exercise over a batch of raw recruits before they can pass muster on parade.'[38] Instead, the idea was slowly evolving that the teacher should be a 'moral regenerator and guide among the poor and ignorant' rather than a badly-paid drill-master, and that only through an interaction of mature and immature minds could there be true education. Yet as R. W. Rich notes, it 'took nearly forty years for the country to realise that a system which deposes the schoolmaster from the post of teacher, and makes him merely a supervisor' could not provide a satisfactory system of education.

The elevation of the 'monitorial system' to one of 'beautiful and efficient simplicity' which, under the National Society's rules, could not be departed from, proved an academic blind alley— a negation of schooling in its broader sense and a denial of the individual instructor's native abilities and skills.[39]

In the Lancasterian schools methods were even more regimented than in those of Bell's. Pupils were marched, in order, to their places and desks. Each pupil was given a number and that number was also used for his hat nail, his desk, and his slate. In addition to the teaching monitors, there was a small army of youngsters for ruling paper, mending quill pens, registration of pupils and other duties. In fact, as Joseph Lancaster himself put it, in these schools the master or mistress was to be 'a silent bystander and inspector. What a master says should be done, but if he teaches on this system, he will find the authority is not personal, that when *the pupils*, as well as the schoolmaster, understand how to act and learn on this system, *the system*, not the master's vague, discretionary, uncertain judgment, will be in practice'.[40] It was the *mechanism* that mattered, not the personnel responsible for the working of that mechanism.

These unsatisfactory and narrow attitudes towards elementary education in England were very different from those adopted by contemporaries elsewhere in Europe. As early as the sixteenth century various German states had organised school systems under Church control, so that as one writer has put it: 'From the time of the Lutheran Reformation the German parent had imposed upon him as a religious duty an obligation to see that his children attended at school for the purpose of being trained in a knowledge of their duty to God and man.'[41] But it was Prussia which became during the eighteenth century the first modern state to establish a national school system free of church control. Under Frederick William I (1688–1740) a new programme of school building was set in hand and all children ordered to attend between their fifth and twelfth years, 'to receive instruction in reading, writing, arithmetic, and the Bible'.[42] This was the beginning of compulsory public education. Under Frederick the Great, in 1763, Prussian schools were made state institutions, through a General Code, while the school leaving age was raised to thirteen. In addition the length of the school year, the schedule for the school day, and the content of the curriculum were prescribed, although supervision was left in the hands of the clergy. Further legislation followed, notably in 1819, so that by the early years of the nineteenth century an effective national system of education had been set up to cater for children aged six to fourteen. Compulsory attendance was imposed and penalties (including fines and even imprisonment) were enforced where parents failed to send their children to school. But the need to use such measures was said to be minimal, because of parents' desire to see their offspring educated.

Likewise in Austria a witness to the Select Committee on Education pointed out in 1834 that 'no man could even marry . . . without producing his certificate of having gone through a regular course of elementary instruction, and in aspiring to any official situation, from the highest to the lowest, nothing can be done without producing this certificate'.[43] Both here and throughout the German states 'the people [were] thoroughly imbued' with the need for education. Austrian school books, too, differed from their English counterparts in that they were not confined to moral and religious themes but were far broader in concept. They covered natural history, physics and the mechanical arts, plus 'descriptions of objects of every day occurrence', and were designed 'to imbue the children with a love of knowledge and a habit of observation'.

In France, under legislation passed in 1833, mass education was also available, every commune being required to establish a primary school for its children. Although in its initial stages this programme left much to be desired—with instruction given in some cases in barns, cellars or stables rather than in purpose-built properties—the defects were gradually rectified, and by the 1860s Matthew Arnold could observe that more youngsters in French agricultural districts were attending school 'than in similar places in England'.[44]

There were equally striking contrasts in governmental attitudes towards teacher training between Britain and her continental neighbours. From an early stage in both Prussia and France the state-supervised training of teachers was set in hand. Unlike the brief and comparatively ineffective courses pursued by students in England at the training centres of the National and British and Foreign Societies, would-be teachers in both of these countries were expected to attend residential seminaries, the first such for primary teachers in the German states being opened at Stettin in Pomerania in 1735. By the middle of the nineteenth century there were 156 training (or 'normal') seminaries in existence in Germany, with 206 preparatory schools in connection with them. By the aid of these seminaries 'a standard of examination in the theory and practice of instruction' was furnished and a strong *esprit de corps* fostered among the teachers. France, too, partly under the influence of developments in Prussia, had an effective system of training schools by the 1830s; in 1834 there were said to be fifty-four of these already in operation, with sixteen more under development.[45] Usually the schools gave a two-year course, students entering at sixteen years, and the regular curriculum included moral and religious instruction, reading, grammar, arithmetic, history, drawing, science, music, geography, gardening, and the drawing up of legal documents.[46] The breadth of topics covered contrasts very strongly with the brief repetitive courses offered by the English training schools.

Holland and Switzerland, too, had well-established training and examination programmes for their teachers by the early years of the nineteenth century. Indeed Dr James Kay, who was later to effect much valuable reform in English education, was particularly impressed with the life and work of students at Kreuzlingen training school in Switzerland. It was under the direction of Johann Jacob Vehrli, who was himself the son of a peasant. His aim was to equip his pupils adequately as schoolmasters, whilst training them at the same time for the 'inevitable simplicity and poverty of the village schoolmaster's life'. The students rose early in the morning, spent part of their days labouring in the fields, and wore the coarsest of clothes, with wooden shoes and no stockings. Such spartan attributes were to inspire Dr Kay's own incursions into the training college field in England during the 1840s.

In the meantime, dissatisfaction with the various aspects of elementary education in England had been growing. The monitorial system, the untrained teachers and the low standards of instruction were all coming under attack, while the continental developments outlined above were widely discussed, usually in very complimentary terms. Even the widening of the franchise in 1832, to cover a broader section of the middle classes, seemed to make the education question one of increasing urgency, presaging as it did a future mass electorate. In 1833 this view was voiced in Parliament by the MP John A. Roebuck, when he pointed out 'that the hitherto subject many are about to become paramount in the State', adding : 'I wish the people to be enlightened, that they may use the power well which they will inevitably obtain.'

Within one part of the British Isles—Ireland—the government had already taken tentative steps towards the assumption of responsibility for the education of the poor. In 1806 a Royal Commission had been appointed to investigate popular education in that country, and when it produced its fourteenth report six years later, one of its recommendations was for the creation of a national system of instruction for the poor which would keep clear 'of all interference with the particular religious tenets of any'. In accepting this view the government decided to support the school programme of the non-sectarian Kildare Place Society, based in Dublin, and its first grant to this organisation—of £6,000—was made in 1816. Subsequently the amount was raised to £10,000 by 1821 and £30,000 ten years later though the programme failed to win the support of the majority Roman Catholic community. During the 1820s, in particular, the administering Society was accused of proselytising on the sly and of favouring Protestant Ulster. So in 1831 the grant was withdrawn and a new Board of Commissioners of National Education was set up to create, with the aid of government finance, a national system of education in Ireland. In schools assisted by the Board, children of all persuasions would receive secular instruction together, whilst denominational teaching could be given separately—on school premises, if necessary—at agreed times. The textbooks used for secular instruction must be sanctioned by the Board as a whole, and those used for religious instruction, by the Commissioners who belonged to the particular denominations concerned. Although this extension of the state's role was the subject of controversy, in England as well as in Ireland, it was eventually accepted, without enthusiasm, by the Irish. Over the years, particularly from the 1870s, the non-sectarianism of the schools was undermined, until by 1900 supporters of sectarian education could declare with approval that the national system 'instead of spreading secularism, was in the greater part of Ireland as denominational as could be desired'. However to some observers this Irish experiment of the 1830s seemed to point the way for possible governmental provisions for elementary education throughout Great Britain.[47]

Nor was it only in Ireland that the state was prepared to dabble in educational matters. For in 1813, when Parliament renewed the charter of the East India Company one of its requirements was that the sum of £10,000 should be devoted by the Company to the encouragement of education among the native Indians.[48] Twenty years later, again under Parliamentary pressure, that grant was increased tenfold.

So it was against this background of discussion and experimentation that new government initiatives were taken in the 1830s and 1840s to deal with schooling in England and Wales. The first step came in 1833 with the provision of a state grant for the building of schools, a modest sum of £20,000 to be divided between the two major voluntary societies, provided they raised an equivalent sum from their own resources. This government aid was, incidentally, not only less than that allowed to Ireland two years earlier but about one-twentieth of the annual education grant of the Prussian government. Next, in 1839 came the setting up of a supervisory Committee of the Privy Council on Education, with Dr James Kay (later Sir James Kay Shuttleworth) as its secretary, and with the first two government school inspectors appointed in November of that same year to report on the educational progress being made and to advise on future developments. Henceforth receipt of a government grant carried with it the obligation to accept school inspection.

Many Anglican clergymen viewed these moves with suspicion and hostility, seeing them as possible threats to the Church's dominance of elementary education (see Appendix 3). In fact the appointment of the Privy Council Committee was matched within the Church itself by the establishment of diocesan boards of education with their own inspectors, who were normally drawn from among local clergy and assigned on the basis of one for each deanery. And the Church's opposition to the state's proposals on the inspectorate was only relaxed in July 1840 when the Archbishops of Canterbury and York were given powers of veto over the appointment of government inspectors working in Anglican

C

schools. They could also withdraw their approval at any time, 'whereupon the authority of the Inspector shall cease, and a fresh appointment take place.'[49] In this connection it is interesting to note that even in the mid-1850s candidates for appointment to an inspectorship in Church schools were still being told that their nomination was conditional on the sanction of the Archbishop of Canterbury being obtained, and on those who were not ordained 'intending to go immediately into Holy Orders'.[50] Not until the Education Act of 1870 was there an end to denominational inspection by the state.

Although the non-Anglican school organisations, somewhat to their chagrin, had less power over the inspectors assigned to them than did their Church of England counterparts, the hostility of the British and Foreign Society towards a report on London schools made by their first inspector, H. S. Tremenheere, led to his transfer to another government post in 1842. A year later the right to consultation about an inspector's appointment was conceded to this Society, too. Such religious bickerings and jealousies were to overshadow the growth of elementary education in England and Wales for much of the nineteenth century and were to lead to considerable sectarian bitterness.

In the meantime, the partial surrender of authority by state to Church over the inspection issue of 1840 was quickly followed by Committee of Council financial support to enable the religious denominations to increase teacher training facilities. Then in 1846 came the institution of the pupil-teacher system, which was to serve the dual purpose of improving the instruction given in elementary schools and of providing a succession of qualified students for the training colleges. Only candidates approved by one of Her Majesty's Inspectors could be apprenticed as pupil-teachers in the schools and during their five-year apprenticeship they would receive a government stipend. Ultimately, if they passed the relevant entrance examination, they were to be given a virtually free admission to a training college. And for the student who successfully passed through the training college course, a government augmentation grant was to be available to boost his or her salary once the first teaching appointment had been taken up.

Although the monitorial system was not eliminated overnight by these government initiatives, they undoubtedly helped to pave the way for a more efficient teaching profession. Among the persistent monitorial schools was that at Staveley in Derbyshire, where even in 1851 the seventy pupils were organised into six classes and were taught by one mistress assisted by monitors.[51] In other cases, as at Lilleshall in Shropshire, a compromise might be reached, with both pupil-teacher and monitors engaged. Here reference to the monitors was carefully omitted in the HMI's report for 1851, while the work of the master and of the pupil-teacher was highlighted, in an obvious attempt to influence the attitude of the school managers: 'The master is certificated, an animated teacher, may do much with perseverance to raise his school. . . . The apprenticeship of a pupil teacher has clearly contributed to the efficiency of the school, especially to that of the lower classes.'[52] By such an approach the HMIs hoped finally to drive the 'monitorial humbug' from every classroom.

Meanwhile among those who had supported the growth of state intervention in education were many who saw the teacher, properly trained and qualified, not merely as an instructor but as an instrument for social discipline, who would combat pauperism, induce self-respect and reduce the high levels of urban and rural crime. This latter role was made very clear in the Commons during the spring of 1847, when one Member claimed that 'without good schools, good schoolmasters, and a good system of education, the State can never hope successfully to combat crime or to diminish its amount'. His colleague, T. B. Macaulay, saw matters in a similar light, declaring that: [The statesman] may see, and shudder as he sees, the rural population growing up with as little civilisation, as little enlightenment as the inhabitants of New Guinea, so that there is at every period a risk of a *jacquerie*'. It was the schoolmaster who was to be entrusted with 'the mind of the rising generation, on whom the prosperity and future eminence' of the nation depended.[53] But perhaps the *Edinburgh Review* summarised the position most succinctly in 1839 when it declared: 'we must build more schools or more prisons'.

Not all contemporaries, however, supported the interventionist stance. In the eyes of at least one sceptic—*The Economist*—this extension of governmental interference was, on its own, unlikely to bring about the desired improvements. Nor was it persuaded by the example of German educational progress:

We are not blind to the faults of our countrymen; but, comparing Jena with Trafalgar, a German *Reisewagen* with a railroad carriage . . . an English foundry, factory, and workshop, with those of Germany, we affirm, without hesitation, that our people are further advanced and better drilled, in the arts that minister to the success of individuals and the greatness of states, than the school-taught Germans.[54]

Although it admitted that existing English elementary schools were unsatisfactory, it considered interference by the national government unlikely to nourish them 'into healthy . . . and vigorous existence', adding: 'Were education left untouched by the State, its own beauties and inherent advantages were so great that the people would be as naturally attracted to it as they are to high wages, and would be as eager to obtain it as they are to get plenty of fine clothing and wholesome food.'[55] But *The Economist* was able to persuade few others to adopt its optimistic *laissez-faire* views and the reforms of 1846 were speedily accepted by most informed observers. Indeed *The Economist* itself modified its attitude over the years and by 1870 was not only accepting the need for state intervention but was pointing out that education was 'not a benefit with respect to which England can, in common decency, be parsimonious'.[56] It was a welcome if belated conversion.

3

Pupil-Teachers

> Mr Cook tells us that from the first institution of the system in 1846 he observed a marked improvement in schools where pupil-teachers were apprenticed, and that subsequent experience confirmed this observation. In his report for 1851, he stated that after a very careful comparison between schools in which pupil-teachers were apprenticed and those in which monitors were employed, he found the improvement of the former uniform.
>
> *Report of the Royal Commission on the State of Popular Education in England* (the Newcastle Commission), Parliamentary Papers 1861, XXI, Pt I, 102, quoting the view of the Rev. F. C. Cook. HMI.

THE POST of pupil-teacher was created in 1846 as a result of action by the Committee of Council on Education. But it had precedents both in the Dutch educational system—where trainee teachers were apprenticed between the ages of fourteen and eighteen to act as assistants, whilst receiving evening instruction themselves—and in experiments carried out at Norwood poor law school in England from 1838. Here the older and more promising pupils were raised first to probationers and then to pupil-teachers, the latter position carrying with it a five-year apprenticeship. Non-pauper private pupils might also be sent to Norwood to train under the same conditions, with one pupil-teacher and one monitor assigned to each class of fifty pupils. James Kay, the inspiration behind this move, saw it as an easy way of meeting the shortage of poor law teachers while, at the same time, imbuing the students 'with a large sympathy for their own class. To implant in their minds the thought that their chief honour would be to aid in rescuing that class from the misery of ignorance and its attendant vices.'[1]

Similar motives lay behind the Committee of Council's decision of 1846. It was an attempt to raise the general quality of teaching in elementary schools and to provide a means of bridging the gap which had hitherto existed between the age of leaving school and the age at which it was possible to enter a training college. Although prior to that date some college entrants had been employed as monitors, many had been engaged in a whole range of trades and occupations before taking up their educational calling, as at the Oxford Training Institute, where of eleven students admitted during 1844, five had been previously employed, three as domestic servants, one as a tailor and one as a compositor. Similarly of eight entrants to Winchester training school in midsummer 1847, six had had a previous occupation —three as servants, two as agricultural workers and one as a shop assistant. While at Borough Road, Henry Dunn considered that the best teachers were recruited from those who were 'intelligent mechanics, or persons who [had] been employed in shops or warehouses'.[2]

Great things were expected of the new generation of pupil teachers. Matthew Arnold, perhaps the most distinguished of Her Majesty's Inspectors of Schools, described them on one occasion as 'the sinews of English primary instruction; whose institution is the grand merit of our English State-system and its chief title to public respect'. While James Kay (or Kay Shuttleworth as he had become on his marriage in 1842) optimistically claimed that thanks to the 1846 reforms:

> A poor man's child may . . . at the age of thirteen, not only cease to be a burthen to his father's family, but enter a profession at every step in which his mind will expand, and his intellect be stored, and, with the blessing of God, his moral and religious character developed. His success will be acknowledged by certificates from authority.[3]

So from the mid-1840s the hallmark of professional ability for a teacher was the possession of a Government certificate, 'gained either by internal examination at the end of a two-year training college course or else by passing the external examination for practising teachers'. The five-year apprenticeship which the young trainee had to serve prior to this, from the age of thirteen, was considered a fitting preparation. And in order to encourage youngsters to take up the scheme, the Government offered a grant to the pupil-teacher during each of his or her training years, ranging from £10 a year for a first-year student to £20 a year for one in the fifth and final year. These sums were despatched annually by postal order from the Education Department in London, and it was hoped that in many cases 'the good conduct of the apprentice' would lead to additional rewards being given by the managers of the school at which the apprentice worked. These might include 'a supply of textbooks on the prescribed subjects of instruction, or an annual grant of clothes, or an addition to [the] stipend'.[4]

However for small rural schools, where the head teachers were unable to train apprentices because of their own limited academic achievements or because of a lack of suitable facilities within the school itself, the new post of stipendiary monitor was also created, for youngsters between the ages of thirteen and seventeen. They were to act as cheap substitutes for pupil-teachers, with the Government paying them an annual stipend ranging from £5 to £12 10s. over the four years of their employment. They, too, would receive a limited amount of instruction from the head teacher of the school at which they worked, while their duties would normally be confined to instructing the youngest pupils only.

Head teachers also secured grants under these regulations, amounting to £5 a year for training one pupil-teacher, £9 for two, £12 for three, and £3 per student per annum for higher numbers. For stipendiary monitors the respective sums were £2 10s., £4, £6, and £1 10s. per head.[5] In addition a master could receive a further gratuity if he instructed a male pupil-teacher in gardening or some other craft-work, while mistresses could benefit if they instructed female trainees in 'cutting out clothes, and cooking, baking, or washing, as well as the more usual arts of sewing and knitting'.

The number of assistants permitted at any single school was regulated by its size. Initially under the 1846 regulations one pupil-teacher was to be allowed for every twenty-five scholars in attendance. But thanks to the rapid rise in the number of recruits, and the consequent increase in cost involved, that ratio was altered within two years. On 25 November 1848, Kay Shuttleworth sent out a circular letter instructing inspectors to exercise 'a more critical discrimination in the admission of candidates for apprenticeship'. In schools where apprentices were already employed, firm limits were to be introduced of one pupil teacher to every fifty children in attendance, unless a potential candidate 'could pass an unequivocally good examination'. Gradually the proportion of one pupil-teacher to every forty or fifty children in regular attendance became the customary arrangement, although in a number of schools staffing was a good deal less favourable. And despite complaints, not until the new governmental Education Code of 1890 was it laid down that one pupil-teacher was to be appointed for an average attendance of thirty pupils, instead of the previous minimum of forty.

School managers who wished to take advantage of the new grants for their school had to meet certain pre-conditions. First of all the master or mistress must be 'competent to conduct the apprentice through the course of instruction' laid down; then the school itself had to be 'well furnished and well supplied with books and apparatus'; and the children in it must be divided into classes, with instruction graduated according to the scholars' age and capabilities. Finally, discipline must be 'mild and firm, and conducive to good order'. Some managers, indeed, seem to have regarded the opportunity for their teachers to take part in the scheme rather as a reward for good behaviour than an academic exercise. At Coleshill in Berkshire, the Earl of Radnor expressed anxiety in 1856 that the boys' school which he supported in the village should become eligible for government inspection so that the master, if he were 'deserving', should have 'some of the advantages provided by the Committee of Council on Education & allowed Pupil Teacher'.[6] He made it quite clear that he was not concerned with the possibility of securing annual government grants towards the cost of running the school itself but merely with benefiting the teacher.

Of course if masters failed in the performance of their supervisory duties the apprenticeship indentures of their pupil-teachers might be cancelled, a decision which left the apprentices concerned high and dry in the middle of their training. For this reason HMIs were often reluctant to take such a drastic step once a schoolmaster or mistress had been allowed an apprentice. And in the early days the only requirement for that duty was that the teacher concerned should be of such 'character and attainments' as would 'enable him to qualify himself for success in an examination at the close of each year of apprenticeship, in those subjects in which the pupil-teachers would be instructed in the ensuing year'. In other words, if a master could cram himself to reach the required standard just a year ahead of his apprentice, he met the minimum qualification. And as mentioned above, once they had embarked on that course most heads were allowed to continue. The action of HMI Watkins in cancelling the indentures of seventeen of his 513 pupil-teachers in 1852, because of the incapacity of their instructors, was the exception rather than the rule. Nevertheless a number of other inspectors had doubts about the suitability of some of their supervising teachers—a fact perhaps not entirely surprising when it is remembered that there were in 1850 only 1,173 certified teachers in the whole of England, Wales and Scotland.[7] Clearly many of those who trained pupil-teachers at this time were themselves unqualified.

Gradually the Committee of Council began to tackle that problem by creating the category of 'registered teacher' in 1854. Members of this new group had to be over the age of thirty-five and to possess 'sound, if humble, attainment'. If they wished to qualify for an apprentice under this dispensation, masters or mistresses must pass an examination of a standard approximating to that of the fifth year pupil-teacher, with an additional paper in geometry or algebra. After 1854 only certificated teachers, or those over thirty-five who were qualified by registration, were permitted to train apprentices.[8]

Before the would-be pupil-teacher was admitted to apprenticeship, he or she had to satisfy certain medical, educational and moral requirements. No candidate was to be accepted who was 'subject to any bodily infirmity' likely to impair his usefulness as an instructor, a very different attitude from that adopted at the appointment of some of the old-style parish teachers. In this connection 'their Lordships' of the Privy Council Committee on Education decided that 'scrofula, fits, asthma, deafness, great imperfections of the sight or voice, the loss of an eye from constitutional disease . . . or an hereditary tendency to insanity' were 'to be regarded as positive disqualifications.'[9] While the manager of a Dorset school was firmly informed that although his candidate for a stipendiary monitorship was intellectually fitted for the task, physically he fell short of requirements, being 'very small, sickly-looking, and deficient in bodily strength'. Such weaknesses were regarded as 'insurmountable' barriers to a successful teaching career.[10]

Moral considerations were covered by the need for managers to testify before the HMI not only as to the character of the apprentice but also that of his parents or guardians. If his (or her) family life did not meet the required standards, the candidate must be boarded out in an approved household. 'Their Lordships' would not allow pupil-teachers to live in a public house, however well conducted it might be. Thus of a Castle Combe candidate, it was noted in 1849 that 'residence in a public house' was 'a very serious, if not insurmountable, objection to apprenticeship', which could only be overcome by the youngster concerned boarding out with an acceptable family.[11] 'Illegitimate children were not admitted, except in cases of outstanding merit, and even so they were required to move to some other place where they were not known.'[12]

Alongside this, an apprentice in a Church of England school had to show that he or she fully understood the catechism, while for non-Anglicans the managers were to certify that the religious knowledge of their trainee was of a satisfactory standard. At the close of each year of training the pupil-teacher (and the stipendiary monitor) must present a certificate of good conduct from the managers of the school, 'and of punctuality, diligence, obedience, and attention to their duties from the master or mistress', while in Church schools the clergyman, and in non-Church schools the managers, must also certify that the candidate had been 'attentive' to his or her religious duties. Failure on any of these counts could lead to a loss of the annual stipend or to the cancelling of apprenticeship indentures.[13] In 1854, it was reported that during the year three out of 556 pupil-teachers had been dismissed for bad conduct. But in general the behaviour of the apprentices was 'extremely satisfactory, and not surpassed by that of any other body of young people in any class of life'.[14]

Nevertheless the responsibilities of the head in keeping his apprentices on the path of virtue occasionally proved something of a trial. Alexander Sargent of Sidbury, Devon, was one sufferer, as the following entry from his log book during 1880 indicates:

Refused to take PT lessons this morning. Pupil Teachers attended last evening a dancing class at the Red Lion public house. I've done my best to keep the girls from evil, and by so doing have brought no end of ill-will upon myself and had numberless unpleasantnesses with E. Sansom whose impudence and daring has been beyond measure. It does not matter how good the girl may be when she enters Sidbury—she is not here long before she is corrupted and set against the school and upheld by those who ought to know better. *Query*: How is E. Sansom and L. Cocks going to do their work and attend a dancing class? From today I hold my tongue, if they go to the bad, go they must, it is not my fault, but as to being answerable for their work, I refuse to be. *I wash my hands of it.*[15]

And in Somerset a desperate head listed a whole catalogue of charges against his male pupil-teacher:

1. Absenting himself from his duties without permission.
2. Sending scholars during school hours for Whiskey.
3. Drinking Whiskey in the presence of his class.
4. Taking and claiming for his own a book belonging to Sidney Rossiter.
5. Being in possession of, and using, duplicate keys to School Cupboards and Sunday School Harmonium.
6. Breaking open a cupboard in the School from which a Missionary Box was lost (contents included).[16]

There were even cases of apprentices absconding, as at Sudbury in Suffolk during 1852. Here two youngsters left the British School, and the reaction of the Committee of Council to the news of their departure was swift and to the point. Not only were their names to be struck from the official register of pupil-teachers but

For the sake of example it would be advisable to keep a placard fixed in the schoolroom for the next fortnight with their names written upon it at full length, and some such notice as the following:
'Thomas Herbert and Frederick Nichols have disgraced their names by dishonestly absconding with payments made to them on the faith of their completing their engagement as Pupil Teachers in this School. A Memorandum of their misconduct has been entered in the Managers' Minute Book and will always remain to be seen there.' So far as the recovery of the fugitives is concerned, and the mode of dealing with them

afterwards, it is for the parties to their indentures, and not for their Lordships to decide upon the course to be adopted.[17]

Fortunately, cases as serious as this were few and far between. But given such possibilities it is not surprising that apprenticeship indentures for teaching—as for other occupations—were couched in sternly moral tones, in order to impress on the trainee the need to avoid temptation and 'faithfully and diligently' to serve his instructor. He must not, except on grounds of illness, absent himself from the school during normal teaching hours. Instead he was to 'conduct himself with honesty, sobriety, and temperance, and not be guilty of any profane or lewd conversation or conduct, or of gambling or any other immorality, but shall diligently and obediently assist in the instruction and discipline of the scholars', under the direction of the teacher.[18] Attendance at divine service on Sunday was obligatory.

The master or mistress had to promise to give the pupil 'daily opportunities . . . of observing and practising the art of teaching', and to devote at least one and a half hours every morning or evening 'before or after the usual hours of school keeping' to the personal instruction of the pupil. In single-sex establishments, the apprentice must be of the same sex as the head, but where, in a mixed school, the latter was a man and the pupil-teacher female, then a 'respectable woman' must be present during the periods of instruction—preferably the mother, wife or sister of the master. Finally, the approval of Her Majesty's Inspector had to be obtained before each transaction could be completed, so that any pupil-teacher engaged before the annual school visit of the Inspector was appointed on a temporary basis only, as a monitor, until the great man had signified his consent.

The required level of educational attainments was very modest, with the successful applicants expected:

1. To read with fluency, ease, and expression.
2. To write in a neat hand, with correct spelling and punctuation, a simple prose narrative slowly read to them.
3. To write from dictation sums in the first four rules of arithmetic, simple and compound; to work them correctly, and to know the tables of weights and measures.
4. To point out the parts of speech in a simple sentence.
5. To have an elementary knowledge of geography.

6. To teach a junior class to the satisfaction of the Inspector.

7. 'Girls should also be able to sew neatly and to knit.'[19]

In addition, in Church schools candidates had to be able to repeat and explain the catechism and show that they were acquainted with the outline of scripture history.

During the course of the subsequent apprenticeship, annual examinations were taken in composition, arithmetic, grammar, geography, history, music and religious knowledge. Girls were excluded from certain aspects of these, such as questions on 'syntax, etymology, and prosody' in grammar, but were instead 'expected to show increased skill as sempstresses, and teachers of sewing, knitting, &c.'.[20] Initially the examinations were conducted in the separate schools by the HMIs, but soon group tests were held each year at specified centres to cater for the pupil teachers of a particular district. Each candidate was required to attend on the appointed day 'with a due supply of pens and foolscap paper' and no doubt an appropriate feeling of trepidation, ready for the annual ordeal.[21]

Educational publishers, alive to the opportunities which this régime offered, hastily flooded the market with books and periodicals designed to guide the apprentices through the various papers and to advise on revision. One such, W. F. Richards's *Manual of Method*, published in 1854, laid down a formidable programme of work:

Monday Evening: Sketch a map and learn by heart facts in Physical and Political Geography. Work examples in one of the Mathematical subjects.

Tuesday Evening: Learn by heart a lesson in the Church Catechism, with Scripture texts. Work examples in one or more of the Mathematical subjects.

Wednesday Evening: Write a short essay upon some subject previously given, or write an account of some reign in English History, or paraphrase a piece of Poetry. Learn a lesson in Grammar or Etymology and learn to Parse from the next day's reading lesson.

Thursday Evening: Prepare for repetition a lesson on the Liturgy. Work examples in one or more of the Mathematical subjects.

Friday Evening and Saturday: Prepare a lesson on Scripture History, and sketch a Map to illustrate the places mentioned in it. Work examples in two or more of the Mathematical subjects.

All this had to be accomplished after a normal day's teaching and alongside the instruction received from the school head. As R. W. Rich points out: 'Nothing can better illustrate the aridity that characterised the "academic" training of the apprentices than the quality of the works produced for their assistance and edification.'[22]

Along with this theoretical training, candidates must also demonstrate their teaching skills before the HMI on the occasion of his visits to the school at which they worked. The tensions to which this gave rise are well brought out by Thomas Hardy in his novel, *Jude the Obscure*. Sue Bridehead had been engaged a few weeks only as a pupil-teacher when the inspector arrived unannounced:

Sue's class was at the further end of the room, and her back was towards the entrance; the inspector therefore came and stood behind her and watched her teaching some half-minute before she became aware of his presence. She turned, and realised that an oft-dreaded moment had come. The effect upon her timidity was such that she uttered a cry of fright. . . . She soon recovered herself, and laughed; but when the inspector had gone there was a reaction, and she was so white that Phillotson [the headmaster] took her into his room, and gave her some brandy to bring her round.[23]

Once the five-year apprenticeship had been completed satisfactorily, the pupil-teacher could sit a competitive examination for a Queen's Scholarship in the hope of entering a training college. Those who passed and were duly selected would then undergo a further period of study for their certificate qualification. Unsuccessful candidates might continue to teach as uncertificated assistants in the schools, a grade formally established in July 1852, or, in the early years, they might be admitted to posts in the lower branches of the Civil Service. This latter concession was withdrawn, however, amid much disappointment in May 1852, two months before the new grade of assistant teacher was offered as an alternative. Then in December 1854, the Civil Service option was clandestinely revived, with HMIs informed that they could recommend the names of a limited number of male pupil-teachers to be brought to the notice of the Lord President of the Committee of Council, 'in the event of an opportunity occurring for the employment of such a youth in the public service.' At the same time it was pointed out that there were ten junior clerkships vacant at the Board of Inland Revenue which might be suitable, although it was stressed that the greatest care must be exercised in the nominations, since should any candidate subsequently 'disappoint the expectation formed of them, the recurrence of any similar offer will be rendered less probable'. Eventually, in March 1855 two former pupil-teachers were recommended for the Inland Revenue appointments. It was hardly a dramatic development and in May 1858 the scheme was wound up for a second and final time. For as all trainees likely to become successful teachers were to be excluded from the list of candidates, the Civil Service appointments, with their relatively high prestige and their pension possibilities, might be regarded as 'equivalent to a prize of demerit' for the less successful pupil-teachers.[24] That was something the Committee of Council was not prepared to allow.

Of course, not all of those who *passed* the Queen's Scholarship examinations went to a training college. For much of the time there were not enough college places to cater for them anyway, while some youngsters could not afford to attend even with the aid of a scholarship.[25] At the Diocesan Training College, Winchester, for example, in January 1875, only thirty-six Queen's Scholars 'with the highest character references' were accepted out of ninety applications for admission.[26] And as late as 1901 little more than one-quarter of the successful candidates actually went to college. Many of the remainder became assistants, or provisionally certificated heads in small schools, if the HMI so recommended.

Provisional certification lapsed at the age of twenty-five, however, and the ex-pupil-teacher had then to revert to an assistantship unless he or she could pass the certificate examination. Despite the difficulties involved, quite considerable numbers of former pupil-teachers, whether they went to college or not, were able to obtain this qualification, often by private study whilst holding down a teaching post, or by taking a correspondence course. During the 1890s former Essex pupil-teachers remember taking the London-based Clough's Correspondence Course. But it was a hard struggle to study after a day's teaching, and even in the early twentieth century failure rates were distressingly high. In 1912, of 2,347 correspondence course and 493 private study candidates who took the acting teacher's certificate examination, about 70 per cent failed. And although the 914 who had taken local authority courses fared a little better, their failure rate of 63.1 per cent was hardly a cause for complacency.[27] Yet in 1911–12 around 43 per cent of all certificated teachers employed in elementary schools had obtained their qualifications externally.[28]

Some pupil-teachers left the teaching profession altogether when their apprenticeship came to an end, even if they could no longer hope automatically to enter the Civil Service. In the late 1850s the Newcastle Commission found that while 87.32 per cent of the apprentices completed their articles, only 76.02 per cent went on to try for a Queen's Scholarship. Office work provided an alternative for a large proportion of the remainder, especially the males.

In many respects the whole elementary school world was meant to constitute a closed system, both socially and educationally, with recruitment of teachers taking place from among the most able of the elementary scholars themselves. And despite the limitations, for girls in particular teaching opened up new horizons. Not only did it offer a guaranteed income during the training period but when that had been completed, the profession offered advantages, both socially and economically, which could not be obtained in, for example, domestic service—the most common employment for working-class girls. Small wonder that the proportion of female pupil-teachers rose. From 32 per cent of the total in 1849, their share climbed to 41 per cent in 1854 and 46 per cent in 1859.[29] Thereafter the trend was sharply upwards until by the mid-1890s an overwhelming 78 per cent of all pupil-teachers were female.

For boys, on the other hand, even in the early days the rate of payment offered during the training period was less attractive, especially for those from the industrial areas. As HMI Watkins, who inspected in Yorkshire, complained in 1843: 'we must take

what we can get, and where we can get it. I do not say it lightly
. . . the maimed and the lame, and the nearly blind, have been
offered at my examinations during the year, and rejected to the
visible and sometimes very audible dissatisfaction of those who
proposed them.'[30] It was pointed out by the Newcastle Commission itself that telegraph clerks on the railway could earn 10s. and
11s. a week, 'with the prospect of increase', and 'other offices,
merchants', lawyers', canals, &c., are almost as enticing to young
lads', so that candidates were reluctant to take on the lower-paid
responsibilities of pupil-teaching. HMI Stewart claimed that
even in such predominantly rural counties as Cambridge, Hunt-
ingdon, Bedford and the adjacent areas it was impossible to find
apprentices 'except the managers are prepared to pay £5 per
annum to eke out the stipend conditionally offered by the
Government'.[31]

Another unsettling feature for young candidates was the knowledge that they could only obtain their government stipend after
they had successfully completed the annual examination, with all
the anxieties that this entailed. If the trainee failed and had to
repeat a year of his studies, he received no government grant for
that second period, a factor which allegedly inhibited inspectors
from failing candidates. The solution usually adopted in such
circumstances in the early days was 'to terminate the indentures
at the time of the inspection' since this permitted payment to be
made for the year's work already completed.[32] If the HMI
agreed, fresh indentures could then be drawn up so that the
candidate could continue his training. But the difficulties to
which failure gave rise are shown clearly in the case of Elizabeth
Pinchon, who failed her second year examination as an apprentice at Upminster British School, at the end of 1880. In a
letter to her father the school managers pointed out that under
the apprenticeship agreement they could pay Elizabeth 'the same
salary as last year, and apply for her term to be extended a year
that she may try to pass next autumn the examination she has
failed in now.' However, another course would be to terminate the
engagement altogether, 'by a six months' notice. . . . We should
regret it on many grounds, but cannot say that in all respects we
are encouraged to think that the life of a teacher is what she is
thoroughly fitted for, or that living where she does, she is able
fully to use the advantages & satisfy the claims of her present

position. We wish to act considerately to her, as well as wisely for the interests of the school'. In these discouraging circumstances Elizabeth had little choice but to leave.[33]

But if low pay and examination uncertainties were two unfavourable aspects of pupil-teaching, the former at least was less of a handicap in the remoter country districts, where average juvenile wages were low. Particularly in the 1840s and 1850s, the £10 offered to a first-year pupil-teacher candidate compared quite favourably with the annual earnings of a young female domestic servant or a male farm worker. While for the sons of rural craftsmen, like blacksmiths and carpenters, in whose trades apprenticeships were customary, the limited earnings which went with the training period were accepted as short-term penalties which would be outweighed by long-term advantages. Only after changes in the system of payment for pupil-teachers from 1862, following government economies, did financial considerations begin seriously to affect the more isolated rural communities, too.

Youngsters who became pupil-teachers were usually from a working-class background. As the Rev. B. M. Cowie, HMI, noted rather condescendingly in the early 1860s, their parents were 'respectable persons, of decent habits, and unimpeachable character . . .; they are the best representatives of the working classes. . . . They . . . exemplify the virtues which thrive perhaps best in a humble station.'[34] In country areas, in the view of a colleague, they tended to be 'the children of small tradesmen, yeomen, or the upper servants in gentlemen's families.' In the towns, and particularly in London, they belonged 'to the better and higher divisions of the operative classes . . . They are the children of respectable artisans, silk-weavers, cabinet makers, etc.'[35] These generalisations are borne out by an examination of training college records. Thus of the first one hundred students admitted to the College of St Matthias at Fishponds, Bristol, between 1852 and 1858, thirty-nine were the daughters of shopkeepers and artisans; ten of servants; and nine of farmers.[36] Similarly of the first fifty students to enter the Hockerill Training College at Bishop's Stortford, Hertfordshire, between November 1852 and January 1855, twenty-one were the daughters of shopkeepers and artisans, nine of servants and eight of labourers. The journal, the *Pupil-Teacher*, emphasised this point too, in 1859 when it declared :

Many a country boy, whose highest ambition, ten years since, would have been to be the village innkeeper or the village blacksmith . . . will now aspire to a profession. . . . He has [now] at least a fair chance of raising himself in the social scale. . . . Many a country girl will now, by becoming a pupil-teacher, be first in her family, for many generations, to be accounted of a higher grade than that of peasants and domestic servants. . . . In short the pupil-teacher system is probably working a social change of far greater magnitude than perhaps even the most imaginative or far sighted amongst us supposes.[37]

Even in the 1870s and 1880s the recruitment pattern was much the same. At Culham College, for example, of forty-two students admitted early in 1871 almost half came from a background of small shopkeepers and artisans, while at Winchester in the same year, of nineteen entrants, eight were the sons of artisans (carpenters, tailors, etc), two of gardeners, one of a labourer, and one of a coachman.

For every young pupil-teacher the first day at work was something of an ordeal. Often the appointment would be taken up at the school which the apprentice had attended as a scholar, and so there were all the problems of adjusting to a new relationship. If the apprenticeship were away from home, then board and lodgings had to be arranged with a suitable family and new friends made. Flora Thompson describes the initiation of one such girl, Charity Finch, in the 1890s. Charity was the daughter of a North Oxfordshire carpenter, and as was customary, until her apprenticeship had been approved by the HMI, she first of all took up an appointment as a monitress in the infant class, with 'her badge of office, a short, light cane, known as a pointer, officially intended for pointing out the letters of the alphabet on the big wall card to her class of infants, but equally useful for banging the desk to give emphasis to her instructions.' In order to support the dignity of her new position,

> her hair, which had hitherto hung loose upon her shoulders, was plaited into a long, thick pigtail. Her skirts were brought down from her knees to her ankles and, over them, instead of a white pinafore, she wore a small black, or coloured apron. Instead of as "Charity" or "Cherry", as formerly, the children

of her class were told to address her as "Teacher", and this trifling rise in status gave her great satisfaction, for she felt she had taken the first step towards realising her long-cherished ambition of becoming the mistress of a village school.[38]

Another girl, who began pupil-teaching in 1886, remembered that one of her first tasks was to look after the 'baby' class, whose members were 'packed like sardines, in a stuffy room taken up largely by a rigid wooden gallery with little floor space. . . . On hot afternoons some of the mites were apt to fall asleep and my first job was to lift them from the gallery, stand them in front of the class and steady them to keep them from falling.' In her experience, 'the main subjects taught were writing on slates (and cleaned with spit ! !) and the alphabet by the teacher banging a letter card placed on an easel and the children shouting the names of the letters (much to the annoyance of the teacher in the next room).'[39]

A third youngster, who began pupil-teaching at the age of fourteen at an Essex Infant School around the turn of the century, started her day by reading Bible stories to her small charges. Next there would be counting beads on a frame and singing : 'Then the children used to play with sand on slates. I was paid a shilling a week and received it once a month. I thought I was very rich with the first four shillings I earned. I gave it all to my mother to help pay for a new white dress for my Confirmation.'[40]

However, as a witness to the Newcastle Commission pointed out, the daily round could be a good deal harder than these examples indicate, especially for female apprentices. During the earlier years of the pupil-teacher system, they were expected to spend over five hours a day, five days a week in instructing the scholars; to that time had to be added the hour and a half devoted each day to their own instruction, plus the period necessary for preparation of lessons and private study. Then there would be home duties to carry out, especially for the daughters of artisans and labourers, who formed the bulk of female apprentices :

Her parents earn from 30s. down to 12s., or it may be less, a week. She is not unfrequently one of several children, sometimes the only girl, or the only girl above infancy. It is a great wrong to her mother, father, brothers, and sisters, if she be prevented from bearing her fair share of the usual household work of her home, and a greater injury to herself if she be excused from this. She ought to bear her part of the family house-cleaning, the family cooking, the family washing, and the family clothes-making and clothes-mending. Otherwise, if she fail to obtain a Queen's scholarship, or if she marry an elementary schoolmaster, or a small shopkeeper, or a small yeoman, she will be anything but a good housewife; or if she become a certified schoolmistress, she will not be the person whom sensible thoughtful parents of humble life will care to entrust with the formation of the character of their girls.

These home duties claim at least on an average an hour a day of her time.

Next, she is an apprentice TEACHER in an ELEMENTARY school. She may have charge of a section of 40 children. She must be engaged in *teaching* daily for not less than $5\frac{1}{2}$ hours; and in preparing the school for her class, and putting things away, &c., for about another half-hour daily.

These school duties claim at least six hours a day, on an average of five days in the week.

Again, those school-managers who have the interests of their female apprentices really at heart, and the interests of the children who are already so much influenced by their example, or who will hereafter be under their care, require the female apprentices, with the assistance of the elder girls and monitors, to do sometimes all the household work of the school premises, sometimes all this, except scrubbing the larger and rougher floors. They also require them to visit, to inquire after absent children, dividing this duty between them and the principal teacher. These duties provide healthy bodily exercise.

These school duties, which are a most important detail in the training which is to fit them for their office, claim on an average another hour a day, or six hours a week.

Already we have taken up *eight hours* a day on an average for five days in the week. But there is yet a claim on their time for one and a half hours daily. They have to spend an hour and a half a day for five days in the week in the class with the mistress; when she is to revise and correct the exercises they have written at home; to hear them [read] the lessons they have prepared for her at home; to submit them to written examinations; to direct them as to what they are to study by themselves; to point out to them the difficulties they will meet, and when they have failed to overcome them without assistance to aid their own efforts to do so; to practise them in arithmetic and English grammar; to improve them in reading and penmanship; to exercise them in the fourth and fifth years in composition on some given subject; to instruct them in the art of teaching; to make up with their assistance the *voluminous school registers and school accounts*; and to give them such admonitions as occasion may require.

This makes *nine and a half hours* a day for *five days* in the week, or nearly *eight hours* a day for *six days* in a week.[41]

In more than one school pupil-teachers were also expected to 'overlook children's play' to make sure the youngsters did not bully one another, while responsibility for 'the care of the flower-beds' might also fall to their lot. Leisure time was minimal and it is small wonder that with such a daunting daily grind many of the young trainees became pale and drawn. As one observer commented when a party of thirty London pupil-teachers was taken to Cambridge to look over the colleges and watch the college boat races, 'it was frequently remarked by the men who entertained them how unenthusiastic they were, and how difficult it was to make them laugh'. They probably felt that life offered them little to laugh about. Only rarely did they fall victim to original sin, like the pupil-teacher and monitor in a Somerset school, who aroused the ire of their headmaster when : 'This afternoon I went into the class-room where they were engaged at 2.40 (lesson began at 2.15). Not a stroke of work had been done, and the teachers were playing round the blackboard.'[42]

With such a humdrum daily existence, it was not surprising that the quality of teaching which the youngsters offered left much to be desired, even if it were an improvement on the old monitorial system. All too often, in the view of one HMI, they fell 'into the faults of meagreness, dryness and emptiness, or the opposite and not less mischievous evils of presumption and ostentation'.[43] Mannerisms had to be kept under strict control. A Wolverhampton headmaster, James Saunders, in his *Practical Hints for Pupil Teachers on Class Management*, published in 1877, warned against 'unnecessary noise' or movement, stressing that the successful apprentice would 'refrain from giving huge raps on the desk or black-board with his pointer, from taking giant strides from one end of the room to the other, from banging the doors after him, from pinching his boys' ears on the sly till they howl again'. (Officially corporal punishment was the prerogative of the head teacher.) Saunders noted, too, that if the apprentice purchased new shoes 'and particularly [if they were] raspish and creaking, he [should] give them a week's exercise out of school before wearing them in it'. Attention must be kept at all times on the task in hand, with a careful avoidance of winking or joking with fellow trainees, since such lapses from grace would be sure to be quickly noted by the scholars and reported to their parents:

> Thus, though the Schoolmaster, perhaps, is unaware of it, the parents know perfectly well . . . how many minutes were employed in reading or writing love-letters; how many times Brown or Williams was sent out to look at the clock; how many sly punches, cuffs, luggings, &c., were bestowed on Robinson.

Instead of this:

> Let your black-boards be clean . . . and provided with chalk and dusters, your easels furnished with pegs . . . your books ready, your slates clean, your pencils sharpened, your pens overhauled, your attendance register at hand . . . your dictation papers at your elbow—in short, everything ready that by any chance you may require; and all this before school commences.[44]

One youngster who failed to meet these standards was the pupil-teacher at Aveton Gifford in Devon, whose 'criticism lesson' was contemptuously described by his head as 'a few facts hastily jumbled together and rapidly discharged at the class'. It lasted only five minutes. But the reproofs handed out on such occasions, especially when given publicly, could have a wounding effect on some of the more sensitive trainees. Margaret Bondfield, later a leader of the Shop Assistants' Union and the first woman Cabinet Minister, began her working career at the age of thirteen as a stipendiary monitor at Chard Board School. She seems to have got on quite well until one day 'she pronounced the word Mesopotamia in a manner that caused [the headmaster] to burst out laughing. He did not tell her how to pronounce it correctly: his laughter was like a searing iron passed over that small sensitive soul'. Shortly afterwards she left to become a shop assistant in Brighton.[45]

But it was in 1862 that the problems of the apprentices were particularly increased when, following the introduction of the Revised Code, government grants both to them and to the heads who trained them were ended as part of a general economy drive. Robert Lowe, Vice-President of the Education Department at this time, excused the cuts by pointing out that one danger of allowing educational expenditure to proceed as hitherto, was that it might become 'instead of a grant for education, a grant to maintain the so-called vested interests of those engaged in education'—of whom pupil-teachers and their supervisors clearly formed a part. Henceforward apprentices had to make their own arrangements with the managers of the schools at which they worked, while supervising teachers were expected to give instruction for one hour a day, five days a week, without payment. The position of the head mistress of a Hampshire school during the mid-1880s is but one of many hundreds which could be quoted; for her £60 a year salary, plus 10 per cent of the general government grant to the school, she was expected to give 'the usual course of instruction to pupil teacher and paid monitor' as well as playing the organ in Church on Sunday, conducting a Sunday School and training the choir.[46]

Needless to say the enthusiasm with which teachers pursued their unpaid duties was not always of the highest, while the special instruction given to pupil-teachers was provided at times designed to suit the head rather than the apprentice, as at one Devon school, where in 1863 lessons began at 6.30 a.m.! Similarly Mrs Frances Anne Bowkett, who was apprenticed at Cherwell British School, Banbury, at the end of the 1880s remembers going for lessons between 7.40 and 8.40 each morning, 'and then we started teaching'; her regular class numbered fifty to sixty children, aged about nine.[47]

Managers, in their anxiety to keep down expenditure, now engaged apprentices on the most economical terms possible rather than seeking to recruit the best candidates for the job. In 1871

HMI Bellairs noted critically that all too often 'managers [had] gone into the market and hired labourers at the lowest price at which they could be had, rejecting often the better agent because it was dearer. In some cases I have heard of £4 per annum as the stipend of a pupil-teacher. In consequence of this the social status of our pupil-teachers has deteriorated, and to some extent the physical and mental condition'.[48] As early as November 1863, the Rev. B. M. Cowie, HMI, was bewailing the shortage of pupil-teachers coming forward for appointment. By 1866, there were only 8,937 youngsters under training as compared to the peak figure of 13,964 employed in 1861. Not until the 1870 Education Act had broadened career prospects was the trend clearly reversed, with numbers again moving firmly upwards.

Confirmation of the poor rates of pay offered to apprentices can be found in surviving pupil-teacher agreements—as at Aldermaston, Berkshire, where in 1869 one girl was engaged on a five-year term 'entirely at her own charge', i.e. without any stipend at all. Her male colleague, engaged in the same year, was paid the small sum of 2s. 6d. a week, or £6 10s. a year. Another female apprentice engaged at this school in January 1872 was to be paid one shilling a week during her first year, with the rate increasing by steps of 1s. per week in the second and subsequent years of her five-year term. But the 5s. per week, or £13 per annum, earned in her final year could hardly be regarded as generous. Countless trainees elsewhere shared these conditions.[49] In fact on a national basis it was suggested in 1869 that in Church of England Schools about one in ten of all male pupil-teachers and about one in six of the females had starting salaries *under* £5 a year; only about one in twenty-five of the females started at over £10 a year.[50] Almost thirty years later complaints on the inadequacy of stipends were still prevalent. In 1897 HMI King claimed that in the West of England £6 a year for a girl and £8 for a boy was 'the average salary at starting', rising to a maximum of £15 per annum. While in Oxfordshire as late as 1904, and despite some improvements in pay over the intervening period, half of the county's forty-two pupil teachers were earning £12 10s. per annum or less. The lowest rate was a mere £4.[51] Yet, as the principal of St Mary's Roman Catholic Training College, Hammersmith, pointed out, male pupil-teachers at the end of their training ought to earn at least £30 a year:

'I do not see how a young man of 18 can at the present rate live respectably and keep up the sort of position a young man should do who is going to be a teacher'.[52] But the rates actually paid to such lads in Roman Catholic schools were, according to his calculations, in the range of £11 to £19 per annum only.

There is little doubt that the poor stipends offered from the 1860s onwards were particularly discouraging to male apprentices, and their numbers declined ever more sharply in relation to their female counterparts and, indeed, in aggregate terms, too, from the later 1870s. On 31 December 1859 there were 6,605 male and 6,253 female pupil-teachers employed in England and Wales; then in the following year, for the first time the number of first-year girl apprentices in England (though not yet in Wales) exceeded that of the males.[53] Thereafter, as noted earlier, the sex ratio changed increasingly in favour of the girls, with 6,384 boys and 8,228 girls employed as trainees in England and Wales in 1870; by 1880 these totals had risen to 10,822 and 21,306, respectively, and by 1896 the position had been reached of 7,737 males and 28,137 females employed as pupil-teachers or probationers—the latter being too young to be formally apprenticed.[54] In rural areas in particular the cheaper female apprentice became the order of the day by the later nineteenth century.

These developments naturally affected the relative numbers of male and female teachers in the schools. In 1869 there had been 48 female certificated teachers and 60 female assistants to every 100 teachers in each category; by 1896 the respective figures were 60 certificated female teachers and 84 female assistants to every 100, and approximately the same proportions were still applicable at the end of the century.[55] In 1872 for the first time the number of certificated mistresses—at 7,778—exceeded that of the qualified males, who now totalled 7,632.

So it was in these circumstances of difficulty of recruitment, especially among boys, that in 1877 the period of apprenticeship was reduced from five years to four. Two years earlier the government had also introduced a new pupil-teacher grant which successful candidates could earn for their school (though not directly for themselves.) This amounted to 40s. a year for a 'fair' pass in the annual examinations and 60s. for a 'good' one.[56]

Meanwhile in the larger towns efforts began to be made to try to cope with the weaknesses in the instructional aspects of pupil-teaching by setting up centres to which the apprentices could be sent each day for their personal education. But in country areas, where schools were scattered and pupil-teachers comparatively thin on the ground, such schemes were not practicable.

The first centres were opened by the rate-aided Liverpool School Board in 1876, the Board having been induced to take this action by the examination successes of pupil-teachers from the city's Roman Catholic schools, who had been receiving some central class instruction from local nuns under a private denominational arrangement. Then in 1878, when changes in the government Code allowed stipendiary monitors to be substituted for the old first-year pupil-teachers, 'the monitors engaged by the board were formed into half-time classes, and a special teacher was appointed for their instruction'.[57] Next, in 1883, all the pupil-teachers in the city's board schools were allowed one half-day per week during school hours for private study, and finally in 1884 half-time provisions were extended to first-year pupil-teachers as well. Similar experiments were carried on in London, where attempts to give pupil-teachers centralised instruction in 1875 had brought the capital's school board into conflict with the Education Department, 'because the Code stipulated that the instruction of apprentices was to be given by the headmasters of the schools in which they worked.'[58] Only when, from 1880, central instruction received official recognition were the Liverpool and London experiments able to function properly. And in 1887 when the Royal Commission on the Elementary Education Acts (usually known as the Cross Commission) was sitting, there were eleven centres at work in London alone, giving instruction to 1,636 pupil-teachers, in addition to the facilities offered by other large towns and cities. Accommodation of every type was utilised by the authorities to house their courses, including disused voluntary schools, private houses, or part of a board school; often the surroundings were extremely uncomfortable. One youngster who attended a London centre at this time, later described it eloquently as a 'rat-hole'.[59]

The Cross Commission gave cautious approval to the innovation, recommending that managers of voluntary (i.e. non-rate-aided) schools should be encouraged to follow the example of school boards and 'to extend the advantages of central class teaching', while 'extra grants should be offered to those managers or boards who successfully adopt that course'. Nevertheless not all of those appearing before the Commission agreed with these suggestions. One witness claimed that central instruction weakened the link between teachers and apprentices, while another, rather ominously, considered it 'far inferior to the old system in dealing with pupil-teachers who require "whipping-up".'[60]

The Majority Report of the Commission also accepted, again in cautious tones, the general principle of pupil-teaching as a mode of training, declaring that there was 'no other available, or, as we prefer to say, equally trustworthy source from which an adequate supply of teachers is likely to be forthcoming; and with modifications, tending to the improvement of their education, the apprenticeship of pupil-teachers, we think, ought to be upheld'.[61]

But a minority of the Commissioners disputed this conclusion. They issued their own Report, disagreeing strongly that there was 'no other equally trustworthy source from which an adequate supply of teachers is likely to be forthcoming'. Instead they called for a broader training course and a prolonged period of preliminary education before students were entrusted with the management of classes. In their opinion the pupil-teacher system was now the weakest part of the educational machinery, and great changes were needed in it if it were to be continued in the future: 'we think . . . that no pupil-teacher should be entrusted with a class till he or she is at least 15 years of age; the first year or two of apprenticeship being almost entirely employed in learning'.[62]

Against this background, pupil-teacher centres proliferated from the mid-1880s. And whilst they undoubtedly raised the academic standards of those students able to attend them, apprentices in more remote areas were placed at a considerable disadvantage, especially when, at the end of their training period, they competed for a Queen's Scholarship. In 1896, HMI Tillard lamented that in Norfolk :

> Outside Norwich and Yarmouth no central classes for pupil-teachers exist nor does it seem likely that they will be formed to any great extent in country districts generally. . . . The supply of country pupil-teachers seems to be still dwindling, and there seems to be a reluctance on the part of teachers to undertake the training of pupil-teachers. Handicapped as he

is in the struggle with his town brother, still the country pupil-teacher will be sadly missed if he disappears, and if the country schools have to depend for their future teachers on the failures of large towns.

(This latter comment referred to the general belief that only those who could not succeed in better-paid urban employment would undertake the running of a country school.)

In West Cornwall, central classes were similarly impracticable:

In some of the small towns the teachers of the schools have combined to give the instruction to their pupil-teachers in common, each teacher taking all the pupils in one subject of the course. . . . Besides this, in several small towns, lectures in geography and history have been given on Saturdays to all the pupil-teachers that could be collected there, on payment of one guinea annually.[63]

But for many youngsters only correspondence courses could provide an answer. And in this connection it is significant that a Report by the Federation of Teachers in Central Classes for 1902 pointed out that of a total of 32,000 pupil-teachers and probationers employed in the schools only 17,000, or just over half, were receiving their instruction in centres. Yet at the 1902 scholarship examinations ninety-one out of the first one hundred successful candidates had been trained in the larger centres.[64] This was a measure of the competition that the rural apprentice had to face.

At local level, there is certainly evidence of the difficulty of recruiting pupil-teachers for village schools at the end of the century. At Yateley in Hampshire, one youngster had to be recruited from Devon for the autumn term of 1897. Unfortunately he proved utterly ineffective, as the master noted in his log book on 10 September: 'E. Wormacott stammers and is quite useless as P.T. here. He leaves today.' An entry in the Managers' Minute Book four days later added that 'Ernest Wormacott was an utter failure and . . . the Chairman of the Managers [has] sent him home again, and paid his fares both ways.'[65]

While at Finchampstead in Berkshire when a new circular on the instruction of pupil-teachers was issued by the Education Department in January 1894, the school correspondent noted:

'I don't see how in a Small School like Finchampstead these Rules can be carried out & therefore I think we shd. avoid engaging another P.T. unless our School should greatly increase.' The requirement to which he seems to have taken particular exception was that: 'The Managers should provide good reference books and text books for the use of the Pupil Teacher, such books to remain the property of the School.'[66]

In these circumstances many managers of smaller schools preferred the cheaper alternative of the stipendiary monitress, whose employment carried with it less managerial responsibility and a lower rate of pay than applied even to pupil-teachers. The motives of economy which led to the employment of monitors are confirmed in many log books, as at one Oxfordshire school where in October 1886 the master noted that the school managers: 'Finding they are likely to be about £50 deficient at the end of the year . . . decided that next year the staff should be reduced—and that a paid monitress should supply the place of an assistant mistress.'[67] At Barton Stacey in Hampshire, where a monitress had been engaged as a replacement to an adult assistant in 1896, the managers discussed in 1898 whether they should replace her by a pupil-teacher but: 'it was agreed that a monitor would meet the requirements of the School, while its circumstances would not warrant the engagement of a pupil teacher.'[68]

Meanwhile, discussions on the merits and demerits of the pupil-teacher system were continuing and in 1896 a Departmental Committee was appointed to enquire once more into the whole question. It reported back two years later, and its views on the desirable future trend of elementary school teacher training are important, as, in the long run, it was they which were to prevail. Hitherto, the Committee pointed out, elementary schools had been the natural recruiting ground for their own future instructors. The knowledge of school routine, familiarity with its methods and discipline, all made it comparatively easy for those accustomed to the elementary school to fall into its ways and associations and to look for a career within its walls. But it was desirable that would-be teachers should have some secondary school experience to broaden their outlook:

The traditions of primary teaching are still, through no fault of the teachers, narrower than is consistent with sound education; and we believe that better methods, greater spontaneity, a wider outlook . . . would result from the more frequent employment in primary schools of persons whose experience has not been exclusively or chiefly primary.[69]

Pupil-teacher centres were one way of dealing with the problem, but they were expensive to run and produced 'professional and social narrowness of aim', while their staffs were often imperfectly qualified and of limited training:

> We look forward to the ultimate conversion of those centres which are well staffed and properly equipped into real secondary schools, where, although perhaps intending teachers may be in the majority, they will have ampler time for their studies and will be instructed side by side with pupils who have other careers in view.

Unfortunately the Committee's report did not immediately lead to reforms, although the basic length of pupil-teacherships in urban, if not in rural, areas was reduced from four years to three in 1900, to encourage trainees to continue their full-time education to the age of fifteen. But thanks to family poverty and a shortage of secondary schools, the Committee recognised that in country districts this recommendation was not practicable: 'pupils could rarely . . . be retained at school to so late an age as 15'. In 1902 the annual examination of pupil-teachers was abolished. Then, with the passage of the 1902 Education Act came the establishment of local education authorities to replace the existing administrative machinery and to be responsible for the maintenance of both elementary and secondary schools. The way was finally opened for the implementation of the Committee's proposals.

Under fresh regulations introduced in 1903, therefore, two important principles for pupil-teacher training were laid down. Firstly, employment in elementary schools was to be postponed, so as to ensure the continued full-time education of the future teachers themselves; and secondly, as far as possible their personal education was to be continued during the period of apprenticeship itself on more satisfactory terms than had hitherto applied. The first aim was achieved by raising the minimum age for the recognition of pupil-teachers to sixteen—although, significantly, in rural areas the lower limit of fifteen was accepted. The second was secured by an insistence that trainees should receive at least three hundred hours of instruction in approved centres or classes for pupil-teachers, with many secondary schools recognised for this purpose. 'The importance of drawing candidates for the elementary teaching profession from among secondary pupils was stressed, as was the aim of utilising the secondary schools . . . for preliminary training purposes.'[70] An increasing number of secondary schools now became involved in this work, and by the year 1906–7, 357 of them were recognised as pupil-teacher centres, alongside 179 independent centres which were still carrying on their work. By this time, too, the curriculum of students had been widened as compared to the mid-nineteenth century position, so that even female pupil-teachers were now expected to study algebra, Euclid, arithmetic, composition, English, French, geography, history, science, drawing and writing as well as the inevitable needlework.[71] They were also expected to prepare appropriate 'notes of lessons' and to give practical demonstrations of teaching. (The surviving exercise book of one Buckinghamshire pupil-teacher shows that the lesson notes were to be presented under three headings—'matter', 'method', and 'illustrations'. A composition lesson on 'The Farm' begins hopefully in the 'method' column : 'I shall first gain the attention of the class by asking them what they would like to be when they grow up. Among the answers given I shall probably get one boy to tell me that he would like to be a farmer.'[72])

In 1907 fresh regulations sought to extend the full-time education of prospective teachers to eighteen years of age, by offering bursar grants to those secondary scholars aged sixteen and above, who 'had been attending a secondary school for at least three years' and had expressed an intention of training for the elementary teaching profession. The grant was to be available for one year and after its expiry the youngsters could either proceed directly to a training college or could serve for a year as student-teachers, in order to gain practical experience of their future profession.[73] By the first World War this method had become the most common mode of entry; in 1911–12, there were 2,858 bursars in training, as opposed to 1,955 commencing pupil-teacher courses.[74]

In rural areas, however, the continuing scarcity of secondary schools and the length of the unpaid training period required made bursaries unattractive to many candidates, and so it was accepted that in villages at least 'the ancient resource' of pupil-teachership 'must continue to be available'. In fact especially in Wales there was a very decided swing back to the pupil-teaching system just before 1914. Welsh supporters of this argued that because of a scarcity of candidates willing to undertake the longer training period and with many small rural schools out of reach of secondary provisions, if 'the children who might be selected and trained for teachers in rural districts are not allowed to enter the profession through a simple apprenticeship system, they will be lost to the profession altogether.'[75] Other critics were afraid that the new developments might mean that elementary teaching became the preserve of middle-class children. In the autumn of 1908, the *Sunday Chronicle* published an article entitled 'A Stolen Profession' in which it claimed that middle-class youngsters rather than the children of artisans were the main beneficiaries of the new system of secondary scholarships and bursaries: 'A useful profession is being stolen from the child of the working man, and while he sleepeth the enemy hath removed his landmark.'[76]

So although by the early twentieth century the *desired* method of entry to the teaching profession had been established as full-time education to the age of seventeen or eighteen, followed by appropriate training at a college, for various reasons in many rural districts this objective proved impossible to achieve. Indeed, thanks to a shortage of qualified staff and to a lack of funds, in many of the smaller village schools it was the untrained *monitor* who provided the only form of assistance for the head teacher. An analysis of Devon staffing records in 1903 (when the county council assumed control of elementary schools) shows that thirty per cent of all assistants at that time were monitors, as opposed to about twelve per cent who were pupil-teachers: 'nine out of twenty assistants in board schools, and eight out of twenty in voluntary schools, were under eighteen.'[77] A similar situation existed in Oxfordshire, where in 1904 twenty-four per cent of all assistant teachers were monitors, as opposed to around seven per cent who were pupil-teachers.[78] The comparative cheapness of this policy is underlined by the fact that monitors might be paid as little as £2 12s. per annum even in 1904.

D

Sadly, too, despite the regulations of the Board of Education, which in 1899 had replaced the Committee of Council as the central administrative body for education, staffing difficulties continued to hit pupil-teachers' educational opportunities in many country areas. At one Hampshire school during September 1903, the apprentices were supposed to attend a pupil-teacher centre at Basingstoke. But on the twenty-first of that month the headmaster noted : 'I cannot spare Edith Nye to attend the P.T. Centre at Basingstoke'. At another school two years later the managers were forced to reduce the number of pupil-teachers who could be released to attend the Basingstoke centre at any one time because of general staff shortages.[79]

So the old system muddled along until after the first World War. Its gradual disappearance from the later 1920s onwards marked the end of an important phase in English elementary education but one which by that date had long outlived its usefulness.[80] From 1927 local authorities wishing to employ apprentices had now 'to apply for special permission' and to 'state fully the reasons' for which they desired to recruit them. In these circumstances pupil-teacher numbers fell from 1,288 appointed in 1926–27 to a mere ninety-five in 1937–38, of whom only eighteen were boys.

4

Training College Life

The efficiency of a Training School is not to be measured wholly or chiefly by its power of communicating knowledge. It is not for the knowledge acquired, or for the exercise of the understanding in the acquisition of it, that it is most to be valued, but rather for that moral discipline of the Students which is associated with the laborious, the faithful, and the punctual discharge of a duty—for that *faithfulness* which must characterize the life of an Institution, of which the ground-tone is dedication to the work of God, and labour, and truth.

Report by one of Her Majesty's Inspectors of Schools, quoted in F. C. PRITCHARD, *The Story of Westminster College, 1851–1951*, London 1951, 20.

The English Normal Training School is founded by the contributions of the Religious Communion with which it is connected. It generally consists of a group of buildings, in a collegiate style of architecture, comprising dormitories, a hall, and a refectory, and domestic offices, as well as a library, class-rooms, and a residence for the Principal, Vice-Principal, and three or four Masters. Immediately adjacent is an elementary school for the poor, with a house for the Master, who is commonly also a teacher of the theory of school method and organisation in the College.

SIR JAMES KAY SHUTTLEWORTH, *Public Education as Affected by the Minutes of the Committee of Privy Council from 1846 to 1852*, London 1853, 72–3. (Kay Shuttleworth had been created a baronet in 1849, on his retirement from the Committee of Council on Education.)

BY THE middle of the 1830s, as we saw in chapter 2, discontent at existing teacher training facilities had become widespread. The limitations of the instruction provided by the National and the British and Foreign School Societies were recognised, the weaknesses of the monitorial system were being ever more strongly condemned, and the examples supplied by European training schemes, notably in Germany, Switzerland and France, were commented upon with growing favour. Henry Brougham spoke enthusiastically in the House of Lords of the French training schools which he had visited and claimed that 'the improvement of the quality of education [had] every where, except in England, gone hand-in-hand with the exertions made for spreading it and augmenting its amount'. To him the seminaries for training masters were 'an invaluable gift to mankind, and [led] to the indefinite improvement of Education. It is this which, above every thing, we ought to labour to introduce into our system'.[1]

Some pioneering work was, admittedly, being carried on in Britain itself—notably by David Stow in Glasgow from the 1820s. Unlike the approach in contemporary monitorial training establishments, Stow insisted 'on the influence of the master upon the children being direct and continuous'. And as a large number of children were to be taught together he utilised a raised platform or gallery for most of his lessons, so that the teacher could see every child, and every child could see him. Learning, Stow insisted, was not cramming but 'doing' : 'What we mean by training is causing children *to do*, whether doing be an exercise of the head, the heart or the hand.' Understanding rather than mere memorising was a key aspect of his work with children, and for teachers seeking to train under his auspices the average duration of the course was eight to nine months—though 'in the case of candidates coming with poor academic qualifications a minimum period of eighteen months was required'. Much emphasis was placed on grounding the trainees in the techniques of their profession, with about two-fifths of the students' forty-hour week devoted to observation and practice in teaching.[2] In 1838 Dr Kay himself was to describe Stow's training institution as 'the most perfect school of this description', and it certainly attracted a number of recruits from England—with the Wesleyan Education Committee alone sending 248 men and 90 women during the period 1841 to 1851. In the latter year they opened their own college at Westminster and the need to use Stow's facilities thereupon ceased.[3]

A further innovation appeared in 1836 with the setting up in London of the Home and Colonial Infant School Society. This had the explicit aim of preparing teachers for infant work based on the principles of Pestalozzi. Once again large numbers of children were taught simultaneously by the teacher and great stress was laid upon self-activity, with the children participating directly in the learning process by the use of personal observation. 'Object lessons' became an integral part of the Home and Colonial system.[4]

However, these endeavours were mere straws in the wind rather than major influences within the teacher training system as it then existed in this country. So in 1838 the National Society set up a Committee of Inquiry to investigate conditions and to make recommendations for possible improvements. Out of its deliberations came proposals for the establishment of specialised diocesan training schools throughout the country, and for the setting up of a Metropolitan Training Institution in the capital itself to replace the Society's existing central schools. It was this report which provided the basis for the diocesan training colleges (or normal colleges as they were sometimes called) that dominated teacher training for the rest of the nineteenth century. From 1839 the first steps were taken to implement the Committee's recommendations, with training establishments speedily set up within the dioceses of Canterbury, Chester, Chichester, Bath and Wells, Durham, Exeter, Gloucester and Bristol, Lichfield, Salisbury, Winchester and Oxford. In their early days these institutions were extremely modest affairs, catering for a mere handful of students who were accommodated in the smallest of buildings. Thus the training school for Bath and Wells was held in the vicarage house at East Brent; that at Oxford in a house on the outskirts of the city, which at its maximum accommodated twenty-five people.[5] One student who attended there recalled that the college buildings comprised two rooms only, 'one . . . serving for lectures, study, meals, and indoor recreation on wet days, and the other over it, for a common dormitory with beds crowded together as closely as possible'.[6] The rest of the house was occupied by the Principal, his large family and their servants. Similarly at Winchester the first college was set up in a small house near the Cathedral, where it was noted that there was maximum accommodation for nineteen students.[7] Although a few scholarships or exhibitions were offered by the diocesan authorities to entrants, most had to pay fees or to obtain private sponsors. One such was the former servant of the rector of Wootton, Oxfordshire, who entered the Oxford training school in October 1849 under the patronage of his old employer. He remained for eight months before leaving to take charge of Wootton school 'for which he came to prepare'. Fees were quite substantial, amounting to £23 a year at Winchester, to cover board and washing (tuition and lodgings being free), while at Oxford they were £20 per annum. At both colleges entrants were also expected to bring sheets and towels with them.[8]

In all of the training schools great stress was laid on the cultivation of the correct moral attitudes by the new recruits. Typical of this philosophy was the comment by the Bishop of Salisbury in April 1814, that 'a good moral character was of more importance to the school teacher than good brains'. While at Cheltenham, where a college was opened with seven students in June 1847, the founders solemnly pledged

> to the Church and to the world that whatever else is done or neglected, this great, this fundamental point shall never be overlooked; namely—the education of the students in those Scriptural doctrines and Spiritual truths which are bound up in the very designation of the Institution: 'SCRIPTURAL, PROTESTANT, EVANGELICAL—in accordance with the ARTICLES AND LITURGY of the CHURCH OF ENGLAND.'

The object was for entrants not merely to acquire knowledge but to develop those qualities of mind which would enable them 'to train up children in the ways of Godliness'.[9] It is small wonder that the Rev. B. M. Cowie, HMI, should see training college graduates in the early 1860s as the 'secular officers of the Church' whose main task was 'dispelling ignorance, and eliciting the dormant powers of self-help and progress'.[10]

In the non-Anglican colleges which grew up at around this time attitudes were very similar—as at the Methodists' Westminster college, which was opened in 1851. When the first group of students arrived in October of that year, they were firmly assured of 'the supreme importance of personal piety', if they were to be successful: 'The cultivation of a vital and practical religion was essential.'[11] Here, as elsewhere, prayers were held morning and evening, with all the students required to attend.

But the religious denominations were not alone in their concern to improve the standard of teacher training. The government, too, began to turn its attention in this direction and as early as 1835, £10,000 was voted by parliament for the building of a training school. That allocation was made, significantly enough, after the speech by Brougham in the House of Lords quoted earlier, in which he drew attention to the government-controlled colleges which were flourishing on the continent.[12] However, any attempt to set up a state-financed college in Britain quickly ran into fierce opposition from the religious denominations, who feared government competition in this field. So in 1839 the cash was handed over to the National Society and the British and Foreign Society in order that they might extend their own facilities. Three years later it was used to defray part of the cost of reorganisation and extension at the British Society's Borough Road premises and to establish the new National Society institution, St Mark's College, at Chelsea. In February 1840 a grant of £2,500 was also approved by the Committee of Council 'for the completion of the building' in which Stow's Glasgow training school was conducted.[13]

One of the most enthusiastic advocates of teacher training reform was James Kay Shuttleworth, who was from 1839 secretary to the Committee of Council on Education. When he realised that the attempts to promote a government training college were foundering he decided, with the help of friends, to establish an institution of his own at Battersea. The college was opened in February 1840 and, as he himself declared, it was intended to act as a model for the future 'and to show that masters trained in the spirit of Christian charity could conduct schools in which the children of all denominations were educated together.'[14] Initially two types of students were accepted; those aged thirteen, who were to be indentured as apprentices for seven years, and secondly, young men, aged between twenty and thirty, who were to be admitted for short courses of one year. However within three years it was decided to end recruitment of the very young entrants and from then onwards, eighteen became the minimum age accepted.

As with its diocesan counterparts, great stress was placed at Battersea on the inculcation of the correct social and moral attitudes. Kay Shuttleworth himself declared in 1843 : 'The main object of a Normal School is the *formation of the character of the schoolmaster.*' Although he appreciated the need for a pro-gramme of broad intellectual training he feared that unless this were accompanied by the strictest of moral guidance, it might foster conceit and over-confidence in the student. The remedy was to be found in religious training coupled with a spartan standard of living and hard physical and mental work. For in his view : 'The path of the teacher is strewn with disappointment, if he commence with a mercenary spirit. It is full of encouragement if he be inspired with the spirit of Christian charity.'

Battersea students (and staff) were from the beginning expected to combine study with domestic duties, gardening and even building operations—Kay Shuttleworth believing that the 'conceit of the pedagogue' was not 'likely to arise among either students or masters who cheerfully handle the trowel, the saw, or carry mortar in a hod to the top of the building.'[15] And when HMI Moseley visited the training school in February 1846 he noted that among the tasks already completed by the students were the erection of a Chinese pagoda, in trellis work, over one of the garden paths, the making of four rustic garden-seats, and the construction of a 'brick provision-house, near the piggery'.[16] From the start it was intended that the school should be as self-supporting as possible and so the growing of vegetables and the rearing of livestock formed an integral part of the daily routine. Only one servant was kept to do the cooking, and all the work of cleaning dormitories and making beds devolved on the students themselves. The day's labours commenced at 5.30 a.m. and after domestic chores had been completed everyone turned out to milk the cows or work in the garden :

> At 7.30 there was a short religious service, and afterwards the superintendent received the reports of the prefects, and frequently gave a short address. Breakfast was at 8.30, consisting of porridge and milk, and at this, as at every other meal, the tutors had the same fare as the students. Half an hour was more than sufficient for this frugal meal, fortified by which the students passed on to three hours' work in classes till noon, the first half-hour being devoted to religious instruction. An appetite for dinner was stimulated by an hour's work in the garden. Dinner was the main meal of the day, and was a substantial, if plain, repast. From 2 till 5 p.m. was spent in class again, with another hour of outdoor activity to follow. At 6.15 supper was taken, consisting of bread and milk, and

at 7 the students turned out for drill. The rest of the evening was spent in miscellaneous but useful activities like copying music, making notes on geography or mechanics, or practising singing. The day came to a close with evening prayers at 9, and all were in bed by 9.20.[17]

As Kay Shuttleworth himself piously remarked: 'By this laborious and frugal life, economy of management is reconciled with efficiency both of the moral and intellectual training of the School, and the master goes forth into the world, humble, industrious and instructed.'

From 1843, following the establishment of eighteen as the minimum age for new entrants, a course of at least eighteen months to two years was envisaged. A summary of subjects studied in the early 1840s shows that in the 'second class', six hours a week were spent on religious instruction; three on geography; eight on reading, etymology and grammar; five on mechanics and natural philosophy; six on music; and two each on English composition; history; arithmetic; pure mathematics and mensuration; and 'Pestalozzi'—a technique which was designed to develop the faculties in a 'natural order'. Gardening absorbed sixteen hours each week, teaching in the village school a further fifteen, and preparation for teaching five hours more. This meant that the students were occupied in one way or another for seventy-four hours a week.[18]

A similar programme was adopted by most of the other training schools at that date. As can be seen, technical education received a low priority, and it is significant that even in the mid-1880s—and despite a general widening of the range of subjects studied—the Royal Commission on Technical Instruction could still complain that the 'teaching of art and science subjects, in the Training Colleges . . . for elementary school teachers, is very defective'. Yet its calls for action to remedy these weaknesses— with art teaching provision described as 'inferior even to that . . . made for science'—were little heeded. Even where teachers did obtain qualifications to teach scientific subjects, the standard was often discouragingly low:

teachers crammed from their text-books, and when they were appointed to a school they adopted the same procedure with their pupils in order to obtain the maximum grant possible. It has been asserted that some candidates were able to pass the examination in chemistry without having had any practical experience in a laboratory and, perhaps, without having seen or used a test-tube. It was also said that the highest number of certificates in agriculture went to young men who had never stirred beyond the precincts of White-chapel.[19]

Most of the Battersea students were lower—or lower middle-class in origin—'the sons of small tradesmen, of bailiffs, and of servants or of superior mechanics'. It was a background which they shared, both then and later, with the recruits of other colleges, as we saw in the last chapter.

Later in the century, as competition for places intensified, the entrants from rural areas dwindled. For, as we have seen, the haphazard method of their early training as pupil-teachers in small country schools handicapped them in the struggle for selection when compared to the opportunities available to their urban colleagues. Once inside the colleges, however, both urban and rural students followed common courses, in order to meet the requirements of the final examination; little attempt was made to cope with the special problems of the small, all-age mixed village school, or the limited financial resources of a country district.

Kay Shuttleworth had intended that the Battersea college should exert a major influence on the development of the teacher training system, and so it proved. For 'it was the type to which all subsequently founded training colleges conformed until the advent of the Day Training College' in the 1890s.[20] But in 1843, for a variety of reasons, he decided to transfer the college to the National Society, and it remained associated with that body to the end of the century.

Battersea's policies regarding discipline, hours of work and academic pursuits were widely imitated elsewhere. This was particularly true of the frugal, closely controlled daily routine. At the Winchester diocesan training college even in the 1880s and 1890s the day commenced at 6.15 a.m., when the bell-man a second-year student, made his rounds. Half-an-hour later the bell rang again, to indicate 'going down'. Those who ignored the regulations faced fines; a failure to make one's bed properly led to a penalty of 2d., with a similar fine imposed for not opening the dormitory window. Smoking was strictly forbidden in the college—a restriction which most of its fellow institutions shared —and anyone caught smoking in the grounds, the college itself, or the city of Winchester was fined the substantial sum of 2s. 6d.

At mid-Victorian Culham College in Oxfordshire, which was opened in 1853 as a successor to the earlier Oxford diocesan training school, conditions were equally stringent. As one former student recalled, he and his fellows had to leave their chill and comfortless cubicles at 6.30 a.m. and were prohibited from re-entering them until they went to bed at night : 'No matter what was forgotten, what might be wanted from our scanty stores, no admittance was the rule, except by special permission.'[21] And he added : 'Oh! the miseries of those dreadfully cold mornings, when with chilblains on our hands, for want of a few pounds spent in heating the College we had to wash and dress in the bitter weather, with no possible chance of warmth, before going in to study for the dreary hour before Chapel, previous to which the student whose turn it was, swept the Class Room and lit the fire; coal, etc. being fetched by another student on similar duty.' At that time what he calls the 'monitorial system' was in full swing at Culham, and the 'duties' required of the students included 'sweeping rooms, fire-lighting, corridor cleaning, garden, postman, chapel cleaning, and town messenger'.

After morning chapel came breakfast. This consisted of bread, a small quantity of butter and an unpalatable beverage 'by courtesy, called "coffee" in the morning and "tea" in the afternoon. Served in jam pots adorned with the College Arms, the flavour of that beverage is with us, even to this day.'

When breakfast was over lectures commenced at 8.45 a.m. and continued until 1 p.m. The afternoons and evenings were taken up with drawing, music, recreation and private study, with a two-hours' stint at lessons after tea each day. Examinations were held every Tuesday afternoon from 5 p.m. to 6.30 p.m. for first-year men and every Saturday morning from 11 a.m. to 1 p.m. for those in their second year.

The 'recreation' period included a little football or cricket, gardening and spells of twenty minutes apiece pumping up the college water supply. This last was a much-hated duty, which, according to Alfred Pittman, a student in 1863–64, might be bartered by some of the more desperate for a 'week's butter' supply.

Culham also had strict prohibitions against speaking to girls or visiting the nearby small town of Abingdon. The punishment book for 1879 reveals that one student was rusticated 'for being in Abingdon, talking to a woman, on Saturday evening', while three others were 'severely reprimanded for stealing food from masters' dinner table'. This last was perhaps a tribute to the solid, uninspiring fare which was the students' lot, both at Culham and at many of the other colleges. According to one Culhamite, Benjamin Bailey, who attended from 1859 to 1861, the main meal each day consisted of 'relays of mutton and beef, and substantial puddings, but on Fridays we had the concentrated essence-of-all-the-week, in the form of a thick brown soup.'[22] Beer was also served but according to Bailey, the only man who took kindly to this beverage was the drill master, a veteran of the Crimean war.

Failure to attend chapel, idleness, reading novels on Sunday, and 'illicit correspondence and meeting with principal's servant maid' are but a few of the many other faults catalogued in the Punishment book. Some of the students formed a 'rule breaking club', to help one another 'in writing impositions and bearing punishments'. Even at the turn of the century the printed college rules include prohibitions on walking or studying 'in the Grounds or the Lane' leading to the college after dark, while 'Students may not make or retain any acquaintance in the neighbourhood of Culham without the Principal's knowledge and consent.'

In the girls' colleges discipline was, if anything, stricter than for their male counterparts. Regulation of dress was a particular feature here—as at Stockwell College, which was opened in London by the British and Foreign Society in 1861. Here all frivolities were firmly condemned :

The Ladies' Committee wish it to be distinctly understood by all candidates for admission that they consider neatness and plainness of dress incumbent on those who undertake the instruction and training of the young; and it is the express wish of the committee that no flower, ornament, or other finery should be worn.[23]

Similarly at the Durham Diocesan Female Training School, first opened in 1858, the principal commented adversely on 'over-dressing and extravagance in jewellery' on the part of some of the students, and he posted a notice 'forbidding the wearing of jewellery other than brooches and ear-rings of moderate size, and extravagance in head-dresses'.[24] In many respects trainee teachers were regarded as superior domestic servants and so it is scarcely surprising that considerable emphasis was laid on the need for the girls (like their male colleagues) to perform household chores; these would provide practical training for themselves as well as helping to cut down on the day-to-day running costs of the colleges. At Brighton, for example, HMI Warburton noted in 1882 :

> Each student makes her own bed, and keeps her own room clean in every respect except scrubbing. She also cleans her own boots, knife, spoon, and fork. Several students are employed daily in sweeping and dusting lecture and dining rooms and class-rooms, staircases, corridors, and governesses' sitting rooms. They wash up cups, saucers, plates &c. used at breakfast and tea, but the dinner plates and dishes are washed by a servant. Several students are engaged in setting tables, making tea, coffee, &c.; they also lay the cloth and wait in turn at governesses' table, and clear away after meals. During the summer they also wash their own collars and cuffs and iron them. Cookery : The second year students get lessons from the lady superintendent in a small kitchen fitted up for the purpose, with gas stove and cottage range. One or two are employed daily in assisting the Cook.[25]

This was a typical arrangement. At Durham even in the nineties, each student carried her own cup, saucer and plate to the dining room for every meal other than dinner, and washed them herself before leaving. All students were responsible for sweeping and dusting classrooms and dormitories, and for taking a turn at ironing in the laundry once a week.[26] At Lincoln, students complained bitterly of the blistered hands and the aching backs which were their lot when turning the mangle for an hour at a time in the laundry.

As in the men's colleges, living conditions were austere, with unheated dormitories and cold water for washing. Not until the

1880s did HMI Warburton insist that warm baths should be provided for the girls at Durham 'at least fortnightly or weekly'. And, as a former student recalled, there was no common room: 'such a luxury as a bed-sitting room was undreamed of; cubicles were not supposed to be occupied during the day time, we took our spells of rest on the seats of the classrooms, sitting back to back for ease and comfort, or propping ourselves against a cushion supported by the partition dividing a long room into two.'[27]

The diet, too, was uninspiring, though few seem to have fared as badly as the girls at Cheltenham college, where in 1858 there was a complaint from an anonymous sympathiser that they were being half-starved. According to a letter written to the trustees by 'A Friend to Students', 'twenty two young Ladies, or more' daily sat down 'to dine off one paltry shoulder of Mutton. The same students get nothing but dry bread for supper, besides being generally stinted in their supply of necessary food. I thought this abominable system of starving students had sunk into oblivion, but am sorry that in a respectable College like yours it shd. be tolerated.' Whatever impact the letter may have had, complaints about the food at Cheltenham certainly continued into the 1860s.[28]

The overall philosophy behind this approach was summed up by HMI Cook in 1854, when he wrote of 'the training of these young woman' as being 'of a peculiarly searching and practical character. From childhood they have been educated under religious influences; they remain in their proper and natural station; the temptations to which they are likely to be exposed are well understood by the superintendents of training schools, and form a special subject of daily admonition and advice; their personal habits are carefully scrutinised, and any dangerous tendencies are soon detected, and repressed'.[29] Throughout the century there was anxiety that trainee teachers should not become 'conceited' or 'arrogant' as a result of their college experience. Thus in 1859 the Rev. George H. Hamilton, Rural Dean and Vicar of Berwick upon Tweed, declared in evidence to the Newcastle Commission:

> Teachers trained in our colleges are sadly deficient, as a general rule, in *moral power* of character. They think they know much more than they do, because they know much more than they

did, and more than their neighbours of the same position in society: they are not humble minded or contented with their lot, and the consequence is that they do not take to their duties as teachers with that hearty interest which is necessary to impress the taught with the character of the teacher.[30]

Miss H. Hope, another witness to the Newcastle Commission, commented on the 'spirit of conceit and self-sufficiency' which was likely to develop among female students if they were exempted from domestic chores: 'It should be required of all young women in an institution of this description to perform every common duty for themselves.'[31] Even the Rev. Derwent Coleridge, principal of St Mark's College in London and in many respects sympathetic towards the aspirations of the elementary teaching profession, nevertheless felt it necessary to point out that it was not the business of the training colleges 'to make second-rate gentlemen and ladies; if we make the attempt, they will be very second-rate'; instead they must 'train schoolmasters and schoolmistresses, men and women, whose occupation it will be to impart in subordinate but harmonious co-operation with their pastors, and other social superiors who may be engaged with them in the same work, not merely the rudiments of book-knowledge, but all the essentials of religious and moral culture'. The young trainees must be prepared for the 'self-denial and self-devotion, the patient zeal, the submissive yet resolute temper' which their future profession would demand.[32] It is significant that at Lincoln as late as 1896 attempts to increase the comfort of the students' living quarters aroused concern at the bad effect this might have on their character. The college magazine, in discussing the possible provision of a common room solemnly observed: 'Let us hope . . . that the Recreation Room, which is one of the latest new fads, may not, with its lounges and luxurious easy chairs and its general state of refined rest and dainty do-nothingness convert steady, working, industrious girls into mere imitations of fine ladies.' By this time, however, recreation rooms were becoming increasingly accepted in most colleges. HMI Oakley, in his report for 1898–99, commented with approval on the change which had taken place in this respect since 1886 when 'there was not a single college which had a recreation room and now there was scarcely a college without one'. These rooms, he said, were well-equipped with a library, a piano and various games, and contributed to the students' general 'comfort and enjoyment'.[33]

Elsewhere, as at Borough Road, the last decade of the century saw a growing emphasis on physical fitness and outdoor games, in the belief that such activity would provide essential moral and character training—particularly for the men. In many respects it was an imitation of the programme of 'muscular Christianity' followed by the public schools over the previous thirty years, notably by Edward Thring's Uppingham.

However, an examination of the reminiscences of former trainees hardly bears out the critics' allegations of the over-confidence and arrogance of college students. In fact—especially for youngsters coming from quiet rural areas—the very size and complexity of a large urban college must have been intimidating. T. J. Macnamara, who had served his apprenticeship in an Exeter school and was later to be an active member of the National Union of Teachers, recalled the daunting impression made upon him when he came to London in 1880 to enter Borough Road college :

> Paddington, and a heavy pall of yellow January fog. The roar and turmoil! The struggle for a four-wheeler! The pale inter-mittent flash of the street lamps through the stifling gloom ! . . . All is so new and bewildering . . . The cab draws up wheezily before a black gaunt jail-like building. The College; and my home for two years ! . . . I find the eighth landing. How cold and clammy ! The newly scrubbed floor is not even dry, and the nauseating smell of disinfecting soap pervades everything. My bedroom, a cheerless cubicle, six paces by three. . . . Down-stairs a hopeless maze of half-dark corridors and brutally cheerless rooms. One of these poverty-stricken chambers serves a double purpose. It is a classroom in working hours and a common-room out of them.[34]

In his view : 'Two years at the Old Borough Road was a fine chastening for any man. It put him through a fire that tested.'

But if one major strand of training college development in the Victorian era was concerned with educating would-be teachers for their appropriate station in life, another was concentrated on the length of their course and the academic standards they were expected to achieve at the end of it. In the early days students were of very variable intellectual quality indeed—like the 'respectable farmer's son' who was admitted to the Oxford diocesan training school in October 1841 and was classed as 'very imperfectly taught & of feeble powers—but wrote well'. Another entrant of similar calibre was the seventeen-year-old son of a ragman, described as 'very coarse in manner & appearance . . . expert as Arithmetn.—but not otherwise of much ability'. Both these men were appointed to headships when they left the training school. And at the recently-opened Chester diocesan training school, HMI Moseley noted that of the forty students in residence in November 1845, eighteen spelt incorrectly; twelve read and eight wrote imperfectly; and ten, 'upon the evidence of the exercises they have sent in, may be characterised as illiterate'. Their position can hardly have been improved by the fact that all of the academic work at this institution devolved on two members of staff. As Mr Moseley pointed out, at no other training college were 'labours like these . . . required. At St Mark's College *four* [instructors] are employed constantly and *five* occasionally, and at Battersea *three* constantly and *six* occasionally in performing those duties, in respect to from 60 to 70 students, which are here assigned to two in respect to 40 students'.[35]

After 1846, however, there came a gradual raising of standards with the establishment of the pupil-teacher system and the provision of Queen's scholarships for the ablest of the young apprentices to permit them to undergo a period of study at one of the colleges free of charge. At the end of each year of their course they were again examined, and the college was awarded a government grant for each successful candidate. This amounted to £20 for a first-year student, £25 for a second-year one, and £30 for those in the third year. Initially it had been hoped that most students would train for three years, but that proved impossibly optimistic, given the pressure of demand for trained teachers at the time and the modest financial resources of many of them. Large numbers in fact remained at college for a single year only and so in 1853 an attempt was made to combat this by establishing two years as the minimum. Under new regulations, grants were only to be paid for students who had remained for at least that length of time, unless they were over twenty-four years of age or could gain special exemption in some other way.[36] The proposal aroused such an outcry from the colleges, however, that it was dropped in the following year. A new scale was then drawn up which sanctioned annual payments to each institution ranging from £13 for a first-year student with a third-class pass to £24 for a second- or third-year man with a first-class pass. (Female students attracted grants of two-thirds of these amounts.) In 1855 the scheme was amended yet again, so that a candidate who obtained a first-class Queen's scholarship now became eligible to receive personal pocket money as well—£4 for his first year at college and £6 for his second, in addition to the grant which, as before, covered his tuition fees. Finally from 1856, students who failed their first-year examination were to be given another chance and permitted to start their second-year course without delay.

Two years before this, in 1854, a common syllabus had been drawn up for the colleges—to cover religious knowledge, reading, penmanship, arithmetic, English grammar, geography, English history, physical science, and music, with geometry, algebra and higher mathematics for male students. School management was covered as well, along with drawing and domestic economy for the girls. So whereas under the old régime the Education Department had been compelled to set separate examination papers for candidates from each individual college it now became possible to have a common programme for all of them.[37]

These changing circumstances led to a sharp increase in the number of students under training—as well as the number of colleges. By 1858 there were fifteen men's colleges, thirteen women's, and five catering for both men and women, under government inspection, while the average number of students under training had reached 2,000—four-fifths of them Queen's scholars.[38] All appeared set fair for further expansion when the situation suddenly altered. At the beginning of the 1860s came the Revised Code, with its withdrawal of state stipends to pupil-teachers and its ending of the Queen's scholarship system as it had hitherto existed. Between 1863 and 1871 even the term 'Queen's scholar' was in abeyance. Although scholarships were still to be allocated to students by the colleges, the total grant payable to a college was to be restricted to a maximum of seventy-five per cent of its annual expenditure, while the sums paid over in respect of the students were to be offered on a retrospective basis only and were to be paid by instalments over a minimum five-year period. None but certificated teachers who had trained for two years and had subsequently successfully completed a probationary period in the schools could bring to their colleges a full grant. Entrance fees for new students would now be required to help make up the deficiency in the colleges' income; and in order to ensure that the latter concentrated their energies on equipping teachers for dealing with the 'basic' skills required in elementary schools, the teacher's certificate syllabuses were pruned by the Education Department, with the grants offered for additional subjects, like higher mathematics and languages, drastically reduced. Political economy became a compulsory subject at the colleges for the first time—perhaps in deference to the views of the Department's Vice-President, Robert Lowe. For in July 1861, in a speech in the Commons foreshadowing the Code changes, Lowe had declared: 'I really think that the schoolmaster should be taught some political economy in these days of strikes; so that the person who is looked up to as an authority next to the clergyman in his village should be able to give some sensible opinion on those melancholy contests about wages.'[39] Finally, the number of students in training was to be limited to 'the number . . . for whom accommodation was provided in 1862'.[40]

In introducing these changes, Lowe pointed to the heavy cost to the government of training college education. He declared that although it had originally been intended that such aid should supplement voluntary effort by the denominations, in the preceding year 'for the training college at Cheltenham the Government paid 99 per cent [of its expenditure], and on the average the amount paid by the Government for training colleges was nine-tenths, 90 per cent'. In his view: 'We had . . . good reason to ask from these colleges an increased subscription.'[41]

Whatever Lowe's intentions may have been, under the new conditions of stringency and financial uncertainty, the number of students coming forward for training dropped rapidly. According to HMI Cowie in 1863 there had been 542 pupil-teachers admitted to training colleges, but by 1865 this total had declined to 316 and two years later it had sunk to its lowest level of 224.[42] Even in 1864 Cowie had commented on 'the position of some of the training schools' as 'one of anxious uncertainty', and had noted that only about one in three of the male pupil-teachers who might have gone on to college in that year had actually done so.[43]

The cut-back can be seen very clearly at college level. At Westminster College in 1864 only forty girls and thirty-five men applied for admission compared with what had hitherto been the normal level of about fifty applications from the girls and eighty from the men, while at Borough Road, where there were ninety-five students in residence in 1862, numbers slumped to sixty-eight by 1866 and sixty-one a year later.[44] At Cheltenham, once government policy became known, the principal, the Rev. C. H. Bromby, speedily expressed a desire to resign, declaring that 'private reasons combined with the great uncertainty now hanging over the Institution induced him . . . to seek preferment in the Church. . . . And that some of his friends were now bringing his case before the Premier with a view to such preferment'. His efforts were rewarded almost two years later with the bishopric of Tasmania. But his successor was faced with serious difficulties as student numbers fell sharply from 156 in 1861 to 109 eight years later, and there was considerable anxiety as to the future.[45] Two colleges—those at Chichester and at Highbury in London—were forced to close, with Highbury's twenty-seven remaining students transferred to Cheltenham in 1864. And in the country as a whole the total of those studying at training colleges dropped from 2,972 in 1862 to 2,403 in 1866.[46]

The fact that the grants available for each student were paid to the colleges retrospectively and were only finally handed over when the student had received his or her 'parchment'. i.e. had successfully passed the certificate examination and had served in an elementary school long enough to obtain satisfactory reports on two successive occasions from the HMI, led colleges to put pressure on their students in order to protect their own financial position. At Lincoln, for example, a girl who left to get married before she had completed her course was made to pay £20 to the college as compensation for the loss of the grants she would not now bring. In 1865 new entrants to this college were required to sign an agreement 'to remain in the college for two years, and placed on record that they recognised that a breach of this undertaking would forfeit any chance of their being awarded a certificate'.[47] Similarly at the Winchester diocesan training college, students entering in January 1863 had to agree that they would remain at college for two years and 'thereafter mindful of the advantages conferred upon us in our Training to follow the profession of a Schoolmaster at least until we have obtained our Certificate'.[48] This approach was encouraged by the Education Department. Indeed in October 1863, HMI Cowie bluntly informed the Cheltenham authorities 'that an agreement must in all cases be drawn up between the College and the student . . . and that although that agreement might not have legal force, it would be morally binding on the student'.[49]

More than twenty years later similar pledges were still being extracted. At Ripon in the mid-1880s every female student had to promise :

> (if life and health be spared) to complete the full term of training over two years, and at the end of that time to accept the charge of a national or elementary school under Government inspection, and to remain in such school (if permitted by the managers) until the issue of my certificate from the Council Office.
> I further declare that I consider myself bound to carry out this engagement in order that the managers of the training school may receive the grant of public money which will . . . be paid on my account by their Lordships the Committee of Council on Education.[50]

Interestingly enough, even in the early years of the twentieth century the Board of Education was following much the same policy. Under new regulations all students admitted to colleges from 1907 had to sign an undertaking which, on the part of a male trainee, committed him 'to serve for seven years in a school receiving grants from the State or in a Training College'. This had to be completed within ten years of his leaving the college and he had to bind himself to refund for every year in default a proportion of the grant paid to the college on his behalf. A woman student was required to pledge herself to give 'five years' service within eight years of leaving' college.[51]

In the meantime, following the passage of the 1870 Education Act, with its widening of elementary school provision and its consequent stimulus to the recruitment of trained teachers, the position of the colleges began to improve. Not only were grants now offered once more for one-year trained teachers (amounting to half the sum allowed for their two-year counterparts), but the system of deferred payments was somewhat modified. The term 'Queen's scholar' was also revived, to apply to any pupil-teacher who came high enough in the examination list to secure admission to a college. It has, indeed, been said that in the early 1870s 'for the first time in their history all the training colleges were full' and were unable to admit in any year 'much over one-half' of the pupil-teachers qualified to enter them.[52] New institutions were opened, so that by 1884 there were forty-three training colleges in existence in England and Wales, catering for 3,265 students; thirty of them were Church of England.[53] Among these was Bishop Otter's Memorial College, Chichester, which was opened in February 1873 to cater particularly for the daughters of middle-class professional men—clergymen, doctors, naval officers, civil servants and the like.[54]

But if the last thirty years of the century saw a lifting of some of the most pressing problems affecting the colleges, certain of the restrictions survived, including those laying down that grants were to be limited to a maximum of 75 per cent of college expenditure in a year and that the full grant for students could only be paid over when their 'parchment' had been secured. This remained the position to the end of the Victorian era, save that in 1890, following the Report of the Royal Commission on the Elementary Education Acts, new day training colleges were authorised, attached to a university or a college of university rank. To them a smaller grant, of not more than £10 per student per year, became payable, as opposed to the maximum annual sum of £50 for a male student and £35 for a female which had applied in the residential colleges for almost thirty years. By 1903 the total of day college students had risen to over two thousand.[55]

Yet if these were the somewhat confused and often unsatisfactory financial facts of life for both trainee teachers and their colleges in the mid- and later-Victorian years, the academic instruction provided also left much to be desired. Even libraries in many of the colleges were poor. At Westminster, for example, 'anything satisfactory in the nature of a Reference Library did not begin till the closing years of the nineteenth century', while at Lincoln as late as 1899 there were only 485 books in the library—and they were stored in a cupboard in the lecture hall rather than in a purpose-built room.[56] Tutors were, therefore, thrown back upon oral teaching, and frequently a lecture consisted of little more than the dictation of notes, which were to serve the purpose of a text-book for the certificate examination. 'The minds of the students became loaded with facts, and the knowledge gained was often highly abstruse, since the tutors had not that deep knowledge of their subjects which renders lively and effective presentation possible. Except in rare instances the whole business was a kind of specialised "window-dressing".'[57] College staffs, especially in the early years, consisted of a combination of clergymen and young ex-training college graduates, whose experience of teaching was strictly limited and whose general knowledge was almost equally so. Not until the 1890s were university-trained teachers widely recruited by the colleges.

Often, too, especially in the earlier years, lectures seem to have consisted of a confusing mixture of religious and secular instruction. The notebook of a student who attended Westminster College in 1855 reveals that his course began with dictated lesson notes on a Bible subject and on the Otter—a somewhat surprising combination :

> That on the Otter stressed what was to be demonstrated in many future lessons—the wisdom and goodness of God. After a general description, its habitation, its food, its structure, its peculiarities and its uses were examined. The Otter is plentifully supplied with its food—fish, because 'fishes cannot see under water.' The Otter is useful to man because 'its skin makes pistol covers and some soldiers' caps, as well as cigar cases. Indians also eat their flesh.' Thus we come to 'The Lesson' which is (i) God has provided them with what they need—hence His wisdom, (ii) Made them useful to man— hence His goodness.[58]

But it was the 'cramming' aspect of the college curriculum which was to be so relentlessly mocked by Charles Dickens in his novel, *Hard Times*—a book first published in 1854, before the Revised Code had added to the uninspiring regimen offered. Dickens describes in ironic vein the newly-appointed master of Coketown School, Mr M'Choakumchild :

He and some one hundred and forty other schoolmasters had been lately turned at the same time, in the same factory, on the same principle, like so many pianoforte legs. He had been put through an immense variety of paces, and had answered volumes of head-breaking questions. Orthography, etymology, syntax, and prosody, biography, astronomy, geography, and general cosmography, the sciences of compound proportion, algebra, land surveying and levelling, vocal music, and drawing from models, were all at the ends of his ten chilled fingers. He had worked his stony way into Her Majesty's Most Honourable Privy Council's Schedule B, and had taken the bloom off the higher branches of mathematics and physical science, French, German, Latin, and Greek. He knew all about all the watersheds of all the world (whatever they are), and all the histories of all the peoples, and all the names of all the rivers and mountains, and all the productions, manners, and customs of all the countries, and all their boundaries and bearings on the two-and-thirty points of the compass. . . . If he had only learnt a little less, how infinitely better he might have taught much more.[59]

Something of the effect produced on the students by this approach is described by James Runciman in his book, *Schools and Scholars*. Runciman was a student at Borough Road College in 1871 and 1872, but his experiences were applicable to those trained elsewhere. He confessed himself 'shocked when he found that he was expected to learn his country's story from a tiny fivepenny book, which contained strings of dates and names arranged in horrifying sequence. Take a single "lesson," of which I give an account that contains not a shade of caricature.'[60]

The historical tutor entered. . . . He was the most conscientious of men, and he stuck to the Government syllabus with a tenacity which left nothing to be desired. His lads all liked and respected him, and many of them loved him, although the memory of his classes was like a nightmare. He took his seat with a determined air . . . The men squatted in the dingy theatre like a set of charity-boys, and awaited the first question. Then the tutor began with a resolute monotonous snuffle, 'What event happened on September 25, 1066? Hands up those who know.' Then the 'men' held up their hands in a childish way. . . . The grand test was reserved till the close of the hour. It ran somewhat in this way : 'Write down what happened in 1086, 1088, . . . 1113, 1139, 1109.' Little slips of paper were handed round; the students scribbled : the teacher cried, 'Change papers.' . . . Then the tutor droned out the exact words of the miserable little book, and each man scored out the errors on the paper in front of him. To omit a semicolon was culpable; to leave out a preposition was worse; to substitute a word for one of those used in the book was worse still; while to omit the day of the month on which somebody signed something, or killed somebody else, was regarded as next door to criminal. . . . Now such tomfoolery as this went on for about three hours per week, and clever young lads spent hours of private study in preparing for the ridiculous ordeal. Slow hands bored and bored till their heads were splitting and their lives were a misery; for they always feared lest some treacherous date should slide away at the most critical moment.

Small wonder that when the students came to teach history in their turn their lessons were as dry as dust. Yet geography lessons at Borough Road were in Runciman's view, even more 'melancholy examples of waste' than the history lectures, with the men committing to memory endless unrelated lists of rivers, capes, heights of mountains, exports, imports and other items, which they little comprehended and which interested them even less. Grammar consisted of cramming 'a little sixpenny text-book of rules and definitions' by heart : 'the men learned nothing whatever about the history and structure of their language. They could give you a correct definition of the subjunctive mood; they could jabber out a list of the different kinds of adverbial clauses; but . . . very few of them could write ten consecutive sentences of plain English.'[61] (See also Appendix 5.)

In fact, as another student at a provincial training college recalled : 'The text-book was the Gospel of truth, the compendium of all knowledge, the only complete and infallible guide to the intellectual Valhalla. This observation applies equally to History, Geography, Grammar and Literature.'[62] To the end of the nineteenth century the colleges remained 'pedant-factories', whose machinery efficiently removed whatever traces of interest in a more liberal culture the scholars had picked up earlier in their careers. ' "Répétez sans cesse," it was said, was the tutor's motto'.[63] Discipline remained rigid and authoritarian, with manners and deportment, especially of female students, strictly controlled. At Durham even in 1907–9, one girl remembered that 'strict silence had to be observed in class between the bell for a lecture and the arrival of the lecturer', while most of the students were 'easily reduced to tears by criticism or censure'.[64]

Alongside these regulation stints on the academic treadmill, the trainees naturally spent a certain amount of time on practical work. Nearly every college had a 'model' or 'practising' school attached to it, where this essential element of the course could be carried out. Not until the Education Act of 1902 were the 'model' schools removed from the direct control of the colleges and a wider variety of practice then became available to the students. But before any of them were allowed to try out their skills on the children, they were carefully guided on the method of approach to be adopted. At Westminster, for example, the trainee was help-fully instructed to 'Try to appear perfectly easy,' and 'Never appear irritated'; he was likewise informed of six ways of 'Securing Good Order, six methods of Restoring Order, and seven General suggestions'. It was as well also to know the eight best ways to Lose Order:

1. Speak in a formal high scolding voice.
2. Give dry lessons.
3. Let the classes be crowded.
4. Let work proceed slowly.
5. Be frequently changing places.
6. Cultivate a stiff manner.
7. Let the lesson be above the capacity of the class.
8. Manifest irresolution.

Repeated stress was placed on good routine and punctuality, 'and several warnings given on not talking to visitors.'[65]

The amount of time devoted to teaching practice varied from college to college, but it was usually comparatively brief. At Salis-bury women's college in the mid-1850s students had by their second year spent only seventy hours so occupied, while at Cheltenham the figure was eighty hours. By contrast, at Bishop's Stortford it was 240 hours. Half a century later the normal arrangement at most colleges was a modest 150 hours of practice during the two years of training. HMI Coward considered it should have been at least twice as long.[66]

The plan of action at Brighton in the early 1880s is described by HMI Warburton:

> Each student is in turn sent into the practising schools for a fortnight at a time, two first year students and two second being always engaged in the mixed girls' school, and one first year and two second in the infant school. . . . Once a week three second year students give consecutive criticism lessons before all the students, these lessons being criticised by the students and by the mistress of method. Once a week the first year and second year students have separately a lesson on school management and on preparing notes and lessons. Once a week the first and second year students have alternately a paper of questions on school management, or an hour's study of the subject.[67]

The criticism lesson was one of the most disliked parts of the whole business, especially by the sensitive student, since he or she was expected to give a lesson on a selected subject before an audience of staff and fellow students and had then to be prepared to receive their frank—and perhaps uncomplimentary —comments. More than one sufferer would have agreed with the former student at Westminster College who recalled how 'the hand of fate' hung heavy upon him when he saw for the first time his name on the fortnightly list for this particular duty:

> Oh the brain-racking thoughts and sleepless nights that passed between then and the dreaded ordeal. . . . And then—a blurred vision of expectant youth and smiling, pitying comrades, an agonising and chaotic twenty minutes, the cry of 'time up' and all was over.[68]

It was just this stress by the colleges on 'practical' instruction, and their neglect of educational theory, which aroused the criticism of an American observer, Charles Judd, on the eve of the First World War. In his view, the theoretical side of pedagogy was treated in 'a very meagre and abstract manner', while the textbooks employed in the theoretical courses dealt with the general science of psychology and with the discipline of logic and ethics, 'rather than with any of those practical applications which are being attempted in our American normal schools and college departments of education. In this respect there is so wide a breach between pedagogical theory and actual emphasis upon practice teaching in English institutions that one is tempted to say that the teachers in English training colleges have not realised the possibility of dealing in a scientific way with the practical problems of school organisation and the practical problems which come up in the conduct of recitations.'[69]

Be that as it may, however, for the individual student such wide-ranging concerns as these could safely be left to the deliberations of his elders and betters. To him (or her) it was the certificate examination at the end of each year which was the real hurdle to be overcome. Because both the student's own future career and the finances of the college depended upon success here, preparation became a relentless, monotonous grind. Coaching was often barefaced. In 1874 the examiners in English reported that the students of one college had 'almost without exception' written out an essay 'which they must all have evidently learnt off by heart'. This was no isolated case. For it was reported of the geography papers in the mid-1870s that one of the chief defects in the answers from all colleges was their mechanical character: 'Indeed, so very close is the similarity in the answering of the students of each college, and so distinct generally is that answering from that of the other colleges, that I would hesitate much before I could charge any two students with copying. The students slavishly reproduce their knowledge in the mechanical way in which it is fashionable to give it at their college. I should say that there is much geography taught at our colleges, but not much intelligently'.[70] As we have seen, this was a view with which James Runciman would have agreed heartily, and yet it was an inevitable outcome of the Revised Code system, with its narrow curriculum and its placing of a premium on the mechanical methods which would bring examination success.

Needless to say in the days immediately before the great ordeal, the students' nerves were at full stretch—as a contributor to the Westminster College magazine of December 1899 made all too clear:

The exam. fever is upon us. The dayroom, hitherto a hall of laughter, is now hushed, save for a gentle murmur like that of the humming of bees. When you enter it, no cheerful voice greets you, but, with downcast eyes, the spectres sit as though petrified. Were it not for an occasional moving of the lips or the motion of a hand as it turns over the page of a book you might imagine they were carved in stone. . . . Before you are aware of it, the dire malady has smitten you, and you, also, have become one of the silent sufferers.[71]

Or, as another product of the system later wrote: 'the main business of our life there . . . was—to us—to do decently in the Christmas class-lists'.[72] For a good certificate 'pass' meant the prospect of a higher salary and more choice when seeking the first job.

Yet if the training college system very largely failed to give its students a broad education, it was at any rate an improvement on the haphazard method of teacher recruitment which had preceded it. At least its products were given some guidance in the art of teaching the three 'r's', which were to form the staple diet of their professional career—particularly in country areas. Some students were even inspired to study further on their own account and, like James Runciman, subsequently read for a degree. But if as a result of these developments, the total of certificated teachers employed in the schools rose sharply, it did not keep pace with the demand. On 31 December 1869, there were 12,027 certificated teachers employed in elementary schools under inspection. By 1900, this figure had increased to 64,038 certificated or provisionally certificated teachers. Yet as the Report of the Board of Education for that year commented:

The extent to which the Training Colleges have contributed to the present supply of efficient teachers in England and Wales is shown by the fact that of 24,557 certificated masters employed in schools reported on last year 16,941, or 69 per cent, had been trained for two years or over, and 710, or 2.9 per cent, for less than two years; while 6,906, or 28.1 per cent, were not so trained. In like manner, of 39,481 certificated schoolmistresses, 18,238, or 46.2 per cent, had been trained for two years or over; 1,079, or 2.7 per cent, for less than two years; and 20,164, or 51.1 per cent, were not trained in colleges.[73]

In other words, over a quarter of all male certificated teachers and over half of all female certificated teachers had not attended a training college. In addition, alongside these figures must be placed the substantial number of teachers who were *neither* trained *nor* certificated. Even the increase in training college provision following the passage of the 1902 Education Act and the abolition of the 75 per cent limit of grant vis-à-vis annual expenditure, which had hitherto applied to residential colleges, could not eliminate them before 1914. Under the 1902 Act, local authorities could set up their own training colleges, and sixteen of them rapidly took advantage of this opportunity; overall training college places jumped from 7,000 in 1903 to 12,000 seven years later.[74]

But many of the more backward rural areas preferred the cheaper alternative of an untrained assistant—perhaps an ex-pupil teacher who had neither attended college nor passed the acting teacher's certificate examination. Or, from 1875 it might be one of the large new class of uncertificated female teachers who became available as 'supplementaries' or 'additional' teachers or, under the Code of 1890, as 'Article 68's'. Originally they had been intended to replace the stipendiary monitors but, in the event, both groups continued to exist side by side. The supplementaries' only qualifications were that they were over eighteen years of age, had been vaccinated against small-pox, and had been accepted by Her Majesty's Inspector as suitable to assist 'in the general instruction of the scholars and in teaching needlework'.[75] Their numbers increased rapidly in the last years of the nineteenth century as many country church schools, under growing financial pressure, sought to cut their staffing bills to the bone. According to the Board of Education's annual report for 1900, there were at that date 17,512 supplementaries employed and their total had increased in 'the last seven years [by] over 100 per cent'. So whereas in 1875 trained, certificated teachers had represented 70 per cent of the males and 57 per cent of the females employed in elementary schools, by 1914 their share had fallen to 66 per cent and 32 per cent, respectively. By contrast, the number of uncertificated and untrained teachers had advanced sharply, especially among the females, where they comprised 13 per cent of the number employed in 1875 but a substantial 41 per cent of the 1914 total.[76]

In 1909 the Board of Education sought to restrict the future employment of supplementary teachers by confining new appointments to infants' classes, or to the lower class of older scholars in a small school in a rural parish. Although the Board granted five years' grace to those supplementaries already engaged in schools for older children, as a result of its action numbers fell a little between 1909 and 1913, from 17,204 to 13,473. But towards the end of the five years, the Board was pressed by many local education authorities to postpone the date on which recognition of supplementaries in departments for older children would cease. Reluctantly it agreed, with a stay of execution granted for a further five years.

This rather casual attitude of 'making the best of things' in the staffing of English elementary schools was, of course, very different from that adopted in Germany. As the American observer, Charles Judd, pointed out, there was 'no possibility of getting into the teaching profession [there] without a thorough-going equipment which [had] been carefully supervised by the State. Every teacher must satisfy State requirements of a very high order, and when the appointment is made in . . . the German school system, it is an appointment for life, and an appointment to a position which is distinctly a Government position. . . . Everything proceeds in the German system with great definiteness and regularity. The result is that the schools of Germany are supplied with a group of teachers of a very high degree of efficiency.'[77] (As other American commentators pointed out, however, this did not prevent schools from being dull and cheerless: 'Row upon row of long, straight-backed benches filled dreary classrooms. Children sprang stiffly to attention when a visitor, the principal or an inspector entered. . . . The formal, serious autocrat of a teacher seemed profoundly conscious of his responsibility to the nation.' He was 'the chief instrument of the ruling powers for training submissive, efficient citizens'.[78] Another critic noted the 'military atmosphere' which reigned: 'The pupil is expected to obey, and for that reason the spirit of independence finds less favourable soil than is offered in American schools. . . . It is obvious that the German method well prepares the pupil for the performing of future tasks; but it does not call forth originality and self-reliance'.[79])

Another difference between Britain and Germany was that

the profession in the latter country was dominated by men—so that of 187,485 teachers employed in the *Volksschulen* in 1911, only 39,268 were females. Women were never employed in the instruction of boys, except in the lowest grades, and even here it was common for the boys to receive their instruction from men. Girls in elementary schools, on the other hand, were usually instructed by male teachers, and in rural schools women were rarely engaged. This may be compared with the English system, where in 1914 about three-quarters of all elementary school teachers were women.[80]

So, despite the efforts of the training colleges and their lecturers, the standard of teaching in the elementary schools of England and Wales remained unsatisfactory in many areas to 1914. Even the training college courses themselves left much to be desired—though from 1891 colleges were allowed to put their students in for University examinations alongside their teacher's certificate courses. A minority only of the students took advantage of this—in the year 1900–1901 a mere thirteen obtained degrees —and the move was castigated by HMI Coward as: 'a system of over-straining, you have a system, to use common and rather vulgar language, of bunkum and shoddy'.[81]

After 1907 the imposition of religious tests by the denominational colleges in the selection of students was ended—at least officially. Yet as H. C. Dent has noted: 'however uninspired and ill-directed the average . . . course may have been, at least it gave the ablest among the children preparing to be teachers a respite of two years from the rigours of teaching; and, for all the dreariness, narrowness, and overwork of college life, an opportunity along with one's fellows to become conscious, and proud, of belonging to a profession which, though it had no great social status had at least the compensation of being socially valuable.'[82] It is to an examination of the daily round of that 'socially valuable' occupation that we must now turn.

1. Dame school, eighteenth century.

2. Village school, late eighteenth century.

3. Patron and patroness's visit to the village school.

4. The monitor commands, 'Show slates!'

5. Boys wearing their sisters' cast-offs.

6. A school group with pupil-teacher (on left).

7. Hands behind backs for good discipline.

8. Horspath Church School, 1907.

9. Children in a public agricultural gang, 1860s.

. A school garden in 1906.

11. A plaiting school.

12. Buttermaking in a tent.

13. Home-taught lacemaker, turn of the century.

5

The Daily Round

Children's education is a great deal more than mere reading, writing, and casting of accounts. I think the formation of character is a great thing in a school, and the teaching of precision and accuracy, and habits of attention and order, are important matters.

THE REV. JAMES SIMPSON, incumbent of Kirkby-Stephen, Westmorland in evidence to the *Select Committee on Education*, Parliamentary Papers 1866, VII, Q.211.

The schoolmistress in charge of the Fordlow school at the beginning of the 'eighties had held that position for fifteen years and seemed to her pupils as much a fixture as the school building; . . . Every morning, when school had assembled, and Governess, with her starched apron and bobbing curls appeared in the doorway, there was a great rustling and scraping of curtseying and pulling of forelocks . . . Reading, writing, and arithmetic were the principal subjects, with a Scripture lesson every morning, and needlework every afternoon for the girls. There was no assistant mistress; Governess taught all the classes simultaneously, assisted only by two monitors—ex-scholars, aged about twelve, who were paid a shilling a week each for their services. Every morning at ten o'clock the Rector arrived to take the older children for Scripture . . . History was not taught formally; but history readers were in use containing such picturesque stories as those of King Alfred and the cakes . . . There were no geography readers, and, excepting what could be gleaned from the descriptions of different parts of the world in the ordinary readers, no geography was taught.

FLORA THOMPSON, *Lark Rise to Candleford*, Oxford 1963 ed., 190–192. 'Fordlow' was the North Oxfordshire village of Cottisford.

1880. Some difficulty is being experienced in getting children to do their homework, as parents state they cannot afford to buy paper for their children to work on.

EDWARD RAINSBERRY, *Through the Lych Gate*, Kineton 1969, 117, quoting from the log book of Long Compton school, Warwickshire.

E

IN THE early years of the nineteenth century, moral and religious instruction formed a major part of the elementary school curriculum, with teachers encouraged not merely to instruct the children in reading and writing but to 'attend to their morals' as well.[1] In many schools, indeed, pupils were taught only to read, since instruction in writing and arithmetic was thought likely to educate them 'above their station' and thus to discourage them from performing necessary but uninteresting manual tasks when they grew up. A typical advocate of this view was the vicar of Yarnton in Oxfordshire, who declared in 1812; 'Reading is a key to the treasures of holy writ and . . . should be put into the hands of all. But writing and arithmetic being qualifications for particular places, services and sorts of business, should be reserved for specific purposes and particular children.'[2] Similarly in 1802 John Randolph, then Bishop of Oxford, considered that the aim in instructing the children of the poor should be 'merely to give them an entrance into a life of daily labour, well fortified with the principles of duty; all beyond that may puff up their tender minds, or entice them into a way of life of no benefit to the publick and ensnaring to themselves.'[3]

Such ideas took a long time to die, and as late as 1856 a speaker at an educational conference of parochial clergy and schoolmasters in the Oxford diocese could declare to the masters present : 'When you have manufactured a steady, honest, God-fearing, Church-going population, then you have done your duty as Schoolmasters.'[4]

Some of this emphasis was, of course, due to the contemporary belief that the duty of educating the people was first and foremost a religious one. In countless rural communities it was the local vicar or rector who assumed responsibility for the establishment of a village school, and who helped to cover its running costs from his own pocket. What this meant in individual terms is shown in a letter written in 1858 by the curate of South Stoke in Oxfordshire to the Dean and Chapter of Christ Church, who were the major landowners in his parish. In appealing for aid to finance the school he noted bitterly : 'with the exception of the Mistress's salary which the Vicar . . . pays, the whole of the expense of the School falls on me the Curate, which I could not afford were it not for the kindness of private friends.' His problem was aggravated by the fact that the principal farmers in the parish were Nonconformists who would not support the church school. Indeed, they had established a rival dissenting establishment at nearby Goring.[5] In such circumstances it was small wonder that HMI Blandford could comment, in the mid-1850s, on the 'great difficulty' experienced in raising funds for the support of schools: 'few persons are really aware what a heavy tax they are upon the parochial clergymen.' Thirty years later the secretary to the National Society was making much the same point, when he declared that clergymen grew weary of 'the incessant canvassing and beating about for money when [they] first [came] to the parish'.[6] Though by that date financial aid from the government had eliminated some of the severest problems.

Alongside these religious concerns, fears of the possibly 'subversive' influence of education in raising children's occupational aspirations were also combated by combining academic instruction with manual labour in charitably financed Industrial Schools. This was an approach recommended by the vicar of Stone in Buckinghamshire, among others, when he appealed to the principal landowner, Dr John Lee, to set up such a school in his parish:

> I am a very Strong Supporter of what is called "Industrial Education", that is learning and working combined . . . let us have a good agricultural teacher who will keep the boys learning during the forenoon and at outdoor work in the afternoon. Schools of this kind would be a real blessing to the neighbourhood.

Dr Lee seems to have agreed with him, for the building of a new school was set in hand in 1861, together with the provision of one acre of land to be 'cultivated by the boys', and for which they received 'small gratuities'.[7]

Similarly Miss Onslow of Old Alresford in Hampshire established an Industrial School catering for thirty-four girls aged from about eleven to nineteen or twenty. Each evening and every Saturday morning were spent by the pupils in reading, writing and arithmetic, while the rest of the day was devoted to laundry work, cooking and house cleaning. The laundry, in particular, was a major operation, taking in washing from 113 local people.[8] But projects like these—although much lauded by contemporaries —remained comparatively rare, partly because of the cost of running them and partly on account of the difficulty of finding suitable work for the children. Far more popular was the simple device of arranging for older pupils to clean the ordinary day school premises—thereby saving the cost of outside labour—on the pretext of providing the girls with 'industrial' training.[9]

A further method of inculcating the correct social attitudes was to teach the pupils reading, writing and arithmetic with a religious slant. This included the provision of biblical arithmetic textbooks, which posed such questions as: 'There were twelve apostles, twelve patriarchs and four evangelists; multiply the patriarchs and apostles together and divide by the evangelists.'[10] Or: 'of Jacob's four wives, Leah had six sons, Rachel had two, Billah had two, and Zillah had also two. How many sons had Jacob?' The latter was suggested by the Central Society of Education in 1838.[11]

Not until the passage of the 1870 Education Act, which laid down that no child was to be compelled to attend religious instruction in any elementary school (church or otherwise) in receipt of a government grant, were religious texts omitted from school readers. Prior to this, as one critic has put it:

> To instruct in religion and in morality was the entire preoccupation of every writer for children. . . . The exhortation, the sermon, the Bible quotation, the hymn, fable and moral tale were the vehicles. They exhalted obedience to teacher, parent, minister; respectfulness to one's betters; industriousness, neatness, cleanliness; kindness to animals. They castigated fighting, quarrelling, lying, stealing, begging, drinking, swearing, gambling, playing cards, keeping bad company and telling tales.[12]

Although such objectives may appear praiseworthy in themselves, when translated into written form they made very dull reading, as an examination of early nineteenth-century textbooks will confirm. Furthermore, even when books with secular themes *did* come on the scene, they often emphasised the virtues of self-help, social subordination and perseverance in language little likely to arouse the enthusiasm of their young readers. Thus in the *Revised Lesson Books*, published by the British and Foreign Society in 1864, it was possible to read in a volume intended for an eight- or nine-year old: 'Capital is the result of labour and savings. Nothing is more certain that that, taking the working classes in the entire mass, they get a fair share of the proceeds of the national industry.'[13] Indoctrination it may have been but it certainly did not make interesting reading.

Much the same lack-lustre impression was, no doubt, made on ten- and eleven-year-olds faced with volume 4 of Chambers's *National Reading Books*, published in 1874—as in the 'Lessons on Animals': 'The order of Carnivorous Animals, or "flesh eaters", is composed of a great variety of important animals, most of which are beasts of prey. This order is divided into *digitigrade* animals and *plantigrade* animals.'[14] Such texts can have done little but bewilder and confuse the majority of village children.

Nor was this all. In most church schools it was customary for at least part of the religious instruction in the school to be given by the incumbent, or by his wife or curate, and in this regard the teacher and pupils were very much dependent on the whims of these outsiders. Thus at Mixbury in Oxfordshire (where the school was built in 1838 over cart sheds in the rectory drive), the incumbent's wife seems to have attended almost every day during September and October 1870 to give scripture lessons, but then appears to have abandoned this routine and to have left the work to the master once more. Elsewhere instruction in other aspects of the curriculum might be taken on by members of the clergyman's family, or by other well-to-do members of village society, as the mood took them. This is shown very clearly at Ellingham in Hampshire, where during 1874 the mistress was aided by the vicar, his daughter, and the daughter of a local landowner—as the following random entries from the school log indicate :

Jan. 17 The Rev. J. G. Glanville visited the School on Tuesday and taught a class . . .

Mch. 6 Miss Glanville visited the School today & taught a class . . .

Ap. 24 Miss Glanville visited the School today & taught a class . . .

June 26 Miss Glanville visited the School on Monday afternoon and assisted with the needle-work . . .

Oct. 23 Miss G. Fane visited the School on Monday & gave a class dictation . . .[15]

In another parish during the mid-1880s the vicar, his daughter and, on one occasion, his son, took the children for a whole range of subjects, in addition to religious knowledge. These included geography, dictation, arithmetic and needlework. In all, during the month of February 1885 the vicar visited this school on eleven different occasions; on four of them he gave a dictation lesson, on five, scripture or catechism lessons; and on the remaining two he instructed in geography. During March of the same year there were eleven visits, and during April, six.[16]

Although hard-pressed teachers may have welcomed such assistance, its spasmodic and unpredictable character must have made its incorporation in the school curriculum extremely difficult. Yet, however inconvenient it might be, protest was normally out of the question if the teacher concerned valued his or her job. This was shown very clearly at Langley Burrell in Wiltshire, where according to the diary of the Rev. Francis Kilvert, son of the rector of the parish, the squire, Mr Ashe, exercised despotic control over the school. On 11 November 1874, Kilvert noted:

> We are in trouble at the school now because a few days ago Mr. Ashe came angrily in to Miss Bland the schoolmistress and ordered her always to keep all three windows and the door of the schoolroom open during schooltime, except in very cold weather when one window might be shut. He said in a fierce determined way, 'This is my school and I will have my word attended to. If you don't do as I tell you, Miss Bland, instead of being your friend I'll be your enemy'. . . . And there are the poor little children crying with the cold. Cruel. Barbarous. And of course the parents are indignant and the numbers of the children falling off.[17]

In such a situation it was all too easy for the teacher to be used as an instrument of social control, to enforce obedience to the existing order—as at Helmingham in Suffolk, where, during the mid-Victorian years, a girl who had omitted to curtsey to the squire's wife remembered being caned for it at school the next day. Then there is the entry in Holbeton school log book, Devon, during 1867: 'Spoke to the children about making obeisance to their Superiors.' Holbeton was very much a 'parson and land-owner-dominated village'.[18] While at Boston Spa in Yorkshire in 1876 a girl of seven was expelled for refusing on her guardian's instructions to curtsey to the vicar's wife, and when the master refused to chastise her for this offence he was 'dismissed by the vicar on the spot, although he had held the post for twenty years'.[19] Few teachers were prepared to stand by their principles in that way and thereby risk losing their position as this man had done.

Another aspect of the problem was the favouritism which some masters and mistresses showed towards the children of the larger farmers or the squire's agent as opposed to those of the labourers or the village craftsmen. As the son of a Welsh shoe-maker later wrote bitterly of his own schoolmaster in Denbigh-shire:

> The cane was in his hand from the opening of the school in the morning to its close at 4 o'clock in the afternoon; . . . But probably what the boys disliked most in him was his obvious favouritisms. These were shown invariably to the well-dressed children of the well-to-do who attended not the Methodist or Baptist Chapel, but the village Church. They were hardly ever caned, even lightly. But the Chapel-going children, and especially those who were poor or slow, suffered many a blow.[20]

And as late as the 1930s a girl who attended school in a Kentish village recalls that during the winter months the seats near to the fire were reserved for the offspring of the farmers and the squire's agent.[21] The rest had to sit 'in the desks in the draught', endur-ing cold hands and feet with as much philosophy as they could muster.

In a number of parishes, however, the discomfort endured by pupils was largely the result of the poor accommodation provided for them. At Benson in Oxfordshire, for example, the school was conducted in 1850 'in an old stable with a cottage attached', for which a rent of £12 per annum was paid. The parishioners were too poor to provide better premises from their own resources since, according to the incumbent, the coming of the railways had deprived them of 'their chief source of employment' by lead-ing to 'the entire discontinuance of 30 coaches that formerly changed horses there daily'. He also lamented that the people were 'much demoralised and careless about religion', with dissent 'very rife'. Only the provision of a good school would remedy these ills and he appealed to the Dean and Chapter of Christ

Church, Oxford, as major landowners in the parish to give him help. Somewhat reluctantly they provided £50 and this, coupled with a substantial grant from the Committee of Council on Education and various private subscriptions, led to the construction of a new school in 1852, at a total cost of £550.[22] But not all parishes were able to overcome their problems as successfully as this. Indeed, as Harry Chester, a former assistant secretary to the Committee of Council, pointed out in 1860, little attention was given in the early days to the planning of even purpose-built schools: 'they were very commonly erected by the village bricklayer and carpenter, by rule of thumb, without any plans at all. The National Society . . . had unfortunately proclaimed that "any shape" would do for a school, and that there was no better model than a "common barn" '.[23] While HMI Sneyd-Kynnersley wrote disapprovingly of a small Welsh village school which he encountered in the early 1870s:

the windows are somewhat low and narrow, and filled with diamond panes; and inside the light is scanty. There is a tiled floor; there are desks for the upper standards only; the other children sit on benches with no back-rails: both desks and benches are evidently the work of the carpenter on the estate. There is no cloak-room, and the damp clothes of the children are hung round the walls, sending out a gentle steam, as if it were washing-day next door, and the water were not very clean. About a quarter of the room at one end is occupied by a platform, which is found convenient for village entertainments.[24]

Often, though, instruction was still being given—as it had been in earlier centuries—in cottages, halls, barns or the church itself rather than in specially built properties of even the dubious quality mentioned by Messrs Chester and Sneyd-Kynnersley. At Leinthall Earles in Herefordshire, HMI Colt Williams reported as late as 1873 that the school was conducted in 'a cottage with a thatched roof which the owner . . . had had . . . repaired previous to my visit in 1871', while at around the same time the church school managers at Adforton (also in Herefordshire) were proposing to use an old blacksmith's shop 'situated at the end of a dirty lane' as their school. A still stranger situation existed at Little Langdale, Westmorland, where a building had been left in trust for a school but, according to the HMI, it was 'fitted for a chapel of ease only' by the trustee, who was also the incumbent. In this case the schoolmistress's kitchen had to be used for instruction, though the Inspector sternly declared that in his view the incumbent should not 'be allowed to continue his breach of trust on a/c of the comparative small no. of chn.', there being only about thirty-three children of school age living at Little Langdale.[25] The difficulties for teachers trying to carry out their duties under such conditions, and often without adequate desks, chairs, benches, or even a blackboard, are easy to appreciate. Not until the passage of the 1870 Education Act, with its requirement that all schools in receipt of a government grant must be provided with satisfactory accommodation, did certain of these problems come to light, with action then taken to deal with them.

There were, nevertheless, some villages where even in the middle of the nineteenth century more favourable circumstances prevailed, and where a broader curriculum also applied than the reading, writing, arithmetic and study of the Church catechism which were commonly held to be 'the aim of all education for the labouring classes'. The better qualified teachers who were now emerging from the training colleges were likewise anxious to experiment with a wide syllabus. So there were schools like that at Osmaston in Derbyshire, where even in 1851–52 the Inspector noted of the most senior class: 'religious knowledge very good; spelling, arithmetic, and geography good; some boys learning algebra; grammar and writing good; fair knowledge of English history.'[26] The second class here also learnt geography and English grammar alongside the customary three 'r's', religious knowledge and needlework for the girls.

But even in relatively enlightened places like this some of the benefits of the broader approach adopted were nullified by the irregularity of attendance of the scholars and the poor quality of the school equipment. In particular the opportunity for employment in country areas rapidly emptied class rooms at certain seasons of the year, with youngsters absent for months at a time. HMI Blandford commented in the late 1840s that 'the children . . . are taken away from school as soon as they can earn anything, and although the boys in the rural districts return to the schools at certain times in the year, when there is no work to be done in the fields, yet they seem to receive little or no benefit from the extra time they are under instruction, in consequence of their general irregular attendance in the course of the year'.[27]

And whilst such reservations as these were being expressed regarding the overall level of achievement in elementary schools, the total cost of education was rising rapidly, following increases in the number of government grants available. There was, for example, the implementation in 1843 of a grant for school apparatus, followed by the institution of the pupil-teacher system and of salary augmentation grants for teachers from 1846, and the offering of capitation grants for scholars from 1853. These latter applied initially to rural areas only, and were linked to the attendance of the pupils; they sought to increase the income of country schools and at the same time to raise attendance levels—without much success. On a national basis, therefore, state education expenditure rose from the £20,000 allowed in 1833, when the aid scheme was introduced, to £663,435 twenty-five years later.[28] The speed with which this sum was growing began to arouse alarm in official circles, and in an effort to ensure that 'value for money' was being obtained it was decided to appoint a Royal Commission (the Newcastle Commission) to 'inquire into the Present State of Popular Education in England, and to consider and report what Measures, if any, are required for the extension of sound and cheap elementary instruction to all classes of the people'.

The Commission reported three years later and concluded that although the system was acceptable in principle, it had a number of serious defects. In the Commissioners' view, many elementary subjects were poorly taught, while attendance in the country districts, in particular, was extremely irregular, with most boys leaving school for good at the age of ten or eleven. However its county reports did confirm that school *provision* in rural areas at the end of the 1850s was superior to that in the rapidly expanding industrialised counties. Wiltshire, Westmorland and Oxfordshire were the three counties with the highest proportion of public week-day scholars to total population, followed by Rutland, Essex and Dorset. By contrast, industrial counties like Stafford, Lancashire and Northumberland were respectively twenty-seventh, forty-first and forty-eighth out of the fifty-three counties listed.[29]

It was in an effort to tighten up on the effectiveness of the grant system, therefore, that in 1862 Robert Lowe, the Vice-President of the Education Department, implemented the new and rigorous device of the Revised Code. Henceforth government grants for elementary schooling, other than building grants, were to be calculated only on the attendance of pupils at school, under a certificated teacher, plus the results of an annual examination conducted by one of Her Majesty's Inspectors and based on the three 'r's'. A grant of 12s. per child was offered for all pupils over six years of age, 4s. of which related to attendance (with 200 attendances per child per annum the minimum accepted), and 8s. to passes in the annual examination in reading, writing and arithmetic. Failure in any one of these subjects meant a deduction of 2s. 8d. from that particular pupil's grant. The infants, who were exempted from the ordeal of the annual examination, could earn 6s. 6d. each—in addition to their attendance grant—provided the Inspector was satisfied that they were 'instructed suitably to their age, and in a manner not to interfere with the instruction of the older children.' The examinations of this latter group were arranged in a series of standards with each child expected to move up a standard every year. Finally, at every school receiving annual grants the head teacher had to keep a diary or log book in which to record the scholars' general academic progress and their day-to-day activities.

Although elementary education had had many unsatisfactory aspects prior to this, the new developments were to intensify them. On the beneficial side, admittedly, the change did mean that every child, and not merely the brightest, would now receive attention from the teacher, since all had to succeed at the annual examination if the maximum grant were to be earned. In addition general reading books had to be provided to supplement the Bible, which had hitherto often served as the sole source of reading material and dictation practice, as well as of religious instruction, purely on account of its cheapness.

But if these were gains, in almost every other respect the new system exerted an adverse influence on the instruction given. Because reading, writing and arithmetic were the grant-earning subjects, they were concentrated upon to the virtual exclusion of all others, apart from religious instruction and needlework, which was compulsory for the girls. Publishers, alive to the possibilities of the situation, quickly produced textbooks which claimed that their chosen volume comprised 'all that is necessary to enable the pupils to acquire knowledge demanded in their Lordships' Minute. It need scarcely be said that any matter which is not absolutely required should, for obvious reasons, be omitted.'[30] This narrow approach to schooling soon became the accepted one.

Teachers protested in vain at the developments. A deputation of schoolmasters who visited the Prime Minister, Lord Palmerston, in November 1861, when the Code was still under discussion, strongly emphasised the limitations of the system, claiming that it ignored 'the moral and religious teaching of their schools. By confining its aid to mechanical proficiency in reading, writing, and arithmetic, the State placed the temptation in the way of the teacher to neglect that training which all felt should form the very foundation of true education.'[31] Lord Palmerston politely thanked them for giving their views and promised that these would 'have the most respectful consideration of the Government in any future legislation on the subject'. But the Code went ahead in the following year in substantially its original form.

Over the years some of the rigidities of the system were ironed out, as efforts were made to widen the curriculum with, for example, the provision of additional payments for 'specific' subjects, such as English grammar, history and geography, in 1867. But the impact of these was limited—with only 3.7 per cent of all the children on the books of elementary schools in 1875 being examined for one or other of the 'specific' subjects. So in that year English grammar, history, geography and plain needlework were converted into 'class' subjects, with the grant earned by the proficiency of the whole group rather than the success of the individual.[32] And from 1871 a new, broader range of 'specific' subjects was brought forward. As the Tory Vice-President of the Education Department, Lord Sandon, optimistically remarked, 'by working into the mere mechanical reading a little grammar, physical geography, a little knowledge of the geography of England, and a certain amount of history, it was thought that the mind of the child would not be over-burdened, and that the teaching would be rendered more lively'.[33] Singing, too, became a grant-earning subject from 1872.

But if these changes did effect some improvements, their influence in country areas remained modest. The three 'r's', combined with average attendance, formed the basis of the education grant up to 1890, and the last elements of the 'payment by results' system did not finally disappear for 'specific' subjects until 1897.[34] Nevertheless, after 1890 the grant for the three 'r's' was replaced by higher payments for attendance and an additional 'discipline and organisation' item. Only with the Code of 1900 was the final liberation secured. This abolished all piecemeal grants. Instead schools received capitation grants of 17s. for infant children, and 22s. for older. 'The inspectors were able to reduce the grants by only a shilling for defects and the only additional payments were for cooking and manual instruction'— neither of which affected most rural schools.[35]

In the meantime for more than one generation of teachers and scholars, the routine of school life became an unremitting grind in the basic subjects, with endless repetition and learning by rote the normal methods of instruction adopted. As one of Her Majesty's Inspectors later noted :

> in those days the average school was a hive of industry. But it was also a hive of misdirected energy. The State, in prescribing a syllabus which was to be followed, in all the subjects of instruction . . . did all his thinking for the teacher. It told him in precise detail what he was to do each year in each 'Standard', how he was to handle each subject, and how far he was to go in it; . . . what degree of accuracy was required for a 'pass' . . . and it was inevitable that in his endeavour to adapt his teaching to the type of question which his experience of the yearly examination led him to expect, he should gradually deliver himself, mind and soul, into the hands of the officials of the [Education] Department . . . who framed the yearly syllabus, and the officials in the various districts who examined on it.[36]

Individual initiative was crushed, and the minimum standard needed to secure a pass became the maximum level of the teacher's ambitions. HMI Johnstone, for example, reported in 1877 that teachers were no longer devoting special time and effort to reading : 'they aim exclusively at what will secure a pass, and the reading is hesitating and laboured, not enough so to cause a failure, but enough to show clearly to the hearer that the boy he listens to will never read alone for his own amusement'.[37] But this man was something of a Job's comforter, for he claimed that good writing was beyond 'the fingers of the rural labourer. . . . The boy that can hold a plough cannot grasp the more delicate handle of a pen'. (Presumably he had forgotten the agricultural careers of the poets Robert Burns and John Clare.) While as for arithmetic, that was a subject 'which seems beyond the comprehension of the rural mind. It is never, except in the rarest instances, mastered; whole classes fail entirely in it, and often pass only by accomplishing the mechanical details of such simple sums as to require no exercise whatever of the intelligence.' The country teacher reading these comments must have felt that his task was well-nigh hopeless.

In fact, thanks to the Revised Code, relations between HMIs and teachers became more strained—a tendency which was reinforced by the differing social backgrounds of the two groups, with the Inspectors recruited from well-to-do families, usually after an education at one of the older Universities. Such men were 'little inclined to regard teachers as in any way their equals', even though they recognised the pressures under which many of them worked.[38]

But it was the *financial* power which the Inspectors exercised over the schools which made them particularly feared. Records show that the government grant was of overwhelming importance in the very survival of some of the smaller schools—like Shutford in Oxfordshire, where in the mid-1880s the various grants were providing over a third of the total school income. It is possible to trace a note of desperation in many log books as the date of the dreaded annual examination drew near. Thus at Weston-on-Avon (then in Gloucestershire) the master noted despondently on 30 January 1879: 'The Government Inspector has announced his visit to Weston School on Monday next 11.45. Do not expect much success under present circumstances'. These latter included an extremely cold school room where, according to an entry in the log book ten days earlier, the master had hardly been 'able to carry the school on properly, the children shivering frequently with cold'. When the visit took place, his worst fears were realised for the HMI observed severely: 'I am disappointed with the results of the examination, and fail to find the improvement I looked for. Very little is attempted and even that little is moderately done. . . . The elder children seem altogether at a loss how to set about their sums. . . . Unless very great improvement is shewn next year, the grant will incur a heavy deduction.'[39] Perhaps not surprisingly, given the attitude of school managers in those days, the master lost his position a few months later.

A Welsh teacher, Hugh Morris, shared many of these anxieties in January 1890 : 'Very bad attendance this week. I feel heartless in trying to continue with such irregular attendance, and such discouraging report from the Inspector is enough to eat the very life out of a poor fellow.' He, too, was eventually dismissed—although in his case excessive use of the cane rather than mere academic shortcomings seems to have been the cause of his downfall. In any event, his final entry in the school log on 31 July 1891, was a bitter one : 'This is the last day I shall teach in this school. I am told my successor will be an angel, not one of the fallen ones, pray, for I declare this locality be overstocked with such fiends already.'[40] Morris also commented on the feelings of the pupils as examination day drew near, with several of them declaring 'they will not come to school again because they fear the Inspector'. On another occasion he noted : 'Some of the children declare they will not come to school any more, because they so dread the Examination.[41]

A third sufferer from the Revised Code was the head of Market Rasen Methodist School, Lincolnshire, who although successful in his examination results, nevertheless felt the pressures of his position. As he confided in his log book in 1883 : 'I observe from the papers that a Master has committed suicide through the overstrain, and I can truthfully say that I, and all the teachers of this neighbourhood are daily suffering from this same pressure. Teachers are expected to perform miracles and try to do so. . . . I have worked hard—labouriously [*sic*] hard. Throughout the year I have felt underneath my work—I have sought change of air, Medical Advice, etc., but my doctor tells me nothing will do me good but complete rest. Query. How can a teacher obtain rest?' In the following year he again gave way to self-pity : 'When I first entered my pupil-teachership teaching had its rosy hues; but alas they have all vanished.'[42] Despite his anxieties, however, he remained at Market Rasen until 1905, completing the formidable stint of twenty-nine years at this one school.

Nor was it just the country teachers who felt in that way. In October 1892, W. H. Pullinger, a London master, wrote despondently to a former colleague, who was now in the inspectorate :

Work at school goes on much the same as usual.—We begin our series of exams. next week. Drawing on Monday, Preliminary Scripture on Friday & so on until the end of the chapter which I suppose we shall reach some time before Xmas. What a farce it all is! We are of course working a bit at high pressure. I have a very dull Standard V to make me feel anxious. They are not bad boys & they have worked very well but there is not a spark of ability among them—the only able boy was put into Stan. VI—& yet my work will be judged by what they can do on examination day. I suppose that in the good time coming Standard Examination will be abolished. I hope you will do what you can to speed its departure . . .[43]

The educational press displayed similar hostility to the Code, especially *The Schoolmaster*, which had been established in 1872 as the organ of the National Union of Elementary Teachers. In one article, entitled 'Teaching under the Code', which appeared in this journal on 18 January 1879, the author bitterly pointed out that the payment by results system was 'a bondage grievous to be borne, of which making bricks without straw is only a feeble emblem . . . at all cost "passes" must be secured. . . . Hence many teachers work over-hours, keeping the feeble and slow back to cram them, examine them, and cram them again. . . . [Many] poor fellows . . . have worked themselves into an untimely grave—martyrs to Codes, and martinet inspectors. Whoever will mix with teachers will be surprised to find what large numbers are suffering from such disorders as are the natural and direct result of over work, and the feverish excitement of annual inspections.'

A majority of heads began to hold tests in readiness for the visit of the HMI weeks, or even months, before his expected arrival, while some altered the otherwise sacrosanct timetable in order to try to eliminate known weaknesses or omissions. At Great Bardfield British School in Essex, the master noted on 12 October 1863, that he had 'changed the school routine for a time in order to work up for the coming examination in reading, writing & arithmetic'. HMI Matthew Arnold eventually visited this school in the following May.[44] Similarly at Claydon in Oxfordshire, mock tests were held on a monthly basis from June of each year during the early 1880s—in preparation for an inspection in the following January.[45] While at another Oxford-shire school not even an epidemic of measles and scarlet fever in the winter of 1885–86 was allowed to stand in the way of preparation. The head merely cancelled the holiday at Christmas and carried on. There are countless other examples. In fact as late as 1924, when payment by results had long disappeared, Sir Ronald Gould, then a young teacher in Somerset, remembers the nerve shattering effect of a possible visit by the Inspector. On his first day at the school there was a knock on the door, and when he opened it, a small boy was standing outside:

> 'Are you the headmaster?', he enquired. 'No', I answered, 'but I can give him a message.' 'My headmaster has asked me to tell your headmaster that the cuckoo is coming early this year.' It was September! The message was passed on. The effect was cataclysmic. The head's face blanched. Panic. 'Tell all the teachers to check registers, weekly forecasts, exercise books, have inkwells cleaned, windows decorated with flowers. . . .' The HMI was expected.[46]

Small wonder that when the Revised Code was at its height the teacher's nervousness transmitted itself to the children and that, as at Joseph Ashby's Tysoe, in Warwickshire, the children would sit uncomfortably on the edge of their seats on examination day, waiting to be called out. The master's worry was under-standable, for at this school, as at many others, his salary depended partly on the level of government grant secured for the school by its pupils. (That policy will be examined in greater detail in chapter 8, when the salaries question is discussed.) Joseph recalled how two inspectors arrived each year to carry out

> a dramatic examination. The schoolmaster came into school in his best suit; all the pupils and teachers would be listening till at ten o'clock a dog-cart would be heard on the road, even though it was eighty yards away. In would come two gentle-men with a deportment of high authority, with rich voices. Each would sit at a desk and children would be called in turn to one or other. The master hovered round. . . . The children could see him start with vexation as a good pupil stuck at a word in the reading-book he had been using all the year, or sat motionless with his sum in front of him. The master's anxiety was deep, for his earnings depended on the children's

work. One year the atmosphere of anxiety so affected the lower standards that, one after another as they were brought to the Inspector, the boys howled and the girls whimpered. It took hours to get through them.[47]

Certain teachers responded to this situation by taking a firm—even brutal—disciplinary line with their charges. HMI Swinburne, who examined schools in the Eastern Counties during the later Victorian years, subsequently described how in one place he was told by the mistress that : 'Love rules without the sword', but when she asked the pupils : ' "Now what did I say I'd do, dears, if you didn't please the nice, kind Inspector?", the reply came : "Please, ma'm, you said you'd caane us !" '[48] 'And there were masters who would not hesitate to flog boys for furtively handing to one another answers in examinations, and yet would themselves . . . hand from school to school [the Inspector's] questions'.[49]

However Swinburne appreciated the difficulties under which teachers laboured. At one school the head mistress fainted in the middle of the examination because she thought her charges were performing badly. Elsewhere for weeks before the inspection 'the children were stuffed and almost roasted—(no wonder they resembled trusssed fowls)—the mistress had sleepless nights, the parson and the squire of the village were in a flutter of anxiety, for so much depended at that time on the verdict of Her Majesty's Inspector.'[50]

The private letters of HMI King, however, reveal a more sympathetic attitude towards teachers' difficulties, when, at the beginning of 1894, he reluctantly left his native Cornwall to take up inspectorial duties elsewhere. He was anxious that his successor, Sydney Marvin, should make due allowances for the poverty and backwardness of the more remote rural parishes. Thus on 14 March he wrote : 'I'm sorry the Treleigh children did badly : they are rough & the poorest of the poor but by coaxing I used to get something out of them. Downing tries his best & he has a good little p.t. . . . I hope the little man at Goonhavern did well—he talks broad Cornish & is a Rad of the first water but a very honest hard working man & his boys & girls are capital. . . . All children are nice creatures but I do miss my little people in Cornwall—at Redruth even—a very barren soil—I had some very special friends.'[51] More than six months later he was still writing to Marvin, offering advice and trying to win his successor's interest for the Cornish schools. But few other Inspectors displayed that sort of personal anxiety over the children's welfare.

Where a good examination result was obtained, teachers naturally took great pride in their achievement and sought to use the Inspector's report as an advertisement to attract pupils to their school, since a larger school roll would often mean a higher salary. At Harpenden British School, during the 1880s and 1890s the headmaster arranged for the final sheet of the children's copy books to be inscribed with printed extracts from a whole range of annual reports—running from 1866 to 1881. Typical of those quoted was the comment for November 1880: 'The high reputation of this School continues to be well maintained.' The extracts were preceded by a brief statement: 'The following Reports on the State of this School are inserted so that the Parents of the Boys may know the Opinions entertained of this Institution by Gentlemen thoroughly competent to judge.'

But among those who were less successful there were, needless to say, many who grumbled at the unfairness of the proceedings —as in an editorial in *The Schoolmaster* of 29 March 1873: 'The zeal of some inspectors has lately led them to expect things nearly impossible in the way of arithmetic . . . The standards set . . . by different inspectors, and even by these and their own assistants, vary so much that a greater uniformity is greatly required'. Similarly adverse comments came from individual heads, too. One man complained that when HMI Collins visited his school at the beginning of 1879, the Inspector was 'not only very near-sighted but so deaf that I failed to make him hear even when I shouted, and was obliged to write on slips of paper every communication I had with him'. After a series of farcical misunderstandings over such matters as the marking of registers and the counting of the number present, Mr Collins proceeded to examine the pupils. Of twenty-five youngsters called forward in Standard II, four failed in reading, two in writing—and eleven in arithmetic. The master then continued:

> The number of failures in reading speaks for itself, for even if he could have heard I think it very unfair that a small child should be required to read from a book held close to an

inspector's nose. As regards the failures in arithmetic, our assistant, who was in the room, declared she could not catch the numbers he gave, owing to his indistinct utterance. . . . Will you allow me to add that in my first standard out of twenty-four examined by the inspector's assistant, twenty-four passed in reading, twenty in writing and twenty-one in arithmetic.

This letter appeared in *The Schoolmaster* on 25 January 1879, and in the following week 'A Teacher of the District' wrote to defend HMI Collins: 'No inspector has sought more earnestly than Mr Collins to work with the teachers of his district.' Whatever the rights and wrongs of this particular case, the correspondence underlines the tensions of the annual inspection and the anxieties involved for pupils and teachers.

Apart from failure in the examination, however, one of the perennial difficulties faced in securing a maximum grant for a school was the fact that when the Revised Code was introduced in the 1860s school attendance was not yet compulsory. At a time when child labour was general, particularly in agriculture, there was a constant battle to ensure that pupils made the requisite number of attendances. Youngsters working in cottage industries, like lace-making, glovemaking and straw-plaiting were ostensibly restricted by the 1867 Factory and Workshops Regulation Act, though, as we saw in chapter 1, many parents ignored the restrictions and continued to keep their children at work.

Only with the passage of the Education Acts of 1870, 1876 and 1880 did it at last become compulsory for every child to attend school at least to the age of ten and thereafter to thirteen or fourteen, as local bye-laws laid down, unless a suitable leaving examination could be passed which gave earlier exemption. This latter concession gave rise to the so-called 'labour certificate'.

Although when the 1870 Act was proposed there is little doubt that the government had Britain's declining industrial competitiveness and the education problems of the new manufacturing towns particularly in mind (like Manchester, where almost twenty-five per cent of the children who might be in school allegedly received no instruction at all), country districts, too, gained from its provisions. Under the Act, each child had to be provided with an elementary school place, and in areas where the existing voluntary schools were unable to meet this need, local ratepayers had to form an elected school board, financed partly out of the rates, to fulfil the obligation. They were also permitted to make bye-laws relating to school attendance and to appoint attendance officers to pursue those who were evading the regulations. But in rural areas relatively few school boards were established—the voluntary bodies in most cases being able to meet local needs. In some parishes, indeed, boards were resisted on the ground of expense—for ratepayers not only had to support a board's school provisions but also pay the cost of the triennial election of its members; in others, and more commonly, there was resistance because the non-denominational schooling they offered might undermine Church influence within the community. At the third annual meeting of the Lincoln Diocesan Conference in 1875, for example, the Bishop of Lincoln expressed the fervent hope that members of his audience would 'do all they could to try to maintain the voluntary and denominational system of education. . . . If they had a godless unchristian education they would have a godless unchristian people. If the system of School Board teaching was spread widely he would tremble for our civil and political institutions throughout the country.' His remarks were loudly applauded.[52] While in Cambridgeshire, the Bishop of Ely headed attempts to raise funds 'whereby the educational requirements of every parish in the county might be provided for'. As a result of these efforts about £1,500 was collected 'and in most parishes the formation of Boards was postponed'.[53] So, in the country as a whole, as late as 1895 more children were still attending voluntary schools than board ones. And even where school boards *were* set up in rural parishes, they were often very unsatisfactory—many not even bothering to draw up the attendance bye-laws they were empowered to introduce:

> Typically, they consisted of the vicar, the churchwardens and three farmers. The vicar had a conscientious objection to School Boards, and the farmers thought that the younger a child started on agricultural work the better for everybody. They gave exemptions to all who asked, and employed illegally those who did not bother to do so. They also, generally, made the teacher's life very difficult.[54]

Certainly HMI King had a low opinion of their work in

Cornwall: 'Small School Boards with little in them beyond petty economy do not form an effective educational machine. I have managed to keep on good terms with them all, but I can be deaf & blind on occasion. Church & dissent are at daggers drawn & one has to be wary—politics also are dangerous ground, but I have always taken the line that a public servant has no politics except in private.'[55]

In 1873, therefore, a private members' bill sought to extend the regulation of child employment and school attendance on a wider basis. Under the Agricultural Children Act no child below the age of eight was to work in agriculture, while between eight and twelve years certain minimum school attendances were required. Unfortunately the Act's lack of a proper enforcement agency proved its undoing. Within weeks of its coming into operation on 1 January 1875, it had become a dead letter.[56] So not until a new Education Act was passed in 1876 were attendance provisions extended in any significant degree to voluntary schools as well. Under this legislation all children from five to ten years of age had to attend school full-time. For those between the ages of ten and twelve a minimum of 250 attendances a year was required, and for youngsters between twelve and fourteen, the minimum was 150 attendances—unless they could pass the relevant leaving examination in the three 'r's' (usually Standard IV of the Code) which permitted earlier full-time employment.

In order to make effective the compulsory aspects of the Act a new type of local authority—the attendance committee—was introduced to cover those school districts which were still without a school board. Parents neglecting to send their children to school could be fined, and despite the laxity of many attendance officers and magistrates, a number were. But even then, a minority of education authorities failed to draw up the necessary bye-laws, so it was left to the Act of 1880 finally to make the adoption of attendance regulations mandatory throughout the country.

If this legislative framework made it easier for teachers to obtain good attendances, the problem was by no means at an end. The ill-health of the pupils continued to be one major difficulty, while, despite the restrictions, child labour—especially seasonal labour—remained an important part of British agriculture for years to come. The mistress of Claydon Board School,

Oxfordshire, was certainly not alone when she wrote despondently in March 1883 : 'If something is not done immediately the "Average Attendance" will be very small & the "Grant" correspondingly so.' Two and a half years later came a similar complaint : 'The attendance of some of my pupils is most distressing.'⁵⁷ In this parish, farmers (including members of the school board itself) regularly employed illegal child labour.

As regards the pupils' ill-health, there are frequent comments in the school log books about the prevalence of coughs and colds, while—as at Yetminster in Dorset in January 1881—more serious epidemics might hit attendances. In this case, whooping cough and scarlatina took their toll, while at Whitchurch in Oxfordshire during the winter of 1887–88 the problem was an outbreak of mumps. In the stuffy overcrowded atmosphere common to most village schools, where the smell of unwashed bodies and, often, filthy clothing was combined with the unhygienic practice of spitting on the slates to clean them, disease spread rapidly. Measles, whooping cough, diphtheria and scarlet fever were all major killers of children to the end of the Victorian era.⁵⁸

Teachers were not exempt from the ravages of disease either. In 1858, the Rev. M. Mitchell, HMI, commented on the adverse effect caused to health in East Anglian schools by 'picturesque lattice windows', which seriously hampered ventilation and proper lighting. He pointed out that there had been 'eleven cases' in his area where the teacher or a pupil-teacher 'had broken down in health or collapsed' after teaching in a poorly ventilated room fitted with lattice windows. The condition of the pupils was not noted! The diary of twenty-one-year-old Albert Brett, an assistant master at Andover British School, also contains many gloomy observations about the effect of teaching upon his health—as on 6 September 1864 : 'Found it very hot and close the air very impure in the class room. I feel very apprehensive as to its effect upon my general health'. And on the following day came another despondent entry : 'My health is not good. Diseases which I thought were already cured have again tormented me. . . . Sometimes . . . I am inclined to think that my life will be short, and I shall die a premature death.'⁵⁹ Training college records confirm a sprinkling of premature deaths among teachers, particularly from tuberculosis. At Culham College, to quote but one example, of forty-two students who began their two-year course in February

1875, three had died from this disease within ten years of leaving, while two of the previous year's intake suffered a similar fate.

But if ill-health was one cause of poor attendance by scholars in the later nineteenth century—and an excusable one—another still more prevalent factor was child labour. This affected country areas more than the towns and as late as 1898, HMI de Saus-marez blamed 'the supineness of the magistrates and the attend-ance committees' for the irregular attendances. He also observed that 'in addition to the regular harvest, children are employed in potato-digging, pea-picking, hopping, blackberrying and nutting, and fruit and daffodil gathering, and where, as in a case brought to my notice a boy can earn ten shillings in one week in picking blackberries, it is not surprising if his parents consider him more profitably employed than in struggling with the analyses of sentences . . . and are willing to take their chance of the law's delay, or if necessary to pay the maximum fine that can be imposed for irregular attendance. . . .' His colleague, HMI Alington, likewise reported from Kent : 'One school in which I found the average [attendance] reduced to about 50 per cent during the three weeks of fruiting, and another in which it fell to 47 and 49 per cent during a rainy fortnight, are not excep-tional.'[60] (See also Appendix 6.)

Only in parts of the north of England, where the wage rates of adult farm workers were higher and, more importantly, oppor-tunities for child employment were limited, were these attendance problems less severe. In Holderness in Yorkshire there was relatively little for children to do beyond helping with the hay and corn harvests, since with no root crops grown, weeding was not required, and for the draining, banking and hedging which formed much of the farm work the youngsters were unsuitable. Hence in this area absenteeism was no great difficulty. Similarly in Northumberland few children began work before the ages of ten or eleven and in this county even in the 1840s parents attached sufficient importance to education to make every effort to send their children to school. No 'greater stigma' could attach to parents than to leave their offspring 'without the means' of basic education.

But against these more favourable examples must be set the fact that in the majority of country districts the truancy problem was severe. Indeed, even in high-wage Yorkshire on the wolds where arable farming was carried on, children's schooling was neglected in favour of bird-tenting, weeding, setting and lifting turnips and potatoes, and harvesting. Whilst in 1887 the National Union of Teachers formed a Special Committee on Rural and Half Time Schools to consider the attendance issue. Of 144 district associations submitting returns to this body, fifty-seven considered that the illegal employment of children in field labour or domestic work was the principal obstacle 'to regular attendance in Rural schools'; and fifty-seven claimed that the neglect of school boards and school attendance committees to enforce the regulations was a severe handicap.[61] Only eighteen of the associations made no mention of child employment within their area.

About four years later, in October 1891, the Union took a further step when it submitted a report on the subject of attendance to the Education Department, appealing for more effective enforcement of the legislation, with the appointment of special magistrates to deal with attendance cases. Its strictures regarding the attitude of farmers were especially severe:

> The exigencies of harvest time, hop-picking, potato-dropping, and fruit gathering seem to leave those persons no time for consideration of the fact that they are breaking the law in employing children of school age. In many instances children are spoken of as helping their elder brothers or sisters, or their parents, in the fields, with the full knowledge, and on the land of members of the local authority. Cover beating several times occurs as a form of illegal juvenile labour.[62]

Despite such protests—and even the offering of prizes for good attendance at some schools—the problem persisted into the twentieth century (see chapter 10). Only with the further mechanisation of agriculture, eliminating tasks formerly performed by children, did it at last cease to be a major difficulty. In other areas, cottage industries had a similar effect, so that at Yetminster, the mistress could complain in October, 1891: 'many of the elder girls were absent, being kept at home to assist their mothers with the gloving. 17 only were present.' And a year later: 'Attendance small on Wednesday & Friday owing to the girls being employed in carrying their mother's work to the gloving master.'[63] While at Puncknowle, also in Dorset, it was netmaking which was the offender.[64]

The position of teachers in these circumstances was extremely delicate, particularly where the children were kept away with the connivance of the major farmers and landowners in a parish. On the one hand they needed good attendances to carry out their professional duties satisfactorily; on the other, they were anxious not to offend members of their management committee or school board who might be making use of the child labour. Most heads accepted the situation with philosophic resignation, hoping to put pressure on particularly blatant offenders but otherwise making the best of a bad job.

Another anxiety, which was pinpointed by a correspondent to *The Schoolmaster* of 6 September 1873, was the failure of children to come to school on the annual inspection day, even when they had achieved their complement of ordinary attendances :

> they are capable of passing; but lo! when the day comes many of them are conspicuous by their absence, although the master may have begged of them to attend, may even have walked miles (as I have done myself) to entreat the parents to send them, at any rate on that day, but they are not there in spite of all this. What is the cause of it? In a great many cases (at any rate in villages), it is the callousness and obtuseness of the parents; they know next to nothing themselves, and cannot appreciate learning in their children; the consequence is that they take no interest in the school, and less in the managers and master. Why, Sir, I have been told repeatedly (and I think the experience of many teachers in agricultural districts will corroborate my statement) that they consider that they are doing the master a favour by sending their children to school at all! . . . Another prolific reason of non-attendance may be some small spite that a boy or girl may have for their master or mistress, for some wholesome correction administered; and they adopt this means of revenge, knowing that the master has some interest in the examination.

For if the child did not complete his examination, then the school lost a major part of the government grant available for him.

Clashes between parents and teachers could, however, take place over other issues than the annual inspection. Home Lessons provided one fertile source of dispute. The master at Keresley, Warwickshire, was not alone when he noted in the later 1860s that when, from time to time, he had set homework he had been told 'by the parents that the books [would] be burnt and slates broken' if he persisted. Likewise at Brailes in the same county the mistress was forced to admit defeat: 'Home lessons suspended to suit parents' views', reads the log book entry for 30 July 1875.[65]

A still more serious cause of ill-feeling was the failure of children to bring their school pence, before fees were abolished in most elementary schools in 1891. Although the Education Act of 1876 had empowered the poor law guardians to pay school fees where parents were unable to do so, not all were prepared to co-operate. At South Ferriby in Lincolnshire, for example, the headmaster noted on 22 January 1886 that: 'The Guardians will not allow the fees except on parents promising to repay.' And on 19 February: 'I have a poor attendance . . . I cannot receive school fees from several parents as they are unemployed. I have repeatedly asked the Guardians but to no effect.' His colleague at Grasby Church School, in the Caistor poor law union was more fortunate—as on 21 January 1881 : 'The Relieving Officer paid the fees of the children receiving parish relief.'

But where there was no such help available and children arrived without their school pence, teachers would often send them home to collect the small sums involved. And if parents were without the necessary cash, they merely kept the children at home. Or, as with one family at Yetminster, the girl or boy concerned might be sent to a competing establishment. In this case, the mistress wrote on 18 January 1889: 'Alice Childs being in debt for school fees has left this school to go to Ryme, where Yetminster children are received free of charge.' But occasionally there were more vigorous reactions. In 1888 a small boy in Hampshire, who was sent home for his fees because 'he was four or five weeks in arrears', quickly returned with a message from his mother that she 'was not going to pay any money' and the teacher might do what [she] liked'. Most parents lacked the courage to show this kind of defiance.[66] But for the sensitive child involved in such a situation, the humiliations of poverty must indeed have been bitter.

One of the most frequent grounds for disagreement between parents and teachers was, however, over the question of school discipline. There is little doubt that among the teaching profession there was a small number of men and women who delighted in keeping their charges subdued and afraid—like the teachers mentioned by HMI Swinburne : 'And there were [those] whose descriptions of their treatment by love so delighted me as I strode along the front rows that I raised my hand in wonder—only to find a dozen boys or girls . . . cower as expectant of a blow'.[67]

Nevertheless even for the non-sadistic majority of the profession, strict discipline was seen as the only way of coping with the mass of children of all ages and abilities who were crammed into the average schoolroom. And unlike the situation elsewhere in Europe, corporal punishment was accepted as an inevitable part of that disciplinary process. (One critic, writing in 1875, called it a 'relic of insular barbarism; . . . that, as a system . . . is no longer tolerated in any of the great European nations except our own'.)[68] But most contemporary writers and lecturers on school management advocated a firm line. Joseph Landon of Saltley Training College, declared, for example : 'It is far safer in matters of discipline to err on the side of strictness than laxity. A child likes good discipline, and respects thoroughly a wise and decided control.' His school management textbook ran into nine editions within thirteen years.[69]

Elsewhere, there was the feeling that if teachers did not secure dominance over their pupils, the youngsters would quickly get out of hand. Flora Thompson remembered one young mistress who came to Cottisford in the 1880s. She tried to be a friend as well as a teacher to her pupils, but to them this smacked of weakness. They would hide her cane, put water in her inkpot, slip frogs into her desk and ask stupid, unnecessary questions about their work. When she replied, they coughed in chorus. 'Several times she appealed to them to show more consideration. Once she burst into tears before the whole school.' One afternoon when a pitched battle was raging among the older boys, and the mistress was unavailingly appealing for order, the rector arrived. His call for silence led to an immediate hush, and the youngsters remained 'wide-eyed and horrified' whilst he had the whole class out and caned each of the boys soundly. But if this solved the problem on that occasion it also meant the end of the mistress's own career at the school. She left shortly afterwards.[70] Another sufferer was Albert Brett, who encountered problems at Andover in October 1864 : 'Had my temper sorely tried by some few boys in Standard VI.' Four days earlier his indignation had been still greater: 'Find the boys many of them rather impudent in the upper divisions. I have had occasion before many times to speak of it & tonight while walking in the street, had another instance of their insolent behaviour. Nothing annoys me so much and never have I had so much of it as I have during my residence here.'[71]

Certain of these discipline problems were no doubt due to the youth and inexperience of the teachers. At the 1861 Census of Population more than one in five of all schoolmasters and mistresses were under the age of twenty-five; forty years later the proportion of youngsters had risen still further, with between one in three and one in four of the men and, still more strikingly, over one half of the women under the age of twenty-five. Although some of this weighting in favour of youth may have been due to the pupil-teacher system, much of it clearly was not —for more than one in four of the mistresses were in the age range 20–24 inclusive, while a number of those aged 15–19 were probably unqualified assistants rather than pupil-teachers.[72] Training college records confirm the early age at which students took up headships. So that of 43 entrants to Culham College in January 1860, no less than twenty-nine became heads immediately on leaving, three of them being only nineteen years of age and thirteen only twenty when they took up their appointments. One of the nineteen-year-olds, who had undergone a one-year course, moved to the headship of Lugwardine in Herefordshire, although the principal had unenthusiastically described him as: 'A rough, heavy & dull person: . . . may prove a useful man in a very rural district'.

On occasion, strong disciplinary action by the teacher might call forth an equally firm parental response. Hugh Morris in Wales noted one such experience: 'A woman gave me a rough scolding on Monday, because I had punished her son slightly for being late coming to school and for swearing.' While on another occasion a 'boy of Cwmdeffydd left the school . . . soon after we commenced school. He whistled in the school very loud and declared vehemently that he did not, and was very impudent, so I gave him a stroke on his hand with one rod, so he rose from his seat and went home. His mother came here and did scold gaily.'[73] Still more dramatic was the case of Alexander Sargent, head of Sidbury school, from 1875–1899. He had scarcely settled into his school before: 'Mrs. B— came . . . and cursed and swore before the children, called me everything offensive she could think about, and interrupted the work of the school for about ten minutes'. This was because of a punishment he had inflicted, and over the years he was to record many similar incidents. In 1883 he even noted a 'threat to murder' him.[74]

But sometimes parental hostility went beyond mere verbal abuse. The volatile Hugh Morris recorded how on one occasion when he was 'going to Pantydwr of Monday evening after school I met with Evan Rees, Bryndrainog, and his son, a boy eleven years of age, with a load of turf. I told him he was breaking the law by keeping the boy from school, so he gave me a heavy blow with his fist on my cheek. I had a club in my hand and he had to feel the weight of it a few times on his back so he scampered off as fast as he could making a very ugly face.'[75] The columns of *The Schoolmaster* confirm that this was no isolated incident. During the six months ending December 1893 there were at least six cases of assault on village school teachers reported in this journal—leading to fines on the parents concerned.

From time to time the older pupils, too, exchanged blows with their teachers. According to George Swinford (b.1887), the master at Filkins in Oxfordshire used 'to glory in giving me a good thrashing for the least thing, but when I got older, I turned on him and kicked his legs, then he used to send my mother [a] note, [and] I had another good hiding.' In the end he proved too unruly for the master to handle and was allowed to leave at the age of twelve, even though he had not passed his leaving examination.[76] Then there was the young master in an Essex town who found, whenever he tried to cane a boy—'the lads got onto him and they literally did used to fight him . . . across the table and he'd always keep getting his cane and hit back'.[77] While Charles Slater of Barley, Hertfordshire, who was born in 1868, remembered the effects of the 1876 Education Act on discipline problems at his school: 'there were some big lads working on the farms and these came back to school, and the school cane was then used freely, but a big lad name[d] Ben Jackson resented this and closed with the schoolmaster and down on the floor they went, and it proved that Ben was as good as his master but the schoolmaster called to one of the boys to fetch Mr

Gordon, the rector and he came and took the cane, and gave Ben a sound thrashing . . . but the schoolmaster was in poor health and the poor man died soon after.' The physical and mental stress which such incidents caused to teachers is easy to imagine. In any event, this master's successor took a firm line from the beginning. On the first day at the school he gave Slater 'a flat smack [on] the head on looking at my slate'. After that, the two got on well together: 'He used to give me two pence a week to fetch his milk and a penny an hour to work for him on Saturdays'.[78]

Even the rivalry between church and chapel could cause difficulties. At Crich in Derbyshire the master of the church school complained to the vicar how his colleague at the nonconformist British school in the village was encouraging his pupils in rowdy behaviour towards the church scholars and teachers. In his log book for 20 June 1883, he noted that fifty of the British school children with their master had 'shouted opprobrious epithets' to himself and his wife, while on the previous day a stone had been thrown at the latter and had cut her face, causing 'much pain'. Not surprisingly, he concluded: 'I rarely go out alone whilst it is light, afraid of intimidation'.[79] And at Littlemore in Oxfordshire, one of the members of a nearby Baptist chapel even wrote to the Education Department in London to complain that the clergyman of the parish and the mistress of the village school had told parents that the children '*must* come to the Church School on Sunday *if* they wish to come to the School during the week, or if they go to our School on Sunday they cannot have them at their Day School (the *only* school in the village for the children to go to).'[80] The incumbent denied the accusation, and the Education Department supported his stance. But such controversies must inevitably have poisoned relations between a school head and certain of his or her pupils.

It was against this general background, therefore, that the daily work of the schools went on—with the teacher under constant pressure from managers and HMI and with a paramount need to keep good discipline if examination successes were to be secured. At the same time, thanks to the demands of the Revised Code, the normal teaching round meant endless drilling of the children in the basic subjects. At Tysoe, Joseph Ashby remembered that in the 1860s:

Right up the school, through all the six standards . . . you did almost nothing except reading, writing and arithmetic. What a noise there used to be! Several children would be reading aloud, teachers scolding, infants reciting, all waxing louder and louder until the master rang the bell on his desk and the noise slid down to a lower note and less volume.

Reading was worst; sums you did at least write on your slate, whereas you might wait the whole half-hour of a reading lesson while boys and girls who could not read stuck at every word. If you took your finger from the word that was being read you were punished by staying in when others went home.[81]

Kate Edwards of the Lotting Fen had very similar memories of her school days:

When we got into school we had prayers, and then set down to the morning's work. There were no playtime or 'break', and even the little child'en worked through till dockey time without being allowed out. First of all we got our slates out and 'made pothooks'—practising our letters with a squeaking slate pencil. . . . After writing we gathered round a big reading sheet and read from it, one word or sentence each. Of course we knowed the sentences off by heart, but the words were harder. We used to chant the sentences as if they were poetry, especially as they happened to rhyme.

> Ann is ill.
> Take a pill.
> Do not cry.
> A hot pie.

We used to sing songs because we had to get them ready for the day when 'the inspector' come, and we all had instructions to come clean and wear clean pinafores.[82]

Like many children who lived too far away from school to walk home at the midday break, Kate brought her luncheon with her —usually bread and lard, washed down with cold water. At her school, as elsewhere, 'there were no supervision by the teachers at all during the dinner time. So as soon as we had ate our dockey, we were free till afternoon school started, to go where we liked and do just as we liked. In the winter we huddled in the schoolroom, or went down to the station to fill our pockets with carrots from the trucks. One pocket was allus full of carrots, and the other of cock-sorrel leaves for chewing. . . . In summer we played either in the river or in the churchyard.'

But perhaps the most depressing tribute to the daily drudgery was paid by a visitor to an infants' school, in 1880. The school catered for children up to the age of seven and when he arrived at 11.30 a.m., two and a half hours after the school had opened, the children were

> in full grind. The highest class, on which Miss X concentrates her attention (and with reason, for they only have to pass the Inspector and he comes in about a fortnight), were engaged in simultaneous spelling from the reading books. They were working at a column of words, taking one at a time, and going on in this way, 'b-r-o-u-g-h-t, brought! b-r-o-u-g-h-t, brought!' till Miss X said 'Next word,' when they went on to the next. Such a grim determined grind I hardly ever witnessed. . . . They kept on steadily . . . as if they were little clocks which could not help going till they ran down.[83]

A few of the more adventurous teachers combined these mass production techniques with incentives, in order to increase efficiency—like the Devon head who in 1871 recorded in his log book : 'Have adopted the following plan when at slate work, hoping it will encourage accuracy and quickness. All stand round a line, with a chair or form in front. All having written their names on their slates, a sum is dictated which each child at once works. As soon as a child has completed his sum, he places his slate on the chair. When all have done this the slates are turned and examined by the teacher. The owner of the first found right goes to the top, the next second, etc. Copying is next to impossible, and little noise is occasioned.'[84] In another Devon school geography quizzes were used to arouse the children's interest, each youngster having to choose a side and ask questions. Those who failed to answer correctly had to take their seat, amid considerable excitement.

But many heads considered that the isolation of rural life was itself one of the most serious obstacles to their work. As the master of Holbeton school observed in 1883 : 'It is a very hard matter to cultivate the intelligence of our children. There is no foundation

F

to work upon, they have seen nothing, the parents do not read or in many cases attend worship. To talk of Railways, Manufactures, Telegraphs, or ordinary Arts of Civilisation is to make sure of not being understood at the very commencement.'[85] While at Austrey in Warwickshire as late as 1894, the master bewailed the 'low' level of intelligence of his pupils : 'the fact constitutes a teacher's chief difficulty in a village far removed from any centre of population. Austrey is absolutely without any concurrent aids to the development of mental capacity.'[86] In order to combat this, object lessons were used in the schools from the 1870s, particularly for the youngest children, to increase their perception of the world around them, and in 1895 they became compulsory for these groups. Unfortunately lack of suitable equipment sometimes rendered them of little value—as at Asthall in Oxfordshire, where the HMI noted disapprovingly that the 'Object Lesson [could] not be given properly because there [were] no pictures for the purpose of illustration.' All too often, the lessons degenerated into a lack-lustre discussion, with the children answering 'in monosyllables and very indistinctly'.

Yet, happily there was a brighter side to village school life than this. Some heads aroused a deep affection in their charges, like the elderly mistress of the small Yorkshire school attended by Fred Kitchen in the 1890s. In his view, she was the

> dearest old lady that ever kept school. There were about sixty scholars when all were present, and I thought she must be very wealthy when on occasions she would send each row in turn to the little sweet shop. . . . Her chief care for our welfare was to teach us morals and manners, most of which I forgot in the surroundings of my after years. One thing I shall always be grateful for is that she taught me to love and reverence good literature.[87]

Then there was the Essex boy who claimed to have so enjoyed school that he was never absent. If 'I had chilblains on my feet I would put my sister's boots on, which were bigger. The Heads of the school bought me a new suit of clothes with collar and bow for three years' attendance with only 3 days' absence.'[88]

In other cases, collections were organised to buy gifts as marks of regard for a favourite teacher. Thus at Skenfrith School, Monmouth, *The Schoolmaster* for 1879 records that the older scholars presented an 'elegant inkstand and address to their master . . . on his resigning . . . after two years' service'. While the head-mistress of a Lincolnshire school was presented with 'a handsome writing-desk, suitably furnished, with other presents' by the staff and scholars 'as a token of their love and esteem'. There were many similar examples.

It was men and women like these who made the country school 'an accepted and valued institution instead of an alien intrusion imposed from without. . . . Their contribution as civilisers as well as instructors was great; the leaven worked slowly, but its effects went deep.'[89] Through their teaching, even within the limited curriculum available, youngsters became aware of the wider world beyond the borders of their own parish. They were encour-aged to strive for a better life than that known by their parents' generation. At Cottisford, Flora Thompson remembered the newly appointed mistress in the late 1880s telling the children that 'it was not what a man or woman had, but what they were which mattered. . . . She even hinted that on the material plane people need not necessarily remain always upon one level. Some boys born of poor parents, had struck out for themselves and become great men, and everybody had respected them for rising upon their own merits.' She sought to inspire her charges with a like ambition and it is significant that Flora's own brother refused to become a country carpenter or a mason, as his parents planned. Instead he wished to travel and see the world—an ambition which, in his case, ended sadly enough with a soldier's grave in Belgium during the First World War.[90]

Henry Winn, a Lincolnshire schoolmaster, made much the same point. When describing the link between education and rural depopulation just before the first World War, he noted that once the children 'got a little education they began to look down on their parents' condition' and to say that they would 'never be a farmer's drudge'. During the years that Winn taught 'nearly all the boys passing through that school were lost to agriculture. One went to London and joined the police force there, inducing his brother to go into the army. One family of four boys entered the Lincoln foundries. Two other brothers engaged in the coal trade, one or two entered into the Railway service. . . . Thus the bone and sinew of our villages go away leaving the old and infirm to do the work.'[91]

And whilst these changes were taking place, literacy levels were also rising. Whereas in 1871 only about 80 per cent of men marrying and 73 per cent of women were able to sign the marriage register, by 1900, the figures had jumped to 97 per cent and almost 96 per cent, respectively.[92] At least part of this was attributable to the increase in school provision which had followed the passage of the 1870 Education Act. As Richard Altick has pointed out, in the two decades before this legislation, the literacy rate rose by 11.3 per cent for males and 18.4 per cent for females, but in the following two the advance was 13 per cent and 19.5 per cent, respectively. He concludes that although the Act did not necessarily *hasten* the spread of literacy as compared to the earlier voluntary effort, what it did do was to ensure

> that the rate at which literacy had increased in 1851–71 would be maintained. Had the state not intervened at this point, it is likely that the progress of literacy would have considerably slowed in the last quarter of the century, simply because illiteracy was by that time concentrated in those classes and regions that were hardest to provide for under the voluntary system of education. In short, the . . . Act was responsible for the mopping-up operation by which the very poor children, living in slums or in remote country regions, were taught to read.[93]

Significantly, too, although governmental expenditure on education fell by more than twenty per cent between 1861 and 1865, thanks primarily to the effects of the Revised Code, by the end of the decade the upward movement had been resumed. By 1886, according to the Cross Commission, the government grant to elementary education had reached £2.9 million; in 1861 the approved parliamentary outlay had been £813,441.[94] Despite the constraints imposed by the payment-by-results system, therefore, elementary schooling was growing significantly in the final three decades of the nineteenth century.

6

Life at the School House

. . . let me warn Teachers of the evil of contracting hasty and unadvised marriages. The choice of a wife may easily be an unfit one, especially if the selection is made at an age when experience cannot be supposed to exist; the temptation to do this in consequence of the solitariness to which many are doomed is very great; but marriage cannot be contracted thoughtlessly and unadvisedly without very great risk. A young man feels the pressure of family cares and troubles coming thick upon him.

JAMES CROSS of Wing School, Buckinghamshire, on 'The Teacher in his Home' in *Report of the Annual Meeting of the Oxford Diocesan Association of Schoolmasters for 1861*, Oxford 1861, 8.

He was painfully soon convinced that her tongue would never have run so easily as it did had it not been that she thought him a person on whom she could vent her ideas without reflection or punctiliousness—a thought, perhaps, expressed to herself by such words as, 'I will say what I like to him, for he is only our schoolmaster.'

'And you have chosen to keep a school,' she went on, with a shade of mischievousness in her tone, looking at him as if she thought that, had she been a man capable of saving people's lives, she would have done something much better than teaching.

THOMAS HARDY, *An Indiscretion in the Life of an Heiress*, London 1976, 36. (The work was first published in the *New Quarterly Magazine* in July 1878.)

FOR MUCH of the nineteenth century it was common for the masters and mistresses of village schools to be provided with a rent-free house or lodgings as part of their contract of employment. Even in 1900 about a quarter of all certificated masters (including those in both town and country schools) lived in 'residences free of rent', while a number of others occupied dwellings rented on favourable terms. In a rural county like Oxfordshire nearly two-thirds of the heads of the county's former board schools were, as late as 1904, provided with a free house;

about a quarter of them had free fuel.[1] One reason for this was the shortage of suitable accommodation which could be rented in the ordinary way. As Lord Wharncliffe, Lord President of the Council, observed in October 1844, a year after government grants first became available for the building of teachers' dwellings, the schoolmaster

> ought to be provided with . . . a house, by no means too large, so as to exalt him too much in the scale of society; but he should be taken out of a cottage and put into a decent residence, which would be calculated to make those persons lower than himself, inclined to show a proper feeling of respect for the schoolmaster who teaches their children.[2]

HMI Bellairs, too, considered that the 'teacher's residence should consist of two sitting and three bedrooms', the latter properly ventilated, 'with chimneys, and a sliding panel over each door'.[3] Unfortunately, as will be seen, many school houses failed to meet these standards.

Yet the Committee of Council on Education recognised at an early stage that free accommodation was a valuable addition to a teacher's cash income. Consequently, between 1846 and 1862, when salary augmentation grants were available for certificated teachers, a condition of their payment was that a rent-free house or lodgings would be supplied by the school managers. Official correspondence makes it clear that this aspect was taken seriously by the authorities, so that the incumbent of Haddenham near Ely was firmly informed in February 1848 that the provision of board and lodgings for the infant school mistress in his own house, together with the payment of a salary of £10 per annum, was not acceptable. 'For altho' the board and lodging is probably equal in amount to £16 which would be requisite to make up the lowest salary which my Lords recognize in a Schoolmistress for augmentation (where a house rent free is not provided) yet this arrangement has all the appearance of putting the Schoolmistress completely in the position of a domestic servant.'[4] Suitable lodgings elsewhere and a higher cash payment were necessary if Committee of Council approval were to be obtained.

Even when salary augmentation grants were abandoned with the Revised Code of 1862, free accommodation remained a valuable perquisite. Thus at Alton National School in Staffordshire, where there was an average attendance of seventy-five pupils, the mistress was paid a basic salary of £30 per annum in 1877, plus part of the government grant to the school (valued at £5 1s. 6d.), a portion of the school pence (amounting to £2 18s. 2d.), and lodgings and coal, which were together assessed at £6 13s. 0d., making a total of £44 12s. 8d.[5] Lodgings and fuel in this case equalled about one-seventh of her annual income. While at Gerrards Cross in Buckinghamshire, the master appointed in November 1879 received a salary of £90 a year plus a furnished house, garden and coals 'and with the prospect of receiving two-thirds of any increase he could secure to the Government Grant'. Then in March 1896, this agreement was modified slightly, with the master's basic salary rising to £100 a year, the extra £10 being paid in lieu of the coal, wood, oil and domestic utensils formerly provided by the managers.[6]

Elsewhere, especially when a woman head was living alone, she might be paid a little extra to accommodate her assistant, as happened at Bix in Oxfordshire in the 1880s and 1890s. Here the headmistress was given an additional £3 per annum, out of which she was to find 'all other necessaries' for her assistant. Inevitably the success of such arrangements depended on the compatability of the personalities involved. The first two mistresses appointed seem to have lived together quite happily for three years until both were dismissed by the school board for inefficiency in the summer of 1888. But relations between a successor, Miss George, and her assistants, proved less satisfactory. From the time that she took up her appointment in January 1893 until September 1894, Miss George had four different colleagues living in the house. The fourth, following 'unpleasantness', eventually complained that 'she was somewhat nervous at night and sleeping accommodation was not what she had been accustomed to', though she declared herself ready to stay on. At this point Miss George herself threatened to resign over the 'behaviour' of the assistant, declaring 'it is impossible to remain in the same house— if she is to remain in it', and so the latter was dismissed.[7] After that, matters appear to have settled down.

A fair proportion of the houses provided under these arrangements were, as HMI Bellairs had recommended, comfortable dwellings, comprising kitchen, living room, and two or three bedrooms; but sadly there were numerous examples of a less favourable kind, too. One disgruntled correspondent to the *School and the Teacher* pointed out in January 1855:

> It is a lamentable fact, that many teachers' houses are a mere make-shift, as if anything was good enough to be inhabited rent free. . . . In many places the three or four rooms constituting the house are under the school; in some places it forms one of a row of labourers' cottages. . . . There may be some school-managers who imagine that I wish teachers to have mansions provided for them; not so, but build your teachers' houses as you would, at least, for a tenant of the middle class . . . you will thus cause the parents of the children to be duly impressed with the importance of your teacher's worth, and of his fitness for it . . . the more you seek to elevate the position of your teacher, the more you will inspire the people with confidence that he is both able and willing to give to their children a sound and useful education.

According to this critic, even houses which had been built with the approval and financial support of the Committee of Council were 'so devoid of arrangement and convenience, that it is a matter of surprise how their lordships were induced to sanction the plans.'

Almost forty years later T. J. Macnamara, the editor of *The Schoolmaster*, was making similar comments in a lecture to the National Union of Teachers on the theme 'The Village Schoolmistress'. His remarks were based on complaints which had been received by the Union on the housing question, and he described how in one case a former coach-house and store-room for wool fleeces had been turned into a school house, even though it was overrun with rats and insects. 'It is exceedingly damp. No cupboards, no washhouses, no out-offices; only one door; no privacy whatever; cold and wretched in winter and stiflingly hot in summer. Height of front room, seven and a half feet.' In another dwelling, built close to a churchyard, the mistress complained that it was so cold and draughty that she had to sit by the fire with a fur-lined cloak around her. 'The water I fetch down over a steep hill. There is no washhouse, no pump, and no place to throw rubbish with safety'.[8]

So seriously did the Union treat the accommodation issue that in 1899 when its Rural and Small Schools Committee produced a special report on country schools, the largest section was devoted to the housing question. Among the forty-six cases quoted in the report was one where the head claimed that his house had been valued at £4 per annum but it was 'in such a disgraceful state that I have refused to live in it, and rent another in the village. It is very little better than a good pig-sty.' In another instance the 'Wall of house forms one side of open drain. Filth from two houses; first, 6 feet away, second 12 feet, emptied into it and soaks through pigsty 2 feet away . . . one surface well, 5 feet, by 4 feet for 14 people. . . . Over 12 holes in roof, one 2 feet square. Roof cracked from chimney to spouting. Nine holes turfed. West gable dangerous. Present state two years.'[9] Most of the other complainants had similar problems, with drainage deficiencies virtually universal.

However, private lodgings, paid for by the school managers, might prove little better. In 1898, the mistress of Affpuddle school in Dorset was reduced to pleading with her managers for a shed, in which to prepare her work, make up registers, etc., because she was unable to secure a private sitting-room at her lodgings. She also stated that if the shed were erected she would 'willingly pay half the cost of the cooking apparatus', which would enable her to prepare some of her own meals. Only after considerable discussion was the Affpuddle incumbent prepared to recommend that her wishes be met. For, as he noted, she was ready to resign over the issue and that 'would be a great misfortune for the School as it is very difficult in these days to get a Mistress of her experience and efficiency for a small village school.'[10]

But even where the housing itself was satisfactory, the furniture and utensils provided in furnished accommodation might leave much to be desired. Macnamara described one dwelling, consisting of two rooms, plus a small pantry and a coal-hole—the latter connected with the solitary sitting-room :

Furniture of Sitting-Room.—Pail, coal-scuttle, fire-irons, and fender; five cane-seated chairs (hardly safe to sit upon) and one easy chair (broken beyond mending); one round table and cover; a few cups and saucers, plates and dishes, knives, forks and spoons, and one cupboard.

Bedroom.—One washstand and towel-horse, dressing table

and mirror, one bedstead, palliasse, flock bed, two blankets, one counterpane, bolster and one pillow, two or three little bits of carpet, and one chest of drawers.[11]

Some teachers, of course, supplemented the furniture supplied with their own possessions, or undertook the whole of the furnishing on their own account. Sun Insurance records reveal that early in 1843 two schoolmistresses from Norton St Philip in Somerset insured their household goods (china and glass excepted) and their wearing apparel, books and plate for the substantial sum of £200; almost twenty years later an Epsom schoolmaster was likewise insuring his household property for that amount.[12] However, few teachers could afford the necessary outlay though the anonymous authoress of a pamphlet entitled 'How a Schoolmistress May Live Upon Seventy Pounds a Year', first published in about 1887, stressed the need for a head arriving at a fresh post to bring with her at least a hamper containing teacups, spoons, a teapot, food to eat, and her own sheets.[13]

More ambitiously, John Knight, when taking up the headship of Wheatley School, Oxfordshire, in 1880, brought a piano with him, as well as books and other items when he moved into his house. And as he was unmarried, he noted that he would also require 'a respectable woman in the morning after breakfast to put things straight and prepare dinner'.

In other households, especially where mistresses were concerned, or where a master was married with young children, domestic help might take the form of a resident servant. But certain of the more ruthless heads utilised the services of their pupils for general cleaning purposes. At Sir William Borlase Bluecoat School at Great Marlow, Buckinghamshire, in 1876 there were complaints from parents that their children were being employed on household duties instead of learning their lessons. The school managers called upon the master and mistress for an explanation, but they were quite unrepentant, declaring 'it had always been the custom for various boys to clean boots knives &c. and occasionally to work in the garden'. Eventually the managers resolved that the pupils would in future only 'be required to clean the Schoolroom, sweep the Front, Clean the Schoolroom window & light the Schoolroom Fire . . . & that these occupations should be carried on out of School Hours'![14] A similar policy was adopted at Blaxhall in Suffolk during the later 1870s and early 1880s, when a girl was employed, ostensibly as a monitress, at a wage of 2d. a week to clean the school, lay the fires, ring the school bell in the morning, and at the weekends scrub the school lavatories. She also received 2d. a week for fetching the schoolmistress's bread and milk. While at another East Anglian school, Kate Edwards recalled washing up, dusting, cleaning shoes, paring vegetables and carrying out other chores in the schoolmaster's house during the morning. For her labours she received each week a 'quarter of an orange peel' and an inadequate education.[15]

Eventually this approach was called into question by the Committee of Council on Education. In 1871 the secretary to the Committee, Francis Sandford, minuted : 'My Lords do not consider that "sweeping the School" after School-hours can be regarded as "industrial work", and would recommend managers not to insist on it as a condition of a child's attending a School.'[16] But countless managers and teachers clearly ignored his advice, until they were faced with a parental revolt. At Cublington the mistress recorded on 11 June 1877 : 'Requested the Rector that a woman may be allowed to do the sweeping. The mothers of the children dislike their doing it and keep them away in consequence.' This protest obviously succeeded for on 15 June came a further entry : 'Mrs Halsey engaged to sweep the school in future for 6d. a week all the year round, this includes lighting fires during the winter season.'[17]

For many head teachers, though, especially the women, home life must have been much like that described by Charlotte Brontë in her novel, *Jane Eyre*. In this, the heroine, Jane, after leaving her post as governess at Thornfield Hall, obtained the position of mistress at a small country school in the North of England :

> My home, then—when I at last find a home—is a cottage; a little room with whitewashed walls and a sanded floor, containing four painted chairs and a table, a clock, a cupboard, with two or three plates and dishes, and a set of tea-things in delf. Above, a chamber of the same dimensions as the kitchen, with a deal bedstead, and chest of drawers, small, yet too large to be filled with my scanty wardrobe.[18]

As her servant, Jane secured an ex-workhouse orphan, who conscientiously saw to the cleaning of the house : 'All about me was spotless and bright—scoured floor, polished grate, and well-rubbed chairs.'

Companionship was more difficult, but Jane got to know the parents of some of her pupils, notably the farmers and their wives 'with whom I passed many a pleasant evening hour in their own homes'.

Sadly, other women found the loneliness of their position harder to overcome. The parish clergyman and his family might invite the mistress to their home from time to time, while some teachers, like Jane Eyre, enjoyed good relations with local farming families. But there were few other leisure activities open to them. They were rarely on terms of social equality with better-off members of their community. At Cottisford, even in the 1880s the schoolmistress, when accompanying her pupils on a visit to the manor house, was sent to the kitchen for her tea. And in another case a vicar's wife, 'in a real dilemma, said : "I should like to ask Miss So-and-So to tea; but do I ask her to kitchen or dining-room tea?" '[19] This social problem was heightened where the women continued to live in or near the communities in which they had been brought up and where their parents or relatives were of humble origins. Among them were mistresses like Caroline Cox, the locally-born head of Yarnton School in Oxfordshire, who in the early 1870s was residing with her mother, 'a pauper'. Or Mary Brown of Haselbury Bryan, Dorset, who was a carpenter's daughter and continued to live at home with her family. The census returns reveal numerous other examples; indeed as Table 1 indicates, even in 1871—and despite the influence of the training colleges—many teachers, both male and female, were still being recruited locally.

A schoolmistress correspondent to the *Educational Guardian* of March 1861 also aired another grievance when she noted that the teacher 'must not dress above her station'. This was 'the cry of the clergyman's family and committee of ladies, consequently the new mistress is subjected to the painfully unpleasant process of analysis, and being pronounced guilty of "dressing as well as themselves", is punished by being made to feel her inferiority in ways too numerous to mention'.[20]

Matrimony, too, presented problems, especially for the women,

Table 1. Teachers in Specimen Country Parishes, 1871 Census

Teachers	Born in parish where teaching	Born in county where teaching	Born elsewhere in England and Wales
DORSET—14 parishes or townships			
5 adult male teachers	–	1	4
21 adult female teachers	4	8	9
WESTMORLAND—10 parishes or townships			
9 adult male teachers	–	2	7
7 adult female teachers	4	1	2
OXFORDSHIRE—12 parishes or townships			
9 adult male teachers	3	2	4
14 adult female teachers	2	6	6
BERKSHIRE—14 parishes or townships			
6 adult male teachers	–	2	4
19 adult female teachers	2	1	16
90 teachers in all	15	23	52

N.B. Dame school teachers and private school teachers have both been excluded. The parishes covered are: *Dorset*: Durweston, Stourpaine, Iwerne Courtney, Pimperne, Tarrant Gunville, Tarrant Hinton, Tarrant Keynstone, Cranborne, Edmonsham, Child Okeford, Ibberton, Hinton St. Mary, Haselbury Bryan, Okeford Fitzpaine. *Westmorland*: Hartley, Winton, Brough, Gt. Musgrave, Worslop, Temple Sowerby, Milburn, Long Marton, Kirkby Thore, Dufton. *Oxfordshire*: Bladon, Clifton, Cassington, Combe, Wolvercote, Wootton, Yarnton, Eynsham, North Leigh, Ducklington, Clanfield, Lew. *Berkshire*: Aldworth, Beedon, Blewbury, Brightwaltham, Chaddleworth, Chilton, Compton, Fawley, Hampstead Norris, East Ilsley, West Ilsley, East Hendred, Peasemore and Upton.

unless they married another teacher. For as one of HM Inspectors pointed out, the mistress's position 'separated her very much from the class to which she had originally belonged, while it did not bring her socially into contact with a different class, and therefore she was very much isolated. She could not marry a labourer, nor an artisan who was not an educated man, and she was not very likely, generally speaking, to marry a person very much above herself.' Thus Miss Rose Knowles of Thorpe Malsor school in Northamptonshire was engaged for a time to the butler at the local hall, though this clearly did not please her mother and the arrangement fell through.[21] A few other women married village craftsmen, like Jane Burroughs of Puncknowle, Dorset, who left at short notice in August 1864 'as she proposed immediately' to marry; her future husband was a carpenter from the nearby parish of Longbredy.[22] Then there was the headmistress of Mapledurham School, Oxfordshire, Miss Mary Ann Barnaby who, in November 1862, married one of the village blacksmiths. Her predecessor, who had taught at Mapledurham for more than twenty years, had married a shoemaker. And at Wootton near Woodstock in the same county the head of the infants' school was the wife of a local sawyer. An exploration of the mid-Victorian census returns will quickly reveal other cases, while in Thomas Hardy's novel *Under the Greenwood Tree*, the flighty Fancy Day of Mellstock school eventually settles down with Dick Dewy, son of the local tranter. Though she at least was proposed to by the vicar as well, rather against his better judgment. In another Hardy novel, *An Indiscretion in the Life of an Heiress*, the entire theme is concerned with the unsuitability of a liaison between a village schoolmaster and the squire's daughter, whom he loves.

The unhappiness to which a teacher's social isolation could so easily give rise was recognised by HMI Bellairs in his book, *The Church and the School*, which was intended as a guide for parish clergy. He advised his readers to

> . . . make the life of the teacher, especially if unmarried, as cheerful and happy as you can. Occasionally, as opportunity occurs, shewing little acts of hospitality and kindness.
>
> These will help a young teacher to dissipate many a train of sad or home-sick recollections, and to bear with contentment, if not with cheerfulness, a more than ordinary lonely life.
>
> The solitariness to which so many elementary teachers, especially in remote rural districts, are subjected, is a point which has strong claims upon the clergy for sympathy.[23]

Nevertheless HMI Bellairs also warned : 'If you take for mistress an unmarried young woman, make arrangements before engaging that she shall not live alone. Many managers are very careless in this, and unfortunate scandals occur.' He advised, too, that the school house should be 'properly painted and whitewashed . . . the drains, spouts, roof, &c. . . . in good order, and the garden well fenced, in sound tillage, and supplied with fruit trees' before a new teacher took up occupation.

Although masters were better placed in social matters than their female counterparts, having more opportunity to join village clubs and societies, the reference to the school house garden by Mr Bellairs touches upon one of the main leisure activities of many of them. Partly for reasons of economy, especially where a master's salary was low and his family large, but also as a way of relaxing after a tiring day in school, countless men took a great pride in their digging and planting. These were activities of which Sir James Kay Shuttleworth also approved. As we saw in chapter 4, students at Battersea training college were regularly involved in horticulture and animal husbandry. For as he carefully observed, a schoolmaster in a rural parish often had a right of pasture for his cow on common land or a run for his pig or goat in a wood : 'and might thus with a little skill, be provided with the means of healthful occupation in his hours of leisure, and of providing for the comfort of his family . . . [Thus] they would be in less danger of despising the labourer's daily toil . . . and of being led . . . to form a false estimate of their position in relation to the class to which they belonged, and which they were destined to instruct.'[24]

Occasionally this interest might mean taking on the secretary-ship of the local horticultural society. At Harpenden in the 1880s and 1890s one former scholar at the local British School remembers his headmaster taking a prominent part in the parish's gardening activities, including the organisation of the annual flower show. His interest also extended to the school itself, where he proved an enthusiastic teacher of botany.[25]

Similarly when a new headmaster was appointed to Wheatley school in Oxfordshire during 1872 one of his first concerns was for the condition of his garden. In a letter to the incumbent he noted anxiously that he had spoken to his predecessor 'about some potatoes which I have, asking him if he would see they were planted, and also to have the garden planted properly & I would pay him whatever it cost'. Eight days later, on 16 April, he wrote again, pointing out that he had 'sent [the] potatoes off by train' on the previous Saturday, and would pay for them to be planted before he took up his appointment.[26]

These agricultural and horticultural interests, when combined with a master's scholastic abilities, also provided country teachers with a means of earning extra cash. Particularly during the spring hoeing season and at hay and corn harvest they would undertake measuring work for local farmers. Alfred Hart, the master of a small private school at Ivinghoe in Buckinghamshire, noted in his diary for 1864, that during the first three weeks of September he had earned £6 3s. 5d. in this manner. Typical of his daily routine was an entry for 8 September : '. . . went & measured some thatching for Mr Tompkins. Afternoon went to North field to measure land for Mr T. Ashby.'[27] Occasionally masters would even advertise their skills in the local trade directories. The *Post Office Directory* for 1847 records that William Webster of Chinnor, Oxfordshire, combined teaching with land surveying and beer retailing, while his fellow heads at Ashampstead and Basildon in Berkshire and at Burton Latimer in Northamptonshire also advertised their land surveying skills—in the case of the latter alongside a grocery business.

These agricultural tasks might be undertaken on such a scale that they interfered with the holding of educational conferences during the summer months. The Lincoln Diocesan Board of Education in 1858 commented on the difficulty masters had in attending meetings whilst the harvest was in progress 'in consequence of the demand made upon their time for land measuring'. Only nine masters and four mistresses from Lincolnshire had attended a diocesan meeting held in August 1858. And it is interesting to note that the response remained so modest despite an offer by the Lincolnshire Committee of the Diocesan Education Board to pay 10s. to every teacher who attended.[28]

Other opportunities for mixing with fellow villagers were provided by the teacher's role in training the choir or playing the organ at Sunday Church services—activities which, as we shall see in a later chapter, were not always welcomed by the masters and mistresses concerned. Night schools were likewise organised in some parishes, particularly during the winter months, and although these might be conducted by the incumbent or his curate, in many cases the village master or mistress would preside. The pupils were usually young men and women who had left school early and were anxious to catch up on their three 'r's', like the scholars described in George Eliot's novel, *Adam Bede*. Here the lame parish master, Bartle Massey, acted as night school teacher :

> The reading class . . . seated on the form in front of the schoolmaster's desk, consisted of the three most backward pupils. . . . It was touching to see these three big men, with the marks of their hard labour about them, anxiously bending over the worn books, and painfully making out, "The grass is green," "The sticks are dry," "The corn is ripe"—a very hard lesson to pass to after columns of single words all alike except in the first letter. It was almost as if three rough animals were making humble efforts to learn how they might become human. And it touched the tenderest fibre in Bartle Massey's nature, for such full-grown children as these were the only pupils for whom he had no severe epithets, and no impatient tones . . . [This] evening, as he glances over his spectacles at Bill Downes, the sawyer, who is turning his head on one side with a desperate sense of blankness before the letters d, r, y, his eyes shed their mildest and most encouraging light.
> After the reading class, two youths, between sixteen and nineteen, came up with imaginary bills of parcels, which they had been writing out on their slates, and were now required to calculate "off-hand"—a test which they stood with such imperfect success that Bartle Massey, whose eyes had been glaring at them ominously through his spectacles for some minutes, at length burst out in a bitter, high-pitched tone, pausing between every sentence to rap the floor with a knobbed stick which rested between his legs. . . . The other pupils had happily only their writing-books to show, in various stages of progress from pot-hooks to round text; and mere penstrokes, however perverse, were less exasperating to Bartle than false arithmetic.[29]

From time to time, teachers would also organise outings for their day scholars, when both they and the children could enjoy themselves. A typical example of this kind occurred at Kidlington, Oxfordshire in September 1877, when the church school pupils, their master and mistress, and the Sunday school teachers were treated to a tea and entertainment. The tea was held in a 'spacious barn' which had been 'gaily decorated for the occasion'. After the meal had ended the children played for an hour in the grounds, 'racing for toys &c., and at seven returned to the barn, where a magic lantern was exhibited'. At the conclusion the senior curate proposed three cheers 'for the Giver of the Feast, and those who assisted', followed by three cheers for the clergy, the teachers and other friends. And as the children departed they were each given a piece of cake to sustain them on the homeward journey. [30]

May day festivities, too, engaged the time and attention of teachers and scholars, with the former helping to make the garlands which the children would carry as they paraded the village, singing songs and receiving small cash gifts from the householders upon whom they called. Later the money would be spent on a school tea. [31]

Other teachers, like Mrs Bowkett of Banbury, spent their leisure hours in organising plays and recitations to be performed by the children. She was head of Cherwell Infants' School from 1898 until 1927, and, with her assistants, regularly made the costumes and stage settings for the children's various entertainments. After seventy years she still remembers the excitement of staging *Cinderella*—one of the most ambitious performances put on by her pupils. These events were open to the general public and with the proceeds from the sale of tickets she financed a shoe club, to provide poorer pupils with footwear. Other donations were given to support the local hospital fund and nursing association. Mrs Bowkett was a great believer in social gatherings: 'I always felt that entertainment was a stimulus to the children.' [32]

But if the scholars regarded such festivities as red letter days in their calendar, many of their teachers no doubt found comparatively sedate events, like the annual choir supper, more to their liking. Perhaps, as at Worminghall in Buckinghamshire in 1871 this would consist of 'splendid joints of beef and mutton, with the necessary accompaniments'. The schoolmaster presided over the festivities here and, according to *Jackson's Oxford Journal* so generous was the supply of food that the participants had to meet again on the following evening 'in order to clear up the remnants of the feast'.[33] Elsewhere, there were men like James Barrett, head of Great Barrington School from 1883 to 1925, who ran the local cricket club and organised the village friendly society. Mr Barrett helped to found the Barrington Working Men's Benefit Society as an insurance against sickness and as a means of covering medical bills. It became one of the great interests of his life.[34]

Sometimes a master's scholastic abilities might lead to his being employed by fellow parishioners on a whole range of small tasks which called for writing or numeracy skills. In this connection it is interesting to note how the official attitude of the Committee of Council changed over the years. In April 1854, the then secretary to the Committee, R. R. W. Lingen, minuted that the task of 'daily keeping School during the ordinary hours, and of instructing apprentices for another hour and a half, is quite as much to undertake as is consistent with a conscientious discharge of each of those duties and with a due regard to health'.[35] But over forty years later, his successor, Sir George Kekewich, took a very different line when the question of the master of Parracombe School, Devon, being employed as a parish overseer was discussed. In this case the school managers had given the children a holiday so that the head could attend the annual audit, and Kekewich wrote:

> I should be sorry to enforce Article 85(e) so far as to prohibit the Managers from giving a holiday under the circumstances of this case. We should not prevent them from doing so, if the master wanted to go somewhere to see his family, or attend to his private affairs, and the only difference between that case and this is, that, this is an annual holiday and the Teacher gets some extra emolument from it. I should be sorry to deprive these country Teachers of the power of adding something to their small incomes, if their Schools are not injured thereby.[36]

The various tasks with which a master could become involved are illustrated by entries in the diary of Alfred Hart at Ivinghoe during 1864:

25 *February:*   'Writing "Peppermint" on Mrs Norris's bottle.'
25 *April:*   'Went over to Mr Groom's to write his name on his new cart this eve.'

30 August: 'Went up town twice to paint Ann Hawkins's grave stone also wrote an application to Directors of S.E. Railway for Cornelius Short, in the eve went to Mr Jolly's Cheddington to take the measuring accts.' (Mr Hart was paid 8d. for writing the letter and 4s. for work on the grave stone.)

16 November: '. . . Mr Green and Mr H. Dimmock called and signed his Will.' (For preparing the Will for Thomas Green, the Ivinghoe wheelwright, he received 5s.)

Hart also shared in the general village festivities, as on 20 July, the date of the local friendly society celebrations, when he 'went and dined with the members in the booth'. Six days later he attended 'the Duck feast . . . at Mr Groom's', the latter being a farmer from the neighbouring parish of Pitstone. And on 13 July he noted that: 'Three nights this week' there had been 'rough music up town J. Cook.' 'Rough music' was the name given to noisy demonstrations by villagers to indicate disapproval of a person's conduct, such as excessive cruelty to a wife or children, adultery, or persistent drunkenness. Very often a straw-filled effigy of the offender would be burnt outside his house and a large group of men and boys would mark the occasion by beating pots and pans in order to disgrace him.

The activities of William Wright, master of Folkingham School, Lincolnshire, from 1839 to the mid-1850s followed a similar pattern. He, too, carried out surveying duties for local farmers, wrote letters, cast up accounts, prepared legal documents and acted as a bondsman. On one occasion, early in March 1848, he even soled someone's boots 'with Gutta percha'; and on another, at the end of November in the following year, he drew up 'a Letter to the Post Master General, London,' on behalf of a fellow villager who was 'applying for Letter carrier's office'. Wright kept pigs, a cow and a few sheep, and there are many references in the diaries to his going 'a shepherding' or helping with the lambing. Gardening was another major preoccupation, but he still had time to 'smoke a pipe' with his friends—the local farmers and tradespeople. Extracts from his diaries for 1849/50 in Appendix 7 provide a picture of his life and that of many other country schoolmasters in his day.[37]

A third diarist was Albert Brett, the twenty-one-year-old assist-

ant master at Andover British School, Hampshire, and his entries
—covering a period from September 1864 to May 1865—indicate a similarly modest range of activities. On 10 September, for
example, Brett noted that he had been 'nutting' with a friend:
'picked enough to fill my carpet bag'. Two days earlier he had
taken part in the children's annual treat: 'Various games were
played by the boys and girls, myself, Mr Marriott, Mr Millard
& Son joining in. We had a game of cricket, but I as usual made
but a poor score. Apples were scrambled for by the children.' On
17 December he returned home to Puddletown, Dorset, for the
Christmas holidays and on 26 December: 'In evening went to
N. Sparks and met with Thos. Hardy. Spent a pleasant evening.'
This was probably Nathaniel Sparks, violin maker, who played
a cello in Puddletown church and was a cousin of Thomas Hardy.
(Hardy himself was at the time based in London, where he was
studying to be an architect.) On the afternoon following Brett
'met with Tolpuddle Ethiopian Serenaders'—a somewhat unexpected kind of entertainment for that out-of-the-way Dorset
parish.[38] In Andover, Brett regularly took part in musical evenings
at the club room attached to one of the public houses and occasionally, as on 30 January 1865, attended penny readings or
similar social gatherings in the town. The January penny readings
seem to have been more eventful than usual, however, for according to Brett, proceedings were 'very noisy . . . [The audience]
would not let the president speak in consequence of his prohibiting the appearance of the Amateur Ethiopians', thereby presumably offending local artistic sensibilities.

Another 'musical' schoolmaster was Josiah Evans, the head
of Clyro School, who in 1871 decided to learn to play the violin,
though according to the curate, the Rev. Francis Kilvert, the
effect produced was the reverse of melodious. Kilvert visited him
on 22 October in that year:

Coming home in the dusk I turned into the school house to
tell the schoolmaster I was going out to-morrow for a few
days and that I should not be at school this week. . . . He
produced the instrument and began to play upon it. It had a
broken string, and there was something wrong with all the
rest, and the noise it made 'fairly raked my bowels' as old
Cord used to say at Wadham of Headeach's violoncello. The

schoolmaster however did not appear to notice that anything was wrong. His wife held the book up before him. 'Glory be to Jesus', sang the schoolmaster, loudly and cheerfully sawing away at the cracked and broken strings, while the violin screeched and shrieked and screamed and groaned and actually seemed to writhe and struggle in his arms like a wild animal in agony. There was something so utterly incongruous in the words and the noise, the heart-rending bowel-raking uproar and screams of the tormented violin, that I smiled. I could not help it. Shriek, shriek, scream, groan, yell, howled the violin, as if a spirit in torment were writhing imprisoned within it, and still the schoolmaster sawed away vigorously and sung amid the wailing, screeching uproar, 'Glory be to Jesus' in a loud and cheerful voice. It was the most ludicrous thing. I never was so hard put to it not to laugh aloud.[39]

On a very different musical plane was J. D. Jones (1827–1870), master at Ruthin British School. He was a prolific composer of tunes and anthems in the Welsh language, as he proudly recorded in an autobiographical fragment : 'before I was twenty I had published "Y Per Ganiedydd", a small collection of tunes for congregational singing.'[40] Other compositions followed until his early death in 1870.

But for those many masters and mistresses in country districts who had no such absorbing hobby, leisure hours offered little variety and little congenial company. By the mid-nineteenth century fewer teachers were finding they had anything in common with the labourers and artisans who lived alongside them, and yet their efforts to associate with the better-off members of rural society were, as we have seen, often rebuffed by those who still saw them as members of an inferior breed. The hardships of this situation have already been touched upon in so far as they related to women teachers, but for the men, too, they often gave rise to many heartaches. *The School and the Teacher* summarised the whole vexed problem in a leading article in September 1855 :

Time was when the parochial schoolmasters of England were only fit for, and when they were content to occupy a very low social position. Raised scarcely, if at all, in intellect or feeling, above the mechanic or the labourer, whose children he taught, he was content to associate with those who were his equals; if he visited at the parsonage, it was the servants to whom his visits were paid, and from among them his companions were chosen. His visitors, when he had any, were the village tailor and shoemaker, and too often he was to be found, 'hale fellow well met', with the frequenters of the ale-house. We do not say that this was universally the case : we know well how many men there were among the older class of teachers who . . . rather than descend to the level of the labourer and the mechanic, who were intellectually, and too often morally unfit for their companions, were content to live a life of solitude, and rather than associate with companions such as we have described, were content to live without companionship at all. But the men were condemned thus to live : they had no status in society : the ignorant tradesman, who had a few pounds in his pocket, looked down on the schoolmaster, and would as soon have thought of asking the *boots* from the commercial inn to spend an evening with him in social enjoyment, as the schoolmaster. . . . There is a strong feeling that the present race of teachers occupy a place in society much lower than what they are entitled to take, . . . but the time is surely coming when the schoolmaster's proper status shall be given him, when his claims to be regarded as a *gentleman* will be recognised by Society at large.

Despite the optimism of *The School and the Teacher* that state of affairs was to be a long time in arriving. In the meantime, as the anonymous author of *The Schoolmaster's Difficulties Abroad and at Home* put it :

the schoolmaster is far too frequently . . . the solitary bee, or wasp of the place. . . . It is, usually, a rare thing to see the good man with a companion, or to hear of his having any friend with him, excepting now and then from some far-distant spot. You do not find he visits his neighbours, or is being visited by them; you may occasionally meet him on a constitutional walk, or in a poor labourer's house inquiring after his scholars, or in some parochial meeting where his presence or assistance is desired; but, too often, when he has quitted the scene of his daily toil, entered his little dwelling, and pocketed his latch-key, he is left completely alone, without any human being to break the social monotony of his existence, for weeks together. Even if married, and blest with children, though certainly in that case possessed of home-resources to put an end to actual solitude, yet his additional cares now form a large offset to his comforts, however amiably and peacefully he and his humble family may be all living together; . . . His wife and children are, herein, partakers with him of the same difficulties in regard to social life. They cannot force themselves upon the courtesy of others, or associate with every one, any more than himself; . . . It is almost a marvellous event in his life to be kindly asked out to dinner, or coaxed home to tea by any of his decent and well-to-do neighbours; though, in some bold effort to break the bonds of his loneliness, he may occasionally press some chatting familiar to share his simple hospitality.[41]

The problem was summed up by the master of Hook Norton School, Oxfordshire, when he wrote in June 1866 : 'I am naturally of a retiring disposition, and my occupation has fostered it and I felt myself pained often by an unwillingness to associate with my equals in age &c.' Chiefly for this reason he had sought to obtain a post in a London bank, but had been 'greatly disappointed at finding that my age (30) precludes it'.[42]

The question of social activities was considered at a meeting of the Oxford Diocesan Schoolmasters' Association in 1861, when some of those present suggested that it might be a good idea to set up a skittles alley in the school to provide a little healthy recreation. But many of their colleagues did not agree with such frivolity. According to *The School and the Teacher*, the idea was opposed 'rather warmly on the ground that, however harmless skittles are in themselves, a youth taught expertness in the school skittle alley in one village would, on leaving, be under strong temptation to exercise his skill in the public-house skittle alley in another; that no recreation more leads to smoking and drinking habits; it is besides a very noisy, dirty, and unintellectual game, and therefore unworthy the patronage of institutions, professedly under the management of church officers'.[43] Far more suitable in the eyes of most of those who attended was, no doubt, the evening entertainment which followed this discussion—namely a 'graphic lecture on Southern Africa'.

Yet it must be confessed that the critics' fears of drunkenness and allied troubles were not altogether without foundation, especially among male teachers. The annual reports of the Committee of Council on Education in the 1890s show a steady trickle of masters who lost their teaching certificate, or had it suspended, for persistent drunkenness. And the embarrassments to which this could give rise are indicated at Handforth in Cheshire, where the school managers noted sourly that the master 'had been frequently seen in a drunken condition and that between the hours of six and seven o'clock this Monday evening he had been seen leaving the Greyhound Public House in the village in a state of inebriation and was followed from there to his lodgings by a number of children hooting him and on being sent for by the Committee a reply was sent that he had gone to bed'. He was dismissed instantly.[44]

Another offender was a former student of Culham College who had been appointed head of Cranbourne Endowed School at Christmas 1869, when he was aged twenty. Just over a year later he 'fell into bad company' and according to the Culham principal, 'in 1872 absented himself, gave no reason, severely reprimanded by Com[ee]. Early in 1873 ran away, found in bad company, dismissed & enlisted.'[45] Even more disreputable was the career of one of his successors at the college. In February 1876 it was reported that 'in a fit of intoxication he had destroyed his furniture, & attempted to strangle his wife. He professed to be a tee totaller but habitually drank secretly.' Thirteen years later he called at the college 'on tramp to London—given to drink, a vagabond. Professed to have returned from Chile where he had been an Electrical Engineer.' Some even showed their drink problems whilst they were still at college, like the nineteen-year-old Somerset youth who left Culham in September 1870 'owing to constant attacks of hysteria, wh. suspicion of being caused by drinking spirits'. According to the principal he then obtained a post as an assistant master. A colleague who was admitted to the college at the same time was within months also severely reprimanded for being found with 'a barrel of beer' in his cubicle; and in his second year, he was 'insolent and disorderly at Easter'. For this offence he was rusticated for two weeks. Many similar examples could be given. Indeed, in March 1880 after some over-enthusiastic clandestine celebrations had been reported in one of the Culham dormitories, the assembled students were solemnly warned by the principal: 'The habit of secret & unnecessary drinking as a pretext for fitly commemorating an event is, in my eyes, an extremely dangerous indulgence, & often becomes low & blackguardly. It must not be tolerated here.'[46] But despite his firm words, offenders continued to be reported.

So it may not have been merely for the benefit of the scholars that in 1909 a pamphlet was issued by the Board of Education giving a 'Syllabus of Lessons on "Temperance"'. One of its sections was devoted to the: 'Evil Consequences of Intemperance to the Individual, to the Home, and to the State', while the avowed object of the whole exercise was to stress 'the manifest advantages of abstemiousness, and the absence of advantage in, and the positive risks and dangers of, any departure from it'.[47]

On the more positive side, however, the availability of cheap foreign excursion tickets, following the example of Thomas Cook, could open up the delights of travel to members of the teaching profession. As John Hurt points out, many schoolmasters must have been able to afford the 36s. needed to go on Cook's four-day trip to Paris to visit the 1867 exhibition held there. And there were men like Edmund Pryer, who left Culham College at Christmas 1877, and wrote to the principal almost two years later 'giving very interesting account of his visit to Boulogne during the summer holiday.' The next year he made a 'holiday trip to Brussels', and again wrote to describe his experiences.[48]

Even the Committee of Council began to take an interest in the leisure question. In its *Memorandum on the Training and Instruction of Pupil-Teachers*, issued in 1891, Sir George Kekewich advised school managers to ensure that their younger teachers—as well as pupil-teachers—were provided with some out-of-school entertainment. Perhaps books could be lent, or a local 'reading circle' established: 'but study and bookwork alone do not complete the education of these young persons for the work and the life which are before them'. So a natural history club, a cricket club, a debating society, a visit to a picture gallery, a holiday excursion and similar activities could also be arranged. In Sir George's view, the 'future usefulness' of a teacher depended not only 'on what he knows and can do, but on what he *is*—on his tastes, on his aims in life, on his general mental cultivation, and on the spirit in which he does his work.'[49] Kekewich consulted the principal of the Borough Road College on this issue, and the latter replied, recommending that young teachers should become involved in organisations like the 'Home Reading Union' : 'A Teacher in a School, the head of a family, any one, may form a "circle", each member paying a very small sum, & receiving from the Union a magazine which gives periodical helps & hints to the circle, wh. meets under the guidance of its "leader" to read & discuss specified great works.'[50] Unfortunately, whilst such initiatives may have flourished in the towns, it is most unlikely that a young teacher would have been able to organise a success-ful literary or debating circle in the average country village.

More hopefully, the emergence of the various teachers' associa-tions and, particularly, of the National Union of Elementary Teachers in 1870, provided opportunities for social gatherings and discussions alongside the organisations' basic concern with the improvement of working conditions. *The School and the Teacher* for November 1860 described one such body—the North-West Oxfordshire Schoolmasters' Association. This had been formed in April 1859 by the rector of the small parish of King-ham, who had invited 'all the Masters in the Deanery of Chipping Norton to dinner, and then proposed its formation'. By Novem-ber 1860 membership stood at twelve, and the masters met once a quarter for a day, 'part of which is spent in discussing some educational topic, introduced by the reading of a paper, and the rest in social enjoyment'. Among papers read at the meetings was one on 'Teaching Spelling' and another on 'Teaching Arithmetic', which were useful though hardly riveting themes. Then there was the Charlbury and Chipping Norton Teachers' Association which was connected with the NUET and which at a meeting on 15 October 1881 combined a discussion of the weaknesses of the government's school code with 'a good tea and a capital enter-tainment'.[51] Later the same group decided to organise a glee club for members. Many other local associations affiliated to the union arranged annual picnics for members, as reports in *The Schoolmaster* attest. In July 1893, for example, the second annual picnic of the Daventry Teachers' Association in North-amptonshire took place at Blisworth Gardens, where after speeches had been made exhorting those present to support the union : 'Various amusements were engaged in during the after-noon, including a ladies' and gentlemen's cricket match, lawn tennis, rounders and dancing.'[52] Most of these junketings followed a similar pattern, and through such events teachers could meet together to discuss common experiences and thereby lose the sense of isolation which so many endured in their own village setting.

Nevertheless as James Cross of Wing School pointed out in 1861 to his colleagues in the Oxford Diocesan Association of Schoolmasters, for many of them self-improvement would be the main out-of-school concern:

> A certain portion of time daily devoted to personal improvement should form part of the plans of every Teacher. . . . The habit of study and observation must always be kept up, whether in the fields, in the town, or at home: we should endeavour to be continually storing up facts for future lessons. . . . Regular exercise in the open air should be taken, always having an object in view, or it will be of little use. Do we walk? Perhaps we may have a taste for Natural History, Botany, or Geology; or do we stay at home? We may be Gardening, Carpentering, &c., something we must do; our usual duties may then be for a time forgotten, for the mind requires refreshment as much as the body. The study of Music may be turned to practical account in a parish, either in the formation of the village Singing Class, or in the Church on Sunday . . . some Teachers in the country are in danger of suffering from isolation, and are liable to sink into apathy, and inactivity from having no excitement for their ideas . . . The pleasures and rewards of the Teacher in this life may be those which we may class under the head of those of an unpretending character, viz: those consisting of a comfortable home and the peaceful enjoyment of domestic life.[53]

Richard Phillotson in Thomas Hardy's novel, *Jude the Obscure*, was, therefore, conforming to an accepted pattern when he took as his hobby the study of Roman-Britannic antiquities. This necessitated his 'going alone into fields where causeways, dykes, and tumuli abounded, or shutting himself up in his house with a few urns, tiles, and mosaics he had collected', rather than in visiting his neighbours.[54] It sounds a very dull and priggish existence for men and women who were, in many cases, still in their twenties. Perhaps it is not surprising that some of the former at least sought consolation in the 'demon' drink. Others, like Mr Marton in Charles Dickens's *The Old Curiosity Shop*, drew in upon themselves. The opening description of Marton gives the essence of his character—and that of many of his fellows: 'He was a pale, simple-looking man, of a spare and meagre habit, and sat among his flowers and beehives, smoking his pipe, in the little porch before his door. . . . In his plain old suit of black, he looked pale and meagre.' In his quiet respectability he was one with countless of his colleagues, who shared the narrow round of his daily life and, perhaps too, his timidity 'of venturing into the noisy world'.[55] Yet by some of their poorer neighbours he and his fellows, in their self-imposed isolation, may well have been regarded with suspicion, and even dislike, as conceited or stand-offish. Certainly John Clare, for one, considered the village schoolmaster to be 'one of the most pretending & most ignorant of men'. While if the anonymous author of a poem which appeared in *The School and the Teacher* is to be believed, the position of 'The Schoolmaster's Wife' was hardly to be envied either:[56]

Of all the unfortunate females in life,
There's none to compare with the Schoolmaster's Wife.
A lady by birth, in her feelings and station,
She still is the veriest drudge in creation.
Her heart must be tender, her skin must be tough;
Her tongue must be smooth, but her hands will be rough.
She must be energetic, yet gentle and kind;
Most thankful for insult, to ridicule blind.
She mustn't make blunders in speaking or spelling;
Must know people's wishes without any telling;
Keep servants in order, talk science and sense;
Cure ringworm and bacon; comb hair, and dispense.
With festers and chilblains must be quite *au fait*,
And carve rounds of beef in a masterly way;
Brew, bake, mend, and make, but be tidy and hearty;
And quite in her element giving a party.
She mustn't know people she meets in the town,
Unless they're alone, or she's in her best gown.
She mustn't be grave—it looks peevish and spiteful;
She never should smile—that is wanton and frightful.
Her style must be cheerful, her morals severe;

Her tone must be rigid, but never austere.
Wherever she visits, her friends will explore
Herself and her garments, behind and before.
She mustn't wear feathers, or flounces, or bustle;
Her shoes mustn't creak, and her dress mustn't rustle.
Her conduct at home, her behaviour at church,
Are suitable subjects for rigid research.
She shouldn't be dark, and she mustn't be fair;
She shouldn't wear caps, nor go curling her hair.
She'll humour her husband, and coddle the boys;
Nor ever object to a scandalous noise.
She'll grow yellow and wrinkled, and bilious and thin;
Find her teeth falling out, and her cheeks falling in;
Till death and dyspepsia seize on their prey,
And she, in her grave, gets her first holiday.

Yet, despite these disadvantages, school teaching still offered to the poor but able boy or girl a chance to escape from a life of manual labour. For that alone, it was valued by many of them.

7

Tenure Problems and Old Age

Clerical managers are all predominant in country parishes; and unless the teachers will tamely submit to Sunday-school, organ, choir duty, and whatever other Church work the clergy choose to put on them, their situations are not worth more than three months' purchase. By a clerical manager I have just been got out of a school, in which I have been for eight years, for no other reason than because I offended him some time since by refusing to have Sunday-school forced upon me.

Letter from 'No Sunday Worry' in *The Schoolmaster*, 23 July 1881.

A schoolmaster furnished evidence with regard to land tenure. The offended landed proprietors arrayed themselves against him and endeavoured to secure his dismissal by the School Board. At first they were unsuccessful. A new Board however was soon after elected, and the dismissal of the master effected notwithstanding his excellent work and the protests of the people of the village. A schoolmaster must not be a village Hampden.

Statement by the President of the National Union of Teachers in *Supplement* to *The Schoolmaster*, 21 April 1900.

IN 1861 the Newcastle Commission concluded that the occupation of an elementary schoolmaster was one

> which requires a quiet, even temper, patience, sympathy, fondness for children, and habitual cheerfulness. It wants rather good sense and quiet intelligence than a very inquisitive mind or very brilliant talents . . . [But if the master's] prospects are not so extensive as in some other walks of life, they are more secure. He is never out of work. He is affected only casually and indirectly by the vicissitudes of trade.[1]

In the Commissioners' view : 'A schoolmaster is sure of a good income, a great deal of leisure, and moderate labour as long as his health lasts.'

Despite this optimistic view, however, the reality was often very different, especially in country areas. On the question of security of employment, in particular, teachers could find themselves at the mercy of irresponsible or tyrannical school managers. And although some of them, through carelessness, inefficiency or wrongdoing may have deserved the summary dismissals which were handed out, in most cases there was little justification for the action taken. A bad report from Her Majesty's Inspector, a refusal to perform extra duties—such as conducting the Sunday school or training the choir—a desire by managers to cut down on running costs by employing a cheaper substitute, dislike of a teacher's outside activities, or, in church schools, even a change of incumbent, could all lead to dismissal. Inevitably the loss of a job in such circumstances carried with it a slur upon the teacher's character and abilities, however unjustified that might be. Even the *Church Times* of 15 December 1894, recognised the injustices that could arise when it declared : 'There is one point of clerical conduct which demands serious attention. We refer to the autocratic and unjust treatment to which the masters of parish schools too frequently have to submit.' It called for the setting up of an official appeals procedure—unfortunately without success.

A similar line was taken by the Annual Report of the National Union of Teachers in the same year when it condemned 'certain flagrant cases of unjust and capricious dismissal of teachers'.[2] And six years later its president declared that the Union was 'giving advice on Tenure troubles at the rate of four applicants per day', out of a total membership of around 43,000.[3] He estimated that the rate at which cases were being dealt with 'suggested that some 60 per cent of teachers might need some advice in the course of a working life.'

Although these comments relate to the last years of the nineteenth century, they were equally applicable to earlier decades as well, for then the isolation of country life and the low status of school teachers rendered many of them vulnerable to arbitrary action by employers. A typical example of this was provided at the village of Coleshill during the mid-1850s. Here the boys' school, which had been opened in 1842, was financed largely by the Earl of Radnor, who was the principal landowner in the parish. However on 21 January 1856, quite without warning, the Earl wrote to the master, Henry Joyner, who had been employed there for about two and a half years, informing him brusquely that : 'As the school . . . does not go on quite to my satisfaction, I should be glad to hear from you that you wish to leave it. Pray mention when you would wish to go.'⁴

Joyner was naturally shocked by this sudden decision and whilst expressing his willingness to move, he nevertheless appealed to the Earl to inform him why he was being dismissed, adding : 'If there is any suspicion of my ever having acted wrongly in any matter—I am sorry for it—but I beg most earnestly to declare that I have never wished to act otherwise than in the most straightforward and upright manner.' He also asked whether the Earl's son, who was a Member of Parliament, could 'procure me a writership or other employment in some public office; as I have two brothers who are serving with credit in government offices in London.' Radnor's response to this was short and to the point : 'I must decline entering into particulars with respect to my reasons for my giving you the notice which I did—but I repeat generally that it was because I did not think that the school went on satisfactorily. My son tells me that it is not within his power to assist you in the way you wish.' Joyner's plea for time to seek a fresh post, as he had a wife and family to support, met with an equally chilling response : 'I do not wish to tie you down to leave at any particular day nor to inconvenience you, but I should wish you not to interpose any unnecessary delay.'

No doubt Mr Joyner's bitterness at this treatment was made all the greater by the knowledge that at the time of his original appointment (which had come about through the intervention of Mr Forss, his predecessor at Coleshill), he had been successfully employed as master of the National School at Calne. The Calne incumbent was lavish in his praise when he informed the Earl in April 1853 that Joyner was 'a young man possessed of considerable talent and ability. He has also a kind disposition and amiable temper. . . . His manner of teaching arithmetic & geography is particularly good, the *first* especially . . .'⁵ So it was only after a flatteringly persistent approach that Joyner decided to move to the Earl's school—and to the disappointments that followed.

Nor, sad to say, did Mr Joyner's immediate successor at Coleshill, William East, fare a great deal better. He was a former student of the Metropolitan Training Institution in London and was appointed to the Earl's school in the spring of 1856.

G

But on 25 July came a visit by HMI Bowstead. He pronounced on the 'inefficiency' of East, whereupon the Earl gave him immediate notice, too. This precipitate action was, incidentally, approved by the Countess of Radnor, for in a letter to her husband written in August, she firmly stated:

> I should be very sorry if you were to be satisfied with having a second-rate schoolmaster. . . . I do not believe there is one school in the neighbourhood now which *we* should be satisfied with & if yours becomes again as I hope it will what it was in Mr Forss's time I believe boys will soon come to it from the neighbouring villages & towns. I think it is a very great object to have a school good enough to attract the sons of farmers & men of a superior class, as I cannot help thinking that mixing with such boys is likely to raise the sons of the labourers almost as much as the actual knowledge they gain at the school.[6]

In the meantime the search for a successor was going ahead, ending eventually with the appointment of the master of Faringdon workhouse school. He had applied too late for the original vacancy in March 1856 and appears to have been a more suitable choice—not least because he showed himself fully aware of his humble station in society. In his initial application, he had concluded his letter in the following meek terms: 'Throwing myself entirely upon your Lordship's favor [*sic*], and begging your Lordship's forbearance should I have made my application too late, I beg to subscribe myself your Lordship's most obedient and humble Sert.'

That this kind of humility was expected by the Earl is shown by the tones in which the first master at the school, Francis S. Forss, felt he must apologise for his temerity in wishing to resign the headship, which he had held for more than ten years. He explained 'most respectfully' that this was partly because his fiancée had 'a strong objection to this neighbourhood—not only on account of her health, but for other private reasons, and consequently I think I should be destitute of proper affection even to wish her to live in a place in which I had any reason to believe she would not be happy.' (In fact Forss married Caroline Belcher, a thirty-three-year-old farmer's daughter from Caversham in Oxfordshire in July 1854, just over a year after he left Coleshill.)

A second reason was Mr Forss's own health, which he considered to be unequal 'to the great exertion necessary for the carrying on a school of this sort successfully'. His letter ended : 'I . . . trust I shall not put your Lordship to any inconvenience by resigning the charge of the School . . . I should be sorry to put your Lordship to any inconvenience and shall not wish to leave till your Lordship shall have found a suitable person to succeed me.' Subsequent correspondence between the two continued in this servile fashion on the part of Forss.[7] On one occasion he even had to apologise for not answering the Earl's letter 'by return of post. I sent an answer by the next post, which I trust your Lordship has received'. But the apology did not prevent a reprimand from his employer.

Messrs Forss, Joyner and East were not the only teachers to encounter problems when working in schools under the control of a single manager. A similar difficulty arose at Thorpe Malsor, near Kettering, in 1888. Thorpe Malsor Hall was the seat of the Rev. C. H. Maunsell and his wife. The latter managed the school, as her husband held a benefice in Brighton, and there had already been skirmishes between herself and Miss Rose Knowles, the school mistress, over a variety of issues. Miss Knowles had even written to her mother in December 1882, advising the postponement of a visit until Mrs Maunsell's return to the parish : 'She generally sacks somebody when she comes and as I have been here the longest it will be very likely me.' Her fears were not realised on that occasion but five and a half years later the axe fell, when towards the end of June 1888, she was sent for by Mrs Maunsell :

> I wished her good morning when I went in, she never spoke so I knew there was something up. She layed [*sic*] my money down and then said there were going to be a great many changes here. She therefore wished to give me two months notice from to-day. . . . I thanked her and asked her if she would please write me out a testimonial, she said yes and that ended it. She did look savage. . . . Mrs M. is going to buy an Organ for Church so they will get some one who will play that, a master I expect.[8]

With difficulty Miss Knowles obtained a fresh post in time for the September term. But as she complained to her mother in

July: 'Mrs M. has been away nearly three weeks. I have not heard anything from her, she has left me no directions; but she has given the Head gardner [*sic*] his directions to lock up every where when I go. Of course they must have some one here competent to play in Church and train the choir. I was not at all surprised only I thought she might have done it more graciously'.[9]

In many cases, though, it was not the whim of a single patron but the results of the annual examination conducted by Her Majesty's Inspector which decided the fate of a teacher. Thanks to the Revised Code of 1862, bad results meant a reduction in the amount of the government grant to a school, and managers generally blamed failures upon the teacher, rather than upon their own unwillingness to enforce the school attendance regulations properly or upon the attitude of the Inspector. One example of this kind occurred at the small village of Bix in Oxfordshire in July 1888. At their meeting on the third of that month the members of the school board agreed unanimously that as the Inspector's report had been 'unfavourable', a 'change of teachers was necessary in the interest of the Ratepayers and children'. The clerk to the board was instructed to give both the headmistress and her assistant immediate notice, with no mention made of the fact that the former had been employed at the school for more than ten years with reasonable success.[10] A similar situation arose in 1893 at a Devon school. Here the mistress, under notice to leave, complained in her log book: 'One always feels that the fate of a whole years' work may hang on the humour or caprice, and absolutely on the stroke of a pen, of some Assistant Inspector.'[11] But sympathy for her is somewhat blunted by the comments of her successor that the time-table was 'in fragments and was made up for 1889. Registers not made up, nor yet names rewritten. . . . Dirt, confusion, and disorder prevails throughout'. Despite the common practice for newly appointed teachers to denigrate the work of their predecessors, in this case at least the charge of gross inefficiency seems to have been well founded.

In another case, a master who lost his post in 1890 after fourteen years, as a result of a bad examination result, was moved to bewail his fate in verse. He denied the charge of incompetency:

And you should also bear in mind
That illness threw us much behind.
For 'influenza' played its part
Just when the children wanted 'heart'.

Then there were the vagaries of the inspectors themselves:

. . . our Examiner was new
And 'failed' the very best, a few
Of whom for certain one can tell
They do their work and do it well:
And 'Grammar' (not our weakest point)
Was butchered—hackled—joint by joint:[12]

His method of protest was certainly original, but it availed him nothing. He still had to go, leaving copies of his broadsheet behind him.

On occasion, though, charges of inefficiency and dishonesty could lead to still severe penalties, such as fines or the loss or suspension of the teacher's certificate. At Gerrards Cross National School the managers were informed on 16 November 1881, that the newly appointed assistant master at the school had been fined by the magistrates at Beaconsfield, 'at the instance of the Vicar', for 'altering a testimonial from Crocker Hall School.' Needless to say his engagement was also terminated.[13] A good deal more fortunate was the head of another Buckinghamshire school at Great Marlow. In 1879 he admitted having 'entirely lost the control of the Boys' at the Sir William Borlase Bluecoat School and wished to send them to the nearby National school because of this; earlier he had been reprimanded for giving 'excessive' punishment to the scholars. Yet, although he was forced to resign his position he was allowed to retire on a pension of £40 a year.[14]

Even the introduction of the acting teacher's certificate examination in March 1847 led to the downfall of some members of the profession, when they were discovered cheating. The Committee of Council took a very stern line on this, as surviving correspondence makes clear. On 18 August 1849, for example, the Spalding incumbent was informed by R. R. W. Lingen, the Committee's Acting Assistant Secretary, of the misdoings of W. H. Granville, master of the local National school, at the examination held the previous Easter: 'their Lordships have been obliged to come to the conclusion that on two occasions in the course of the examination he copied his answers from those of Mr Gray, the Master of the Newbottle School who sat next to him . . . Mr Granville has added to his fault by refusing to acknowledge it.' In these circumstances he would 'not be admitted to any examination for Certificates of Merit before 1852. Nor can their Lordships any longer continue to recognise a School entrusted to his charge as a fit place for the training of a Pupil Teacher, and if he is to retain his situation, my Lords will not feel justified at the end of the year in considering the conditions as fulfilled which would empower them to sanction the payment of any stipend or Gratuity.'[15]

The loss or suspension of a certificate affected a small trickle of teachers only, but where it occurred the principal offence was concerned with errors in the registration of scholars. Where such mistakes were wilful they were designed, no doubt, to boost a school's income from attendance grants in cases where the head's salary also depended partly upon the amount of the school grant. Each year a number of teachers were punished in this fashion—as in the twelve months ending 31 August 1890, when there were twelve registration offences leading to suspension of a teacher's certificate or cancellation of the government grant to a school, out of a total of eighteen offences of all kinds reported. Other matters leading to suspension in that year included drunkenness and 'misrepresentation of tenor of HM Inspector's reports'. One offender, who had been employed at Witney Wesleyan School, had his certificate cancelled for 'presenting a forged testimonial'.[16] Of eight teachers who had their certificates cancelled or suspended in the year ending 31 August 1891, three were concerned with registration offences.

In a number of cases, though, these errors were committed unwittingly by head teachers who were overburdened by the large size of their schools and the lack of effective assistance. They simply allowed their registers to get into a muddle and then were unable to extricate themselves. Occasionally this might have tragic consequences as the day of the annual visit of the HMI drew near. In January 1879, the young headmistress of a Birkenhead school was found drowned, having committed suicide a few days before the inspection of her school was due to take place. The inquest was told that she had 'of late been sitting up frequently till half-past three in the morning making up her school registers', and had often confided to her colleagues her fears that the Inspector would take her certificate away.[17] In commenting on the case *The Schoolmaster* pointed out bitterly that it was by no means the first suicide to have occurred 'in which the dread of an approaching examination had been the supposed cause.'[18]

In some cases, changes in governmental regulations or the passage of fresh legislation could also lead to loss of employment, without any actual inefficiency being proved. Under the Revised Code of 1862, only schools with a certificated head teacher were eligible for the payment of a grant, while the 1870 Education Act laid down that schools with qualified heads would alone be recognised as 'efficient'. Both measures undermined the position of the long-serving uncertificated master or mistress and whilst they were undoubtedly in the best long-term interests of education, they created short-term difficulties for the individuals concerned. The Government itself to some extent recognised this by laying down in the New Code of 1871 that teachers over thirty-five years of age, who had taught in elementary schools for at least ten years and could prove their efficiency to the HMI might be awarded third-class certificates without taking any examination.[19] Subsequently the age limits were reduced, so that under the Code of 1876, acting teachers who were above twenty-five years of age and had taught in elementary schools for at least five years with satisfactory results could be awarded a third-class certificate. Yet, despite the concessions, a number of teachers lost their posts as a result of the 1870 Act. One casualty was Samuel Harris, the head of Bampton National School from 1840 to 1873. In the latter year he was obliged to leave because he could not obtain a government certificate, and thus found himself at the age of fifty-seven without either job or prospects. He and his wife travelled to the Isle of Man, where their son had settled, and were helped by 'kind friends' into a small business. Unfortunately Harris's health then gave way and the business had to be sold, along with most of his personal possessions : 'Ill and penniless, I could no longer remain . . . so my wife and I made our way back to Oxfordshire to get an order to admit us into Witney workhouse.'[20] Once in the workhouse their luck changed. Harris was recognised, and Assistant Inspector Thomas Eley was contacted by the authorities. Eley visited him and sympathised with his plight. He wrote to *The Schoolmaster* appealing for subscriptions to support the couple in 'decent lodgings' while help was sought for them from the 'Schoolmasters' and Schoolmistresses' Benevolent Institution'.

A similar example of premature dismissal as a result of the 1870 Act occurred at Brinkley in Cambridgeshire, where the former master of the school was given a pension of £17 per annum, payable from 6 January 1871, and was appointed Parish Surveyor.[21] But not all elderly teachers in need received such timely assistance as these two had done. For many, 'dame school' instruction or the poor law remained their only resort.

Nor were these the only hazards to be faced by Victorian teachers. Especially in the smaller schools, where financial resources were limited, even good results in the annual examinations and the possession of satisfactory qualifications might not be sufficient to prevent dismissal. At one Berkshire school an entry in the Managers' Minute Book for October 1875 states that because of the 'necessity of diminishing the expenditure of the school' notice was to be given to the headmaster. His assistant was similarly treated in the succeeding month. Their replacements—a headmistress and assistant—were appointed at salaries of £52 per annum and £20 per annum, respectively, in place of the £60 a year plus the children's school pence and £30 obtained by their predecessors.[22]

About a decade later in Hampshire, the same cavalier disregard for the well-being of staff was displayed. Here the man concerned was a Mr Butcher, who had been appointed to Yateley school on 21 May 1884, at a salary of £120 a year, with his wife acting as infant mistress at £20 a year. At a Managers' meeting almost two years later the financial position of the school was considered:

> After considerable discussion . . . it was thought that too much money was being spent on Teachers' salaries and it was thought that there might be a saving of £40 a year under this head.
> It was therefore proposed by the Chairman and seconded by Mr J. P. Stilwell that three months' notice be given to Mr and Mrs Butcher on May 1st. This was carried unanimously.[23]

Mr Butcher had also acted as organist at the Church and so it was decided to advertise for 'a lady to teach infants and needle-work and to take the organ in the Parish Church, thus giving the Managers a greater choice of Masters'. Eventually on 14 July, it was reported that a replacement assistant had been appointed at an annual salary of £20, with £5 for lodgings, while the new head-master was to receive £60 a year plus a quarter of the government grant to the school and two-thirds of the pupil-teachers' grant (this latter at most amounting to £2 per pupil-teacher per annum). It was further resolved that 'if these items should not reach £90 per annum, the managers will make the salary up to that sum.' In this way the managers were saving about £30 a year on the master's salary; and although in most years the new man received a rise of £5 it was not until September 1894 that he managed to achieve the level of pay obtained by his predecessor a decade earlier.[24]

Mr Butcher's combined appointment as schoolmaster and organist on Sunday was a common arrangement in rural Church schools, as an examination of advertisements of staff vacancies in the educational press makes clear, although in urban areas it was a good deal less usual, since there alternative musical talent was available. Thus, to quote one of many possible examples, the Rector of Selworthy near Taunton advertised in *The School Guardian* of 24 May 1879 for 'a certificated Master, with Wife or Sister to superintend infants and sewing. Sunday school, organ and choir. Salary £95, with house and garden, for school; and £10 additional for organ and choir.' Even in the last years of the century the same attitude persisted, so that of thirty-eight advertisements for heads of voluntary schools which appeared in *The Schoolmaster* of 12 July 1890, fifteen mentioned extraneous duties, all of them in villages. And of thirty-four vacancies adver-tised in the issue of 2 August in that year, fourteen—again all in rural areas—specified that extra duties would be required. Other issues of the newspaper followed a similar pattern.

Yet it was 'extraneous duties' which often generated the most bitterness between school teachers and their clerical managers. This resentment was clearly shown in the letter written to *The Schoolmaster* which was quoted at the head of the present chap-ter, and there were many complaints along the same lines in the columns of that journal and elsewhere. In February 1886, 'A Country Teacher' angrily pointed out: 'Within the radius of twelve miles I know two masters and one mistress who are obliged to leave their positions because of the clerical tyranny brought to bear upon them. . . . Should a teacher annoy the parson by word or deed he has notice to quit, and has no appeal whatever. A short time since I knew a man who was dismissed because he made an application for a better post; another has had notice to quit because he voted for the Liberal in the general election; and an assistant master has had to suffer a reduction of a fortnight's salary, the reverend gentleman stating that he would only pay for work done.' Much the same hostility was displayed by T.C., another *Schoolmaster* correspondent, when he declared : 'I know some of the clergy think no more of their teachers than of a dog, and I quite agree with what appeared not long ago, when a teacher wrote and said, "if his parson came and told him to go and sweep his (the parson's) yard, he must do it or leave".'

Not all teachers, of course, objected to the performance of extra duties. At Wheatley, Oxfordshire, John Knight, a twenty-three-year-old applicant for the post of head, informed the incumbent in August 1880 : 'I have been used to large organs, and to taking any kind of service', adding in a subsequent letter : 'With regard to the Sunday School it would give me great pleasure to assist.' Mr Knight was duly appointed to the post. A similarly co-operative attitude was displayed by the successful applicant for the position of headmistress of the girls' school at Wheatley at the same time : 'I shall be pleased to give any assistance I can in the Sunday Schools.'[25] And at Great Barrington in Gloucestershire, James Barrett combined forty-two years as head of the local Church school with fifty-seven years as choirmaster and organist at the church itself. The latter feat is marked by a commemorative plaque in the church.[26]

Given this emphasis on choir and organ duties, it is perhaps not surprising that a lack of musical talent could prove a serious handicap for any master or mistress seeking promotion, no matter how satisfactory his or her academic achievements. Training college records confirm the problems that could arise—as with one former Culham student, who was appointed to the headship of Okeford National School in Devon at the age of twenty-two. Although his principal had classed him as 'excellent—refined & of good tone' when he left in December 1872, he lost his position at Okeford within six months because he was 'not equal to the Organ duties'. Several months passed before he obtained a fresh situation. Another student, who was appointed to a school in Dover during June 1870, filled his classrooms 'to overcrowding' by his successful teaching, but once again music proved his Achilles heel. According to the Culham principal he was not good at this subject: 'ought never to undertake training of a choir'. But he was compelled to do so and thanks to his exertions was forced to leave in 1872, 'quite broken down in health'.[27] In fact it is significant that when the principal wrote to the incumbent of an Oxfordshire country parish to give a testimonial concerning another, more successful, candidate for a headship, he noted that the man was 'a most admirable fellow, very good trainer of a choir & organist, & a good teacher . . . he is also a man, who would thoroughly enter into your work, & of a deep, religious tone, fit for a sub-deacon, if we had such an office'. The order of priorities in this list of favourable qualities is instructive.[28]

Yet if failure to perform extraneous duties satisfactorily was one cause of insecurity of tenure for school teachers in Church schools, another might arise as a result of an incumbent leaving the parish or dying. Records show that at least one former student at Culham College was unfortunate enough to lose his job on these grounds twice in two years, between December 1854 and 1856. Reports in the educational press show that his experience was not unique.

Even out-of-school activities could endanger employment, as an assistant mistress at Whitchurch near Reading discovered in February 1886. An entry in the school log book reads: 'Revd. Canon Slatter called and reported that "The Managers had decided on giving Miss Stowe a month's notice as they were not satisfied with her conduct out of school." ' Nor were the men exempt from such restrictions. In 1867 the master of Diseworth School, Leicestershire, was given notice to quit because 'a child was born to him three months after marriage'. Only with difficulty did he eventually obtain a position at a village school in Buckinghamshire.[29] Thomas Hardy's novel, *Jude the Obscure*, deals with the same theme, when the schoolmaster, Phillotson, is dismissed by the School Committee because he had 'condoned' his wife's elopement with Jude, by allowing her to go away freely. Although Phillotson maintained that his domestic affairs were no concern of the managers, they sternly overruled him, 'insisting that the private eccentricities of a teacher came quite within their sphere of control, as it touched the morals of those he taught.'

Strong political or trade union affiliations might also lead to dismissal, as Mr B. Tunnicliffe of Wimlington school found to his cost in 1892. Tunnicliffe had aroused the anger of the local school board because he had been active in the Liberal interest at the general election held in that year. When he refused to apologise for his actions they gave him three months' notice. The National Union of Teachers decided to give him financial support when the notice expired, in order to demonstrate to rural teachers 'the value of combination' and to give the school board electors a chance to change the board's composition, since a poll was due to be held early in the following year. But despite attempts by the Union to influence ratepayers in Mr Tunnicliffe's favour, the constitution of the board remained unchanged by the election and the Union and he had to accept defeat.[30]

Similar problems were faced by Thomas and Annie Higdon, the master and mistress of schools at Wood Dalling and, later, Burston in Norfolk in the early years of the present century. The couple first came to Norfolk in April 1902 and very quickly, under the headship of Mrs Higdon, standards in the Wood Dalling school improved. Both she and her husband were intolerant of the neglect by the managers of attendance regulations and, outside the school, of the poor living conditions of the local farm workers. Between 1906 and 1910 Tom Higdon actively promoted a branch of the Agricultural Labourers' Union in the village and also successfully encouraged a number of the men to stand for election to the parish council. As a result of these actions, relations between the Higdons and their managers—several of whom were farmers—steadily deteriorated. At last, in 1910, the couple were threatened with dismissal because it was claimed that Mrs Higdon had called the managers liars after a dispute over the timing of school holidays and the heating of the school, among other matters. In the event, Mrs Higdon apologised for her outburst and in January 1911, instead of being dismissed she and her husband were moved by the Norfolk County Education Committee to the school at Burston. Here similar difficulties soon emerged, with Tom Higdon again taking a prominent role in local politics and trade union affairs. Then in March 1913 came the parish council elections. Undeterred by the fact that a campaign such as he had waged at Wood Dalling would bring him into conflict with the rector and the leading farmers of the village, Higdon set to work to get sufficient labourers nominated, along with himself and a sympathetic smallholder cum bricklayer, to win control of the council. Thanks to the energy he displayed, victory was secured, but at considerable cost to himself. The rector of the parish, who had been one of the unsuccessful candidates, and other members of the management committee of the school now displayed growing hostility to the couple. Ultimately Mrs Higdon was charged with having unreasonably caned one of the scholars. Although no satisfactory evidence was brought to support the claim, she and her husband were dismissed. Many of the villagers suspected the charge had really been brought because of Mr Higdon's political and union interests, and so when the couple were forced to leave the school on 1 April 1914, most of the children, with the approval of their parents, refused to attend any more. Instead a temporary school was established, under the Higdons, in a former carpenter's workshop. And thanks to the publicity which the children's 'strike' gained, sufficient funds were eventually collected to make possible the construction of a new purpose-built property, in 1917.[31]

Fortunately head-on clashes like these were rare. And although, when they did occur, the managers normally emerged victorious, as they did in the Higdons' case, some teachers *were* able to withstand threats of dismissal, particularly if the managers were not united. One such case arose at Aston National School in Staffordshire during 1898. In June of that year the Rev. G. Brown, incumbent of Aston, abruptly announced that he had dismissed the then headmaster, Mr J. Plant, and had appointed a replacement to start in the coming September. His action was challenged by HMI Yarde, who queried Brown's managerial rights. A new committee of managers was appointed and it was agreed that Plant should remain at his post. But matters did not proceed as planned. Brown declared that he would not surrender possession of the school building and obtained an injunction to confirm him in occupation. Meanwhile the headmaster whom he had appointed took office. Mr Plant, however, still had the backing of the other managers and the HMI, so a school was temporarily started in his house, and most of the children of the parish attended it. The dispute dragged on until at the end of March

1899, the Education authorities in London supported Mr Plant's claim to the headship, and despite the incumbent's continuing opposition, the two schools were eventually merged in May 1899.[32]

A similar case arose at nearby Longsdon, in July 1902, when the headmaster, who had served nearly nine years at the school, was given notice by the new vicar. Two years previously, when the latter had first arrived in the parish he had suggested that the master should leave, explaining that 'a new clergyman always got on better with a schoolmaster of his own appointing'. He also claimed that the master 'had influence with the young men of the parish which rightly belonged to the church and that the master's resignation was imperative to the success of his ministry'. Then on 7 July 1902 came the attempted dismissal, when the vicar handed over a note saying that he had been requested 'by the Managers of the School to let you know privately that they think a change of Schoolmaster would now be beneficial for the school, as you have now been here a fair number of years. They do not desire however to do anything which might in any way be prejudicial to you, so they have asked me to intimate to you privately that in their opinion by far the best and pleasantest plan will be for you to send in your resignation as they wish to treat you with courtesy and consideration'. When the other managers were approached on the matter, however, they denied all knowledge of the proposed dismissal. So with their support, the master was able to stay on.[33] But that was not quite the end of the affair. The unfortunate rivalry between master and incumbent appears to have continued for a number of years until eventually in 1910 the vicar exposed the master for irregularities in the completion of the registers. As a result of this, the latter's certificate was suspended for a year, while his assistant, who had also 'adjusted' her registers to achieve good attendance figures, was struck off permanently. In the end, therefore, both master and assistant lost their jobs—though at least at that stage it was for an officially justifiable cause.[34]

The tenure issue was also one which the National Union of Elementary Teachers pursued vigorously from its inception in 1870. A union survey in 1891 showed that around one in three of the sample of one thousand two hundred teachers investigated depended for the tenure of their post on the performance of outside duties, like playing the organ, training the choir, or some similar parochial function. While a report produced in June 1899 by the union's Rural and Small Schools Committee underlined the range of tasks required still more clearly. Thus one board school head noted : 'To suit Wesleyan : Sunday school superintendent and treasurer, and secretary of Band of Hope. To suit Church of England : secretary of reading and recreation rooms; librarian; secretary and captain of cricket club.' Another unfortunate complained of 'Organ, Sunday school (twice), choir and practice, clothing club, penny bank : . . . Present vicar forbids going away in holidays without finding substitute. Son in choir, not to go away without permission.' In this case the unqualified assistant teacher at the school also had to clean it. A third head felt there was : '*No* security of tenure. No feeling of safety. Cannot tell from one quarter to another when I may have notice to quit. 18 years' service.'[35] It would be tedious to catalogue all the complaints recorded, and it is perhaps hardly surprising that in 1900 the union President chose as the theme of his annual address : 'A Plea for Reasonable Security of Tenure for the Teacher'.[36] Among the examples quoted was that of a mistress who was dismissed because she refused to attend early morning communion, and a Southport schoolmaster who had been driven to 'a premature grave' by the worry of a tenure battle, leaving behind a wife and family of young children.

Union weapons in fighting unfair dismissals included a black-list of schools, which members were advised to boycott until the original teacher had been reinstated. Those who ignored the blacklist risked having their union membership withdrawn, and thereby losing the social and legal benefits which that organisation could provide. Rural teachers, in particular, would find this a blow.[37] Another method was to give legal advice and assistance to members wrongly dismissed, while electoral pressure was applied in the case of recalcitrant school boards, since with these triennial elections of members had to take place. One case where this method was successful occurred in the Llandovery area of Wales, where the board was 'completely Nonconformist'. The chairman had persistently opposed the head from the time he took up his appointment, while another board member—described as 'an ultra Baptist'—had objected to the master holding school concerts. According to the union investigator, there were no grounds for dismissal other than caprice. The head's character was good and he had achieved adequate results, 'given the exceptionally difficult conditions and absence of proper help. . . . Talley is a scattered rural parish, the small village being about nine miles from a railway station. The people are nearly all Welsh speaking and Nonconformists.' Thanks partly to union efforts a new board was subsequently elected and the head was reappointed.[38]

But attempts by the union to press the Education Department to intervene on the tenure issue remained, for long, unsuccessful. Patric Cumin, secretary to the Department from 1884 to 1890, in evidence to the Cross Commission firmly rejected the idea of allowing teachers to appeal to the Department in controversial cases of dismissal:

> That is a subject that I have a very strong opinion about, and I will explain why. When I was Secretary of the Scotch Education Commission, in Scotland the parochial schoolmaster had a freehold of his office; and the result was that an enormous number of most incompetent teachers continued in office, and you could not get them out. In the same way in the endowed schools one of the most crying evils was that masters had a freehold in their office, and that consequently the endowments were wasted, or at all events very inefficiently used. In consequence of that, with considerable difficulty the law was changed in order to leave it to the managers, or to the governing body, to make a bargain with their teachers as to the tenure of their office . . . and in all the schemes passed by the Endowed Schools Commissioners, from the beginning they laid down this principle: that there is a contract to be made with the master or mistress, and with him or her only, and that the sole judges of whether or not that contract has been fulfilled are to be the governors or the managers, subject of course to the opinion of a court of law.[39]

During the 1890s the union's efforts were intensified, though the most that could be achieved was an addition to Article 71 of the 1897 Code stating that any agreement entered into between managers and teachers must be in writing. A model form of agreement was also provided for the appointment of the head teacher in a school. Then, with the passage of the Superannuation

Act of 1898 the need for reform became more urgent, since 'future pension as well as present job might now be at stake'. In January 1898, therefore, the National Union of Teachers appointed a standing committee for the sole purpose of dealing with tenure questions—something towards which it had been moving from 1892, when its Law Committee began to take an increasing interest in the issue.[40] Detailed discussions were held by the new Committee on particular cases—at its first gathering on 21 January 1898, eleven were considered—and soon numbers built up. So that at the monthly meeting held on 15 July, it was noted that advice had been given in fifty-one cases since the previous meeting, with seventeen more discussed by the committee itself.[41] On a broader basis, too, every opportunity was taken of stressing that in 'almost every country where there [was] any pretence to a national system of education there also [would] be found some means of appeal against the capricious dismissal of teachers'. In the President's address to the 1900 conference a number of foreign precedents were mentioned.[42]

Yet, despite these efforts, not until the passage of the 1902 Education Act, giving local authorities overall control of elementary schools within their area, were some of the uncertainties removed. Then, thanks to the influence of the NUT, an amendment was carried requiring the consent of the local education authority if a teacher were to be dismissed 'unless the dismissal be on grounds connected with the giving of religious instruction in the school'. In the following year a new edition of the School Code tackled the extraneous duties issue as well. Fresh agreements had now to be entered into with all teachers in voluntary schools, prohibiting the imposition of extra tasks as a condition of employment. Among the authorities complying with this was Hampshire County Council which in October 1903 provided a typical specimen agreement for the voluntary schools and teachers within its area. Perhaps the most telling clause laid down that: 'The Teacher shall not be required to perform or abstain from performing any duties outside the ordinary School hours or unconnected with the ordinary work of the School.'[43] Although a trickle of complaints continued thereafter, one of the main problems connected with the tenure battle had been overcome.

The new freedom was of particular benefit to those anxious to take part in political activity and although the clause did not provide cast-iron guarantees of individual liberty—as the case of the Higdons was to show—many teachers did gain from it. This was particularly true in the hard-fought general elections of 1910, when feelings on both sides of the political spectrum were running high. Thus from Sudbury in Suffolk early in 1910 there came complaints to the Board of Education from Liberal supporters that a number of headmasters in church schools were acting as sub-agents for the Conservative candidate and that this was 'detrimental to the best interests of education, & liable to place the children of Nonconformists, whose parents [were] known to be Liberals, under a new form of annoyance & probably persecution'. The Board replied tartly that as long as the work did not interfere with the teachers' duties in school, such political activities were quite in order.[44]

Of course, some of the local authorities displayed vagaries of their own—like that at Plymouth, where in August 1903 a resolution was passed that the marriage of a mistress in their employ was to be 'equivalent to three months' notice to terminate the engagement'.[45] Fortunately few others appear to have followed their example.

So far, attention has been focused on those teachers who lost, or were in danger of losing, their employment as a result of capricious action by school managers and school boards, or as a consequence of their own actions. But for the many who continued in the profession without such difficulties there still remained the residual problem of old age. Admittedly it was a problem which they shared with most other workers at that time and one which was increasingly to exercise the minds of politicians and social observers in the second half of the nineteenth century. Nevertheless under the Committee of Council Minutes of December 1846 a rather vague promise was made that 'a retiring pension may be granted by the Committee of Council to any schoolmaster or schoolmistress who shall be rendered incapable by age or infirmity of continuing to teach a school efficiently. Provided that no such pension shall be granted to any schoolmaster or schoolmistress who shall not have conducted [an] . . . Elementary school for fifteen years, during seven at least of which such school shall have been under inspection.' All applications had to be supported by a report from HM Inspector and from the trustees and managers of the school at which the teacher worked, covering his character and conduct, and the manner in which he had carried out his professional duties. The amount payable was to be determined on the basis of this report but was in no case to 'exceed two-thirds of the average amount of the salary and emoluments annually received by the applicant during the period that the school has been under inspection.'[46] As can be seen, the language was extremely cautious, making the award of a pension a purely discretionary matter. In fact R. R. W. Lingen, who succeeded Kay Shuttleworth as secretary to the Committee of Council on Education, subsequently claimed that the whole object in framing the Minutes had simply been to facilitate the removal of inefficient teachers, as the new training schemes got under way and raised standards in the profession.[47]

Nevertheless many teachers—not unnaturally—ignored the cautious provisos and interpreted the Minutes as a promise of a pension. Their optimism continued despite the fact that in 1851 a new Minute placed an upper limit of £6,500 on the funds which could be disbursed in any one year for the pensions, i.e. twenty payments of £30 each; one hundred of £25 each; and one hundred and fifty of £20 each, with the remaining £400 to be distributed in the form of donations or special gratuities. At the same time teachers were warned against 'calculating on the minutes as affording a substitute for the economy which is incumbent upon them, in common with all other workers, while their strength lasts'.[48]

So, despite these restrictions, the decision of the Education Department to withdraw all pension rights following the introduction of the Revised Code of 1862 caused great bitterness and a deep sense of betrayal among members of the profession. Significantly the National Union of Elementary Teachers listed the 'Establishment of a Pension Scheme' as one of its earliest objectives, and in 1872 noted seven distinct reasons for teachers to be given such aid—including the fact that 'Civil Servants, Soldiers, Policemen, and various officials receive retiring pensions, after a certain length of service', and that :

The office of Elementary Teacher involves a great strain upon the energies of both mind and body, and hence, as a rule, cannot be efficiently filled late in life, while the remuneration is generally too small to admit of any adequate provision being made for old age.[49]

The anxieties to which advancing years gave rise are revealed in the diary of John Horrocks, a Wandsworth schoolmaster, who decided to purchase a shop early in 1863 'with a view to providing a nest for declining years'. And in order that the school should not suffer from this he provided out of his own pocket a qualified assistant master to supplement his work. Nevertheless by the end of the year he admitted that 'the added labour of the new business' had been 'at times too much'. Not surprisingly, two years later he decided to resign his teaching post in order to devote himself fully to business matters.[50] By this time he was in his mid-forties.

It is, in fact, interesting that even before the Revised Code was formulated, HMI Watkins was deploring the insecurity of the teacher's position in old age :

Many have now reached middle life, some are going down its hill. Every year will add to this number, and carry some on to old age. Many of them will then have served their country well and faithfully for a long term of years, all the best years of their existence. Are they to have no reward for their work, no help when they are unable to help themselves? Is there to be no encouragement thus offered to others to labour and persevere in the course of duty? If some such provision be not made, some of the most valuable teachers, practical and experienced persons, both male and female, will be lost to the cause of education. Such persons, schoolmasters especially, have many offers of clerkships, receivers' and accountants' places made to them with higher salaries and less responsibility than their present posts. They often refuse them from the right feeling that they ought to continue in the vocation to which they have been called. They are not yet without hope, that in any modifications or extensions of the present educational system their claims will be recognised, either by the extension and enlargement of the pension list, or by their appointment as officers under your Lordships' Committee.[51]

In fact, the reverse occurred and, as we have seen, the already inadequate provisions were brought to an end.

Nevertheless, thanks to pressure from the NUET, in 1872 a Select Committee was appointed to examine the possibility of a restoration of pension rights. William Lawson, secretary to the union, was among those who gave evidence. He claimed to know of several cases where teachers had been reduced to utter destitution as a result of losing their post from overwork or illness: 'a case was mentioned to me the other day, in which a man after teaching up to the age of 50 or 60 in the neighbourhood of York died in a workhouse; and I had a letter recently from a schoolmaster in North Wales who said that he was nearly blind, that he was afflicted with rheumatism, and that he was almost deaf; "but", said he, "I am obliged to hold on, because what can I do; if I give up teaching there is nothing else for me but the workhouse." '[52] How his pupils regarded this he did not say! Even Sir James Kay Shuttleworth told the Committee that it had been 'improperly done' in the Code to strike out the entire pension scheme. Yet despite these arguments the Committee concluded that the Minutes of 1846 had not intended to promise general pensions for teachers, and it made no recommendations for their provision in the future.

However the Committee of Council itself decided to make a small concession by restoring pension eligibility to those teachers who had entered the profession before 1862—subject to the pre-1862 limit that the total cost of this should not exceed £6,500 a year. In 1884 that financial limit was removed altogether in regard to pre-1851 entrants, but was retained for those who had come in between 1851 and 1862. Those who had entered the profession since 1862 were still without assistance.

Thanks to these moves, the amount spent on pensions began to rise sharply in the last years of the century. The age limit which applied was sixty for a man and fifty-five for a woman, and those covered, apart from being employed as certificated teachers in an elementary school prior to May 1862, had to have been recommended by the Inspector and the managers of the school at which they worked. The pension was paid half-yearly and, as noted above, the number awarded was unlimited for those who had 'entered on the charge of a school before 1851'. Teachers who had entered between 1851 and 1862 continued to be restricted—so that under the Code of 1890, there were available seventeen pensions of £30 each; eighty-six of £25 each; and 129 of £20 each, plus £340 for donations or special gratuities. In that year the sum so expended amounted to £5,580.[53]

But in the meantime the London School Board had from 1885 been examining ways and means of establishing a pension scheme for its own teachers and this led in 1891 to a special London School Board Superannuation Bill being introduced into the Commons. There it was submitted to a Select Committee, which had instructions to review the whole pensions issue. Although the Committee recommended the rejection of the London Bill, in the following year it urged adoption of a *national* superannuation scheme. In reaching this decision its members may have been influenced by evidence like that of Ernest Gray, a London headmaster and chairman of the Parliamentary Committee of the National Union of Teachers. On 15 March 1892, he informed the Select Committee that 'England [was] the only country of Europe, with the exception of Spain and Norway, which [was] without a superannuation scheme for its teachers; . . . In Belgium the teachers pay nothing whatever towards their pension fund'. While George Kekewich, the secretary to the Committee of Council, considered there should be a small pension of £50 per annum assured to every teacher 'to prevent the scandal of those who have taught for many years being practically chargeable upon the poor rate'.[54]

Under the Select Committee's recommendations, a fund was to be established by the State to which male teachers would contribute £3 a year and females, £2, interest at 3 per cent being guaranteed. 'In addition to the annuity purchased from these contributions, each teacher should on reaching retiring age also qualify for a pension at the rate of 10s. per annum for each year of service.' Compulsory retirement was to take place at the age of sixty for men and fifty-five for women, as provided for under the existing piecemeal provisions. The plan followed the line taken by NUT representatives before the Committee and the union campaigned strongly for acceptance of the recommendations. Eventually on 24 February 1893, the Commons agreed without a division that it was 'desirable that a national state-aided system of superannuation for teachers in public elementary schools in England and Wales should be established at an early date.'[55] Shortly after, the government appointed a Departmental Committee to consider the 1892 Select Committee's recommendations. This second body reported in 1894 and after the seemingly endless round of discussion and debate the Elementary School Teachers' (Superannuation) Act was passed in 1898, based broadly on the findings of the two most recent Committees, although with sixty-five set as the retirement age for both men and women.

The new legislation came into operation on 1 April 1899, and applied compulsorily to all certificated teachers who entered the profession after that date, although those already employed had a choice whether to take advantage of the scheme or not. Uncertificated assistants were not covered. In the event, just over a quarter of certificated teachers in service decided not to accept the offer, partly because by doing so they subjected themselves to a compulsory retirement at the age of sixty-five, and the 'obligation to contribute to the deferred annuity fund, while if they did not accept it, they could remain in employment till death, or till their employers dispensed with their services'.[56] For those who did join, annual contributions of £3 for a man and £2 for a woman were required, with the proviso that if average salaries increased by ten per cent or more, the contributions were also to be increased, while the whole question was in any case to be reviewed after seven years. At the age of sixty-five, a contributing teacher was entitled to an annuity based on his contributions to the appropriate fund, plus a superannuation allowance from the Treasury at the rate of 10s. for each complete year of recorded service, just as the 1892 Select Committee had suggested.[57] Disablement pensions, too, were allowed of up to £20 a year for men with ten years' service—plus one additional pound for each year of service above ten; for women the total was £15, with 13s. 6d a year added on for extra periods of service.[58]

The proposals, though hardly generous, were supported by the NUT as a means of establishing the principle that teachers were public servants *entitled* to superannuation—something for which they had been fighting for almost thirty years. Later, pressure could be exerted to improve the level of payments.

And despite the smallness of the allowances under both this and earlier schemes, some at least of those who received them were grateful for their good fortune. John George, who had been a student at Culham College in 1853, thankfully informed the principal in January 1899: 'The Committee of the dear old

College will rejoice to learn, that the *First* Student . . . to quit your walls, after working 44 years, 7 months in Church Schools, has been awarded a Pension by the Department. . . . I am still in good health, and though too old for the Government, could still undertake *non* Departmental work: If any member of your Committee, can put me in the way of earning a small sum to augment my present income (£25) I shall be thankful for the suggestion. I am not in want of money, but am anxious to make some provision for my wife and family (3 sons).' At the time of writing he had reached the retirement age of sixty-five.[59]

Another former Culhamite, Edmund Barfoot, was rather less enthusiastic. When writing to the principal in August 1900, he noted that the superannuation he was receiving, 'with a trifle from the Annuity Fund, is £45 16s. 4d., not half the salary I had been receiving, and now I have house rent and rates to pay. It is rather a small income, but still it might be much worse, and with health and strength, I hope to be able to keep the Home for my wife and self. . . . So far, I have managed to increase my income a little by private teaching.[60] No doubt he also derived consolation from the fact that in *pre*-pension days his position would have been a good deal more parlous.

8

Bread and Butter Issues

> Trained teachers would be far more satisfied with their profession and their social position than they usually are, if those who have to do with them would talk less about the high dignity of their calling, and show more by their practical conduct that they have a real sense of it.
>
> Evidence of the REV. J. W. BLAKESLEY, vicar of Ware, Herts., to the *Royal Commission on Popular Education (England)*—the Newcastle Commission—in *Parliamentary Papers* 1861, XXI, Pt V, 90.

> 'He who can, does. He who cannot teaches.' George Bernard Shaw.

One of the major aims of teachers in the second half of the nineteenth century was to improve their standing in society—to obtain recognition for themselves as members of a respectable profession, able to mix on terms of equality with solicitors, clergymen, bankers and others in similar occupations. Yet the battle was an uphill one, not merely in the field of social relationships, which has been touched upon already, but in the economic sphere as well. The origins of the elementary teaching profession, lying as they largely did with men and women who were too old, too sick or too inefficient to earn their bread in any other way, served to detract from the achievements of their mid-nineteenth century successors. Significantly even those closely concerned with education shared many of the reservations on their status. Thus the report of the British and Foreign School Society for 1846, in discussing the brief period of tuition received by most students at the Borough Road training college, concluded sadly that an extension of that period beyond six months was, under present circumstances, most unlikely :

> The time devoted to preparation *for any work* will always be regulated by the amount of personal or pecuniary advantage,

by the money or the position in society, which, if not immediately attainable, may yet, one day, be hoped for, as the reward of labour and talent, diligence or devotion. But the employment of a teacher does not as yet offer these inducements to enterprise or ambition. It is a profession which has no prizes; and under such circumstances, it is not to be expected that any large number of persons can be found willing to devote *much* time to preparation for its duties . . . while the office of an elementary teacher is so little respected, its mortifications so many, its emoluments so small; while no link, however slight, unites the village school and the professor's chair . . . and nothing but the love of learning, the love of children, and the love of doing good remain, as inducements to adopt or to retain the office of a teacher : so long, your Committee are convinced, preparatory training will be imperfect, and permanent attachment to the work comparatively rare.[1]

Even at government level, among those responsible for the administration of the elementary school system there was little interest in, or concern for, the teachers and their charges. According to Sir George Kekewich, who entered the Education Department in 1868, as an examiner, and who became its secretary in 1890 : 'The staff of distinguished and aristocratic scholars from the Universities treated elementary education and elementary teachers with contempt. Their cherished creed was that no education mattered or was of any real value except classics and mathematics. . . . They had no use for village Hampdens.'[2]

Small wonder that more than one country teacher should bewail the fact that 'society' had 'not yet learned how to value them'.[3] On the other hand, a number did accept their inferior status with humble resignation. Among them was John James Graves, a founder and first president of the National Union of Elementary Teachers, who primly declared in his presidential address in 1870 : 'What is the use of men sighing and pining for elevated society—for the company of squires and clergy—if they are not fitted for it?'[4] In his obituary, written in 1903, Mr Graves was said to have always displayed humility towards those whom he considered his 'superiors' in village society : 'To him, the village schoolmaster was a dependent, or retainer, of the squire or parson, or both; not a gentleman among gentlemen.'

Graves remained master of the small parish school of Hanging Houghton in Northamptonshire for more than fifty years. He was not college trained and this may have heightened his sense of inferiority.

But increasing numbers of his colleagues were less prepared to accept this lowly position. Instead they pressed determinedly for what they felt was their rightful place in society. Their discontent took a variety of forms. Firstly, there was bitterness against those who seemed to be thwarting their claims or treating them in a manner they deemed unsuitable. This found expression in the writings of such men as James Runciman, a former student of Borough Road college who subsequently took an external London University degree and then turned to journalism until his premature death, at the age of thirty-nine, in 1891. In *Schools and Scholars*, which was published in 1887, Runciman described in thinly disguised fictional form what had clearly been his own encounter with a local clergyman. Of the hero, Palliser (i.e. Runciman), he declared :

> He knew he was a scholar; he had been brought up a gentleman; at home he was accustomed to consort with refined folk, and, even in London, he was mentioned in certain educational circles as a man who might have been Senior Wrangler. And now this squeaking being [the clergyman] presumed to talk to him as if he were addressing a peccant workhouse boy.[5]

Runciman may have displayed undue sensitivity, but there can be no doubt that clashes did occur between teachers and those well-to-do members of society who saw them as trying to move 'above their station' just because they had received a college education or were employed in a 'white collar' occupation, when their parents and grandparents had been labourers, craftsmen or small tradespeople.

Out of this situation there arose complaints that teachers were conceited or were setting themselves up as 'second-class ladies and gentlemen'. Among the critics was a former HMI, Dr Frederick Temple, who in evidence to the Newcastle Commission claimed that they had 'too exalted a notion of their own position and of what they have to do and that they gradually acquire a sort of belief that the work of a schoolmaster is the one great work of the day and that they are the men to do it'.[6]

Not surprisingly, the question was also taken up by other Inspectors at around this time, and in his report for 1854–55 one of them, the Rev. H. L. Jones, displayed little sympathy with the pretensions of the profession, declaring: 'The teacher who is not pleased with his social position, and lends an ear to the insidious suggestions of periodical publications, calculated only to render him unhappy and dissatisfied, should throw up his employment at once, and give place to men of humbler minds, whose hearts would be in their work, and who are the only persons who can raise the profession of the schoolmaster in public estimation.' He conveniently ignored the fact that past humility had done little to 'raise' the teacher's position or to bring him greater financial reward. On the other hand, his colleague, the Rev. W. J. Kennedy, took a more charitable view, accepting the justice of some of the complaints put forward on teachers' occupational prospects. He admitted that although qualifications had been improved, thanks to the introduction of the certificate system, status had not advanced proportionately: 'The dissatisfaction to which I refer, is, I think, two-fold; partly at the low rate of remuneration, and partly at the want of social status and influence. . . . By the stimulus and aid of the Committee of Council on Education all that is necessary is being done, in order to form the master before he teaches. What I venture to believe is not yet done, nor in the course of being adequately done, is the providing due honours and rewards for him when he is compelled to cease from his laborious vocation.'[7]

A third Inspector, the Rev. M. Mitchell, agreed with this: 'If medals and crosses are considered prizes worth all price by those engaged in defence of the country, I see no reason why they should not be equally valued and stimulative to those who make that country worth preserving. The patient labour of a man who toils to raise up a troop of young children for the great battle of life, may be compared . . . to that of the officer who labours to perfect the discipline of a regiment for the war.'[8]

These varying opinions were discussed by the educational journal, *The School and the Teacher*, in October 1855, when much resentment was expressed at HMI Jones's remarks. The magazine denied that the schoolmaster was trying to 'elbow and wriggle himself into the company of his superiors'. Instead he wished 'to render his own professional name a badge, not of inferiority to all men, but of honor [*sic*] . . .' It, too, took up HMI Mitchell's suggestion with regard to medals as a reward for service : 'We have military orders, legal and clerical degrees, titles to adorn our scientific men, and gratify our artists, is it impossible to devise an hononary reward for the educator, or are his labors [*sic*] of less value than any of these? . . . What in short the teacher desires is, that his "calling" shall rank as a "profession", that the name of "schoolmaster" shall ring as grandly on the ear as that of "clergyman" or "solicitor", that he shall feel no more that awful chill and "stony British stare" which follows the explanation that "that interesting young man" is only the "schoolmaster".'[9]

But this was only one aspect of the status battle. Another was concerned with the relations which existed between the teacher and his or her school managers. That affected not merely the appointment and dismissal of teachers—matters which were considered in the last chapter—but their supervision whilst they were employed. Daily visits by managers to a school were quite common, and in some parishes, like Chevening in Kent, there were rules that the classes were to be open to 'all persons desirous of inspecting or visiting the same'. Similarly at one Wiltshire school in March 1875 no less than nineteen different people visited the school in a single day, with a disruption of normal routine only too easy to imagine.[10] Nevertheless an active interest in the school by its managers was encouraged, particularly by the National Society, who saw it as a means of keeping teachers alert and enthusiastic. Much the same approach was advocated by HMI Blakiston in his book, *The Teacher: Hints on School Management*, first published in 1879 :

Where managers have a due sense of their grave responsibilities, they will take every care that religious teaching receives the thought and attention which its paramount importance deserves.

Such managers would no more leave everything to teachers than would the colonel of a regiment leave all to its adjutant and subalterns. They will depute one of their body to inspect the school daily, if possible, inquire into absenteeism, insure and test accuracy of registration, enforce cleanliness and tidiness, give advice and encouragement to their teachers—exercise, in short, a real and thorough supervision.[11]

But perhaps most resented by teachers was the right of *outsiders* to examine the scholars when they wished. William Wright of Folkingham School indignantly recorded in his diary for 30 January 1852 : 'Monstrous! . . . [The Managers] came to a Resolution that eight Parishioners form a Committee . . . to examine the Free Scholars.—*Not at my school* but privately at their own Homes or somewhere and Report to the Trustees their opinion thereon.'[12] Five days later came the bitter comment : 'The Blockheads' Committee met at 6 and adjourned to the Greyhound inn to examine the progress of some who have left School 7 years.' However Wright outfaced his critics—including what he called 'the Lies and Libels of the Blockheads Committee and Boys, Parents &c.'—at a meeting on 15 December in that year. He defended himself strongly before the trustees, noting in his diary, with satisfaction, that he 'went and soon decided in one Hour all they had done in two hours. They'd not a leg to stand on.'

At Bedhampton in Hampshire, though, the mistress seems to have felt sufficiently incensed over the 'examination' issue to resign her post. On 7 November 1874, Mr Snell, a member of the school board who had earlier been involved in the illegal employment of one of the pupils, reported that he had tested the children in the three 'r's' and that : 'the reading . . . was unsatisfactory . . . the writing from dictation was unsatisfactory as to spelling but that the children wrote legibly and with ease and . . . in the arithmetic two or three children were correct but most were wrong'. Nevertheless it would seem that in this case there was some justification for the criticisms, for the next head reported that 'owing to the backwardness of the children in dictation and arithmetic those subjects [should] be substituted in the Timetable for geography and grammar during the remainder of the present School year.' Her proposals were accepted by the board.[13]

The managerial right of interference was also strongly disputed by *The School and the Teacher*, in January 1855 :

True the master is the servant of the school managers, he is engaged by them to perform certain duties; but he is supposed to be competent to their performance, or he would not be engaged. We claim only that for the teacher, which every gentleman concedes without questioning to his lowest menial. Who ever heard of a gentleman telling his cook how to do the work of the kitchen? or, where, we would like to know, is the competent cook who would not resign rather than submit to such interference? Let the same be conceded to the teacher and we are satisfied.

But if anxiety to improve the standing of the teaching profession in the eyes of society at large and clashes with school managers over the running of a school were two aspects of the status question, a third related to the desire of elementary teachers to be free to move up the promotion ladder to better-paid employment elsewhere. Here three areas received particular attention, namely the desire to take holy orders and enter the church; the wish to enter the inspectorate; and the desire to become teachers in middle-class grammar and endowed schools. Of the three, the most controversial and widely discussed was that relating to the inspectorate, since teachers were by no means united over this issue. From the beginning inspectors had been recruited primarily from graduates of the older universities. They were men who by family background and education had little in common with either the staff or the pupils of the schools in which they worked. Many of them, especially during the 1870s when their numbers increased rapidly from 62 in 1870 to 134 ten years later, were very young when they obtained their first appointment. Or, as one disgruntled teacher put it, they had come 'fresh from the university' and had 'never seen the inside of a public elementary school, and . . . were babies in arms when I entered it myself'.[14] Initially there were demands that teachers should be appointed as sub-inspectors, to work alongside the HMI; but soon, as the question became one of prestige, pressure was exerted for their right of appointment to the full inspectorate.

As early as February 1854, there were some teachers, like J. J. Farnham of London, who were calling for 'every office connected with education' to be 'open to the elementary schoolmaster'.[15] But others adopted a more equivocal stance. *The School and the Teacher*, for example, in October 1854 firmly demanded the promotion of elementary teachers to these positions: 'The fittest persons to be appointed inspectors of schools are men who have made the education of the young their daily study, and have spent their best days in practising what they have learnt.' But by August 1861, its attitude had changed, and it now expressed the view that teachers in general would not approve of this development: 'Unenviable would be the position of those who accept the office. Their antecedents would be commented upon, their decisions would be impugned, and an unfavourable report given by them would be compared with what they themselves had achieved when elementary teachers. . . . In what a painful position would he be placed when called upon, as he must necessarily be, to adjudicate upon the merits of a school conducted by an intimate friend, who is possibly a worthy man but a poor teacher.'[16]

Some argued too, that school managers would not treat an inspector who had risen from a lower rank in society than themselves with the respect which the office demanded, and this view was supported by the Newcastle Commission itself:

> As to the specific complaint that [teachers] are not made inspectors, we think that they would not be fit for the office. It is absolutely necessary that the inspectors should be fitted, by previous training and social position, to communicate and associate upon terms of equality with the managers of schools and the clergy of different denominations. It is one of the alleged grievances of the schoolmasters that these persons do not recognise them as social equals; and that state of things, with which no public authority can interfere, is in itself conclusive against the suggestion that they should be made inspectors.[17]

Other critics considered that the limited academic background of elementary school staffs fitted them poorly for a position which demanded the capacity to examine the broader aspects of educational development. Even James Runciman, critical though he was of teachers' inferior status, nevertheless felt it would be 'a sorry day for education' if all HMIs were 'promoted schoolmasters', though he did think that every inspector should be 'a practical teacher. Let the young honours men from the universities be required to teach in school during at least a year before beginning their duties.'[18]

The controversy over whether teachers should or should not be

14. The written excuse for absence.

15. An Oxfordshire school, built 1854.

16. Another Oxfordshire school, built 1838.

17. Mrs Frances Bowkett graduating mid-1890s.

18. Good attendance medal.

Oxford Diocesan Training College,
CULHAM.

⬤ General Rules ⬤

FOR THE DIRECTION OF STUDENTS IN RESIDENCE.

1. Students must not go out of bounds, except after dinner till the following times:—on Sundays till 6 p.m.; on Wednesdays and Saturdays till 6.30 p.m.; on other days till 4.30 p.m.

The whole of the Quadrangle corridor is within bounds, so also is the Lane at the back of the College from the garden gate to the Railway Bridge, and the Eastern front Paddock. Both the Entrance Drives and the School Path are out of bounds. Those parts of the College grounds which are always out of bounds are shown in a plan in the Entrance Hall.

Students must not walk or study in the Grounds or the Lane after dusk.

2. No Student may absent himself from Chapel or Hall without permission of the Principal, or (in his absence) of the Vice-Principal; nor from Lecture without the permission of the Lecturer. Strict punctuality is required.

3. No Student may go to the Dormitories during the day, except at the hours stated on the notice board, without the written permission of the Vice-Principal, or (in his absence) of the Senior member of the Staff in College.

4. Every Student must retire to his cubicle immediately after prayers at 10 p.m.

No Student is allowed to have a light in his cubicle, except the General Monitor, the Dormitory Monitor on duty and the Bell Monitor. It is strictly forbidden for any Student to enter the bedroom of another at night; nor may he do so during the day except with the occupant's permission, and when the occupant is himself present.

The lights in the Dormitories are extinguished twenty minutes after retiring; the Monitors may have their lights till 11 p.m.

Strict order and quietness must be observed in the Dormitories at all times; no noisy conversation is allowed, and all conversation must cease when the Dormitory lights are extinguished.

Before leaving their bedrooms in the morning Students are required to strip their beds, and to open the window.

No boxes or luggage may be kept in the Dormitories.

5. In the Dining Hall, Lecture Rooms, and Dormitories, the Monitors are held responsible for order, quietness, and neatness, and Students are required to respect and support their authority. No Sporting materials are allowed in any of the College Rooms.

6. All Students are required to take some form of active exercise every afternoon.

7. It is strictly forbidden to enter any Public house for any reason, in Culham, Abingdon or the neighbourhood.

8. Smoking is not permitted in any part of the College buildings, except in the Common Room at stated hours, and in the Hut.

9. Students may not make or retain any acquaintances in the neighbourhood of Culham without the Principal's knowledge and consent.

10. Students are required at all times when away from College, whether in term or vacation, to conduct themselves in an orderly and gentlemanly manner, remembering that the reputation of their College is in their hands.

A. R. WHITHAM,
Principal.

19. Rules for training college students.

. The criticism lesson.

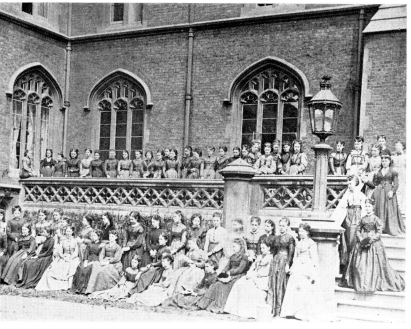

. Women at Westminster College, *c.* 1870.

22. Westminster College orchestra, 1888.

23. A dormitory cubicle at Cheltenham Training College, *c.* 1904.

24. Girls in the laboratories at Cheltenham.

5. The Common Room, *c.* 1912.

26. John James Graves, first president NUT.

27. Three headmasters on strike, 1914.

appointed to the inspectorate rumbled on for the rest of the century. It was, needless to say, an issue in which the National Union of Elementary Teachers quickly became involved. As early as the fourth annual conference in 1873, the president bluntly declared:

> The promotion of teachers to the inspectorate is one of those questions the justice of which commends itself to every thinking mind. [Yet] . . . we have gentlemen who have entered on *another* calling, brought from the profession of their choice to take the prizes of *our* profession. . . . The great difficulty in our way is the system of patronage. Lucrative posts, with pensions attached, are convenient gifts in the hands of Government officials, and hence all our energies . . . will be needed to ensure success.[19]

His successor returned to the topic in the following year, pointing out that while 'the head of the clergy is a clergyman, the commander-in-chief a soldier, the Lord Chancellor a lawyer, it is manifestly unfair that the schoolmaster should be debarred from forming part of the inspectorial staff.'[20]

Nor were the comments on patronage entirely sour grapes. For some of the inspectors clearly owed their preferment at least in part to their friends and connections. Thus the Rev. C. J. Robinson, appointed to the inspectorate in 1859, had beforehand been a curate at Hatfield, the home parish of the Marquis of Salisbury, who was at that time Lord President of the Committee of Council on Education. Another appointment in the same year involved a friend of the Lord President's son. Eight years earlier Matthew Arnold, perhaps the most eminent of the Inspectors, had been promoted through the influence of the then Lord President, Lord Lansdowne, to whom he had been acting as private secretary for three or four years. Arnold wanted to marry, and it was to provide him with a secure livelihood that Lord Lansdowne made the recommendation. Yet, as one of his biographers has noted, at the time of his appointment 'he had few qualifications for the post. . . . Rugby and Oxford did little to prepare him for the problems of giving the working classes basic instruction, and his only teaching experience was a few months with the Lower Fifth at Rugby.' When he took up his office he was ' "a very gentlemanly young man with a slight tinge of the

H

fop" and a reputation for flippancy'.[21] Neither attribute would appear particularly appropriate for his new career. A fourth beneficiary was A. J. Swinburne, who secured his position in 1875 'through the patronage of the Duke of Richmond which was procured for me by Lady Wynford, a friend of my aunt Mrs Vicars'. But perhaps the frankest admission of the use of influence was made by E. M. Sneyd-Kynnersley, who freely conceded that he owed his appointment in the early 1870s to the fact that his father was friendly with a member of the Cabinet in Gladstone's first administration, during 1868–74. These cases were by no means isolated. Even the Treasury felt it necessary to warn the Committee of Council in January 1876 that with the large increase in the number of inspectors it was 'more than ever desirable to act on a system, which will secure that in every case of nomination . . . there is clear & sufficient evidence of the possession by the nominee of qualifications fitting him for the post he is to occupy'.[22]

Nevertheless, despite the continuance of these underlying causes of resentment on the part of teachers, some changes were made in the inspectorial system following the introduction of the Revised Code of 1862. Thanks to the extra examining duties now placed upon the HMIs, a new grade of inspector's assistant was recruited to help with the mechanical aspects of examining, although with no general powers of inspection. These assistants were to come from the ranks of the certificated teachers. Each Inspector who was to have a helper nominated a possible candidate, who was obliged, in turn, to meet certain qualifications. He had to be under the age of thirty when appointed—in 1886 this was raised to thirty-five—had to pass a qualifying examination conducted by the Civil Service Commissioners, based on the sixth standard of elementary school work, and was paid at a considerably lower rate than his senior colleague. In the early 1860s assistants received a basic salary in the range of £100 to £250 per annum at a time when the full inspectors secured £200 to £600 a year, plus a £250 annual allowance to cover travelling and other expenses. Yet despite the limitations, the new posts proved popular, not least because they offered a pension on retirement at a time when elementary teachers themselves had lost the opportunity for this under the Revised Code. By 1871 twenty-eight inspectors' assistants had been appointed. Indeed, after the 1870 Education Act had been implemented, numbers leaped to 116 by 1880 and 150 by 1885.[23] Most of them had worked in big urban schools before their promotion rather than in lower status country districts, with their limited opportunities for advanced work.

Among members of the teaching profession these poachers turned gamekeepers were regarded with dislike and suspicion. For all too often they were inclined to borrow 'the tone and grandeur' of their HMI in dealing with former colleagues, even though their own official role was a humble one.[24] F. H. Spencer, who was a pupil teacher at a Swindon school during the early 1880s, remembered them arriving on the first morning of the examination 'arrayed in frock coats or black morning coats and top hats, with Government satchels filled with examination schedules and arithmetic cards'. In the afternoon they took the finished papers off to mark 'at the second-rate hotel they patronised. Only HMI himself stayed at the "Goddard Arms". He seldom arrived at the school until 10 a.m., and often did not appear till the second day of the examination'.[25]

Occasionally, even with these comparatively lowly positions, patronage reared its head. Although in December 1884, in a gesture towards open competition, the Education Department ceased to require nomination to the post of assistant to be made by an HMI and also raised the qualifying standards, that did not eliminate the problem. Among the new conditions were that candidates must have a first-class certificate gained after two years' training and must be head teachers. Nonetheless, exceptions were made. One such was F. S. Marvin, who in 1890 obtained a vacant assistantship largely through the influence of his friend and mentor, the barrister and positivist thinker, Frederic Harrison. Harrison knew the Department's secretary, Patric Cumin, and intervened with him on Marvin's behalf early in July 1889. His protegé came from a middle-class family and had been educated at St John's College, Oxford, before going on to teach in board schools at Oxford and at Bow in East London. But he had been teaching for only about two and a half years when he was nominated for the assistantship; in addition he ran into difficulties with the qualifying Civil Service examination he was required to take, only succeeding at the second attempt. Not until January 1890 did he take up his post as assistant. About two years later, at the instance of the Department's new secretary, George Kekewich, he was raised to a full inspector—the first assistant ever to be so promoted. Not surprisingly his sudden elevation ahead of older and more experienced colleagues caused a good deal of resentment. One critic noted in *The Schoolmaster* of 20 February 1892 : 'it is well known that . . . the rules of the Department were flagrantly and openly broken to admit him into the inspectorate, although his position in the certificate list was far from good, and notwithstanding that he cut a sorry figure at the Civil Service examination'. In fact a question was even asked in parliament over the issue.[26] Among Marvin's friends and fellow assistants, feelings were mixed, as one former colleague indicated when he offered his congratulations :

> How delightful it must be to be lifted out of a position which by our Secretary's showing is destitute of dignity, and devoid of responsibility. Your apotheosis will prove a great, and perhaps legitimate grievance to most of our colleagues . . . I shall not be one of the aggrieved, but in all future discussions will do my best to justify the action of the Dept., *in this case only.*[27]

Another assistant was rather more bitter : 'till the natural ossification by class feeling sets in, pray let me know how you get on & what are your "impressions" from your Olympian standpoint?'

W. H. Pullinger, a teacher friend from Bow, was also cautious in sending his good wishes :

> I think that under the present system of appointing Inspectors, of which you know I am not an upholder, the appointment is the very best that has been made, as you are the only Inspector that I ever heard of who has had *real* experience in school as well as experience as an Inspector's Assistant, & in the eyes of teachers these experiences will count for more than the highest University qualifications. I suppose however it is your somewhat unique position, as holder of these, to the Department, essential qualifications in addition to your experience, that you owe your promotion. I think it will appear in this light to the N.U. grumbler, of whom I suppose I may be taken as a fair representative, there will be no suggestion of jobbery & if there be any complaints which I doubt they will be directed against the system & not against you in particular.[28]

Pullinger was not to know that at the time of Marvin's original appointment Frederic Harrison had sought—and obtained—assurances from Cumin that taking up an assistantship 'would not stand in the way of [his] advancement to a full inspectorship'. In this casual fashion Cumin was promising to overturn the hitherto sacrosanct departmental policy of not recruiting inspectors from among assistants because of their allegedly limited educational background and the fact that they often approached their work 'in a narrow technical spirit'.[29]

However, about a decade earlier, in 1882 a small step *had* been taken to meet the aspirations of the assistants by the creation of the new position of sub-inspector, to be recruited from among the most senior of them. The appointment carried with it many of the duties of the HMI himself, although the sub-inspectors remained under the overall jurisdiction of the inspectors to whom they were attached. By 1888 thirty-six of them had been nominated, though it was not until 1893—following the Marvin controversy—that the first of these was promoted to the full inspectorate. Then, between 1894 and 1902 six ex-elementary teachers were similarly advanced. But the gain was to prove short-lived. In 1901 the whole system was reorganised once more and further hopes of promotion from the elementary ranks were shattered. As Asher Tropp writes, under the new dispensation: 'No more sub-inspectors were to be appointed. . . . instead a new grade of "junior inspectors" was instituted. By November 1901 it was obvious that the department intended the junior inspectors to be recruited solidly from Oxford and Cambridge.'[30] In taking this élitist line it was probably following the wishes of the old-style HMIs. Certainly in 1892 one of them, T. G. Rooper, who was a friend of Marvin (and owed his own appointment to the patronage of the Duke of Bedford), wrote to congratulate the younger man in terms which expressed little sympathy with the ambitions of elementary teachers:

> I am really delighted with the news . . . I felt much discouraged by the reception which Kekewich gave you some time ago & I feared that he was perhaps going to . . . disconnect Elementary Education & the Universities. Now I believe in the Universities & if men say there is not much learning in them (which I deny) at any rate elsewhere there is none at all. If the

teachers want to be made inspectors, they must get a University Training.[31]

Not until 1913, following further changes, were the junior inspectors themselves replaced by a fresh class of assistant inspectors, who were to be recruited from qualified elementary school teachers with at least eight years' teaching experience—some of this, if possible, as a head teacher.[32]

Nevertheless that belated concession did not satisfy the NUT. As its president sourly pointed out in 1914, the conditions attached to the upgrading of fifteen of his elementary colleagues showed 'that it [was] but a grudging concession after all. The upward limit of forty-five years of age means that the position is not regarded as the natural, but as the merely incidental, outcome of teaching'.

However, some of the coolness on the part of the Union may also have been due to a conflict which had arisen three years earlier between its members and the Board of Education, over the inspectorial role. It had developed over comments made by the Chief Inspector for Elementary Schools, Mr E. G. Holmes. In a confidential memorandum concerning local inspectors employed by individual education authorities, mostly in the larger towns, Holmes had mentioned the fact that the majority of these men were ex-elementary school teachers, whom he classed as 'uncultured and imperfectly educated' and as 'creatures of tradition and routine', incapable of tackling the problems of elementary education with the 'freshness and originality' shown by men 'of the Varsity type'.[33] It was decided to distribute this memorandum, marked *Strictly Confidential*, to over a hundred of Her Majesty's Inspectors for their information. But a copy somehow reached Samuel Hoare, Conservative MP for Chelsea, and when he disclosed its contents in the House of Commons on 21 March 1911, it provoked a political storm. The NUT leaders were touched on a particularly sensitive nerve by this crude denunciation of their colleagues and it was largely as a result of their pressure that the Board of Education's permanent secretary, Robert Morant, was eventually forced to resign. For it was he who had signed the order to print and circulate the memorandum, and his generally arrogant and abrasive temperament had already made him many enemies among the teaching profession. Holmes, the author of the circular, had resigned in November 1910, before the controversy blew up. Although with the departure of Morant much of the ill-feeling died down, it is likely that for some time a residual bitterness and suspicion of Board of Education attitudes remained to sour relations between the central administration and elementary staffs.[34]

This unsatisfactory outcome to the long debate over the role of teachers in the inspectorate perhaps justified the unenthusiastic comments of *The School and the Teacher* made as early as 1861 :

> The appointment to some thirty or forty inspectorships, tenable for life and dependent . . . in no small degree upon influence and patronage will be but a sorry illusion for the thousands of teachers, all equally well qualified for the post, but for whom room cannot be found.

However, that journal's own solution to the promotion problem was not very fruitful, either. It suggested that outlets should be sought in the schools of the middle-classes and that instead of positions being filled by the clergyman 'unfitted for the pulpit' or 'the man with barely sufficient ability to pass the ordeal of the College examination', lucrative posts as heads of endowed schools should be taken up by elementary teachers : 'The parents of the middle classes are longing to obtain better education for their children, they are ready to receive us as their co-helpers, and who can dispute that they have the power to accomplish their desire?'[35]

Despite these optimistic comments, relatively few teachers were able to gain secondary school posts, although by 1914 it was thought that about one-third of the men and one-fifth of the women in grant-earning secondary schools had either begun as elementary teachers or had received an elementary training. But for most ambitious men and women, the best that could be hoped for was a headship within the elementary system itself.

Outside the sphere of education more opportunities did exist. Especially in the early and mid-Victorian years, when literacy levels were still low, the man who could read and write fluently and handle figures easily, was much in demand in business, and there was a steady flow of teachers into posts as company secretaries, accountants or senior clerks in commercial undertakings. As a writer in the *Quarterly Review* pointed out in September

1846, until conditions inside the schools were improved, increased training facilities for teachers meant that the colleges might 'turn out nurseries for railway clerks'.[36] This was confirmed by HMI Watkins in 1861, when he declared that schoolmasters had 'many offers of clerkships, receivers' and accountants' places made to them with higher salaries and less responsibility than their present posts.'

Training college records confirm the trend—as at Peterborough, where of 591 schoolmasters trained over the period 1859 to 1885, thirty-two had abandoned teaching for business or one of the commercial professions by the later date. Likewise at Westminster College, of thirty-one men trained in 1862–63, five had left to go into business within a few years.[37]

For those able to obtain senior clerical posts, career and salary prospects could be good. With the North and South Wales Bank, for example, the salary for a first appointment as branch manager in the 1850s and 1860s was about £150 per annum, rising to perhaps £500 or £600 per annum, while head-office posts, such as those for tellers or corresponding and security clerks, could yield between £150 and £250 a year. In fact, B. G. Orchard in his survey of *The Clerks of Liverpool*, published in 1871, concluded that men working for banks, insurance offices and other public companies would 'reside in a fairly genteel neighbourhood, wear good clothes, mix in respectable society, go sometimes to the opera, shrink from letting their wives do household work, and incur, as unavoidable, the numerous personal expenses connected with an endeavour to maintain this system. At 28 years of age they receive about £150 and hope some day to reach £350 or more'. Even lowlier clerkships, averaging £80 a year 'and unlikely ever to exceed £150', might prove attractive to some teachers in country schools— especially when allied to the 'gentlemanly' status which attached to clerical positions.[38] Only at the end of the century, following a general growth in literacy levels and an increase in the number of smaller clerkships did that position change, as the salary and status of elementary teachers began to improve and that of the minor clerks to diminish.

However, perhaps the most deeply felt ambition for many male teachers, particularly those trained at Anglican colleges, was to take holy orders and enter the church. Francis Forss, head of the Earl of Radnor's School at Coleshill, gave this as one reason for resigning his post when he wrote to his patron in April 1853 : 'I think of entering some College for two or three years so as to qualify myself for the church, and then take Holy Orders; and under the blessing of God to become Curate of some village Church. . . . And in that sphere, I hope to have another opportunity of carrying out our system of education, & of proving to others what can be done . . . I am convinced that more may be done by the clergy than by the Government . . . [I] trust under the blessing of God, I may yet have an opportunity of doing much good'.[39] In his case the ambition was achieved, for after studying at King's College, London, he was ordained a priest in 1858, at the age of thirty-six, and by the mid-1860s had become perpetual curate (later vicar) of Winsley with Limpley Stoke in Wiltshire, at a stipend of £160 per annum—as opposed to just over £90 per annum secured as headmaster of Coleshill. Forss remained at Winsley until his death in 1892, by which time his income had risen to £284 per annum and he was assisted by a curate at £60 a year. Nor did he forget his earlier educational interests for soon after his arrival in the parish he set in hand the provision of an efficient school, often putting 'his hand in his pocket' to cover its outgoings.[40]

It will be remembered, too, that in Thomas Hardy's novel, *Jude the Obscure*, the motive of Richard Phillotson in leaving his small country school for a post near Oxford was so that he might become a university graduate and then be ordained. Although he did not achieve his aim—even his secondary hope of entering the church as a licentiate was frustrated—others, like Forss, fared better. This is borne out by training college records. At Peterborough eleven of the 591 schoolmasters trained between 1859 and 1885 had taken holy orders by the later date, while at Culham, there was also a steady trickle of students who were eventually ordained. Even those who did not meet with the approval of the Culham principal whilst at college might be able to make the transition later—like the Welshman 'who after all the time he has been here, is yet so utterly provincial that he would be unfit for any school out of Wales. Rather given to smoking & not wanting in cleverness—but very uncouth & rustic.' Yet this 'rustic' Welshman was ordained in 1870, less than eight years after he left Culham, and became a B.D. of Lampeter College in 1887.[41] An even more unsuitable character, who was admitted to the college in February 1873, had to be expelled just over a year later when he was 'detected in writing letters of a most disgraceful character to a dormitory maid'. Nevertheless, he managed to pass his acting teacher's examinations whilst in employment and was appointed to a school in Radnor. Five years later, in 1880, he was ordained deacon by the Bishop of Winchester, a development which aroused the ire of the Culham principal, who debated whether or not the question of his 'moral fitness' should be raised with the appropriate authorities. Subsequently this particular candidate became for a time a Unitarian minister, before returning to the church in 1897. Happily most of those who moved from the profession of teacher to that of clergyman had a less eventful career than he.

Yet these developments were little more than straws in the wind and for the mass of teachers the 'status' problem persisted, with prejudice against the profession particularly strong among the comfortably off middle classes, who perhaps feared the rise of a new 'meritocracy'. As late as May 1899, Harold Hodge, writing in the *Fortnightly Review*, could contemptuously describe the average elementary teacher as 'not likely to be a person of superior type'. In his view, the schoolmaster was a 'small middle-class person . . . with all the usual intellectual restrictions of his class. He is, in other words, unintellectual, knowing hardly anything well, parochial in sympathies, vulgar in the accent and style of his talking, with a low standard of manners. He is withal extremely respectable, correct morally, with a high sense of duty, as he understands it, and competent in the technique of his calling. . . . The existing elementary teacher is a competent instructor within very narrow limits; he is usually not much more. . . . What is wanted is educated ladies and gentlemen as teachers . . . At present, elementary school teaching is not thought a good position—it is not recognised as a "liberal" profession—ladies and gentlemen are not expected to take it up. The sentiment—about as false as sentiment could be—could easily be removed by the action of those in high places socially.'[42]

Even in the new century the middle and upper classes had not entirely lost their hostility towards the 'pretensions' of the profession. In July 1903, Winston Churchill's 'bugbears', according to Beatrice Webb, were 'Labour, NUT and expenditure on elementary education or on the social services'.[43] Many others shared that attitude. Yet, at the same time, teachers *were* making advances in public esteem, especially in country areas, where they gave leadership in social organisations and on parish councils. While, as C. F. G. Masterman wrote in 1909, they were also

> raising families who exhibit sometimes vigour of character, sometimes unusual intellectual talent. A quite remarkable proportion of the children of the elementary schoolmasters is now knocking at the doors of the older Universities, clamouring for admittance; and those who effect entrance are often carrying off the highest honours. This process is only in its beginning; every year the standard improves; these "servants of the State" have assured to them a noteworthy and honourable future.[44]

In achieving that goal there remained the important question of financial reward. In January 1840, in their first *Instructions to the Inspectors*, the Committee of Council on Education had stressed that one of the tasks of the HMI when visiting a school was to ascertain 'the probable amount of stipend' of the head teacher, since the total emoluments 'ought to be such as will enable a well qualified Schoolmaster to live in comfort and respectability, if he devote his whole time to the duties of his vocation'.[45] But the investigations of the Inspectors were soon to show that that was far from being achieved. As the Rev. John Allen, the first of the HMIs to be appointed, wrote in the early 1840s: 'If the village schoolmaster is worse paid than the village carpenter or blacksmith, what hope is there of finding any but the most incompetent person in the former situation?'[46] And in 1845 he reported that of 340 schools he had visited in the Home Counties he had found only one master earning as much as £100 per annum.

A year later, with the issuing of the new education Minutes providing for additional payments from the government to certificated teachers, salary levels for qualified staff began slowly to improve. Under the 1846 provisions the augmentation grant varied, for men, between £15 and £30 a year, according to the length of their training and the standard at which they had passed their certificate examination; for women, it ranged between £10 and £20 per annum. However, these sums were only payable if the trustees and managers of the school provided the teacher with a rent-free house and a salary 'equal at least to twice the amount of this grant'. So the minimum pay of a male certificated teacher ranged from £45 to £90 a year and for a female, from £30 to £60. Uncertificated men and women were, as before, left to make their own arrangements with their managers, and these might be very poor indeed. A former woodman, who left Winchester diocesan training college in 1848 to take up the headship of a small school in Hampshire, was paid £20 per annum only, plus the children's pence, 'after the first 50'. While a twenty-year-old colleague who had previously worked as a shop assistant received £40 for 'self & sister with house & perquisites', when he became head at another small Hampshire school.[47] They were not alone in their unhappy financial fate.

Just over a decade later, however, the Newcastle Commission's investigations showed that the average salary of a sample of 3,659 certificated masters was £94 3s. 7d., while for 1,972 certificated mistresses the average stood at £62 13s. 10d.[48] Uncertificated masters' salaries averaged £62 4s. 11d. and uncertificated mistresses', £34 19s. 7d. Although these payments—as regards the certificated teachers—were higher than the minima envisaged by the 1846 Minutes, there were considerable regional variations, so that a certificated master in a church school in Cornwall, Devon, Dorset or Somerset might average just over £81 per annum, while his counterpart in Lancashire and the Isle of Man secured almost £100 per annum. And the Newcastle Commission itself recognised that pay was still a prime cause of dissatisfaction. This, however, it complacently attributed to the fact that teachers' remuneration 'begins too early and rises by too steep gradients':

A lad, the son of a day labourer earning 10s. a week, finds himself at the age of 20 in the receipt of £80 or £90 a year. A young lawyer at that age is beginning his professional education. At 22 the young schoolmaster is probably earning £100 or £110 a year. The young lawyer is earning nothing, and does not expect to pay even his professional expenses till he is 30. But the schoolmaster may never earn more. He reaches in early life a table land, and may tread it till he dies. If the emoluments of the young schoolmaster were smaller, those of the older schoolmaster would appear greater, and there would be no complaint of the absence of promotion.[49]

But most teachers would no doubt have retorted that few 'young schoolmasters' were earning £100 or £110 a year, even on the Newcastle Commission's own evidence, while the upper salary achieved by the lawyer was likely to be very much in excess of that attained by even the most efficient elementary school teacher.

Furthermore, in countless schools, managers were only too anxious to pay their staff the lowest rates possible, and this added to the uncertainty of the salaries position, especially following the implementation of the 1862 Revised Code with its ending of all government augmentation grants. Rural school managements in particular responded to this by making part of the teacher's income dependent on the school's success—or lack of it—at the annual inspection. And this was an approach welcomed by some of the HMIs, including the Rev. H. W. Bellairs, who declared : 'It seems important that a teacher should have a sufficient part of the income fixed to meet necessary expenditure; and at the same time should have some pecuniary interest in the success of the school'.[50]

As a consequence of the changes, the average annual salary of certificated teachers dropped—in the case of men, from £94 in 1860 to £87 in 1865, and for women, from £62 to £55 over the same period. Not until the end of the decade was the upward movement resumed.[51]

Around these 'averages' there were naturally wide variations, according to the skill, age, sex and qualifications of the teachers themselves, the size of their schools, and the resources of their managers. In 1873, for example, the incumbent of Groby, Leicestershire, advertised for a certificated master at a salary of £45 a year, with 'a good house and garden', half the government grant and 'half the fees and night-school pence'. A colleague from Hanborough, Oxfordshire, in the same year, also advertising for a certificated master, offered £80 a year and one-eighth of the grant. Only experience would show which bargain was the better, although most teachers preferred the security of a high basic payment, rather than the uncertainties of a share in the school grant or the children's pence.[52] And where economy was the order of the day, women teachers would normally be employed. In March 1873, one typical appeal for a certificated mistress was at an Essex school for 130 children. The salary offered was a mere

£50, without any share of the grant. For an efficient male teacher almost double this rate would have been needed.

Yet, despite the variations, once the initial impact of the Revised Code had been lost, the salary rates of most masters and mistresses edged slowly upwards again, particularly after 1870, when the new Education Act increased the demand for teachers. By the late 1880s the Cross Commission was commenting that the average salary of a certificated master was £120 per annum, and of a certificated mistress £74 per annum. Even an ex-pupil teacher acting as an assistant mistress could expect to earn in the range of £35 to £50 a year by the later 1880s—at a time when the general retail price level was falling. The Commission also noted with approval that the system of variable salaries, with grant sharing and children's pence, was now giving way to that of fixed payments. Under the old regime, in the Commission's view, the result of relating salaries to the amount of grant received had been 'to make the teacher "look upon the school as a money-producing machine", and very much to increase the teacher's anxiety in view of the annual examination.'[53]

In bringing about these improvements the National Union of Elementary Teachers played but a limited role, since it was unable to exert pressure on the vast number of separate school boards and management committees who comprised the employers of its members. However, in 1893 the annual conference of the Union passed a resolution favouring direct action to increase salaries 'and suggesting the formation of a special sustentation fund for teachers "who refuse to work for a miserable pittance" '. But when the local associations were asked to approve a proposed levy of 3s. per member to finance the fund, the idea was rejected by a majority of more than five to one.[54] The Tenure Committee met with similar failure when in September 1898, it tried to discover how many of its female members were earning less than £45 per annum and of its male members less than £70, for a government report had shown that in 1897 there were sixteen certificated headmasters earning less than £50 per annum and 626 receiving between £50 and £75 per annum; of the headmistresses, 64 earned less than £40 a year, while 143 secured between £40 and £45 per annum. By January 1899 a number of low salary members had been located, but Union efforts to encourage them to ask for a rise in pay—coupled with an offer of financial support should this be needed—were unsuccessful. The individuals concerned probably shrank from the publicity that would inevitably attend a 'test' case, and so the Tenure Committee had little choice but to let matters rest.[55] Increasingly, therefore, the Union saw greater financial support for elementary education from the central government as the only way to deal effectively with the salaries issue.

Meanwhile, the pennypinching life endured by the low salaried teacher is brought out in the correspondence of Miss Rose Knowles, the uncertificated head of the small Thorpe Malsor school. Miss Knowles was also helping to support her widowed mother, who was a dressmaker in London, and her anxieties show through many of the letters she wrote to the latter, as on 13 February 1888 :

> I don't know which way to turn. I cannot let you have a sovereign but will send as much as I can when I get it. You must tell Mr B. you will pay him up between this & the 28th of the month perhaps you will have an order & be able to pay some of it yourself. As soon as I get mine I will send what I can ... I could have gone out to a tea party & dance the other evening for 9 pence but had not got it so could not go.

(Mr B. was probably George Bushnell, her mother's London landlord.) Again, on 28 March she noted that she had sent her mother 'seven shillings & paid away all the rest. . . . All my coals are gone again I had to pay half of them away & have not any more till next November. I should have paid in money but could not. I knew how I should be.'[56] When Miss Knowles lost her position in June 1888, she was forced to accept an even more badly paid post in another small Northampton parish—which she herself described as 'a village about Noah's time'—as the only alternative to destitution. Her mother was to leave London to live with her, but even this economy was not sufficient to allay her fears : 'If I should not suit what we shall do I do not know. I shall always be worrying. . . . The worry over one thing & another has [made] me feel quite ill, be sure & come nicely dressed else I shall send you back again.'[57]

With the passage of the 1902 Education Act, however, NUT pressure over the salaries question intensified. Following the creation of the local education authorities it now became the

Union's aim to press for the introduction of salary scales to replace the old haphazard system of payments which had shown such wide variations from one school to another, even within the same county. It also sought to bridge the gap which had hitherto existed between the salaries paid in rural areas, where teachers' organisations had been weak, competing employment opportunities limited and financial resources small, and larger urban school boards, where the monetary position had been more satisfactory. Thus in Devon in 1903, when the new local education authority took over, there were only three headmasters in the whole county who earned £150 per annum or above (two in voluntary schools and one in a board school); no Devon headmistress earned £90 per annum, although twenty-five earned between £80 and £89 a year—and two, at the other end of the spectrum, under £50. Similarly in Oxfordshire there were only ten headmasters, all in voluntary schools, who earned £150 a year or more; and although twenty headmistresses, again in voluntary schools, earned £90 per annum or more, there were four, at the other extreme, who earned less than £50. By contrast, the *lowest* rate of pay for the headmaster of the smallest school under the Leeds School Board was in the range £150 to £175 a year, while for women the minimum range was £90 to £100. In other words, the *minimum* rates in Leeds in almost every case exceeded the *maximum* rates in Devon and Oxfordshire. Before the local education authority was set up the average salaries of Devon's adult *assistant* teachers—usually women—had been £45 for certificated, £40 for uncertificated and £27 for supplementary teachers. The new scales introduced by the county council were substantially in excess of these, so that a trained certificated male assistant earned in the range £80 to £110 a year and his female counterpart £70 and £95, while for the uncertificated assistant, the rates were £55 to £75 and £40 to £60 for men and women, respectively. Even female supplementaries were placed on a scale of £20 to £45 per annum.[58]

Certain of the local education authorities resisted the pressure for better pay, however, and there were even unsuccessful attempts by some adjacent authorities to reach joint agreements to keep salaries low. But progress was clearly being made. And in 1913, at a time when retail prices were increasing once more, a special Salaries Committee was set up by the NUT to 'formulate and put into operation, a national campaign to secure the adoption of the Union Scale of Salaries'. The venture met with considerable success, and there was an improvement in pay in 149 out of 321 local authority areas.[59] Nevertheless it was becoming clear that only a *national* scale, backed by state resources, would answer the teachers' needs and finally eliminate the problem of the cheeseparing authority. That step was not achieved before 1914.

In their efforts to secure improvements in members' incomes just before the first World War, the leaders of the NUT ran into difficulties with some low wage authorities—the most notorious of them being Herefordshire. As early as 1904 the Herefordshire teachers had pressed for the introduction of a salary scale in their county, but without success. Then in the summer of 1913 the matter was taken in hand by the NUT. When the authority refused to meet the teachers' demands, almost 240 of them placed their resignations in the hands of the Union executive, threatening a mass withdrawal of labour from the schools at the end of January 1914 if no concessions were made. Although negotiations continued up to the eve of the strike, agreement proved impossible. So at the beginning of February more than sixty schools in the county were closed by Union action, while the local authority's attempts to recruit replacements for the striking teachers proved largely unsuccessful. In their stand the latter enjoyed a great measure of public support, including that of the Bishop of Hereford, who as early as December 1913 had written to the Board of Education appealing for help in settling the dispute :

> For the sake of the children and for the credit of the County, which is low enough educationally, I am very anxious to see a settlement arrived at, but I feel quite helpless in the matter as neither side seems at all in the mood to make any concession. My own opinion . . . is that the teachers have a reasonably good case and that a scale might be granted to them. Our L.E.A. contains members on whose arbitrary discretion I should be very sorry to be dependent for an increase of stipend if I were a teacher, and so I think the teachers need the protection of a scale.[60]

Even the Board of Education itself, although anxious to maintain a neutral stance, reminded the local authority of its duty 'to adopt such a standard of remuneration and such a reasonable procedure for dealing with grievances as will enable them to secure for their area a constant supply of efficient Teachers'.[61] And in a further letter, written after the strike had commenced, the Board's President noted : 'I think the Teachers feel, not without some reason, that the procedure of the Education Committee has not worked well or fairly for them in the past . . . I have myself had some investigations made from the Returns in the Office for the last 9 years . . . It appears that, out of 106 Head Teachers who have served in the same Department throughout the 9 years, 59 had till quite recently received no increment at all. . . . It also appears that only 87 out of the 320 persons who have served as Head Teacher in the County during the period have received any increment.'[62]

On 10 February a meeting took place in London between the President of the Board and a representative of the local education authority, at which a rough salary scale was drawn up, and after further negotiations the dispute was at last settled on 25 February. Significantly, agreement was only reached after the secretary to the Board had sent a further letter warning that if the dispute continued 'the Board's exercise of its ordinary powers is bound to result in an ever-increasing loss of Grant to the Local Education Authority'. In the same letter he also expressed blunt reservations on the authority's approach to the dispute :

> The teachers so managed the controversy as to enlist the sympathy of practically everybody except the local ratepayers. There had apparently been little of that personal knowledge or contact between the Education Committee and the teachers which in Westmorland (which is also an area of small schools) has enabled the authority to keep its teachers contented. The practical consequence of your bad tactical position is that you have now to pay a good deal more heavily to get out of it than you would have if the justifiable discontent of the teachers had been tackled in good time.[63]

The NUT President later referred to this intervention by the Board as 'epoch-making'.[64]

As a result of the agreement, the minimum salary for a male head of the smallest Herefordshire schools, i.e. those with up to fifty pupils, was fixed at £100 to £120 a year, and for females in the same category at £90 to £110; in the next group, with between 51 and 100 pupils, the rates were £110 to £140, and £90 to £120, respectively. Further gradations followed, until in schools with 121 pupils or more a minimum salary of £140 a year for men and £120 for women was established. Certificated male assistants were at the same time to be paid £85 to £130 a year and certificated females, £75 to £110, with annual increments of £5 for 'good service' payable, in all cases, within these ranges. Reinstatement was offered to the striking teachers and there is little doubt that the NUT felt satisfied at its first attempt at mass industrial action in support of a pay claim. For prior to the dispute there had been at least sixteen headmasters in Herefordshire earning less than £100 per annum, and the education committee itself had boasted of having the lowest elementary education rate in the whole country.

The Herefordshire children, too, had joined in the dispute by refusing to be taught by 'black-leg' teachers imported by the local authority to replace the strikers. As the *Daily Citizen* reported early in February, it was 'a strike within a strike, for the children would not work. In some cases they locked out the new teachers and organised demonstrations for the old. Disheartened masters and mistresses gave up the task in despair, and the children held high revel.' In one village the scholars filled a black stocking with straw and fastened it to the door of the replacement headmistress's house 'thus signifying their contempt for a "black-leg", as the *Daily News* put it.[65] At Bromyard the school managers attended to escort the children into the building, and a policeman stood guard outside to keep an eye on those who boycotted the proceedings. But it was at the small towns of Ledbury and Ross that the worst scenes of violence occurred. Here riots took place in the schools, with desks overturned and ink spilt, while notices in support of the striking staff were chalked on the walls of the school buildings and elsewhere within the town. At Ross, the new teachers employed at the boys' school were pelted with turfs and other missiles, as were the police who were sent to maintain order, while some of the pupils who had been rounded up and marched into the class rooms, escaped again by climbing through the windows. The *Hereford Times* called 'the disturbance and chaos which prevailed in the boys' department' at Ross 'almost beyond description'. And Archdeacon Winnington

Ingram of Bridstow Vicarage was one of several people who wrote to the Board of Education in alarm, pointing out that: 'Nearly every qualified teacher, who has applied for a post, has resigned as soon as he became aware of the position, and the children in the towns are rioting, and refusing to go to school! . . . *Somebody* must intervene, and that soon, or the children will suffer irreparable damage.'[66]

Significantly, the national press, which had been sympathetic to the teachers' case throughout the dispute, also welcomed its eventual settlement. According to the *Manchester Guardian*: 'The Herefordshire teachers have won handsomely in their fight for better conditions, and their victory will be generally popular.' While in the view of *The Nation*: 'The most satisfactory strike news of the week comes from Hereford, where the teachers have won their battle, and extorted from the County Council a reasonable scale of salaries. The battle has been short and sharp, and the result excellent, not only for the Herefordshire teachers, but for education generally.'[67] To members of the profession it must have seemed that at last their importance within the community was receiving the recognition which most of them felt it had always deserved.

9

Combination and Trade Unionism

There is plenty of work for Teachers to do, both individually and collectively. Our profession is made up of a multitude of individuals, and the character of the whole takes its colour by reflections from the characters of its several units. . . . All must be united; we must join together, first in our local associations, and secondly in an aggregate of associations. We must remember that our character, our interest, our independence, our prosperity, are all in our own hands. If we want to have any power in educational matters, we must think for ourselves, speak for ourselves, act for ourselves. . . . If we want anything, we must try to get it for ourselves and trust to our own energies, our own exertions, and use our own best efforts.

From an address by JOHN J. GRAVES, Master of the Lamport & Hanging Houghton Endowed Charity School, Northamptonshire, and first President of the National Union of Elementary Teachers, at the Union's first conference on 10 September 1870.

Elementary teachers, of all other professions, are by the nature of their employment called upon through the natural instinct of self preservation to join together in some bond of Union and fellowship. There are special conditions in the vocation we have chosen, which render us liable to fall victims to petty tyranny of many descriptions. Comparatively isolated and scattered as we are, the teacher as a single unit counts for nothing in the eyes of those possessed with a little brief authority. Often he is regarded as the legitimate drudge of the parish, as a fit and proper recipient of the venomous spleen of an irate parent. . . . These are . . . dangers lying in the path of every teacher . . . against which the only effective remedy is combination.

The Culhamite, November 1892, 72.

FROM THE early years of the teaching profession it was customary for some of its members to meet together informally to discuss problems connected with their day-to-day working life, or with their economic and social conditions. Later more formal structures were established. There was, for example, a mutual improvement group organised in 1712 for teachers in Bath, 'that they might consult the best methods of teaching their children'.[1] While in London a Society of Schoolmasters was instituted in January 1798 with the object of establishing 'a fund for the benefit of the widows and children of deceased schoolmasters, and for the occasional relief of such schoolmasters themselves as age, infirmity, or misfortune may render incapable of pursuing their occupation.'[2]

In the mid-1830s London-based teachers in connection with the British and Foreign School Society likewise began to organise for self-improvement purposes, meeting quarterly for the reading of papers at Borough Road College. And in 1838 a small group of the city's *church* schoolmasters decided to follow their example : 'Each undertook to read in his turn an original paper on some topic connected with teaching, which was to be followed up by a friendly discussion.' Out of these latter gatherings there developed the Metropolitan Church Schoolmasters' Association, which by 1843 claimed a membership of over 150 and 'a regular code of laws and a full staff of officers. The association held monthly conferences, owned a reading room and library, organised occasional lectures, series of lectures and regular classes for instruction and incorporated small district associations'.[3] In this it enjoyed the support of both the National Society and the London Diocesan Board. While at Portsea in Hampshire by the late 1840s the church schoolmasters had formed an association 'for mutual improvement' which met 'every Saturday for the purpose of preparing for [the] . . . General Examinations for Certificates of Merit', i.e. for the acting teacher's certificate examinations to which they had been admitted from March 1847. Their initiative was welcomed by Kay Shuttleworth at the Committee of Council and he warmly praised the 'admirable and useful object' which they had in view. However their appeal for financial help to buy textbooks and equipment to aid their studies was regretfully rejected : 'their Lordships' of the Privy Council had no funds which could be applied 'towards the general expenses of such an association'.[4]

Whilst these activities were under way among town teachers, in country areas, where the profession was more scattered, the initiative tended to come from the clergy or from Her Majesty's Inspectors rather than from teachers themselves. Asher Tropp quotes the case of the Bath and Wells diaconal board of education which resolved in February 1842: 'That the schoolmasters and mistresses within the deanery, whose schools are conducted on the principles of the Church of England, be requested, with the permission of the several parochial clergy, to form themselves into an association to be governed by rules framed by the board'. Shortly afterwards the first annual meeting was held and the Schoolmasters' Union for the Bedminster Deanery, Diocese of Bath and Wells was duly launched.[5] It was claimed that one of 'the chief though unobtrusive advantages of this union . . . is that it is an opportunity of showing and strengthening the union of mind and heart between the clergy and the gentry on the one hand, and the body of schoolmasters and mistresses on the other . . . although assigned to different ranks of life, we meet on these occasions as brother church people, engaged in one holy work'.

A similar motive led to the holding of an educational conference of parochial clergy and schoolmasters in the Oxford Diocese during the summer of 1856. At its inaugural meeting the chairman, a local clergyman, stressed that its aim was to consider how clergy and teachers could 'best carry on the work in which we all have so large and common an interest—this *Christian training* of the young.'[6] But it is clear from the nature of the papers presented that a substantial part of the enterprise was concerned with the raising of teaching standards, too. Among the lectures given was one on 'Order in Schools', and another on 'Detail in School Management'. Shortly afterwards the Oxford Diocesan Association of Schoolmasters was formally set up to promote educational improvement and to organise annual conferences.

A little earlier than this, in February 1854, the Hampshire Church Schoolmasters' Association (or the Hampshire Church School Society, as it soon became) had developed under the auspices of the Winchester Diocesan Board of Education, with the headmaster of Winchester College as its chairman. From the start all clergy, schoolmasters, schoolmistresses and their assistants in the county were eligible to join, while annual conferences were to be held. These latter would commence with a service in the Cathedral and would then proceed to lectures and discussions, terminating 'with a conversational tea meeting'. Prizes were to be offered each year for the best essay on a selected topic written by a master and a mistress, respectively.[7]

In East Yorkshire the first attempt at professional organisation was the Hull and East Riding Schoolmasters' Association established in 1823, with the aim of assisting aged and infirm members and of providing pensions for their widows and orphans. There is no indication of its membership or of its duration but it was soon followed by other local bodies which, like their contemporaries elsewhere, were connected with the Church of England.[8]

In its early days this combination movement was encouraged by Her Majesty's Inspectors. Thus in February 1854, HMI Brookfield, speaking at the annual dinner of the Metropolitan Church Schoolmasters' Association, proposed as the toast of the evening, 'Prosperity to the association'. He expressed pleasure 'that the time had arrived, when the schoolmaster, at the close of his day's toil could put on his hat, and, crushing it down, exclaim, "By the grace of God, there is a man under it." The advantages of an association like the present [were] numerous, and would, amongst other things, help to shew every man his real position. . . . They were of benefit also in promoting the intellectual improvement, and independence of the schoolmaster, and in assisting to raise his status in society.' Brookfield concluded his speech by 'urging the desirableness of multiplying associations in every part of England'.[9]

In the East Midlands, also, HMI Blandford welcomed their appearance, 'so long as the work of the teacher, and not the teacher . . . is put first. The formation of these associations is so far satisfactory as being an indication of life, and of an anxiety on the part of the promoters for mutual improvement; their success and usefulness will be in proportion to the prominence given to the discussion of subjects strictly connected with the profession of a teacher, and of those "common things" which should be taught in elementary schools'.[10] In this cautious approach he was following the line of the Committee of Council itself. In 1852, R. R. W. Lingen, its permanent secretary, had warned the inspectors against encouraging schoolmasters' meetings which were 'employed for purposes of general discussion, and not simply for mutual improvement in technical and professional matters . . . I am instructed to add emphatically that it is Their Lordships' wish that HM Inspectors should not encourage the idea of independent action and deliberation on the part of

Teachers, by correspondence with them in collective capacities, or as independent of the Managers of their several Schools.'[11] Presumably it was feared that such activities might encourage school staffs to an unhealthy self-reliance or to rebellion against their subordinate position in the school hierarchy!

But by that date efforts were already under way to extend the scope of the organisations into a national movement. The immediate cause of this upsurge of interest was a Committee of Council Minute, issued in 1852, which gave the clergy the right to dismiss a teacher 'on account of his or her defective or unsound instruction of the children in religion, *or on other moral or religious grounds*'. It also bestowed on them the right 'to suspend such teacher' pending reference of the matter to the local bishop, who now became the final arbiter in the matter. Some of the more militant London teachers immediately formed a Committee of Metropolitan Church Schoolmasters to oppose the measure and began to appeal to church teachers throughout the country for support. Deputations were organised from a number of country associations and eventually in April 1853 the offending Minute was cancelled by the Committee of Council, which was now under a new Liberal government.

Although the teachers' hostility was not the sole cause of this retraction—Nonconformists and the Liberal Party had also played their role in condemning the 1852 developments—to members of the profession it seemed that their unified action had resulted in a positive achievement. For the first time, too, they had acted 'not only in independence of, but also in opposition to, the clergy.'[12]

By the spring of 1853, therefore, the Liverpool and Manchester church schoolmasters' associations were taking the initiative in pressing for a national union, and eventually at the end of December in that year the first annual meeting of the 'General Associated Body of Church Schoolmasters in England and Wales' (usually shortened to ABCS) was held in London. A membership of 400 was claimed, with eighteen local associations sending representatives, including those from rural areas like the Isle of Wight and West Hertfordshire, while seven other groups signified their support without sending delegates. The president was, appropriately enough, a Liverpool master, Mr A. Boardman, since it was he who had helped to set the whole enterprise in motion, while the treasurer was Mr B. Simpson of Northampton, and the secretary, Mr J. J. Farnham of London.[13]

It is noticeable that from the beginning members were anxious to give the impression that their organisation was 'respectable' and moderate in its aims. *The School and the Teacher*, which became the organ of the new association, declared in its first issue in January 1854 that the programme put forward was 'so eminently practical, and there is such a careful avoidance of "controversial" topics in it, and of everything which would lead the friends of the schoolmaster to fear that he was "taking a lesson" from the ignorant and misguided among the labouring classes, and was desirous of forming a schoolmasters' "Trades Union" to enable him to place himself in antagonism to the "powers that be" and organise a gigantic strike (!)—that any surmises of this nature must be completely dispelled, and the promoters will not have the painful feeling that their actions and motives are misconstrued.' This cautious approach was also echoed in an article on the new association which appeared in the journal during the following month, when it was emphasised that the aims of the association were the promotion of the cause of education, encouragement of the provision of suitable books and apparatus in schools, publication of deserving literary papers and essays, and 'to maintain inviolate the principle that religion should be the basis of all education':

> It is *not*, as some few have insinuated, to place the schoolmaster in a position for resisting the will of the clergyman. It is *not* for the purpose of enabling teachers to demand either an equalised, or a higher rate of payment for their services. It is *not* to further the interested views of a party, either political or religious. It is *not* to dictate either to societies or individuals. It is *not* to foster the germs of insubordination and conceit, as some may have imagined. It is *not* for any of these purposes we ask for union.[14]

However, despite these disclaimers some at least of the members took a rather more robust view of the aims that would be desirable in the new organisation. There were calls even at the first conference for the introduction of compulsory education and for a widening of the opportunities for promotion within the profession.[15] And as early as 1853, the ABCS had sent a memorial signed by 725 church schoolmasters to the Committee of Council on the subjects of 'promotion to sub-inspectorships, superannuation and the need for lists of text-books and classification of subjects for the pupil-teacher and certificate examinations.'[16] The memorial was presented to the Committee by HMIs Moseley and Kennedy.

A further problem was to arise shortly afterwards over the role of the clergy within the new organisation. At the beginning of 1855 the Doncaster district association decided on its own account 'that . . . managerial power should be confided wholly or principally to the schoolmasters: it was thought that there would be more freedom of speech and action if the attendance of the clergy were dispensed with at the majority of the meetings'. Several of the clergy members of the Doncaster association agreed with this view and it was eventually decided that clerical supporters should be invited to the four quarterly meetings only, and that the other eight meetings held 'should be exclusively schoolmasters' meetings'.[17] Strictly speaking, this was a matter for the Doncaster association alone to decide, but John James Graves, headmaster of the small village school at Hanging Houghton and leader of the Northampton district association, decided to raise the whole question at the annual conference of the union in 1855. In August of that year he wrote a letter to *The School and the Teacher* mentioning five resolutions which his own district meeting had adopted—number two of which was that 'the clergy would best promote the objects of the Associated Body by becoming members of that body. . . . By admitting the clergy, the schoolmasters would rise in the social scale, and gain the respect of the general public. . . . The pecuniary condition of the society would be greatly improved, and on this thing alone must it depend for attaining several of the objects at which it aims.'[18] The Northampton Association to which Graves belonged had been founded with clergy support in 1846, and met monthly for lectures and demonstration lessons.[19] As with most of the country associations it was very much under clerical influence in its outlook and interests.

Yet however justified on pragmatic grounds Graves's approach may have been, it was firmly rejected by many other teachers. Matthew Shirley of Rawmarch, Rotherham, for example, wrote to *The School and the Teacher* for October 1855, pointing out that the ABCS was essentially 'a church *schoolmasters'* association, founded for the benefit of *schoolmasters* alone; if the clergy were admitted it would lose this characteristic . . . the admission of the clergy would hinder that freedom of discussion so necessary to carry out the objects of the association.' To the Sheffield association of which Shirley was a member 'the pecuniary consideration' was 'too contemptible, grovelling, and servile, to require the slightest comment.' An even fiercer denunciation came from another schoolmaster correspondent in the same issue of the journal. Although he admitted that the clergy deserved respect as spiritual pastors 'that esteem should have its limit, and not descend into a favoring [*sic*], cringing course of conduct so contemptible in the eyes of any man of independent principles . . . if the clergy knew our feelings on the subject they would not be led away by a few fawning sycophants, to imagine that their co-operation is at all desired by the general Associated Body.'

Ultimately, after a long discussion the Northampton resolution was rejected at the third annual meeting of the ABCS, and an amendment passed by a large majority :

> That while cordially recognising the value of the countenance of the clergy, and their co-operation with the teacher, in the education of the young, and while anxious to cherish that important and desirable connection, this meeting is nevertheless of opinion, that the general working of the ABCS would necessarily be impeded by the admission of members of any other profession whatever.[20]

In spite of the length and bitterness of the debate there were no secessions from membership. Indeed, Graves himself became secretary of the ABCS in 1857, while, as Asher Tropp notes, even after the banning of the clergy from formal membership, the district associations continued to invite clergymen to attend as speakers at their meetings. At the annual conference itself proceedings opened with a prayer, and an address from a prominent clergyman was invariably included in the general programme.

Up to 1870, then, sectarian feeling remained sufficiently strong among church teachers to prevent their entering into union with those with whom they had denominational differences. So when on 31 December 1853, the first annual meeting of another teachers' organisation, the non-denominational United Association of Schoolmasters (UAS) was held in London, to embrace 'all teachers (public and private) who acknowledge the essential doctrines of Christianity, and the sufficiency of Holy Scripture, as the rule of faith and practice, and who regard the Bible as the only sure basis of true education', the ABCS refused to co-operate with it. As one member declared in a letter to *The School and the Teacher* of February 1854, agreement was impossible because the united group would never be able to decide 'upon where the religious element should begin or cease in elementary school education; whilst I hold that no education is worth the name without it.' At local level, too, 'circumstances offer almost insuperable obstacles to the uniting in bonds of sympathy and co-operation teachers of different denominations.' Despite initiatives by individual ABCS members, agreement between the two unions proved impossible. Perhaps the church schoolmasters felt that their higher membership—450 as opposed to the UAS's 250 in 1855—gave them greater influence or perhaps the religious differences in themselves provided a sufficient barrier. Another problem was that the UAS had a large metropolitan membership, and for this reason may have become an object of suspicion for the provincial masters and mistresses who made up a major part of the ABCS. From whatever cause, then, unity remained out of reach even when the profession was faced with the challenge of the Revised Code in 1861–62.

The introduction of the payment-by-results system, coupled with the ending of government grants for teacher's certificates and pupil-teachers' stipends, and the dropping of the pension proposals, were all greeted with intense hostility by members of the ABCS. In Northamptonshire, John Graves wrote indignantly to the *Northampton Herald* pointing out that if children came to school regularly 'not one week in four only—any diligent teacher may teach them to read, write, and work sums, if not after the most scientific methods. But when half the children attend only half the school time, no person ought to expect so much as if they attended regularly.' The West Cornwall Schoolmasters' Association took a still stronger line, rejecting the Revised Code as 'unjust and impracticable and totally subversive of all popular education'. After due discussion it passed a resolution 'that each teacher carefully prepare an estimate of the result of the Revised Code upon the Government grants in his own school, and lay the same before the managers, and that measures be taken for convening an early public meeting of managers, and teachers, and the friends of education to discuss the Revised Code.'[21]

But the most forceful response came, as might be expected, from London teachers. Here a Central Committee of Schoolmasters was established, to which secretaries of many country associations—ranging from Northumberland and Durham to Lincolnshire, Cambridgeshire, Cornwall and Shropshire—sent support.[22] And in November 1861 a deputation from the Central Committee visited Lord Palmerston in order to express opposition to the Code. *The School and the Teacher*, too, whilst recognising the importance of 'free and unfettered . . . local action' and of sectarian principles, nevertheless called for a more united approach. It quoted the example of a large friendly society, the Manchester Unity of the Independent Order of Odd Fellows, as a possible organisational model for the profession. This would permit much local autonomy and yet would permit the mustering of mass support when the situation demanded it : 'We trust that one of the "effects of the New Code" . . . will be the consolidation of professional unity.'[23]

But despite these exhortations, the ABCS kept aloof from other bodies. Its membership jumped to over 1,200 from the 600 or so claimed before the controversy began, while the petition it presented to Parliament on the issue had 4,519 signatures. Yet although the government made some minor concessions from its original proposals—so that children under seven were now to be exempt from the annual examinations in the three r's which were to be taken by their older fellows—the major principles of the measure remained intact. The teachers' struggles had been in vain. And for that they never forgave Robert Lowe, the vice-president of the Committee of Council, whom they blamed, not entirely justly, as the architect of the scheme. When he died in 1892, aged eighty-one, *The Schoolmaster* reported maliciously : 'It is enough that Robert Lowe lived to see his specific for the improvement of Popular Education utterly discredited on all hands; lived to see the Primary School Teachers—once flouted with contumely—exercising their rightful influence in the educational politics of the country.'[24]

The first reaction of the profession to the 1862 humiliation was to blame their organisations for the ineffectiveness of the protests. The old Metropolitan Church Schoolmasters' Association and the AUS both seem to have been destroyed in the struggle while the leaders of the ABCS were attacked as cliquish and dictatorial. Graves resigned as secretary of the organisation in 1863, only to resume office three years later, when some of the bitterness of defeat was beginning to subside. But for a time the ABCS seems to have confined its central activities to the holding of annual conferences, leaving the district associations to their own devices.

Yet despite their defeat, elementary teachers' organisations were not entirely inactive in these years, for between 1862 and 1867 they 'played an important part in the first stages of the movement for professional self-government' by co-operating, for a time, with the College of Preceptors, a middle-class organisation of private school teachers formed in 1846. The aim was to establish a Scholastic Registration Association which would control entry to the profession, along the lines of the General Medical Council, by providing a register of qualified teachers. Significantly, this interest in professionalisation was also being matched by other groups, like the chartered accountants, who were incorporated in 1875 and the bankers, who followed suit four years later. Among the elementary school associations giving support to the idea of professional self-government in the 1860s were those for Essex and Suffolk, and for Norwich and East Norfolk. Unfortunately the clash of interests between the elementary staffs and the supporters of the College of Preceptors, who considered themselves socially 'above' their colleagues and yet were without any recognised certificate of efficiency, made worthwhile discussions between the groups impossible. The attempt at cooperation collapsed and in 1873–74 the Scholastic Registration Association itself was wound up.[25]

In the meantime, though, as the disappointments of 1862 lost their sting, interest began to rise once more in the elementary teachers' own organisations. In 1866 the ABCS decided to form a committee 'to devise plans to make the association more worthy of the support of teachers.' A circular was sent out to all teachers in church schools appealing to them to unite in one effective body. This action led to the ABCS being attacked for seeking to revive sectarianism when what was needed was a general union of *all* teachers. But Graves rejected the charge. He pointed to the failure of the non-denominational UAS and the survival of his own organisation as proving that unsectarian associations were not feasible. At the same time, in accordance with contemporary 'self-help' doctrines, he stressed the sick benefit society proposals which it was intended to incorporate in the remodelled ABCS as a further attraction to teachers. So when the fifteenth annual meeting of the union was held in January 1868, over 600 teachers were represented, and the name of the association was changed to the General Association of Church Schoolmasters.

Nevertheless members were anxious to achieve more than a revamped version of the old society. Dissatisfaction at the Revised Code and its methods remained strong, and teachers all over the country were becoming increasingly aware of the importance of educational politics. At the 1868 general election many of them 'canvassed candidates on scholastic registration, payment by results, pensions and security of tenure'—issues which affected church and nonconformist teachers alike. Although sectarian differences and 'vested interests' slowed down the process of co-operation between the two sectors of the profession, by the early months of 1869 efforts were being made to draw the groups together. Eventually in April 1870 both the ABCS and a committee of Metropolitan teachers put forward schemes for unity, and on 25 June in that year a meeting of about one hundred teachers was held in London 'for the purpose of taking steps to bring about a union among elementary teachers throughout England'.[26]

In these hesitant steps towards unity the Education Act of 1870 itself played a part. By its adoption of the 'conscience clause' for all schools in receipt of government grants—thereby permitting children to be withdrawn from religious instruction if their parents so desired—it paved the way for compromise among the teachers too. The Act also saw the ending of denominational inspection in the schools and in this way, again, it helped to pave the way for a diminution in sectarian feeling. Finally the emergence of a new class of employer, the non-sectarian school board, provided a further push towards unity. So it was that in September 1870 the National Union of Elementary Teachers was born (it dropped the 'Elementary' in 1889), with John Graves of Hanging Houghton as its president.

In his address to the first general meeting of the new body, Graves stressed the importance of the step taken, with elementary teachers for the first time sinking their differences and uniting both for the good of their own profession and for that of education in general. He pointed to the benefits which it was hoped would accrue as a result of the passage of the 1870 Act, but criticised the failure to provide for the additional teachers who would be needed to implement it properly. He also believed that suitably qualified elementary school teachers should be eligible to become masters in grammar schools and to enter the inspectorate —ambitions which, as we saw in the last chapter, had long been dear to the hearts of members of the profession. In addition, teachers should press for necessary reforms to the Code and for a satisfactory superannuation scheme. But most vital of all for the success of the new enterprise was the necessity to banish petty differences and religious controversies:

> We ought to leave off servility, and take a more manly position in matters educational than we have yet taken. To do this we must be content to forego some of our own cherished crotchets. There is still too much of petty jealousy, exclusiveness, narrow-mindedness, and prejudice among Teachers . . . We must trust our own leaders, place ourselves under our own banner, follow our own tactics, fight our own battles against ignorance and crime on the one hand, and personal opponents and prejudicial interference on the other. . . . We inaugurate, in founding this "National Union of Elementary Teachers", no aggressive association. We desire to assail nobody. We do desire to think and act as reasonable and educated men, to advocate improvements in our educational schemes and machinery, to look after the welfare of the nation as far as Elementary Education affects it, and at the same time try to advance our own interests, convinced that by the elevation of the Teacher we elevate the value of education, and accelerate the progress of civilization.[27]

Out of the conference's deliberations, nine basic aims emerged for the new Union:

1. Control of entrance to the profession and teachers' registration.
2. The recruitment of teachers to the Inspectorate.

I

3. The gaining of a right of appeal.
4. Superannuation.
5. The revision of the educational code.
6. The gaining of security of tenure.
7. Freedom from compulsory extraneous duties.
8. Adequate salaries.
9. Freedom from 'obnoxious interference'.[28]

In addition, social benefits of one kind and another were to be established in the course of the next few years. Thus at the 1875 conference the setting up of 'Provident, Benevolent, and Annuity Funds' in close association with the NUET was reported—though the funds were to be administered separately; in the following year an added objective was to 'establish and support an Orphanage for the Children of Teachers'.[29] Eventually the Teachers' Benevolent and Orphan Fund admitted non-union members and provided old-age pensions, widows' annuities, temporary financial aid, and hospital care. The Teachers' Provident Society, a friendly society limited to union members, provided sickness and death benefits. All of these were great attractions at a time when state sickness and pension benefits were not yet available.

Considerable effort was expended in ensuring that the Union remained a non-sectarian body pledged to pursue professional and educational ends only. As W. Osborn, union president in 1872, declared at the annual conference in that year : 'We don't meet here as *Church* teachers, *British* teachers, *Wesleyan* teachers, or *Catholic* teachers, but simply as TEACHERS; and so long as we continue to drop these distinctive peculiarities, we shall be able to show an undivided front, and become an undaunted power for the advancement of our professional interests and aims'.[30]

The central organisation established by the Union comprised a standing committee, whose members were drawn from local bodies of London teachers plus the secretaries of the various provincial associations. Then in 1873 the name of this steering body was changed to executive committee, with the election of most members taking place at the annual conference. Over the years other minor administrative changes followed, but throughout a major role was played by the local associations. These could be formed in a district by any five elementary teachers. By the time the annual conference met in 1871, forty-eight local associations had been established with more than 2,000 members in all; but some of the associations in the more scattered country areas were very small indeed—like that at Kendal in Westmorland, which had only fourteen members, or the East Lincolnshire Church Teachers' Association with eleven members, and the Norfolk British Teachers' Association with nineteen members. With few exceptions, certificated teachers only were allowed to join and those elementary teachers ineligible for membership remained unorganised until the formation of the National Union of Uncertificated Teachers in 1913. Although this policy was part of the NUET's campaign to raise the standing of the profession, it was a potential source of weakness at a time when so many teachers were in the uncertificated category. Indeed, in the early days membership of the Union rose slowly—from 5,054, divided among 107 local associations, in 1872, to 16,100, divided among 356 associations, in 1890. Only in the last decade of the century, when a more dynamic leadership came forward and when there were further discussions over proposed new legislation, was an upward spurt achieved, to a level of 43,621 members in 1900, or about two-thirds of all certificated teachers.[31] By 1914 over 80 per cent of the more than 109,000 certificated teachers in the country had become members of the National Union of Teachers, as it became known from 1889. (The dropping of the word 'Elementary' from the title was part of an attempt to broaden its appeal within the profession.)

As regards the Union's basic aims, the success of teachers in securing all but the first of the objectives set out in 1870 has been discussed in earlier chapters. Suffice it here to point out that only with the passage of the 1902 Education Act was progress made on the sensitive 'tenure' and 'extraneous duties' issues—both of which were of particular importance to country teachers, especially those in Church of England schools. The 'payment by results' system, however, had gone by 1900, and the change in public opinion on this issue was attributed by at least one writer to 'the power of the Union' which had 'entirely changed' the general view. According to him : 'Without a Union teachers could not give *forcible* expression to their opinions; . . . every petty board or committee would have power to dismiss them with impunity; and for punishing an unruly child they would [be] more likely than at present, to be unjustly fined.'[32]

So it was only the ambition to control entry to the profession which remained unrealised by the first World War. And even here an attempt had been made to deal with the problem, with the setting up in 1877 of a sub-committee of the Union to deal with the 'Certification and Registration of Teachers'. As in the previous decade, efforts were made to co-operate with teachers in higher and middle-class schools but again with little success. Indeed in 1879 when a Bill was introduced in the Commons to provide for the registration and organisation of teachers it expressly *excluded* those working in elementary schools from its provisions. The NUET naturally opposed the measure as setting up 'a distinct line of separation between the certificated teachers and all other parts of the scholastic profession'; and, working through its local associations, it put pressure on MPs and the promoters of the Bill until eventually it was withdrawn. 'It was publicly admitted that the Bill had been stopped by the action of the elementary teachers.'[33] And in 1893 when a similar measure was brought forward, again seeking to exclude from the register certificated teachers in elementary schools, the NUT used 'extraordinary efforts . . . to obtain the repeated blocking of the Bill'. Once more it was successful. Nine years later, when a registration authority, the Teachers' Registration Council, at last began to bring a register into force, an immediate point of controversy was that there were to be two columns to the register—column A for certificated elementary teachers and column B for those who were graduates or had an equivalent qualification. So the old animosities were revived. The NUT strongly condemned the 'injustice which [would] be inflicted on the primary teachers of the country by the introduction of the Register in two lists.' In 1907, a year after it had been implemented, the register was abolished and all further attempts at registration proved unsuccessful. As Lee Holcombe notes, teaching remained unique 'among the professions in that an effective professional register was never created.'[34]

But if registration proved beyond reach, in achieving most of its other aims the NUET became a formidable political pressure group. Although country teachers did not, after the presidency of Graves ended in 1871, play a very active role in this, they were nonetheless substantial beneficiaries from its successes. As a gauge of the role of rural teachers in the leadership of the Union it may be noted that up to 1890, Graves remained the sole representative of the country members elected to the executive committee by the annual conference. Then in that year country members began to wage a more determined campaign to draw attention to their special needs. In July 1890 a Federation of Rural Teachers was formed, recruited primarily from NUT members but working independently of the Union itself and with the objective of representing 'the opinion of rural teachers'. Norfolk and Oxfordshire were particularly prominent in this development, and as early as 18 January in that year *The Schoolmaster* published a letter from Francis Gale, honorary secretary of the Norfolk Confederation of Rural Associations, calling for 'a proper and real representation of the rural and semi-rural interests' on the executive committee. There was resentment, too, at the dismissive way in which the poorly paid country teachers were sometimes spoken of by their more prosperous urban colleagues. In the event, two rural candidates were successful, in addition to Graves, at the 1890 election. The new recruits were William Muscott, who had been head of Garsington National School, Oxfordshire, for about twelve years, as well as an active Union member in the Abingdon, Witney and Oxford areas, and J. S. Jenkins of Highworth School near Swindon, who had worked at his school since 1863. A few years later Jenkins himself was, incidentally, to appreciate the problem of insecurity of tenure at close quarters when a newly-elected school board, composed mainly of Noncomformists, decided to dismiss him. For most of his teaching career he had worked in cooperation with the local clergy and as one of the new school board members declared, 'the Church had had an innings for thirty years; it was time the Chapel had a turn'. So at the age of fifty-five, after thirty-two years' service, he found himself out of a job.[35]

In the succeeding years, rural representation on the executive committee made only limited progress. By 1894 there were four country members among the twenty-four elected to the committee, viz. Graves, Jenkins, Muscott and Francis Gale of Norfolk.[36] However the setting up in June 1899 of a special Rural and Small Schools Committee by the parent body did mean that at least by the end of the century a more positive interest was being taken in the special difficulties of country teachers. In particular, the Committee's 'Rural Charter' of 1899 proposed to increase the financial resources of village schools by making 'the cost of Rural Education practically a National charge', instead of its being, as hitherto, partly rate-supported, partly state-supported, and partly dependent on the contributions of local well-wishers and subscribers.[37]

In their more vigorous approach to representation in 1890 the rural teachers may have been influenced by the militant 'new union' movement then burgeoning among dockers, gasworkers, miners and others. Letters in *The Schoolmaster* during the early months of 1890 certainly refer to the need for a 'New Union' for the teachers, too, and to the fact that 'insecurity of tenure' was still their greatest grievance.[38] In fact on 15 November 1890, one correspondent, writing from London, not only observed that 'new unionism [was] at hand', but plaintively asked : 'surely we teachers are not going to be left behind by the miners of Durham and Yorkshire and South Wales'. Significantly, it was also at around this time that the principal union offices were taken over by a new generation of younger, more active men—like J. H. Yoxall (1857–1925), a former Sheffield schoolmaster, who in 1892 took over the general secretaryship, and T. J. Macnamara (1861–1931), who had taught at Bristol and in the same year became editor of *The Schoolmaster*.

Women teachers, on the other hand, played little part in the running of the NUT, even though, numerically, they dominated the elementary teaching profession. In 1894 there was only one woman elected by conference to the executive committee. And although by 1902 this number had increased to five, the executive itself had grown to a membership of thirty-seven as compared to the twenty-four elected in 1894. Only one of the women taught in a rural school. Presumably the women's limited role was due to their diffidence in taking a lead in what was still very much a male-dominated world.

One of the principal ways in which the Union could press for reforms was by direct approaches to the Education Department, using letters, memorials, petitions and deputations. But between 1884 and 1890, during the secretaryship of Patric Cumin at the Department, relations were virtually non-existent, as the Department studiously ignored the NUET's representations and refused to recognise it as a negotiating body. Only when George Kekewich succeeded Cumin were friendly relations restored.

Then, thanks to the new secretary's change of approach, direct relations with the teachers were entered into by the granting, for the first time, of official recognition to the Union and its officers. As Kekewich later wrote:

> From that day until I finally left the Office, my relations with the teachers constantly grew more cordial and intimate, and I owed to the advice of the Union officials, and the expression of opinion and the resolutions passed at the Union Conferences, numerous and excellent suggestions for the improvement, from time to time, of Departmental regulations.[39]

Another method by which the NUET influenced affairs was through pressure on Members of Parliament. One such Parliamentary lobby was organised on the pensions issue in 1875, when 'no fewer than 435 members of the House of Commons [were] interviewed by the officers of the Executive . . . or by representatives of local associations'.[40] The demand for pension provisions had similarly led to organised lobbying in 1872, with delegates from such rural counties as Derbyshire, Pembroke and South Devon among those taking part. In addition, signatures to the pension petition presented to parliament were received from West Cornwall and Kendal, among other areas.[41] And at the parliamentary elections in 1880 and 1885 local associations were requested by the Executive to organise deputations to all candidates. From 1888 a still more systematic campaign was waged:

> A complete register was formed of the constituencies within the district of each local association, of their representatives in Parliament and of "prominent politicians" who were interested in educational matters. These "prominent politicians" were sent information on educational matters and it was hoped that they would act as a further pressure on MPs and prospective MPs. In 1890 'Parliamentary Registers' were prepared in which every promise made by a Member of Parliament was registered for future reference. Parliamentary correspondents were appointed in a large number of constituencies, to keep the executive fully informed as to any educational action taken in the constituency.[42]

Nor was the NUT executive satisfied with reliance on this carefully orchestrated indirect approach to parliamentary influence.

Direct representation was planned as well, and in 1885 it was decided to support two teacher candidates at the coming general election. Neither was successful, but ten years later James Yoxall, the general secretary, became Liberal Member for the Northern Division of Nottingham, and a London teacher, Ernest Gray, who was secretary of the union's education committee, became Conservative member for North West Ham. Both men quickly made it their business to speak on behalf of the Union. In fact, *The Times*, writing on the education debate of 1895, mentioned as 'perhaps the most remarkable feature of the discussion' the 'intervention of the two able representatives of the elementary school teachers who have found seats in the present parliament.'[43]

At local level, the opportunity for direct influence on the composition of school boards was restricted by the 1875 Education Code, which prevented elementary teachers from becoming members of a board. However, ex-teachers and private school teachers *were* eligible. For the rest, it became the task of the Union to persuade non-teacher representatives, where possible, in favour of their policies. But some of the greatest problems arose on the smaller five-member school boards which operated in rural areas. In many cases their members were people who were educationally and temperamentally quite unfitted for their role, and who were often elected solely to keep the rates down. It was in schools under these boards that the cases of oppression and insecurity of tenure which were examined in chapter 7 were most characteristic, and where Union influence on policy was likely to be at its weakest.

Nonetheless, by the early years of the twentieth century the NUT had achieved a good deal. It had a substantial membership —of over 91,000 by 1914, as compared to the 43,621 recorded in 1900—it had three 'representatives' in Parliament, for T. J. Macnamara, editor of the union newspaper, had entered as a Liberal Member in 1900, and it had 'developed its legal work and "teacher politics" to a high degree of efficiency'. Indeed, there were fears among some members of the general public and the press that the Union had become too powerful. As early as 1880 *The Times* had called it 'a Frankenstein's monster which has suddenly grown into full life'. But perhaps an anonymous writer in *The Citizen* best expressed the pros and cons of the union position when it declared in March 1897 :

Some observers resent its activities, dub it a trade union, and charge it with narrowness and party spirit. But, whatever may be the dangers of the situation, there is no doubt that the position which the union now enjoys has been earned by unceasing effort and devoted labour. To it, and almost to it alone, the country owes the destruction of vicious theories about state interference with the work of the elementary schools which were rampant twenty years ago, and are still cherished in a sneaking kind of a way by many people who ought to know better. But victories of this kind are not bought for nothing. Fighters have not the virtues of students, and are apt, indeed, to lose perceptions which are necessary to the most far-seeing statesmanship. 'Every country', says the proverb, 'has the foe it deserves', and when a critic dwells on the failings of the N.U.T., it is well to remind him of the kind of policy against which the Union had so long to protest.

The Turn of the Century

The purpose of the school is education in the full sense of the word: the high function of the teacher is to prepare the child for the life of a good citizen, to create or foster the aptitude for work and for the intelligent use of leisure, and to develop those features of character which are most readily influenced by school life, such as loyalty to comrades, loyalty to institutions, unselfishness, and an orderly and disciplined habit of mind.

The Board of Education's *Suggestions for the Consideration of Teachers and others concerned in the work of Public Elementary Schools*, 1912 ed., 5. This pamphlet was first published in 1905.

The village school, then, has it seems to me a high function to fulfil . . . Its work is national, not to say imperial, rather than parochial. Its business is to turn out youthful citizens rather than hedgers and ditchers; and it should, in its humble way, give a liberal rather than a technical education.

Report of the Board of Education for 1899, Parliamentary Papers 1900, XIX, 254. Report on Oxfordshire schools by EDMOND HOLMES, HMI.

The great thing we always impressed was Character. You must try and impress the children to be honest and upright and truthful. It was Character; in all we did we had to keep that in mind.

MRS FRANCES A. BOWKETT (b.1874), headmistress of Cherwell Infants' School, Banbury, from 1898 until 1927, in an interview with the author, 29 March 1977.

Whatever you earn, try to save something. What you cannot pay for try to do without.

Sentences from the copy book of ANNIE FIGG, a pupil in 1893. Each sentence had to be copied five times.

ALTHOUGH education, even at the end of the nineteenth century, was still seen very largely in moral terms rather than purely academic ones, it is interesting to note how the emphasis on religious instruction—once so pervasive—had given way to a more secular approach by the 1890s. Now 'scripture' lessons were seen as only one part of the training process. In fact, as early as 1874–75 Her Majesty's Inspectors of Schools had been instructed to satisfy themselves that the children were being brought up 'in habits of cleanliness and neatness' and were being impressed with 'the importance of cheerful obedience to duty . . . consideration and respect for others, and . . . honour and truthfulness in word and act.'[1] After 1899, under the newly established Board of Education, this approach was intensified. As one former pupil recalled :

> headmasters and teachers were for many years expected to preach the blessings of temperance, thrift and other virtues. Many teachers took the Board's texts seriously and [I remember] a very able and sincere headmaster who quite usually kept the whole school standing to attention for anything from one half to one hour, whilst he inculcated the virtues of obedience, loyalty, courage and so on.[2]

No doubt much the same motive lay behind the entry in a Lincolnshire log book on 12 February 1897 : 'Our constant effort is to train boys and girls that they have a chance of improving their positions and to be law Abiding Citizens'.[3] School text books, too, stressed the links between education and a virtuous life—like volume 6 of Thomas Nelson & Sons' *Highroads of Literature*. This optimistically began :

> Of all the amusements which can possibly be imagined for a hard-working man, after his daily toil, or in its intervals, there is nothing like reading an entertaining book. . . . It relieves his home of its dullness and sameness, which, in nine cases out of ten, is what drives him out to the ale-house, to his own ruin and his family's . . .[4]

Yet, as the comments of HMI Holmes, quoted above, indicate, some observers saw education as having a still broader function than this. In the last years of the century it became increasingly popular to stress that children were being trained for an *imperial* mission rather than a purely national one. Perhaps this was partly a result of the Boer War, since thanks to the availability of cheap newspapers and the effects of mass elementary schooling, the campaigns waged in South Africa between 1899 and 1902 were eagerly followed even in isolated village communities. One of His Majesty's Chief Inspectors noted its effect in rural Derbyshire in 1901 :

> I cannot conclude this report without adverting for a moment to the war, which has been ever present to the minds of all. It has its awful evils, but in schools it has exercised a very educative influence.
> Maps of South Africa hang on the walls marked with flags indicating position of friend and foe; the route to the Cape has been often traversed; the topography of the Transvaal and Orange River Colonies has become familiar as that of Derbyshire; the names of the actors in the campaign, British or Boer, are—
>
> 'Familiar in his mouth as household words . . .'
>
> and to show that even 'babes and sucklings' have babbled of the war I must relate in conclusion one incident.
> It occurred in a school in a remote Peak village. The teacher was giving a lesson on Guy Fawkes to a first class of infants. She had forgotten a point, and recovered herself with the query, 'By the bye, children, where *are* the Houses of Parliament?'
> Silence for a moment, and then in a high treble voice came the answer. 'Please, Miss, at the Front!'[5]

HMI Henderson described a similar situation in Suffolk, when he pointed out that one 'small country school' could count 'fifteen old boys who served at the front in South Africa, and at my last visit the idea of placing a board with their names on the walls of the school was mooted. Many a country school can boast of old boys who have served with credit, or even distinction, or done honour to their school in other walks of life, and I am sorry that their names and example should be lost.'[6] Against this background it is perhaps not surprising that in 1902, the anniversary of Queen Victoria's birthday—24 May—was officially designated Empire Day, to be celebrated throughout the British Empire as a means of training school children in good citizenship.

Nor was this patriotic zeal confined to official circles. Mr F. W. Brocklehurst, who attended school at Sheldon, Derbyshire, at the end of the 1890s, is one pupil who remembers the deep sense of national pride cultivated by the mistress. The youngsters were not only taught all the appropriate songs, like *Soldiers of the Queen, Hearts of Oak* and *There's a Dear Old Flag to Fight For*, but each morning before lessons began she would read them the latest news from the battle front.[7] Gaius Carley in Sussex similarly recalled how he and his fellows 'loved to read about the soldiers fighting in South Africa. . . . The Relief of Ladysmith, Mafeking and Kimberley were great days for us, a half day holiday. We marched or shuffled around the small village with our whistle pipe and band . . . and back to Mr Bottomleys [*sic*] Mansion, who gave us lots of things to eat and drink.'[8] In Devon the war gave a great impetus to various forms of military drill. Some schools engaged servicemen as drill sergeants, and at Thurlestone the boys were provided with toy guns, white sailor suits, and two airguns 'in the hope of making them good marksmen', under the direction of the local RNVR Coastguard.[9] Fortunately, few other school managers and teachers took their patriotism as far as that.

However if one change compared to earlier years was the shift of emphasis in moral training away from a reliance on religious instruction alone, a second of equal significance was the broadening and humanising of the curriculum. There was a growing anxiety to make elementary schooling more 'relevant' to the children's day-to-day life, so that under the 1895 Code, cottage gardening was added to the list of 'specific subjects' which could be studied by boys; two years earlier dairy work and housewifery had been included for the girls. The 1895 Code also provided that : 'Visits paid during the school hours, under proper guidance, to Museums, Art Galleries, and other institutions of educational value approved by the Department may be reckoned as attendance' up to a maximum of twenty hours in any one year.[10] Although such concessions were more widely utilised by town schools than country ones, there are occasional references in rural school log books to visits to exhibitions or similar excursions.

The disappearance of payment by results during the 1890s was designed to give greater financial stability to the schools and to permit the drawing up of a 'more liberal and practical' curriculum. As HMI Wix pointed out in 1900—the year the block grant system was introduced—for 'the first time for forty years teachers will be free in arranging their time-tables to consider the educational worth rather than the supposed money value of a subject; for the first time the Code . . . draws up a curriculum which lays down the foundation of a "liberal" education'.[11] To this end a circular was issued by the Board of Education in April 1900, desiring school managers to see that the teaching in their schools was 'more consonant with the environment of the scholars' than had hitherto been the case.[12] The master of Bromsberrow School, Gloucestershire, was one who clearly acted on this recommendation, for an entry in his log book for 12 April 1900, the day the circular's arrival is recorded, adds : 'All the boys have witnessed the operation of Grafting fruit trees while some have performed the operation themselves in the garden adjacent to the school. One of the parents of the scholars has promised to lend me a chain for the purpose of measuring land; and as the farm-labourers find a difficulty in estimating the various areas of ground upon which their work has been done, both in spring and Harvest, they are very anxious that their boys should be taught land-measuring.'[13] Subsequent entries indicate that this enthusiasm was maintained.

Publishers were equally alive to the changing times and soon books on school gardening made their appearance, alongside more traditional texts. As one of them, John Weathers' *The Practical School Garden*, published in 1912, hopefully observed : 'Gardening in connection with School Work is now such an important part of our educational system, that the time has come when some attempt should be made to systematise it.' This the author aimed to do.[14]

Such developments went some way towards meeting the criticisms of farmers and others that country schools were failing to interest their pupils in rural life. Thomas Plowman, secretary of the Bath and West and Southern Counties Agricultural Society, was one who deplored the policy of teaching children to differentiate between a lion or a whale, 'in case', as he ironically observed, 'they should meet either of them on their way home from school; but . . . do not teach them the difference between turnip-seeds and charlock, how to graft or prune, or any of the hundred-and-one different subjects which would make agricultural life more attractive to them, and help to retain them on the land'.[15] He went on to describe how, under the Local Taxation Act of 1890, county councils had had funds placed at their disposal for the promotion of technical education and several of them had appealed to the Bath and West to conduct dairy schools on their behalf. They had also made monetary grants available for that purpose. Within a short time the Society had set up nearly 170 buttermaking schools and fifteen for cheesemaking—the former operating on a migratory basis, with sessions held in different districts, and the latter remaining fixed in one place for the whole of a cheesemaking season and then moving on the next year.[16] However, given the growing importation of cheap foreign dairy produce in these years and the increasing importance of liquid milk sales by British farmers, the project was of limited value only. Futhermore, most of its students were the daughters of farmers—and even country clergymen—rather than the offspring of agricultural workers and village craftsmen, who together formed the bulk of the rural population.

One of the first counties to cooperate with the Bath and West on this project was Somerset. Indeed the first Bath and West butter school was set up in Shepton Mallet in 1888 before additional government financial support became available, and was followed in 1890 with a cheese school in Wells. Other rural courses were promoted in the county, too—including those for sheep shearing, thatching, hedging and ditching, and farriery. Unfortunately the efforts did not always meet with the cooperation of agriculturists, and a number of classes had to be abandoned when farmers refused to provide sheep for shearing or when men able to give instruction refused to do so 'in case they should thereby aid their future competitors'.[17] Technical instruction committees elsewhere followed a similar line, as in Lincolnshire, where courses in thatching and sheep dipping were promoted.

Not all educationists, though, were persuaded of the wisdom of this approach, at least for pupils in elementary schools. One of His Majesty's Inspectors of Schools, writing in 1902, welcomed 'any . . . teaching which may make country children understand and love the country better', but considered that 'in any specialisation . . . of country schemes of instruction it must be remembered that, as the "rural exodus" is largely due to a desire for higher wages and better prospects, so it would be unfair to a country child to make his curriculum differ so widely from that of the town child as to disable him from competition, if his future lot should be cast in a town'.[18]

From the teachers' point of view, the various changes meant they now had greater independence in drawing up timetables, even though these still had to be approved by HMI. Every encouragement was given to them to extend schooling beyond the three 'r's', or even such additional academic subjects as geography, history and grammar. In order to train the children's powers of observation, HMI Tillard suggested 'outdoor lessons, collections of wild flowers . . . use of rain-gauge and thermometer at school, and the keeping of a school naturalist's diary (in which interesting facts of natural history observed by the children are noted down under the teacher's supervision)'. At Marnhull in Dorset the head of the Roman Catholic School was advised that the children should keep diaries in which they could record 'Nature Study developments', weather changes and similar matters; these could later form the basis of 'oral composition lessons'.[19] School 'museums', with the children collecting suitable specimens, were another popular development. While Chief Inspector Fitzmaurice thought that every rural school ought to include one or more of such subjects as cottage gardening, treatment of grass land, knowledge of the habits of the horse, cow, sheep, pig, and the management of poultry and bees, in its general curriculum.[20]

But Fitzmaurice noted, too, the progress which had been made by 1900 in regard to the order and cleanliness of schools and their pupils, as compared to earlier years :

> Children are not now found spread about the schoolroom in chaotic groups round their teachers, as was not infrequently the case. . . . The dirty habit of spitting on slates is disappearing. Writing on paper is more widely used, and where slates are retained effective methods of cleaning them are adopted.[21]

In these years the Inspectors displayed a growing concern for the physical welfare of the children. Although that was not an entirely new departure—comments on the insanitary condition of the 'offices' or the lack of ventilation and fresh air in classrooms can be found in log books from their earliest days—the tone in which the remarks were now being made was more sympathetic to the children. HMI De Sausmarez, for example, quoted with approval the policy adopted at Upton St Leonards in Gloucester-shire, where hot cocoa was provided during the luncheon break to long-distance children at ½d. a pint. The youngsters here were also permitted to eat their meal in the classroom in cold weather rather than being forced to spend the time in the playground.

In other cases, penny dinners were supplied by the school authorities or local well-wishers, largely financed by charity.[22] Perhaps the most successful of these were at Siddington in Cheshire and at Rousdon in Devon. At Siddington, during 1903–5, a dinner consisting of hot stew with vegetables was supplied from November to March at a charge of 1½d. per meal. While at Rousdon, under the influence of the local squire, a school dinner scheme was in operation from 1876. The meal was served throughout the year in a specially provided dining-room and all the children were expected to attend. The menu was very varied, including meat, soup with vegetables and bread, suet pudding with treacle, jam or raisins, rhubarb and apple puddings, and rice. The charge was a modest 1d., with a reduc-tion in cases of large families. Not surprisingly such developments were prized by the scholars. One Essex head recorded the depar-ture of a young pupil for a neighbouring school : 'The attendance officer informs me that a soup dinner of excellent quality is supplied there three times each week and apparently this little chap has gone to sample it.'[23]

Physical exercise also became accepted as essential for improv-ing the physique of the children, and after 31 August 1895, a school failing to provide 'suitable physical exercises, e.g. Swim-ming, Gymnastics and Swedish Drill' was no longer able to earn the maximum grant.[24] Swedish drill, with its stretching of arms and graceful body movements, substituted the 'harmonious development of every muscle at once' for the over-developed biceps which were the product of earlier drill based on the use of dumb-bells.

The anxieties over children's health were not, of course, con-fined to the countryside. The puny frames and poor health of many working-class men from the industrial towns, who had offered themselves for service in the army during the Boer War, had aroused widespread fears of general racial decline. That concern was reinforced when the 1904 Interdepartmental Committee on Physical Deterioration emphasised grave defects in the nutrition and health of the nation's children. Such weaknesses could only be countered by a vigorous campaign to maximise 'physical efficiency' through the provision of better food and increased medical attention. There were European precedents for such an approach. By 1880, France had a well-organised system of school canteens, while in 1883 the first school doctor was appointed at Frankfurt-am-Main in Germany. Two years later Switzerland appointed a school medical officer for Lausanne and soon after medical inspection was introduced in all the schools of France.[25] In England, the London and Bradford school boards had appointed medical officers by the early 1890s, and in the next decade or so were to be followed by a trickle of other authorities. Concern about the health of children was also a standard feature of Independent Labour Party and Social Democratic Federation programmes in these years. From its inception in 1884, indeed, the latter body had advocated the provision 'of at least one wholesome meal a day in each school'. And when a school meals bill was eventually passed in 1906 it owed something to Labour party pressure and interest.

Others supporting child welfare policies on a national scale within Britain included Sir John Gorst, MP for Cambridge University and the last Vice-President of the Committee of Council on Education, from 1895 to 1902. But his proposal to throw upon local authorities the duty of feeding as well as educating school children was condemned by many as a 'dangerous and far-reaching change in [the] social system', which would fatally undermine the parental sense of duty and independence.[26] Though some observers, including doctors and trade union leaders, shared his anxieties, and as early as 3 June 1904, he noted that he had received a memorial from the Royal College of Physicians of Edinburgh 'to the Sec : of State asking what power may be given to [local authorities] to feed children'.[27]

Out of these deliberations there emerged in 1906 the Education (Provision of Meals) Act, authorising the supply of school meals by local authorities. It was followed a year later by the institution of a nationwide school medical service. Both ventures were to be financed primarily out of the rates, and perhaps for this reason, and also because of local inertia, their impact in rural areas before the first World War was limited.[28] For many ratepayers in country districts still adhered to the self-help, *laissez-faire* policies of Britain's mid-Victorian hey-day. By 31 March 1909, more than two years after the school meals legislation had come into force, only 113 local education authorities out of 328 had set up school canteen committees, and these were overwhelmingly in urban communities. Two exceptions to this in 1908–9 were the counties of Worcestershire, which had provided 512 children with breakfasts, and Brecon, which had supplied breakfasts to 65 children. However the food offered at these meals was uninspiring in the extreme, with cocoa and milk plus bread and margarine featuring prominently on the menu.[29]

On the other hand, in Gloucestershire, despite the fact that the Director of Education had referred in 1905 to 'the mischievous effects upon children of insufficient or improper feeding, especially when compelled to attend school, and pressed to work beyond their strength', virtually no progress was made. Not until 1914 did the Education Committee authorise the expenditure of £34 13s. 5d. to provide 5,770 meals for the children of unemployed miners in the Kingswood district, who were 'unable, by reason of lack of food, to take advantage of the education provided for them'.[30]

This reluctance to act on the part of the authorities was clearly not the result of lack of *need*, for cases of malnutrition were being reported in country districts as well as in urban ones. The Annual Report of the Chief Medical Officer of the Board of Education for 1912 showed that 18.6 per cent of children examined in Dorset were suffering from the effects of poor feeding; in Gloucestershire the percentage was 12.7 and in Somerset, 12. Nevertheless, these figures pale into insignificance beside the 31.4 per cent registered by West Hartlepool or even the 26.3 per cent of Norwich.[31] Throat infections and adenoids were felt to be major causes of ill-health among country children, with the 'dampness arising from the subsoil water' considered a possible factor in this. In the view of a Rutland doctor, 'nearly one half of the cases of malnutrition in his area' were due to the unhealthy condition of the nose and throat—'conditions probably preventable and easily remedied'.[32] But sadly, although all local authorities were required to make *some* provision for a school medical service, the response of most, preoccupied as they were with keeping down the rates, was modest in the extreme. Somerset was one of the more active of the rural counties in this respect, with an early employment of school nurses, the provision of spectacles at cheap rates 'and possibly on the payment of instalments by the parents', and treatment of defective teeth and 'chronic diseases of the throat and nose and ears'. But even here it was noted that the county councillors, 'having regard to their duty towards the ratepayers, intend to exercise their powers very cautiously, and only in cases that are reported by the Sub-Committee to be urgent and necessitous'.[33]

In Gloucestershire the main effort was concentrated on the elimination of 'dirty heads'. In 1908 almost one-quarter of the elementary school children examined in the county suffered from infestation—a percentage which had been halved by 1922. In neighbouring Oxfordshire, where about one-fifth of the children examined suffered from the same problem, a determined campaign of compulsory cleaning had reduced the scale of the difficulty by 1914. And in an attempt to tackle the high level of tooth decay among children, Oxfordshire Education Committee decided in 1909 to supply cost-price tooth brushes which parents could purchase from the respective head teachers.[34] Yet, although these measures helped to improve the children's health, they could hardly be regarded as dramatic. The growth of an effective child welfare service remained painfully slow in country areas up to 1914.

And if in the matter of health care, the position of elementary children left a good deal to be desired on the eve of the first World War, in the academic field, too, weaknesses remained. Admittedly there were some teachers, like Mrs Bowkett of Banbury, who believed that 'the secret of success in any subject [was] the happiness which attends it'. She sought to make learning a pleasure and, in particular, taught her young pupils to read by the use of letter games. Rhymes were employed to this end :

> Here is letter "a"
>   Looking stout and fat,
> His head is hanging down so low,
>   He cannot wear a hat.

The teacher would recite the rhyme and then draw the letter "a" on the black board. She would direct the attention of the pupils to its form, and the youngsters would all don hats. 'One child personates "a" and wears a giant "a" round his neck. They go for a walk, the children's hats keep on, but "a's" hat continually drops off to the evident enjoyment of all.'[35] A similar approach was used for the other letters of the alphabet, and from this Mrs Bowkett proceeded to teach the children to read, using a phonetic method based on principles similar to shorthand. Her ideas were so successful that she was encouraged by the Oxfordshire Education Committee to give lectures on Saturday mornings to infant mistresses from the surrounding North Oxfordshire villages.

But elsewhere, despite the exhortations of the Inspectors and the circulars of the Board of Education, methods and curricula followed along lines similar to those in operation during the days of 'payment by results'. At Sheldon, Mr Brocklehurst recalled that under his elderly mistress : 'We had no nature study rambles, or anything out of school. It was reading, writing, arithmetic, dictation, composition, drawing, memorising poetry, and scripture till 10 o'clock, and knitting and needlework for the girls'. The situation at Austrey in Warwickshire was very similar. Here in the early years of the present century the girls were expected to knit their own vests and stockings from wool provided by their parents, and my mother, who was one of the pupils, still remembers the boredom of knitting interminable pairs of black stockings. Rather more enlightened were the plasticine maps produced for geography lessons, with small pieces of coal marking the coal fields, cotton and wool indicating the relevant textile areas, and grains of wheat to indicate agricultural districts. Each morning session ended with the singing of grace—'Be present at our table, Lord . . .'—in readiness for the midday meal.

But perhaps the most depressing tribute to the persistence of the old ways is provided by Professor H. C. Dent. He was a 'pre-adolescent pupil' in an elementary school in 1904 :

Like millions more, I intoned my way monotonously (and uncomprehendingly) through the multiplication tables; I was bored to nausea by the one and only 'Reader' we were allowed each year—which had to serve the dual function of giving us practice in the mechanics of reading aloud . . . and of being our introduction to English life and letters. I wrote, endlessly, in 'copy-books' morally elevating maxims—'A stitch in time saves nine', 'Too many cooks spoil the broth'—but I never composed, much less wrote, in class a single original sentence. I memorized, in rhyme, the names and idiosyncrasies of the English kings and queens

> William the Conqueror long did reign,
> William his son by an arrow was slain . . .

and I memorized (though not in rhyme) the names of the capes, bays, county towns, mountains and rivers, literally all round Britain. And once each week I painted blobs (we called them flowers), and wove wet reeds into work baskets: the school's sole concessions to 'activity' . . .

And this experience of mine, I must emphasise, was not in the class of a cynical, dull or apathetic teacher, but of a lively, intelligent, warm-hearted woman, who as a person did us boys and girls a world of good. Did she know no other way to teach? Or was she bound by the school time-table?—that sacrosanct nineteenth-century visual aid, put up 'in a prominent position' (as the Code required) by the new head teacher when he arrived, and never taken down until he left, it might well be thirty years later . . . Such teaching as I endured went on for many years in many schools after 1904. The spirit outlived the fact of 'payment by results' in the practice of teachers who could not change their ways, even when they wanted to.[36]

Punishments, too, remained severe. As a former pupil from Essex recalled: 'class punishment was to be made to sit bolt upright with closed eyes and hands clasped on our heads'; while in another school 'speaking to teachers without permission was considered bad behaviour and was often punished'.[37] A whole week's play could be jeopardised if children were discovered talking to one another in class, as happened at Braintree Manor School in November 1899. Canings were common, especially for the boys. A surviving punishment book for Burford Council School, Oxfordshire, shows that in 1910, '3 strokes' were administered for truanting and deceitfulness, and for 'Temper' towards the teacher, while six strokes were given for 'Dishonesty, etc. After much private talking & encouragement'.[38] As in the Victorian era, some of this severity was attributable to the large size of classes; the rest to a belief in the need to inculcate self-control and orderliness in the new generation, even if this meant repressing normal childish instincts.

Where the daily routine was so limited it was small wonder that pupils waited anxiously for the end of the last lesson so that they could run outside to enjoy the fresh air and, in due season, to play appropriate games—whips and tops, marbles, bowling the hoop, skipping—or could search for birds' nests in the spring and gather nuts and berries in the autumn. Equally welcome were the occasional half-holidays, perhaps granted, as at Ivinghoe in Buckinghamshire during the autumn of 1903, because there was a 'meet of Stag Hounds' in the village, or because a circus had made its appearance.[39] A Band of Hope meeting—to promote the cause of temperance among children— was another excuse for a holiday at Ivinghoe in 1903.

Resistance to new and more exciting teaching methods was, of course, particularly prevalent in those rural areas where classes were large and where the range of age and ability of the children was wide, and where assistance primarily took the form of monitors, pupil-teachers or the untrained, unqualified 'supplementaries'. Not until the early years of the present century did the Board of Education at last begin to insist that these latter should at least spend a fortnight 'observing' the school routine before they commenced their duties. 'Supplementaries' were also poorly paid and it was that aspect which made them attractive to hard-pressed voluntary school managers in country districts, with limited cash resources.

It was partly to combat financial weaknesses in the voluntary sector that in 1897 the Voluntary Schools Act was passed, providing for extra government aid to be given to these schools and also requiring them to join together in local Associations, so as 'to promote the better organisation of the schools as a whole'. In the case of the Church of England, the area of an Association was to be the diocese or archdeaconry, while for Roman Catholic schools it was the diocese and for Wesleyan and British schools an agreed geographical district. But the scale of financial assistance provided was inadequate to meet their cash needs. In 1902, a 'strictly confidential' memorandum issued by the secretary to the Board of Education estimated that '56 per cent of the voluntary schools in the counties were "under water"' in 1900, with their income falling far short of their expenditure.

Their premises and equipment were also inferior to those of the board schools, and only thirty-eight per cent of their teachers were fully certificated, as compared to a level of fifty-one per cent for the boards.[40]

It was in order to meet this situation and to provide rate aid for *all* elementary schools, not merely those under school boards, that the 1902 Education Act was passed. New local education authorities now became responsible for all elementary schooling, and as was seen in chapter 8, one of the effects of this was gradually to raise the salary levels of rural teachers nearer to those of their urban counterparts. It was hoped thereby to make country schools more attractive to certificated instructors.

But if the measure was welcomed by Anglicans and Roman Catholics, whose schools were major beneficiaries from its provisions, to school board supporters and many nonconformists it was far less attractive. To them it represented an unwelcome encouragement of sectarian education. Opposition was particularly strong in Wales, where nonconformist feeling ran high and where the local education authorities themselves sought for some time to evade their responsibilities to 'maintain' the voluntary sector. In Caernarvon and Barry, for example, this hostility took the form of a refusal of rate aid to church schools—what has been called the 'Slow Starvation Policy'. While in Montgomeryshire in July 1905 the local education authority even withheld the salaries of all teachers in voluntary schools for the preceding quarter. Somehow the managers kept the schools going, though skirmishes continued until January 1906, when, with the return of a Liberal Government, the Montgomeryshire authority resumed its functions in the hope that the hated 1902 Act would be repealed. In the end that did not occur but, following administrative changes, opposition gradually died down. By 1911 it had been established that the elementary system in Wales, as elsewhere, would follow the lines laid down by the 1902 legislation.[41]

Another problem which plagued village schools to the end of the Victorian era and beyond was the irregularity of attendance of scholars. In 1893 the minimum school leaving age had been raised from ten to eleven, and in 1899 it was raised again to twelve, although in country areas eleven still seems to have been accepted.[42] But these changes did not solve the problem. Even in the late 1890s cases were quoted of schools which could achieve only three-quarters of their potential attendance because the children were kept away on one pretext or another, while HMI Boyd Carpenter claimed to know of an Essex school where 'an average attendance under 70 per cent was considered good by the managers'.[43] And when in 1898 the Education Department circularised all the elementary schools of England and Wales on the matter of child employment it found that about half of the managers who replied admitted having pupils at work. In a number of the remaining cases the Department itself considered the returns to be 'defective' because the names of children who were not in *regular* employment, or who worked for parents or others without wages, were omitted. The returns included the names of 5,462 children aged eight years or less who were at work. Agriculture was a major user of their labour, although for the girls, domestic service and 'minding baby' were common occupations, too. Among the youngest workers mentioned were a six-year-old boy in Cornwall who worked twenty-four hours a week, without pay, helping on a farm, and another six-year-old in Wiltshire who spent twelve hours a week 'cow-keeping', for the princely sum of 6d. Five Wiltshire girls, all aged six, were recorded as 'minding baby' for 1d. week, while a five-year-old girl from Worcestershire spent fifteen hours a week in season picking peas, for a weekly wage of 1s. 3d.[44]

Small wonder that HMI De Sausmarez could conclude at the end of the century that the 'real bar' to educational progress was 'the general irregularity of attendance, for which parents, local authorities and magistrates must share the blame'. One of his colleagues, Chief Inspector Currey, agreed, noting the way that the school year was broken up for a whole variety of agricultural pursuits—'pea-picking, seed-picking, potato-picking, hay-making, and harvesting, to say nothing of epidemic sickness. It thus becomes difficult for some schools to open the necessary 400 times', i.e. on two hundred days per annum.[45]

Furthermore, in that period of intense interest in game preservation, when the *grande battue*, patronised by parties of distinguished gentlemen, was regarded as a high point in the social calendar, one of the most persistent problems during the winter months was caused by the recruitment of boys to act as beaters. This was a difficulty which particularly incensed HMI Milman :

In a small school of fifty children I have found as many as twelve boys away 'beating'. I have seen a letter addressed to a master by an attendance officer asking how many boys he would let a keeper have for 'beating'. I have also seen a letter addressed to the same attendance officer by a keeper, saying that if he would let him have three boys from a certain village he would send him a brace of pheasants . . . I have . . . had a letter from a clergyman saying that the tenant of the large house in his parish would not give his annual subscription to the school or his contribution to the new classroom unless he could have boys when he wanted them for shooting.[46]

These generalisations are borne out by entries in school log books, as at Boughton Monchelsea in Kent, where an entry for 29 January 1903 notes: 'Fifteen boys absent beating for Mr Kleinwort.'[47] While at Elmdon in Warwickshire, another village badly affected by the requirements of shooting parties, an entry for 8 January 1901—one of many similar items—reads: 'Gave a holiday today as Squire Alston wanted all the boys for bush beating.'[48]

Even the new craze for golf could have its effects on school attendance, as Chief Inspector Willis noted in 1902 : 'The trouble connected with the employment of children as caddies at golf . . . has recurred, and in a somewhat aggravated form; children of nine, eight, and even seven years old having been employed to drag clubs round the links. The punishment of delinquent players as "employers of labour" would be the best remedy.'[49]

Yet however disruptive these activities might be for the routine of the school, by no means all observers were convinced even at that late stage that child employment was invariably a bad thing. Such doubts were shared by a minority of the Inspectors, including the Rev. C. F. Routledge, who reported from Kent, where, in his view, it was 'absolutely necessary to close the schools altogether during the months of August and September, but the variety of agricultural operations—such as hop-tying, bird scaring, etc. interferes with the attendance of children in the months of May, June, and July. Would it not be possible during this time to be content with a *morning attendance* only, say, from 8 to 12, with a break of one-quarter of an hour at 10 o'clock? The hours of attendance during the winter and early spring might then be slightly increased. It would be quite possible to keep school open from 8.30 to 12, and again from 1 to 3.30, without interfering with the habits of the parents.'[50]

Still more unexpected was the stance taken by one of the Chief Inspectors, who reported on schools in the West Central division of England:

> Education is a large matter. Schooling is but a part of it. There are occasions when schooling must step aside in the interests of education. The sight of soldiers cheered off to war will probably waken more thought in a lad's mind than the perusal of his Citizenship Reader; a day in the woods with the beaters is not an unwholesome change in the dull monotony of country life. A School Board takes advanced ground in education when it gathers the girls to sweep and dust under direction; it is hard to look on the mother keeping her daughter to help her in the house as anti-educational. It is, I believe, allowed that the lack of physical employment is a dangerous evil in our present schooling. These casual employments may not be an unmixed evil.'[51]

Needless to say, where officials adopted this attitude, teachers found it hard to bring recalcitrant non-attenders to book. Indeed, some of them, like Mrs Bowkett, reluctantly recognised that family poverty might make child employment necessary from time to time. In her case certain of the boys would visit the cattle market held on Thursdays in order to earn a few pennies 'minding the calves'.[52]

Teachers' difficulties on the attendance issue were also aggravated by the fact that most farmers even in the early twentieth century regarded the education of labourers' children as a waste of time. Certainly when E. N. Bennett came to write on the *Problems of Village Life* in 1913 he concluded that compulsory education was held by some agriculturists to be 'responsible for restlessness and the willingness to listen to "agitators" ', which they claimed to find among many of their workers: ' "Over-education of the labourers' children," is a phrase constantly on the lips of rural employers.'[53]

Nor is it surprising that in the autumn of 1914, shortly after the outbreak of the first World War, bye-laws relating to school attendance were again relaxed in order to permit children not otherwise qualified for agricultural employment to be so engaged. Some local authorities even granted attendance exemptions to children below the age of twelve, to the consternation of the Chief Medical Officer of the Board of Education, and in 1916, in England and Wales alone the number of youngsters between the ages of eleven and twelve who were employed in agriculture almost trebled.[54] The idea that children were small adults, who must be involved in the money-making process as quickly as possible, took a long time to die. While among the scholars themselves there were some who felt it a disgrace not to be allowed to work when they had reached the age of eleven or twelve. Fred Kitchen, who lost his father when he was twelve, remembered people saying 'it wer' a scandless shame as a lad couldn't leave school afore he wer' thirteen to help his mither', and he himself grumbled 'at being held back from helping to keep the house'.[55]

Alongside these continuing difficulties for elementary schooling, the early years of the twentieth century did at least see an increasing interest in secondary education. Under the 1902 Education Act not only was the patchwork of independent village boards and committees replaced by a single local education authority for the county but this latter body was allowed, for the first time, to establish rate-aided secondary schools. Through the scholarship system an educational ladder could be provided for the ablest elementary scholars. Unfortunately, although a move in the right direction it proved totally inadequate, especially when hamstrung by the various regulatory Codes issued by the Board of Education. Under these it was from the start accepted that the majority of children would receive elementary schooling only, and that secondary provision would be restricted to youngsters who showed 'promise of exceptional capacity' or whose parents could pay fees. These latter were normally fixed at a minimum of £3 per child per annum, and given the economic circumstances of the time, even such a comparatively modest sum as that inevitably excluded most working-class children, other than scholarship holders, from the secondary sector. With 'startling frankness', Robert Morant, the secretary to the Board of Education, had summed up his own philosophy towards secondary schools as early as 1897 when he 'accepted the view that working-class children must not be given an education which would give them too ambitious an outlook.'[56]

Although the number of scholarships was increased from 1907, under the 'free place' system, even in 1924 it was estimated that only about five per cent of the entrants to secondary schools in rural areas were the offspring of agricultural labourers.[57] Nor was academic ability the sole criterion involved in selection. In some cases, children lived too far from the nearest secondary school to be able to attend, even if they won a scholarship, and in others, family poverty prevented them from taking up free places when the chance was offered. Expensive school uniforms were a particular problem in this regard.

These generalisations are borne out by research carried out by Kenneth Lindsay in Oxfordshire, which shows that even in 1924 only forty elementary schools out of 212 in the county sent pupils on to secondary education. Among them were eighty-four free-place or scholarship children—of whom a mere eight were the offspring of farm workers. Yet agriculture employed over a third of the occupied male population above the age of twenty-five in the county. By contrast, over a quarter of the successful candidates fell into the lower middle-class 'small tradesmen' category.[58] As Lindsay wrote in 1926 : 'the unskilled and lowly paid worker, the farm worker and all casual labourers are as yet not really touched by the scholarship system. Individuals undoubtedly are, but the mass remains unaffected.'[59] At that time, in the nation as a whole just under ten per cent of the age group 10–11 was proceeding to secondary schools, one-third of them exempt from fees and two-thirds as fee-payers.[60] Not until the passage of the Education Act of 1944 did secondary education become a reality for most country children. Prior to this, despite reorganisation in the 1920s and 1930s, large numbers had still to attend the all-age elementary schools which had in earlier years catered for their parents' and grandparents' generation. Up to the outbreak of the second World War only about twenty per cent of rural schools had been reorganised, 'and the principle of reorganisation was by no means generally accepted by country people'.[61] Not until the disruptions of the war and its aftermath did the demand for secondary education become as universal in country districts as it had been earlier in the towns.

Teachers, needless to say, found the limitations of the 1902

Act a disappointment. Through the NUT they accused the Board of Education of 'thwarting and hindering the higher educational interests of the children of the working classes'.[62] And the Board's policy of encouraging high fees in the secondary sector was looked upon as a 'deliberate attempt to "fend off" from the secondary schools proper all but a few of the children of the workers'. One speaker at the 1911 NUT conference bitterly summarised the Union view:

> The old liberal policy . . . was to provide an open road with no unbridged moat for every scholar able and willing to continue his education. The policy of some of the permanent officials was the medieval plan which barred the road to the masses, picked up here and there a clever lad of lowly birth, took him out of his order, fitted him with the education of the ruling classes, and made him one of them—a system which has been described as providing a handful of prigs and an army of serfs.

There was more than a germ of truth in his comments.

However, a still more sweeping change was getting under way in countless country parishes even before the passage of the 1902 Education Act—that of rural depopulation. By 1901 less than a quarter of the population of England and Wales still lived in rural areas, as opposed to almost one half in the middle of the nineteenth century. And as people moved away, school rolls also fell, as at Holbeton in Devon, where the master complained in 1890 of men 'being discharged from Flete and Membland where they have been employed all their lives, and are obliged to go about the country to search for work—a state of things unheard of in the history of the village.'[63] Landowners and farmers in other counties, hit by the effects of agricultural depression, reacted similarly. While young country people themselves, as their knowledge of the outside world increased, became unwilling to accept the low pay and limited prospects that all too often went with rural employment. An Oxfordshire schoolmaster told Rider Haggard at the turn of the century that in his parish 'three-quarters of the young men and all the young women left the village at nineteen or twenty years of age, only the dullest staying at home'.[64] C. F. G. Masterman, writing in 1909, made much the same point : 'All the boys and girls with energy and enterprise forsake at the commencement of maturity the life of the fields for the life of the town. A peasantry, unique in Europe in its complete divorce from the land, lacking ownership of cottage or tiniest plot of ground, finds no longer any attraction in the cheerless toil of the agricultural labourer upon scant weekly wages.'[65]

Ultimately, under the new local education authorities this migration of population was to lead to school closures. For on financial grounds the maintenance of the smallest of them could no longer be justified. In Gloucestershire, where there were 473 elementary schools when the local authority took over in 1903, seventy-seven had closed by 1936, with sixteen going between 1921 and 1925 alone.[66] In Devon at least fifty-three rural schools had gone between 1903 and 1936 and in Oxfordshire, thirty-three. The time when every village could expect to have its school was now past and in the inter-war years and beyond, the trickle of closures became a flood.[67] Motor transport enabled children to be conveyed to another village and, at the same time, a declining birth rate and the building of separate secondary schools reinforced the trend of falling elementary rolls. Unlike their mid-Victorian predecessors, children from the 1930s onwards could no longer automatically expect to receive their early education in their home community. At the same time, with the loss of the school a focal point of village life also disappeared. It was just one of the penalties which had to be paid for the growing urbanisation and industrialisation of twentieth-century Britain.

Appendices

Appendix 1

RULES OF THE HASLINGFIELD NATIONAL SCHOOL FOR GIRLS—*c*.1840s
(At Cambridge Record Office)

1. The Children must be sent to School with their hands and faces well washed, and their hair combed and brushed, clothes clean and neat, and they are not allowed to come to School wearing ornaments, feathers, artificials, or any unnecessary article of dress.

2. The School is opened in the morning with prayers, immediately after the Church clock strikes Nine, by which time all the Children must be in School and remain till Twelve o'clock; in the afternoon the Children must be in the School by the time that the Church clock strikes Two, and remain, throughout the year, till Half-past Four o'clock, when the School is closed by prayers.

3. Children of Labourers pay One Penny weekly; Tradespeople's Children, Twopence; and the Children of Farmers and other Parishes, Threepence.

4. Girls are admitted into the School at Seven years of age, and *no Child* is admitted under that age, nor till the Trustees are satisfied that any arrears have been paid which may be due to the Infant Schoolmistress. The admissions from the Infant School take place Quarterly.

5. The Mistress is required to keep a register of the attendance of each Child, and also the amount paid weekly by each Child.

6. Any Child coming to School late, who is inattentive, disorderly, or guilty, of using bad language, destroying the Property of the School, or otherwise misconducting herself, will be punished by the Mistress at the discretion of the Trustees, and is liable to be discharged from the School.

7. If any of the Parents or Friends of the Children interfere in the regulations made to maintain discipline, and enforce obedience to the Mistress or others in authority, the Children of such persons cannot be allowed to remain in the School.

8. The Mistress is required, in secular instruction, to teach the

Girls Reading, Writing, Spelling, English Grammar, Tables, Arithmetic, General History, and Geography, and such subjects of useful knowledge as may from time to time be directed or authorised by the Trustees; in Religious Instruction, Bible Reading and Bible History, the Catechism, Articles of the Church of England, and general knowledge of the Liturgy.

9. The Mistress is required to teach the Girls every kind of plain Needlework, Marking, Stocking and Plain Knitting, Stocking Darning, &c., &c.

10. The Children are allowed to work one week in four for their Parents, but no Child is allowed to bring to the School, under any pretence, any description of Fancy Work, and during the other three weeks, *all the Children* will do any Work, not Fancy Work, which can be procured. The afternoon only of each day is allowed for Needlework.

11. Any sum that may be received for work done at the School will be appropriated for the benefit of the Children.

12. The Children are required to attend the Sunday Schools and also Divine Service at the Parish Church, and the Mistress is required to attend and teach the Children on the Sunday morning from Half-past Nine to a Quarter before Eleven, and in the afternoon from Two till a Quarter before Three, and also to superintend their behaviour during Divine Service at Church.

13. One week's holiday is allowed at Christmas, and five weeks at Harvest, and Saturday in every week.

14. Annual Prizes are given to those Boys and Girls under 14 years of age who show on Examination the greatest proficiency in the repetition and general knowledge of the Church Catechism; and to those Children under 15 years who show the like proficiency in the Articles of the Church of England.

15. The Mistress and Teachers are required, so far as is practicable, to set the Children an example in dress; and all the above Rules, where practicable, are to be applied to the Sunday School.

16. The School is subject to the visitation and inspection of Her Majesty's Inspectors of Schools, and of the Diocesan Inspector, and the National Society's Inspector.

17. Any of the above Rules, where practicable, are to be applied to the Sunday School.

K

Appendix 2

(a) CONDITIONS AT THE CENTRAL SCHOOLS OF THE NATIONAL SOCIETY FOR MASTERS AND MISTRESSES IN TRAINING
(pp. 28–9 of the *Twenty-second Report of the National Society*, 1833)

Every master in training is required to examine the *Orderly Book* on first entering the School in the morning, to see what duty is assigned to him for the day; and to wait his dismission by the School Master, previous to his leaving the School morning and afternoon.

The object of the attendance of the masters in training upon the School being to secure their speedy and perfect attainment to a knowledge of the National System, every master is desired on his first entry to attend one of the junior classes for his more ready initiation in the manner of giving out and saying a lesson, there to remain until such time as he is perfectly master of it, or rises to the top of the class. He then proceeds in a similar manner through the higher classes until he rises to the top of the division. If deemed necessary he may have to repeat this course a second or third time.

No master is on any account allowed to take charge of any class, or be placed in any responsible situation, until he has been examined as to his competency, and pronounced sufficiently acquainted with the National System to be qualified for such charge, and none is entitled to receive promotion until he has been a week in his charge, and conducted himself therein to the satisfaction of the Clerical Superintendent.

The preceding Regulations apply to mistresses as well as masters. And the mistresses are also required to be neat and plain in their manner of dressing, and to avoid every sort of ornament unbecoming the station they are looking to fill. Particular directions on this subject are entered in the Time-book and copied out by each mistress during the first week of her attendance.

In addition to the above, the masters in training assemble in the class-room certain evenings of the week (as appointed), at a quarter before seven o'clock, and occupy themselves there, under the inspection of the School Master, until nine o'clock, in studying and preparing the subjects determined on by the Clerical Superintendent;—the mistresses are required to study and prepare themselves in like manner at their private abodes;—both the masters and mistresses assemble every Saturday morning for examination in these subjects by the Clerical Superintendent, from *a quarter before nine* until *one o'clock*,—the masters in the class-room, and the mistresses in the committee-room. . . .

Two descriptions of persons are officially received for Instruction at the Central School.

1. *Masters and Mistresses in training*, who are to be provided with appointments to Schools in Union, if their conduct and ability prove such as to justify recommendation.

2. *Masters and Mistresses from the Country*, who have already obtained appointments to Schools in Union.

Persons desirous of becoming *Masters or Mistresses in training* are required to produce . . . satisfactory testimonials of their *Moral* and *Religious* Character, from three respectable householders to whom they have been personally known for a considerable length of time. They are also examined as to their proficiency in Religious Knowledge, Reading, Writing, Arithmetic &c. And if approved they are, in the first instance, received as *Probationers* only, and until promoted (after further examination and trial) to the rank of *Candidates for a Situation*, they are liable to be discontinued by the SOCIETY, as unsuitable for its purposes. The *Candidates for a Situation*, unless they forfeit their claims by subsequent misconduct, are appointed to Schools, as opportunities may offer, not in the order of their admission, but according to their qualifications and eligibility . . .

Masters and Mistresses from the Country, are received for Instruction on producing the . . . form properly filled up, together with their appointments signed by the Secretaries or Managers of the Schools for which they are intended; they also undergo an examination on admission.

In all cases the Instruction afforded by the SOCIETY is *gratuitous*; and a certain number of those *Masters in training* who have most distinguished themselves by application and intelligence receive a weekly allowance of half-a-guinea.

N.B. Schools are supplied with masters and mistresses, *for a limited period*, at a guinea-and-a-half and one guinea a week respectively. Assistant boys and girls are also sent, if required, to be paid at the rate of one guinea a month, besides their board and lodging. All expenses are comprised in these payments, except those for travelling, which are *usually* defrayed by the parties applying for assistance.

[On p. 25 of the *Report* it was also noted : *Religious exercises* occupy the principal portion of the school-hours. Every child, as it rises to the higher classes in the School, is expected to know perfectly by heart, and be able to explain and answer questions on, —'the Lord's Prayer,'—'Grace before and after Meat,'—'Prayer on entering and on leaving Church,'—'a Morning and an Evening Prayer for private use at home,'—'the second and third Collects for the Morning and Evening Service,'—'the Church Catechism', &c.— Other subjects are read and studied from books selected out of the Catalogue of the Society for Promoting Christian Knowledge.]

(b) SPECIMEN CORRESPONDENCE CONCERNING ENTRANCE TO THE BOROUGH ROAD TRAINING SCHOOL OF THE BRITISH AND FOREIGN SCHOOL SOCIETY

(preserved at Borough Road College)

(i) To Henry Dunn, Secretary to the British and Foreign School Society

Blagdon
May 25th 1842

Sir,

I beg your assistance to help me to procure what I have for some time past most ardently wished for; Admission into your valuable Institution to be trained for a Teacher. I have been previously occupied as a Carrier; but do not like that line of life, it being such a dissipated one, I have for some time given it up; Steadfastly purposing in my heart to follow some kind of employment in which I may mix with the People of God, instead of those of the world. I hope my natural disposition is suited to the training of the young, whose welfare I feel greatly Interested in, and should God please to prosper me in this my undertaking, I will endeavour (He being my helper) to do all I can for the good of both the Souls and Bodies of those committed to my charge.

I am a Member of the Church of England, and was for nearly five years Teacher in the Blagdon Sunday School.

O may the Lord give me his grace to act like Caleb, to follow him all the days of my life, looking for the sanctification of his most Holy Spirit, and for his Strength to help me in every time of need; so that I may be a useful member of Christ's Church here upon earth altho' a poor unworthy sinner in myself. This is my motive for wishing to become a British School Teacher.

I trust the accompanying testimonials to my character will meet with your approbation.

I am Sir
your most Humble Servant
Willm. Bennett Caple.
P.S. I am now twenty five years of age.

(ii) to Henry Dunn, Secretary to the British and Foreign School Society.

Cheddar Mills
Somerset 3/7 1842.

Dear friend *Henry Dunn*,

Absence from home &c have prevented me from replying earlier to thine of the 21st ult.

I have known W. B. Caple for several years as the driver of a public conveyance & have always had occasion to consider him as steady & well principled.—From some conversation wh· I had with him a day or two since I find that he has for some months past felt desirous of being engaged as a teacher. The education afforded him in the Sabh· Schools was of course very limited but for several years he had some instruction given him by Edmund Dyer, late of Blagdon—now the Independent Minister of Windsor to whom you can apply if you think it desirable.

I have no means of judging what W. C.'s abilities are but he appears to be possessed of energy and firmness & there is withal a kindness & gentleness of manner about him.

As regards his religious character you could not have a better informant than the clergyman whose letter is enclosed & whom I have known for some time past as a zealous & devoted labourer.

On the whole my impression about Caple is very favourable.

I mentioned to him that there must in any case be some delay in admittg· him & pressed upon him the desirableness of making use of the interval in improving himself further & this he seems quite disposed to do.

He would be glad to be informed as early as may be whether his application is likely to be recd·

Thine very truly,

Wm· Tanner

(The clergyman's letter referred to above is not with the collection, having been sent by Henry Dunn to Lord Ebrington in August 1842 —presumably for his comments.)

(iii)

Berriew Augt· 4/48.

Sir,

My age is twenty-one years. The state of my health is I believe upon the whole tolerably good. I have no definite employment; my Father is a Wheelwright Joiner &c. occupies a small farm upon which stands a Corn Mill : my time has been occupied sometimes by working with my Father, sometimes in the Mill, and other times on the farm.—I am not married—I think that I understand the four

first rules of Arithmetic, and a few others. I have a little knowledge of English Grammar and Music, but my knowledge of Geography and History is very limited and superficial. As the School to which I am appointed is to be established as soon as possible after harvest, I cannot devote more than three months to the work of preparation —I have had some practice in communicating instructions to children in a Sunday School but never in a day School—
I am yours respectfully
David Jones
David Jones
Livior Mills,
nr. Garthmill,
Berriew,
Montgomeryshire.

(iv)

Berriew July 27th 1848
Sir,
This is to certify that Mr. David Jones is a member of our church in connexion with the Calvinistic Methodists meeting at Pied House, Berriew, Montgomeryshire. That he has as far as we are aware conducted himself hitherto as becometh a christian always manifesting a very strong disposition to acquire useful knowledge and very active in the cause of Temperance and the Sunday schools and well adapted after a proper training (in our opinion) to make an efficient Teacher in a British School.
We are Yours
Sincearly,
Rich. Powell   Preacher
John Davies   Preacher
Thomas Turner   Preacher
Rich. Baxter   Preacher
(This application was endorsed by Henry Dunn : 'He has a School —to come up at once.')

Appendix 3

A PETITION AGAINST STATE INTERVENTION IN EDUCATION, 1839

To the Honorable [*sic*] the Commons of Great Britain and Ireland in Parliament assembled—
    The Petition of the undersigned Inhabitants of the Parish of Garsington in the County of Oxford—

Humbly sheweth—

That your Petitioners cannot but view with unfeigned sorrow and alarm the scheme of National Education recently proposed to Parliament by which it is intended to place the whole Instruction of the present and future youth of the country entirely under the direction and control of an official Board of Laymen, and from which the Heads of the National Church are systematically excluded.

That such a Scheme appears to your Petitioners to be based on a visionary principle of attempting to unite all sects in religion, whilst it virtually gives support and encouragement to none.

That the Scheme, instead of having any claim on the support and recommendation of your Petitioners, seems to be an ill-advised and ill-constructed imitation of the machinery of Normal Schools in France, under the management and direction of a Minister of Public Instruction, appointed by the Government for the time being; which, however well adapted to the circumstances of that great continental kingdom, convulsed to the centre by a succession of revolutionary movements, where Religion is only a secondary object in the contemplation of the State, cannot but be considered as totally inapplicable to the situation and condition, the habits, the opinions, and the feelings, of the great body of the people of this country.

That a similar Scheme of Normal Instruction, in opposition to the supposed exclusiveness of the Established Church, has already been introduced as an experiment into Ireland; where "Scripture Lesson-Books," as they are called, to conciliate all denominations of Christians, have been substituted for the authorized version of the Bible; in which are found not less than 1102 variations from the usual printed text of Genesis only, and 1680 variations from that of one of the Gospels : and your Petitioners have reason to believe, that in that unhappy country every concession made to conciliate has only tended to produce more exorbitant demands, and that this experiment of Normal Schools, under the direction of a mixed Board of Commissioners of Public Instruction, has completely failed in its object of uniting those of opposite views and persuasions.

Your Petitioners therefore earnestly deprecate the adoption of similar experiments on a large scale, throughout the whole of our parochial system; and, as Diocesan Boards of Education are now formed, or forming, and parochial Schools established in most parts of the Kingdom, your Petitioners humbly pray your [Right] Honourable House not to lend the sanction of your votes, [and the aid of the public purse] in support of a Scheme, ultimately, if not immediately, subversive of the national church, as by law established, productive of no solid or saving knowledge, and calculated only to engender discord, confusion, and every evil work.

And your Petitioners shall ever pray &c.

(signed by 36 inhab^{s.} viz.*

J. Ingram	Rector		
W. B. Pusey	Curate	Tho. Radford	Gent.
R^{d.} Quarterman	Farmer	Wm. Aldsworth	Farmer
R^{d.} Clinkard	Overseer	Wm. Sillar	Shoemaker
Thos. Smith ⎱	Farmers	John Walker	Carpenter
R^{d.} Harper ⎰		Wm. Childerhorn	Farmer
Wm. Turrill	—	Jos. Turrill	Butcher
Jas. Turrill	Clk. Sch'master	Robt. Surman	Farmer
Wm. Aldsworth ⎱	Church w^{s.}	Wm. Wheeler	Mason
Thos. Poulton ⎰		R^{d.} Turrill	Mason
Thos. Cooper	Schoolmaster	Jas. Colson ⎱	Masons
Ch. Godrey	Baker	Tho. Colson ⎰	
Jas. Jannaway	Wheelwright	John Quarter-	
Thos. Fellow	Shoemaker	main	
Wm. Pike	Farmer	Robt. Druce	Shoem^{r.}
Wm. Druce	Carpenter	John Turrill	Mason
Thos. Druce ⎱	Smiths	George Holloway	Farmer
Jno. Druce ⎰		Thos. Hedges	
		Billing	Baker

Appendix 4

EDUCATION IN WALES, 1847

Report by Jelinger C. Symons on Education in Brecknock, Cardigan and Radnor for the *Commission of Inquiry into the State of Education in Wales*, Parliamentary Papers 1847, XXVII, Pt II

(*a*) p. 29

The notion that there is any necessity that a schoolmaster should learn his business is quite in its infancy in Wales. The established belief for centuries has been, that it requires no training at all; and that any one who can read and write, if he be disabled from every other pursuit, can be a schoolmaster at pleasure. That this is a practical belief is further evidenced by the almost total absence of any schoolmaster who has not been brought up to another and dissimilar calling, which he followed, in most cases, up to the time that he became a schoolmaster. A large portion of them are broken-

*In practice, only 34 signatures are shown. A note at the end of the Petition observes: 'The same Petition—mutatis mutandis—sent to the House of Lords—the word votes and the following words in brackets not being applicable to the House of Lords.' The word 'authority' was substituted for 'votes' in the case of the House of Lords.

down farmers, who, in Wales, are a far poorer class and lower in station than in England. In the counties on which I am reporting, out of 140 schoolmasters there were 33 previously farmers, 7 attorneys' clerks, a relieving officer, a plasterer, a flannel-manufacturer, a postmaster, a parish clerk, an assistant-clerk to a union, a farm-bailiff, 5 drapers and shopkeepers, 2 marines, an auctioneer, a gardener, 2 hatters, 2 soldiers, a harper, 3 carpenters, a clergyman, 3 grocers, a stonemason, 4 Baptist ministers, 8 labourers, a currier, a collier, a timber-merchant, 2 tailors, 2 shoemakers, a miner, a preacher, 2 weavers, 5 farm-servants, 7 excise-officers, 3 menservants, 2 sailors, a florist, a paper-maker, a music-master, a cabinet-maker, a builder, 2 students, a clerk in a countinghouse, and a painter and glazier; 21 only had been brought up as assistants or ushers in schools.

Of 49 schoolmistresses, 7 had been sempstresses, 6 governesses, 1 dairymaid, 10 milliners, 9 housekeepers, 12 ordinary maidservants, 2 shopkeepers, and 2 only were originally in schools.

The previous occupation is not the only element in the unfitness of the existing race of schoolmasters for their office. They are often aged persons. . . .

The great majority of the masters derive incomes from their vocation ranging from £18 to £25 per annum; and many have less than £15. In these extreme cases, however, it is very usual to find that their livelihood is aided by gratuities, chiefly in food, from the farmers or shopkeepers, who pay in kind for trifling services, and not infrequently for teaching their sons to read, cipher, or write. The position of the majority of schoolmasters is one midway between a pauper and an able-bodied labourer. Nor does there appear to be any *general* desire to raise the standard of schoolmaster. The Rev. Mr. Bevan, of Hay, whose school is endowed simply to the amount of £4, having resolved to support a good school, gave his master £70 salary, and informed me that he was expostulated with for his extravagance ! . . .

(b) Evidence on Llanbister School, Radnor, pp. 180–1

There is a day and Sunday school here in connection with the parish church, held in the west end of the church partitioned off. This makes a lofty, unceiled, cold and comfortless room. It is paved with stones, and has only one window in it. The walls were dingy, and presenting rather the uninviting appearance of a prison, than a suitable place to teach the young ideas how to shoot. I was nearly stiff with the cold whilst examining the scholars, and so was the master, though the sun shone warmly outside. When I entered the schoolroom all the scholars who could read the Scriptures were engaged in reading the 36th chapter of the Prophecies of Isaiah.

The reading was in the style in which the men cry the last dying speech in the streets, only in rather more drawling and monotonous style. After the reading was ended, which was formally announced by the scholar who read the last verse saying here endeth the reading of the 36th chapter of Isaiah, containing twenty-two verses, the interrogation was then commenced by the master asking each scholar in rotation what struck him or her in the reading. This was answered by the first and second, and one or two lower down from the top of the class, reading each a verse of the chapter. The others answered that nothing had struck them. This was the master's mode of questioning and obtaining answers, instead of requiring them in their own language, to state what might have attracted their attention during the reading. I then examined them as to the facts contained in what they read, the persons mentioned, and the meaning of some of the words; but I soon found they were unaccustomed to this kind of exercise, for I could not obtain a single answer to the questions I asked. They did not know who Hezekiah was. They did not know the meanings of the words "prophet," "city," "scribe," nor "captain" which they read in the chapter. They did not know who Abraham, Saul, David, nor [*sic*] Solomon was, nor the names of Jacob's twelve sons. A girl who stood third from the top of the class did not know who Jesus Christ was : though she could repeat the Apostles' Creed, I had to make her repeat it *three* times before she answered me who Jesus Christ was. The writing was very indifferent, and arithmetic was only taught to two boys. One of them answered that 8od. was 2s. 6d., and neither could tell for a long while how many farthings there were in 3d. The poor little unfortunates who were not able to read in the Scriptures were doomed to sit down, all day, book in hand on a form, without any change of position, except the few moments when they go up to the master to say their lesson—a mode of proceeding enough to tire and disgust the most ardent aspirant in the pursuit of knowledge. The children are very quick and apt to learn, or they would acquire nothing under all the disadvantages arising from the want of suitable books, uncomfortable schoolrooms, and the want of properly trained and educated teachers. For there appears in none of the schools that I have yet visited in this county any system of teaching, classification of the pupils, nor any regular plan of proceeding.

(Signed) Henry Penry

Assistant [Commissioner]

October 29th, 1846

Appendix 5

THE STUDENT'S POINT OF VIEW

Extracts from material collected by the Board of Education and published in the *Report of the Board of Education for 1912–13*, Parliamentary Papers 1914, XXV : from James Runciman's *Schools and Scholars*, published in 1887. Runciman (1852–1891) refers to himself as Annesley and the extracts are from those printed on 48–51 of the Board of Education *Report*. The college concerned is Borough Road, London, *c.*1871–72 and Runciman himself was born, the son of a coastguardsman, at the village of Cresswell near Morpeth, Northumberland.

A company of lads stood about in sheepish fashion in a long, bare corridor, which was shrewdly searched by eddying draughts; but as the evening wore on the passage was deserted, and the motley company took shelter in a long low room, which was fitted with deal tables and lengthy forms. A squalid room it was. The floor was passably clean, and so were the walls, but the aspect of the place was unspeakably forbidding. Not a picture relieved the chill blank of the plaster—not a sign of comfort appeared; the sprawling ill-lighted apartment was like the common room of a workhouse. Some of the young men were gossiping; some sat sadly apart. Here and there a loud-voiced braggart told stories of his own exploits to a circle of meek admirers.

At half-past nine a bell rang, and the young men, to the number of a hundred and twenty, trooped into a lecture-room, which looked like a squalid model of one end of the Coliseum. Tiers of rickety, narrow desks rose from the floor and sloped upwards to a height of about fourteen feet. The walls were greasy, leprous, bedizened with tattered maps. A vast blackboard stood in one corner, and an oaken table curved within the lowermost row of desks. It was hard to sit in the queer seats, for they were contrived, like everything in the building, with a view to combining discomfort and ugliness in the most appalling proportions. A man in clerical garments entered, and solemnly waited for silence; then a hymn was sung, and the fine thunder of trained male voices thrilled Annesley's nerves.

The stairs were bare, and the hoarse winds that moaned around the building forced their way in, and swept shrieking over the cold stones. Annesley was much interested when he saw the rooms on the first landing. Long lines of cells stretched like rows of horse-boxes from right to left. Each cell was open at the top, and the men were only separated from each other by a low partition, so that privacy was practically unknown. . . . In Annesley's narrow little den everything was spotlessly clean, but the general aspect was depressing and cold—oh, so cold! No candles were allowed, and the men who were farthest away from the gas had to grope their way to bed amid lurching shadows and chance lights.

A bell rattled with impatient clamour; a dragging chorus of yawns resounded. Thumps on the floor showed that the reluctant youngsters were rising, and the splash of many basins tinkled oddly. The British notions of cleanliness were sternly set at naught at the . . . College; each youth washed himself as best he could in a minute basin, but the cold tub was unknown. The pious founders apparently considered that washing takes the stamina out of a man, and they arranged so as to let every student cleanse himself in the orthodox way about once a month.

Annesley found his first day's experiences partly droll, partly humiliating. At breakfast-time he took his seat on a form of the workhouse pattern, and made the best he could of the hunks of bread and the mysterious coffee. The utter want of refinement, the savagery of the whole meal, somewhat revolted him, and the unearthly cold of the big feeding-shed cut him to the bone.

Annesley never in all his time heard an indecent word or an oath from any man of either year. In truth, the students were not like young men at all; they affected an air of solemnity, and each one tried to look as though he had been invited to an interview with a ghost, and wished to adjust his features to the occasion. They addressed each other as "Mister," and the politeness generally observed was very funny.

There was not a picture or an ornament in any room; the asceticism of a workhouse was blended with the solidity and ugliness of a gaol, and the combination formed the abode of a hundred and twenty eager, hopeful lads.

The students lived the repressed, arid, bleak life of charity-children. No man could have a moment of privacy until he was in bed. The barren, foetid rooms, with their greasy forms and notched desks, were the only places where a letter could be written, and many a poor fellow, sick with heartache, had to sit down in a miserable class-room and compose his letters, while lively comrades shouted and carried on horse-play all round him. If a man had tried to go up to his bedroom for an hour of quiet thought, he would, in all probability, have been dismissed for the offence. It was hardly possible to read out of class hours, and Annesley often wandered into lonely streets and tramped up and down with his volume of Shelley or Carlyle. . . .

Smoking was regarded as a crime too serious for mention, but, of course, the men who had learned to smoke could not be prevented from taking their pipes after hours. No grounds were attached to the melancholy place, but at the back there was a narrow, flagged yard, like the square in which Millbank prisoners take exercise, and there the smokers gathered when the weather was warm enough. On bitter winter nights the school of smokers hid themselves in any filthy corner where they happened to be secure from observation, and they chatted and puffed with doleful satisfaction.

At dinner the position of refined men was humiliating. Silence was enforced, and the rows of students sat like images on the mean forms, and the food was passed down in rough platefuls. The meat was of the best, and an unwholesome mouthful of any kind never appeared on the table; but the mode of serving was brutally coarse. Manners were forgotten, and the greediest men grabbed at the vegetables with silent vulture-like eagerness. An ugly white mug was placed down beside each plate, and only water was allowed. . . .

Appendix 6

CHILD WORKERS IN AGRICULTURE—AND THEIR TEACHERS—IN THE 1860s

(*a*) In the sparsely populated Eastern counties of England, particularly from the 1840s, large public gangs of women, young persons and children were employed under the charge of a gangmaster to carry out weeding, stonepicking and other agricultural tasks. They operated on a migratory basis, working first on one holding and then on another. As a result of disclosures of the conditions under which they worked, an Agricultural Gangs Act was passed in 1867, prohibiting the employment of children under the age of 8 in public gangs; outlawing gangs of mixed sex; and laying down that gangmasters must be licensed by the local magistrates. By the Agricultural Children Act of 1873 the minimum age of gang members was raised to ten. Thanks to these measures some of the evils of the system described below were eliminated, but the Gangs Act did *not* protect children employed either in private gangs, recruited by a single farmer, or in other areas of agriculture—as items (b) and (c) below will confirm.

From the *Sixth Report of the Children's Employment Commission*, Parliamentary Papers 1867, XVI. *Evidence on Agricultural Gangs collected by Mr. J. E. White in 1866*, 139.

Mr. John Harris, National Schoolmaster, Eye, Northamptonshire :
. . . A large number of the children here work in a gang under the
gangmaster and his son, boys and girls working together. A week
ago there were 72 in it, 35 boys and 26 girls being between the ages
of 7 and 13, and five boys under the age of 7. Now (31st May) the
gang is much larger. Cases of children under 6 years old are rare.
I know of two only from the school, but have been informed of
others. Within the last twelve months a fine boy of 5 years old was
sent out to work. He was an illegitimate child, and so they thought
much of keeping him, and as soon as he could earn anything he
must. When he first went, he used to be carried home from his work
by the others. On inquiry, I am informed on good authority that six
or seven cases of children equally as young are to be met with in
the gang, most of whom have never attended school. The children
are paid for at so much a score. I see them begin to assemble at
this corner at about 6.15 a.m., and start at 6.30, and see them come
back about 6 p.m., not together, but in groups, as they please.

The school attendance is very much affected by the absence of
the children at work, chiefly in the gang. It is my usual practice
when a child is absent from school to inquire why, and to put the
reason against his name. Looking hastily at the attendances within
a year past I see four weeks in which the numbers were respectively
from 94 to 97. February is the fullest time. By now, May, the
numbers have fallen to 70, and will drop till the end of July, when
there will not be more than, say, 30 or so; then comes a month's
holiday . . .

The distances to which the children go to work are so great
('from half to five miles. Sometimes waggons meet them half-way
in the long distances.' . . .) that they could not come to school for
half days. . . . Many parents though professing and appearing to be
really anxious to keep their children at school, still when the working time comes let them go off again. The attraction of the earnings
is no doubt too strong for them. I have, however, known several
cases, though these are comparatively rare, in which the children
of labourers at 11s. or 12s. a week have gone to the gang only on
Saturday, when there is no school, to earn their 4d. to pay their
school 2d. or, with copy book, 3d. . . .

(*b*) From the *First Report of the Royal Commission on the Employment of Children, Young Persons and Women in Agriculture*, Parliamentary Papers 1867–68, XVII. Evidence submitted by Mr George
Culley on Bedfordshire.
Walter Browning, head of Biggleswade Boys' British School. Has
been master for nine years.

Boys usually withdrawn before 10. Out of 150 children 100 belong to agricultural labouring class. If a boy began his attendance at 5, and attended school regularly up to 10, he would be able to pass in Standard 3 of the Revised Code. I hardly think four winter months' attendance would do, better alternate days or weeks throughout the year (harvest excepted); many boys attend my school for three winter months between 10 and 13. Boys attend very irregularly after 6 or 7 years of age. They go out for a month in spring, potato dropping and field keeping, at 7 years. Later in the year they go to onion peeling. I was pupil teacher at Croydon before coming here, and I find the children here very much more difficult to teach and much slower than the children in the neighbourhood of Croydon. This difference of aptitude to learn has struck me very forcibly. A good many labourers in the town do not send their children to school at all after they leave the infant school. Many children are sent to plait schools. The parents do not care about their children learning. I am afraid it would put a serious burden upon many parents if attendance was made compulsory up to 10. Even well-disposed parents seem obliged to withdraw their children from school at 8 or 9.

(*c*) From the *Second Report of the Royal Commission on the Employment of Children, Young Persons and Women in Agriculture*, Parliamentary Papers 1868–69, XIII. Evidence submitted by the Hon. Edwin B. Portman on Cornwall in 1869.

Mr Martin, master, Gulval Mixed School.

The children have been out lately putting down potatoes. Some boys of 8 years old have been out, and some girls. Small holders of land work their children very young, e.g.—William Row (7 years old) has been out putting down potatoes for two years for his father who holds four fields, two in grass for his cow, and two in gardens. The boy looks after the cow, and when he cannot his sister does, who is 9 years of age. He is very irregular in his attendance at School.

If any law was made for enforcing school attendance, I should like the penalty to be put on the employer as well as on the parents in case of neglect. I think that attendance at school should be encouraged, as well as absence from work compelled.

T. Oliver (7 years old).—I have been out putting down potatoes; got fourpence a day; worked from 6 a.m. to 6 p.m., half-an-hour being allowed for dinner.

Ellen Pierce (11 years old) very irregular in attendance.—I have been out pulling radishes at 7d. a day, hours of work from 8 a.m. to 6 p.m. I go home to dinner from 12 to 1 o'clock. Men, women, boys and girls all worked together potatoing; we were seven girls, five boys, three women, and one man to fill in the drills; the women get 10d. a day. The older girls go away early from the morning school to cook or carry dinner for their mothers in the gardens. My aunt works in the gardens, gets 5s. or 6s. a week. 10d. a day is the wage for day work and 1s. a day for tut [piece] work. In my cottage we have one kitchen, one bedroom, and a dairy, where mother, aunt, grandmother, and myself live together.

Appendix 7

EXTRACTS FROM THE DIARIES OF WILLIAM
WRIGHT, MASTER OF FOLKINGHAM FREE SCHOOL,
LINCOLNSHIRE

1849
December
10th, Monday. A fine morning but damp. Arose at 7 and Mr C. called of me to go up to the Pits to measure [the] Stone Heaps. Upwards of 200 yards this time and the last for which twice I am not paid; we settle at Mich^s. In the Evening I read the Sunday Times. Called at Clifton's and at Mr. Chambers's. Gone from Sleaford to Boston . . . 12th, Wednesday . . . I went to Mr. Chambers's to choose 2 pigs. Dan brought them in the afternoon. Dry day, but cold and froze at night and very windy. I went after tea to Mr. Banks's on Business.
13th, Thursday . . . After School Mr. Banks drove me in his Carriage down to Horbling respecting his Mortgage and Accounts . . .
14th, Friday. A finer morning but damp atmosphere. Folkingham Rent Day. I went to pay my Rent and Mrs. Brothwell's about 10 o'clock. At noon I went to Mr. Banks's to write him a Notice to Messrs. Smith and Wiles respecting his Mortgage. He saw Mr. Wiles and delivered it to him. A cold night. Read News.
15th, Saturday. A fine morning. I went to Newton to survey. It began to rain very fast indeed before I got to Walcott I got wet by [the time] I got to Newton; got dried at 11 o'clock. Had an early Dinner & M^r. W^m. Ellis & I started in the Rain to Survey we Surveyed 17 acres & 14 acres Arable and part of Mr. Welby's Garden by 5 o'clock, fair at night, we both got wet; and almost up to the knees. I arrived home about ½ past nine o'clock . . .
16th, Sunday . . . Went to Folkingham Church in the morning. In the afternoon I went a shepherding to both places; Took the Cow

up for good. Mrs. Chambers called in the afternoon to nurse. . . .
Mrs. Howitt called to see Baby. [Wright's only son had been born
in the previous November.]

17th, Monday . . . Wonderful wet time as ever was known.

18th, Tuesday . . . Broke up at 10 o'clock and went to Newton to
Survey. It began to rain before I got to Walcott and rained wonder-
fully all the time I was surveying got twice wet through, dined at
Newton, after dinner I drove to Folkingham, took up Mother and
Dawson and went to Donington. Dawson took the Mare back . . .
Smoked a pipe with my Friend Dolby and staid until 11 o'clock . . .

1850
June

3rd, Monday. A very fine morning indeed and hot. Cottam called
me between 3 and 4 o'clock and his Boy helped me to weed my
Potatoes until breakfast time. Mr. Miller who came yesterday, called
with Mr. Chambers as they went up to the Farm. Whittaker clipped
8 Sheep for me, and I had the 2 Ewes in the front paddock washed
and put into the Sleaford Road Field. Mr. and Mrs. Walton of
Rippingale and the little Boy and Girl called in the Evening as they
returned from Sleaford . . .

4th, Tuesday. A fine hot morning. The 11th Anniversary of my
Appointment to the Mastership of Folkingham School . . . Went a
shepherding at night. . . .

5th, Wednesday. A very fine hot morning. After shepherding I
mowed the front Grass plots; Hilling Potatoes. A great fight expected
to come off at Thistleton Gap, between Bendigo, the Champion of
England and a Londoner Parrock for £400 a side and the Cham-
pionship. Bendigo, the former Champion, of Nottingham was the
Winner.* They fought 49 Rounds in 59 Minutes at or near March,
Cambridgeshire on some Nobleman's Estate by permission . . .

6th, Thursday . . . Planted my Sheep Cabbage in the morning early.
In the afternoon I went up to measure fencing at Mr. Chambers's
Farm and Mr. Owen's, done by Mr. Briggs of Swinstead. Upon Mr.
Chambers's Farm 70½ Acres of 3 and 4 Rail Fencing and upon Mr.
Owens's 6½ nearly Acres of 3 and 4 Rail Fencing. Showery after-
noon, finished about 7 o'clock. A fine shower about 8 for about ¼ of
an hour. Went a Shepherding after the Rain . . .

7th, Friday. A windy morning. I arose as usual at 5 o'clock &

---

* 'Bendigo' was a well-known early Victorian prize-fighter. His real name
was William Thompson and he was the nineteenth child of a poor Nottingham woman. Eventually after his career in the ring had ended he was
converted to 'religion' and became a mission preacher with a special vocation to London cabmen.

shepherded. Read Newspaper. Had W^m. Bland to weed the Mangold Wurzel. Finished Hilling Potatoes; . . . Read Newspaper at night . . . Sent M^r. Ellis 2 large cabbages by Thomas Swann.

September
23rd, Monday . . . The Chapel Tea drinking . . . Thomas Swann gave up coming to School as he is going to his Uncle at Tetney next Sunday to be a Draper and Grocer. William Johnson also did not come . . . 140 at the tea party besides the children. In the Evening I and Mr. Wilson settled the Balance due to me £5 4/4. I recd. the £5, the 4/4 goes into the next Account . . .

Appendix 8

MEMORIES OF THE EARLY TWENTIETH CENTURY
AS SCHOLAR AND TEACHER

The reminiscences of Mrs Stella Elliott of Denbury, Devon. Mrs Elliott was the daughter of a Dartmoor farming family and first attended school in September 1911, at the age of four. She was an uncertificated teacher from 1925 until her marriage in 1935 but the conditions she describes in those years were, in many respects, equally applicable to country schools before 1914.

I have lived in this village of Denbury all my life. I began going to school at the age of four years. The classroom was too small for the size of the class (about forty) and we were obliged to sit very close together on long forms—seating and work surfaces combined. We used slates and slate pencils, bead frames and shells (cowries) for number work. Every day commenced with a hymn and prayers (the door between this classroom and the seniors' schoolroom being left open so that we could all join in). Then the registers were called and kept open until 10 a.m. for any late comers to be marked in (red mark for those on time, black mark for the late comers). After 10 a.m. anyone who came was considered absent. This often happened because children had to walk two and often two-and-a-half miles from outlying farms or hamlets.

A scripture lesson followed and this was very important because once a year a clergyman, appointed by the Diocese of Exeter came to examine the whole school in Religious Knowledge. We learnt passages of Scripture, Psalms, hymns by heart. Reading (primers with large print—at, cat, mat type), writing—pothooks to start with —some physical exercise, mainly marching and arm exercises and heel raising and lowering, all followed in the mornings.

The afternoons were given over to drawing (first using slates and then little sheets of paper about 3″ x 4″), object lessons on a remarkable range of subjects—coal, rice, leather, water, etc. etc.—and always a story to finish the day, when the teacher would show us large pictures half as big as the black board—of a nursery rhyme character or a fairy tale. School ended at 3.45 for infants, 4 p.m. for seniors, after an evening hymn (often Now the day is Over or Jesus tender Shepherd hear me) and prayers. Then good afternoon Ma'am and a *curtsy* and home.

At 7 or 8 years of age (according to the standard reached) we were moved to the big schoolroom (where the intermediate 7–11 and the seniors 11–14 were all taught, about 40–45 altogether). This meant two teachers and two classes all working in one room without any partition at all. A sliding screen was added some years after I left.

As well as the studies followed in the infant class we now commenced History, Geography, mental arithmetic, dictation, needlework, knitting, poetry (a separate lesson for learning poems by heart), singing, including tonic solfa.

At all times the students had to be silent until spoken to. It was an offence to talk or even whisper and if detected would mean losing the quarter hour playtime or staying on after school. I remember having to hem pillow cases of very strong calico at the age of seven years, doing a run and fell seam, and making a harsh calico night-gown, with eleven tucks each side of the front opening! I also remember an Inspector—HMI Mr England—calling me out to the front of the class to cut out, by eye only, a chemise for myself—in paper first. I well remember looking up to find him and all the girls in the class laughing at me because I always worked with my tongue out if I was engrossed in anything.

At twelve years of age my mother decided I ought to take the voluntary scholarship examination for possible entry to Newton Abbot Secondary School, as it was then called. The teacher was not inclined to let any children sit this examination—I could never think why—but mother insisted that I should.

So at the age of thirteen I began school at Newton Abbot which meant me cycling the four miles each way every day. I remember the cold, the gales and the rain and snow I had to go through and the nervous stress I went through when I got into the, to me, large school of 240 pupils. Our village teachers had all been so friendly and even motherly. We had the greatest confidence in them. We had a Mr Perry, Miss Evans, Mrs Slader, Miss Little in succession, all of whom lived in the village and would help in all sorts of ways in village life—sports committees, fêtes, money-raising efforts, church life, etc. I remember they have helped in drawing up of wills even, especially the gentleman.

I went to Newton Abbot Secondary School for five years and managed to get seven passes in the Oxford Senior examination and exemption from the London Matriculation. My parents decided I must leave school and go to earn some wages.

I did one year's student teaching from 1924 to 1925. This meant teaching for four days a week and going back to the Secondary School on Fridays, for lessons. We were expected to read one classic—a Dickens or Brontë, etc.—during the week and have it summarised by Friday. I was sent to three different schools during that year. (1) Highweek girls'; (2) Bovey Tracey Junior; and (3) Kingskerswell Junior. We were sent to these schools by the County— we did not apply directly. We had *no* training or instruction in teaching.

At Highweek I was placed in charge of Standard III as the mistress of that class was away ill and there I remained for my three months although I think I ought to have been given experience in all standards. I received 12s. 6d per week salary.

At the end of that year I had to try to get myself a job. I had interviews for Membury, near Axminster and Abbotskerswell near Newton Abbot. I was fortunate enough to get to Abbotskerswell as Infant Mistress in 1925 after an interview with the school managers —chairman, Rector of the parish; clerk, the blacksmith; also two farmers and two ladies of means.

I had the most wonderful Head Mistress to work with, who remained my very dear friend to the end of her life. She was absolutely dedicated to her work and was an influence for good to all her pupils.

The children were poorly clothed and rather dull compared with today's children. The Head teacher was quite an authority on botany and there was always a 'specimen table' and children were encouraged to bring any flower or shrub and name it and give all information on it in a book kept for the purpose. This Head Mistress (Miss G. Hull) was very keen on celebrating Empire Day. As many of the pupils as possible were told to represent a Colony— some most remote and tiny. The national costume, produce, customs, music, flags were as far as possible studied and provided for a procession through the village on the afternoon of May Day and very colourful and interesting these processions were.

Miss Hull and I together trained the children in Maypole dancing every year for the village Flower Show and Fête. We were able to give a great deal of time to this in school hours and after school, as we had a maypole in the school yard.

Miss Hull even started making soup for some of the poorest children to have at dinner time—she had six of a family of fourteen children at the time.

Together we put on some very successful concerts while at Abbotskerswell, making all the clothes and properties ourselves. We got enough money to buy a piano for the school and other extras.

When I was a pupil at the village school here at Denbury and also while I taught at Abbotskerswell, discipline was always strictly maintained. The cane was used (on the hand) in cases of serious ill-behaviour, but only for boys. Other punishments were detention, loss of privileges or little favours.

Absenteeism was rather high—boys would stay at home to help on farms, especially at harvest time or at 'brushing', beating for game shoots. Girls would stay at home to help mother or look after younger children. I remember, too, that toddler brothers and sisters were allowed to come to school in any emergency in the home—birth of a baby, etc. As boys reached the age of 12 or 13 they would start to work (mornings and evenings) for any local farmer who would employ them, hoping that when they eventually left school at fourteen they would be taken on as permanent employees. The little money they could earn would have to go towards the expenses of their home and family.

As children we all had to work from about the age of nine or even earlier. I myself had to milk cows both morning and evening before taking my scholarship and help in the evenings with yard work or digging weeds, etc.

The attendance officer came to the schools about once in ten days or a fortnight to look into attendance registers. He would visit the parents of bad attenders and reprimand them. This usually had the effect of improving attendance. Only in very bad cases did the County take the offending parents to court.

Also a County Council State Registered Nurse would visit the schools about once every month to examine all the children regarding their skin condition (ring worm was common) cleanliness of clothing, and condition of hair, as fleas and nits were very often found in children's hair then. I remember when the fashion of "bobbed" or short hair came in, this reduced the trouble of vermin very much.

March 1977.

Notes

Chapter 1
SCHOOLS AND TEACHERS OF THE
OLD TYPE
(pp. 1–29)

1. M. St Clare Byrne, *Elizabethan Life in Town and Country*, 7th ed., London 1957, 179.
2. A. H. Dodd, *Life in Elizabethan England*, London 1961, 93.
3. Joan Simon, *Education and Society in Tudor England*, Cambridge, 1967, 151.
4. Simon, *Education and Society*, 236.
5. John Lawson, *Mediaeval Education and the Reformation*, London 1967, 84.
6. Lawrence Stone, 'The Educational Revolution in England, 1560–1640', in *Past and Present*, 28 (July 1964), 44.
7. Simon, *Education and Society*, 203, notes the lamentations of Oxford University in 1539 that thanks to the withdrawal of monastic residents and students, 'the number of students had been halved'. While at Cambridge at around the same time, though some of the colleges were lively enough, the university as such was hardly flourishing (207).
8. Stone, 'The Educational Revolution', 71.
9. Simon, *Education and Society*, 329.
10. John Lawson and Harold Silver, *A Social History of Education in England*, London 1973, 119.
11. Lawson, *Mediaeval Education*, 104. See Lawrence Stone, ed., *The University in Society*, vol. I, Princeton 1974, 20, for mention of some poor men's sons who became undergraduates.
12. Simon, *Education and Society*, 292, quoting from a paper by J. E. Neale, reprinted in *Essays in Elizabethan History*, 1958, 230–1.
13. At Willingham in Cambridge, for example, the inhabitants endowed a school by public subscription in 1593. Even landless cottagers managed to contribute 8s. or 10s. to the common fund.

See Margaret Spufford, 'The Schooling of the Peasantry in Cambridgeshire, 1575–1700' in *Land, Church and People*, ed. Joan Thirsk, *Agricultural History Review Supplement*, 18 (1970), 132.

14. Lawson and Silver, *A Social History of Education*, 69.
15. Simon, *Education and Society*, 303.
16. Quoted by Diana McClatchey, *Oxfordshire Clergy 1777–1869*, Oxford 1960, 135.
17. Simon, *Education and Society*, 321.
18. Lawson and Silver, *A Social History of Education*, 113.
19. Lawson and Silver, *A Social History of Education*, 191. Christopher Hill, *The Century of Revolution 1603–1714*, London 1961, 163, notes of the Parliamentary educational measures of 1649 : 'The original Puritan hope of devoting the whole of the proceeds [of the sale of Bishops' lands and Dean and Chapter lands] to the promotion of religion and learning was not realised : the demands of the Army were too great. Nevertheless, over £30,000 a year from Dean and Chapter lands went to augment stipends of ministers and schoolmasters.'
20. A. C. F. Beales, 'The Struggle for Schools' in *The English Catholics, 1850–1950*, ed. G. A. Beck, London 1950, 365.
21. John Bossy, *The English Catholic Community 1570–1850*, London 1975, 273 and 276. For details of East Yorkshire schools see J. Lawson, *Primary Education in East Yorkshire 1560–1902*, East Yorkshire Local History Series No. 10 (1959), 18.
22. Lawson and Silver, *A Social History of Education*, 113, quoting the comment of Charles Hoole.
23. Byrne, *Elizabethan Life*, 182–3.
24. Spufford, 'The Schooling of the Peasantry', 126.
25. Lawson and Silver, *A Social History of Education*, 114.
26. Lawson and Silver, *A Social History of Education*, 187.
27. The Rev. H. A. Lloyd Jukes, ed., *Articles of Enquiry Addressed to the Clergy of the Diocese of Oxford at the Primary Visitation of Dr Thomas Secker, 1738*, XXXVIII, Oxfordshire Record Society (1957), 19.
28. Clergy Visitation Returns for the Oxford Diocese for 1759 at the Bodleian Library, Oxford, MSS.Oxf.Dioc.Pp.d.555–7.
29. Lawson and Silver, *A Social History of Education*, 192.
30. W. H. G. Armytage, *Four Hundred Years of English Education*, Cambridge 1964, 40.
31. M. G. Jones, *The Charity School Movement*, Cambridge 1938, 39.
32. Jones, *The Charity School Movement*, 41.
33. Lawson and Silver, *A Social History of Education*, 184.

34. Jones, *The Charity School Movement*, 98, quoting from *Account of the Charity Schools*, 1704.

35. Derek Robson, *Some Aspects of Education in Cheshire in the Eighteenth Century*, Manchester: The Chetham Society, 3rd Series, XIII (1966), 32–3.

36. Bernard Mandeville, *The Fable of the Bees*, first published in complete form in 1724; Penguin ed. 1970, Phillip Harth ed., 296.

37. Lawson and Silver, *A Social History of Education*, 185.

38. Thomas Charles to William Wilberforce, written in 1793, and preserved at the Bodleian Library, MS.Wilberforce d.17, 36. In a letter to Henry Thornton, also written in 1793 and preserved at the Bodleian Library, MS.Wilberforce d.13, 110, Charles noted that after his appointment of the first teacher 'the Lord has wonderfully raised up Friends one after another to assist us. Mr Barham of Hardwicke in Shropshire was the first who stepped forward & several Times relieved our necessities. Since his death we have met with Friends; & last year we were quite set up by charitable contributions conveyed to us by Mr Grant from you & others.'

39. Jones, *The Charity School Movement*, 89–90. The parish of Artleborough is also known by the name of Irthlingborough.

40. N. Rowley, *Education in Essex c.1710–1910*, Chelmsford 1974, Document 16.

41. Robson, *Some Aspects of Education*, 33.

42. F. A. Wendeborn, *A View of England*, II, London 1791, 132.

43. *A Schoolmaster's Difficulties Abroad and at Home*, London 1853, 2. This anonymous booklet is preserved at the British Library in London.

44. Richard D. Altick, *The English Common Reader*, Chicago 1957, 147.

45. William Reitzel, ed., *The Autobiography of William Cobbett*, London 1967 paperback ed., 11–12.

46. Manuscript reminiscences of Thomas Hall of Farnborough (b.1817) in the possession of the Misses Hall of Stratford-on-Avon.

47. *The Life of Thomas Cooper*, introduced by John Saville, Leicester 1971, 7. This book was first published in 1872.

48. *The Life of Thomas Cooper*, 75–6.

49. *A Narrative of the Life and Adventures of William Brown*, York 1829, 120–22.

50. *Hansard*, 3 Series, XCI, cols. 1016–1017.

51. *Hansard*, 3 Series, XCI, cols. 1058–1059.

52. *Minutes of the Committee of Council on Education for 1841–*

42, Parliamentary Papers 1842, XXXIII, 162. Report by the Rev. John Allen on schools in the County of Derby.

53. See documents on Begbroke parish at the Bodleian Library, MS.D.D.Par.Begbroke d.4.

54. G. N. Maynard, 'Recollections of Whittlesford School and Schoolmasters in the Eighteenth and Nineteenth Centuries' preserved in manuscript at Cambridge Record Office, Maynard MSS. Vol. VI, R.58/5/6, 73. The account was written by Mr Maynard in 1886.

55. Maynard, 'Recollections of Whittlesford School', 85.

56. William Blackstone, *Commentaries on the Laws of England*, Boston 1962 ed., 206. In *R. v. Hopley* a private schoolmaster in Sussex was found guilty in 1860 of the manslaughter of a pupil because he had inflicted 'immoderate and unreasonable corporal punishment', but the schoolmaster's right to use 'corporal punishment to a moderate extent' was reaffirmed. See G. R. Barrell, *Legal Cases for Teachers*, London 1970, 220–2.

57. *Reports of the Commissioners of Inquiry into the State of Education in Wales Appointed by the Committee of Council on Education*, Part III, Parliamentary Papers 1847, XXVII, Report by Henry V. Johnson on North Wales, 12.

58. *Reports of the Commissioners of Inquiry*, 15.

59. Charles Freeman, *Pillow Lace in the East Midlands*, Luton Museum and Art Gallery 1958, 18–19. Mr Freeman notes also : 'Our earliest local references to the training of children at lacemaking is . . . the Eaton Socon overseers' entry of 1596, when Goodwife Clarke was paid 2d. a week for teaching each child, and the children were to receive what they earned.'

60. *Appendix to the Second Report of the Children's Employment Commission*, Parliamentary Papers 1843, XIV, a.55.

61. *Appendix to the Second Report of the Children's Employment Commission*, a.50.

62. *First Report of the Royal Commission on the Employment of Children, Young Persons and Women in Agriculture*, Parliamentary Papers 1867–68, XVII, 547.

63. *Report of Robert Baker, Inspector of Factories for the Six Months ending 30 April 1871*, Parliamentary Papers 1871, XIV, 54–55.

64. Clergy Visitation Returns for the Bucks Archdeaconry at the Bodleian Library : in 1866 for Linslade, MS.Oxf.Dioc.Pp.c.331 and in 1872 for Edlesborough, MS.Oxf.Dioc.Pp.c.337.

65. Quoted in William Marshall, *The Review and Abstract of the County Reports to the Board of Agriculture*, 4, York 1818, 515.

66. *Minutes of the Committee of Council on Education for 1845*,

Parliamentary Papers 1846, XXXII, 298. Report by the Rev. Frederick Watkins on schools in the Northern District.

67. A. Platts and G. H. Hainton, *Education in Gloucestershire: A Short History*, Gloucestershire County Council 1954, 69.

68. *Minutes of the Committee of Council on Education for 1842–43*, Parliamentary Papers 1843, XL, 9. Second Report by the Rev. John Allen on schools in Derbyshire.

69. Notice and admonition to John Charville preserved at Cambridge Record Office, P.17/25/12.

70. Angela Black, *Guide to Education Records in the County Record Office, Cambridge*, Cambridgeshire and Isle of Ely County Council 1972, 25.

71. *Minutes of the Committee of Council on Education for 1842–43*, Parliamentary Papers 1843, XL, Report on the Endowed School at Yaxley, Hunts., 2.

72. *Minutes of the Committee of Council on Education for 1842–43*, Second Report on schools in Derbyshire, 9.

73. *Minutes of the Committee of Council on Education for 1843–44*, Parliamentary Papers 1845, XXXV, Report by the Rev. John Allen on schools in Bedfordshire, Cambridgeshire and Huntingdonshire, 4.

74. Quoted in W. F. E. Gibbs, 'The Development of Elementary Education in Dorset from the Early Nineteenth Century to 1870', Southampton University M.A. thesis 1960, 132.

75. Gillian Sutherland, *Elementary Education in the Nineteenth Century*, Historical Association Pamphlet G.76, 1971, 13–14; E. G. West, *Education and the Industrial Revolution*, London 1975, 41. Professor West's optimism concerning literacy rates seems greater than is warranted by the facts because his figures appear to be based on *male* literacy estimates and ignore the lower *female* returns normally applicable. For the earlier literacy figures see L. Stone, 'Literacy and Education in England 1640–1900' in *Past and Present*, 42 (February 1969), 101–2. David Cressy, 'Levels of Illiteracy in England, 1530–1730' in *Historical Journal*, 20, No. 2 (March 1977), 1–23.

76. H. C. Barnard, *A History of English Education from 1760*, London 1961, 66, quoting the Whig politician, Henry Brougham.

77. Calculated from *Education Enquiry: Abstract of the Answers and Returns*, Parliamentary Papers 1835, XLI–XLIII. Complaints have been made that this enquiry *underestimates* the number of schools but there appears to be little evidence for this outside the larger towns and cities. Furthermore, the county comparisons are valid, as similar errors and omissions would, no doubt, apply to all of them. For consideration of

this point see West, *Education and the Industrial Revolution,* 76 and Sutherland, *Elementary Education,* 11. For the late 1850s position regarding Wiltshire and Brecon, see *Royal Commission on Popular Education (England),* Parliamentary Papers XXI, Pt. I, 595.

Chapter 2
THE MONITORIAL SYSTEM
(pp. 30–54)

1. Rex C. Russell, *A History of Schools and Education in Lindsey, Lincolnshire, 1800–1902,* Pt 2, Lindsey County Council Education Committee 1965, 12–13. Myers's comments were written in 1789.
2. M. G. Jones, *Hannah More,* Cambridge 1952, 173.
3. Richard Allen Soloway, *Prelates and People,* London 1969, 359.
4. Soloway, *Prelates and People,* 364–5.
5. Soloway, *Prelates and People,* 350.
6. Soloway, *Prelates and People,* 351. Indeed, in the view of Joan Simon, 'Was there a Charity School Movement? The Leicestershire Evidence' : 'it was the Sunday schools that paved the way for the mass daily school . . . At the opening of the nineteenth century the great majority of parishes were dependent on schoolmasters taking a fee, or schooldames who did little but mind children; well under a quarter had a competently endowed daily school. Clearly there was no system of charity schools, run on well defined lines, inherited from the days of the S.P.C.K.' See Brian Simon ed., *Education in Leicestershire 1540–1940,* Leicester 1968, 94–5. See also Roger Smith, 'Education, Society and Literacy : Nottinghamshire in the Mid-Nineteenth Century' in *University of Birmingham Historical Journal,* XII, No. 1, (1969), 49–53 for a discussion of the role of Sunday schools in mid-nineteenth-century Nottinghamshire.
7. Diana McClatchey, *Oxfordshire Clergy 1777–1869,* Oxford 1960, 148.
8. *The Autobiography of Mary Smith, Schoolmistress and Nonconformist,* London 1892, 36–37.
9. Sybil Marshall, *Fenland Chronicle,* Cambridge 1967, 94.
10. John Lawson and Harold Silver, *A Social History of Education in England,* London 1974, 243.
11. *Hansard,* Vol. IX, 1807, col. 1177.
12. Bishop Randolph's notes on the foundation of the National Society are at the Bodleian Library, MS.Top.Oxon.b.170.
13. Pamela and Harold Silver, *The Education of the Poor,* London 1974, 8–9.

14. Calculated from the *Report of the Royal Commission on the State of Popular Education in England*, Parliamentary Papers 1861, XXI, Pt I, 592. In 1858 there were 19,549 week-day schools (or departments) associated with the Church of England in England and Wales, as opposed to 1,131 associated with the British and Foreign School Society, 743 with the Roman Catholics, 445 with the Wesleyan (Old Connexion), 388 Congregational, 144 Baptist and 54 Unitarian; these, with other smaller groupings, gave a total of 22,647 schools in England and Wales in 1858.

15. Christ Church Estate Records preserved at the Library, Christ Church, Oxford, Ms.Estates 60.244, letter from the incumbent to Dr Samuel Smith at Christ Church, 21 January 1823.

16. S. J. Curtis and M. E. A. Boultwood, *An Introductory History of English Education Since 1800*, London 1964, 10.

17. *Report of the Select Committee on the State of Education*, Parliamentary Papers 1834, IX, Evidence of Henry Dunn, secretary to the British and Foreign Society, Q.229.

18. *Report of the Select Committee on the State of Education*, Q.363.

19. *Report of the Select Committee on the State of Education*, Evidence of the Rev. Joseph C. Wigram, secretary of the National Society, Q.784–785.

20. *Report of the Select Committee on the State of Education*, Evidence of the Rev. W. Johnson, clerical superintendent of the National Society's central school, Q.79.

21. National Society Records at Northampton Record Office, Bundle IX, 1839, letter dated 29 June 1839.

22. F. Crampton, 'The Old and New Schoolmaster' in *The School and the Teacher*, VII (1861), 202–3.

23. *Report of the Select Committee on the State of Education*, Q.232.

24. *Report of the Select Committee on the State of Education*, Q.331.

25. G. F. Bartle, *A History of Borough Road College*, London 1976, 15.

26. R. W. Rich, *The Training of Teachers in England and Wales during the Nineteenth Century*, Cambridge 1933, 20.

27. Correspondence at Borough Road College; letter from Peter Tyler, Baptist Minister of Haddenham, dated 14 July 1836. Tyler had been baptised (as an adult) at Princes Risborough, Buckinghamshire in 1804, but subsequently moved to Haddenham where he remained as pastor of the local Baptist Church for nearly fifty years, until his death in 1859.

28. Correspondence at Borough Road College; application from William Carmalt dated 21 February 1838 and letter from the referee dated 28 March 1838.

29. Andrew Bell, *The Madras School or Elements of Tuition*, 1808, quoted in P. H. J. H. Gosden, *How They Were Taught*, Oxford 1969, 2 and 6–7. See also David Salmon ed., *The Practical Parts of Lancaster's Improvements and Bell's Experiment*, Cambridge 1932, 69.

30. Lawson and Silver, *A Social History of Education in England*, 242. Curtis and Boultwood, *An Introductory History*, 10.

31. Rules of Bampton National School at the Bodleian Library, Oxford, MS.Oxf.dioc.Pp.c.433. Among those who emphasised the importance of 'mixing industry with education' was William Davis, interviewed by the *Select Committee on the State of Education* on 6 August 1834. Davis noted that in schools following his plan the children were 'seldom employed more than three hours in the day, and never taken to work by any sort of coercion; they are all volunteers; . . .' (Q.2706). The pupils were engaged from the age of nine or ten in rope making, straw plaiting, gardening, knitting and printing.

32. Gosden, *How They Were Taught*, 2–5, quoting from John Poole, *The Village School Improved*, 1813.

33. Lawson and Silver, *A Social History of Education in England*, 246.

34. *Fourth Annual Report of the Oxford Diocesan Board of Education*, Oxford 1843, 16 and 26.

35. *Fourth Annual Report of the Oxford Diocesan Board of Education*, 27.

36. John Hurt, *Education in Evolution*, London 1971, 89.

37. *Minutes of the Committee of Council on Education for 1845*, Parliamentary Papers 1846, XXXII, 298–299. Hurt, *Education in Evolution*, 90 for the comment by H.M.I. Morell.

38. Quoted in Asher Tropp, *The School Teachers*, London 1957, 7.

39. Rich, *The Training of Teachers*, 2.

40. Rich, *The Training of Teachers*, quoting from J. Lancaster, *Improvements in Education*, 1808. See also Joseph Lancaster, *The British System of Education*, London 1810.

41. Gilbert Stone, *A History of Labour*, London 1921, 349.

42. Theodore Huebener, *The Schools of West Germany*, New York 1962, 4.

43. *Report of the Select Committee on the State of Education*, Evidence of Professor Pillans, 37.

44. Gillian Sutherland (ed.), *Matthew Arnold on Education*, London 1973, 83.

45. *Report of the Select Committee on the State of Education*, 38.
46. Rich, *The Training of Teachers*, 29.
47. James Murphy, *Church, State and Schools in Britain, 1800–1970*, London 1971, 15–16. Hurt, *Education in Evolution*, 26. S. J. Curtis, *History of Education in Great Britain*, 7 ed., London 1967, 209. Donald H. Akeson, *The Irish Education Experiment*, London 1970, 86–90 and 360. Brian Inglis, *The Story of Ireland*, 2nd ed., London 1965, 189–191. Norman Atkinson, *Irish Education*, Dublin 1969, 90–94.
48. Rev. James Johnston, *Our Educational Policy in India*, 2nd ed., Edinburgh 1880 pamphlet, 10–11.
49. For details of the negotiations between the Church and the Committee of Council see Minutes of the Committee of Council on Education 1839–41 at the Public Record Office, Ed.9/1.—notably meetings on 4 June, 15 July and 6 August 1840.
50. Fremantle papers at Buckinghamshire Record Office, D1FR. no. 14—Lord Lansdowne to Sir Thomas Fremantle, 2 April, 1855.
51. Marion Johnson, *Derbyshire Village Schools in the Nineteenth Century*, Newton Abbot 1970, 72.
52. Quoted in J. P. Dodd, *Rural Education in Shropshire in the Nineteenth Century*, Birmingham University MA thesis 1958, 111.
53. *Hansard*, 3rd Series, Vol. XCI, debates on 19 and 22 April 1847, cols. 1012, 1017, and 1185.
54. *The Economist*, 13 March 1847.
55. *The Economist*, 3 April 1847. On 17 April of the same year *The Economist* also commented in ironic vein : 'To replace the soldier, the gaoler, and the constable, by the schoolmaster, is wholly to get rid of government. We are not prepared to expect such vast alterations from the schoolmaster.'
56. *The Economist*, 22 January 1870. See also Arthur J. Taylor, *Laissez-faire and State Intervention in Nineteenth-century Britain*, London 1972, 28, for a discussion of *The Economist*'s laissez-faire stance from 'its beginnings in 1843 . . . until 1859, when its founder and first editor, James Wilson, retired'.

Chapter 3
PUPIL TEACHERS
(pp. 55–84)
1. R. W. Rich, *The Training of Teachers in England and Wales during the Nineteenth Century*, Cambridge 1933, 57.
2. *Report of the Select Committee on the State of Education*, Parliamentary Papers 1834, IX, Q.299. Records of the Oxford

Training Institute, preserved at Culham College, Oxford and of Winchester Diocesan Training School at King Alfred's College, Winchester.

3. J. Kay Shuttleworth, *The School in its Relations to The State, The Church and the Congregation*, London 1847 pamphlet, 36.

4. Kay Shuttleworth, *The School*, 35.

5. *Minutes of the Committee of Council on Education (England and Wales) for 1846*, Parliamentary Papers 1847, XLV, 5.

6. Correspondence concerning Coleshill school, Berkshire, in 1856 at Berkshire Record Office, D/EPb E.146.

7. John Hurt, *Education in Evolution*, London 1971, 126

8. Hurt, *Education in Evolution*, 127. Rich, *The Training of Teachers*, 131–2.

9. Pupil Teachers' Broad Sheet preserved with Coleshill school records for 1856 at Berkshire Record Office, D/EPb E.146.

10. Copies of Letters Selected from Old Letter Books, 1847–58 at the Public Record Office, Ed.9.12. The Committee of Council wrote to the Portland manager on 14 February 1848.

11. Copies of Letters Selected from Old Letter Books, 1847–58, item no. 133.

12. Asher Tropp, *The School Teachers*, London 1957, 21–2.

13. *Minutes of the Committee of Council for 1846*, 4, and Rich, *The Training of Teachers*, 120.

14. *Report of the Royal Commission on the State of Popular Education in England*, Parliamentary Papers 1861, XXI, Pt 1, 100. (The Royal Commission is referred to hereafter as the Newcastle Commission from the name of its chairman.)

15. Roger R. Sellman, *Devon Village Schools in the Nineteenth Century*, Newton Abbot 1967, 83.

16. P. F. Speed, *Learning and Teaching in Victorian Times: An Elementary School in 1888*, London 1964, 86.

17. Letter dated 5 June, 1852 to James Wright of Sudbury in Copies of Letters Selected from Old Letter Books, 1847–58, item no. 280.

18. Apprenticeship Indenture of Thomas White of Fordington, Dorset, with the Managers of the Dorchester National School, dated 1 October 1855, and preserved at Dorset Record Office, D381/1.

19. *Minutes of the Committee of Council for 1846*, 2.

20. *Minutes of the Committee of Council for 1846*, 3.

21. See entry in Enstone School Board Letter Book at Oxfordshire Record Office, T/SC.1, dated 5 January 1876.

22. Rich, *The Training of Teachers*, 144–5.

23. Thomas Hardy, *Jude the Obscure*, London 1957 paperback ed., 116.
24. Letters from the Committee of Council to HMIs, dated 14 December 1854, 18 January and 7 March 1855 and 22 May 1858 in Copies of Letters Selected from Old Letter Books, 1847–58, items no. 330, 332, 337, 340 and 378.
25. HMI King noted in 1897 that half the pupil-teachers in his area did not go to college, in many cases because 'they [could not] afford it'. Q.852 in *Minutes of Evidence of the Departmental Committee on the Pupil-Teacher System*, Parliamentary Papers 1898, XXVI.
26. *King Alfred's College, Winchester*, Vol. 3 of a typescript history of the college which is preserved in the library there, 45.
27. Charles H. Judd, *The Training of Teachers in England, Scotland and Germany*, United States Bureau of Education Bulletin, No. 35, Washington 1914, 36.
28. Judd, *The Training of Teachers*, 39.
29. Tropp, *The School Teachers*, 22.
30. Quoted in Hurt, *Education in Evolution*, 135.
31. Newcastle Commission, 101.
32. Hurt, *Education in Evolution*, 137.
33. Upminster British School Minute Book at Essex Record Office, D/Q 32/1, letter written in January 1881.
34. Hurt, *Education in Evolution*, 110.
35. Hurt, *Education in Evolution*, 122–123.
36. The entrance book of the Diocesan Training Institution, Fishponds, Bristol is preserved at the College of St. Matthias.
37. Quoted in Hurt, *Education in Evolution*, 125.
38. Flora Thompson, *Still Glides the Stream*, Oxford 1966 impression, 83–84.
39. Old People's Reminiscences at Essex Record Office, 'My First Job', T/Z 25/254.
40. Old People's Reminiscences at Essex Record Office, 'My First Job', T/Z 25/332.
41. Newcastle Commission, 104–105.
42. Speed, *Learning and Teaching*, 86. See also Rich, *The Training of Teachers*, 238–239, and Dr. T. B. Shepherd, ' "School Observation" in 1855' in *The Schoolmaster* 2 September 1955.
43. Quoted in Rich, *The Training of Teachers*, 140.
44. James Saunders, *Practical Hints for Pupil Teachers on Class Management*, Wolverhampton 1877 pamphlet, preserved at the Bodleian Library, 23–24 and 28–29.
45. Mary A. Hamilton, *Margaret Bondfield*, London 1924, 38–40.

Miss Bondfield was born in March 1873, the youngest but one of eleven children. Her father was a lace designer.

46. Letter from the Rector of Upper Clatford to a prospective head teacher, 15 May 1885, at Hampshire Record Office, H.M.51. For Robert Lowe's comments see *Hansard*, 3rd Series, Vol. CLXV, 1862, col. 211. His speech was made on 13 February 1862.

47. Reminiscences of Mrs. Frances Anne Bowkett (b.1874) in an interview with the author on 29 March 1977. Sellman, *Devon Village Schools*, 82.

48. *Report of the Committee of Council on Education (England and Wales) for 1871*, Parliamentary Papers 1872, XXII, Report by H.M.I Bellairs, 34.

49. Aldermaston School Records at Berkshire Record Office, D/P 3/25/9. Similarly at Finchampstead school, also in Berkshire, the young female pupil-teacher appointed on 1 January 1896 had a commencing salary of £10 per annum only, rising to a maximum of £16. See Miscellaneous Documents of Finchampstead Church of England School at Berkshire Record Office, C/E Z.3, memorandum of agreement between the managers of the school and Nellie E. Townsend, pupil-teacher. Under the 1862 Revised Code pupil-teachers were no longer apprenticed directly to their head teacher but to the school managers.

50. *Report of the Committee of Council on Education (England and Wales)*, Parliamentary Papers 1870, XXII.

51. Calculated from Return of Oxfordshire Elementary Schools at Oxfordshire Record Office, CER.I/1 and *Minutes of Evidence of the Departmental Committee on the Pupil-Teacher System*, Q.709 and 711.

52. *Minutes of Evidence of the Departmental Committee on the Pupil-Teacher System*, Q.6083.

53. Hurt, *Education in Evolution*, 124.

54. *Report of the Committee of Council on Education (England and Wales) for 1896*, Parliamentary Papers 1897, XXVI. Probationers were recognised from 13 to 16; pupil-teachers from 15 (or 14 in rural schools) to 19 by 1900. The probationer class was abolished in 1905.

55. *Report of the Committee of Council for 1896*, xxxiii, and *Report of the Board of Education for 1900–1901*, Parliamentary Papers 1901, XIX, 28. In 1900 for every 100 teachers of each class there were 62 female certificated teachers; 84 female assistants; and 81 pupil-teachers who were female.

56. *Report of the Departmental Committee on the Pupil-Teacher System*, Parliamentary Papers 1898, XXVI, 2.

L

57. *Final Report of the Royal Commission on the Elementary Education Acts*, Parliamentary Papers 1888, XXXV, 91.
58. Rich, *The Training of Teachers*, 236. See also P. H. J. H. Gosden, *How They Were Taught*, Oxford 1969, 209–11.
59. Rich, *The Training of Teachers*, 237.
60. *Report of the Royal Commission on the Elementary Education Acts*, 91.
61. *Report of the Royal Commission on the Elementary Education Acts*, 88.
62. Quoted in J. Stuart Maclure ed., *Educational Documents England and Wales 1816–1968*, London 1972 ed., 138–9.
63. *Report of the Committee of Council on Education for 1896*, 78.
64. Quoted in Rich, *The Training of Teachers*, 244–5.
65. J. C. G. Lawson, *The Impact of the 1902 Education Act On the Church of England Schools of the Yateley Area*, M.Ed. Dissertation, University of Reading 1975, 27.
66. Finchampstead school Miscellaneous Documents at Berkshire Record Office, C/E Z.3.
67. Whitchurch School Log Book at Oxfordshire Record Office, T/SL.58/1, entry for 19 October 1886.
68. Barton Stacey School Committee Minutes 1893–1903 at Hampshire Record Office, entry 17 May 1898.
69. *Report of the Departmental Committee on the Pupil-Teacher System*, 7.
70. P. H. J. H. Gosden, *The Evolution of a Profession*, Oxford 1972, 201.
71. See Pupil Teacher's Report Book of Zoë May of Hartwell and Stone School who attended the pupil-teacher centre at Aylesbury Grammar School from 1 August 1908 to 31 July 1910 at Buckinghamshire Record Office, D/X 516/4. Gosden, *The Evolution of a Profession*, 201.
72. Notes of Lessons of A. C. Young, first-year pupil-teacher, at Buckinghamshire Record Office, D/X 516/6, for the year 1909/10.
73. Judd, *The Training of Teachers*, 21.
74. Gosden, *The Evolution of a Profession*, 209.
75. Judd, *The Training of Teachers*, 12.
76. Gosden, *The Evolution of a Profession*, 205.
77. Sellman, *Devon Village Schools*, 84.
78. Calculated from Return of Oxfordshire Elementary Schools and School Staffs, 1 March 1904 at Oxfordshire Record Office, CER/I/1.
79. Lawson, *The Impact of the 1902 Education Act*, 56.
80. Gosden, *The Evolution of a Profession*, 276.

Chapter 4
TRAINING COLLEGE LIFE
(pp. 85–114)

1. *Hansard*, 3rd Series, Vol. XXVII, 1835, cols. 1320 and 1322.
2. Lance G. E. Jones, *The Training of Teachers in England and Wales*, Oxford 1924, 15. See also John W. Adamson, *English Education 1789–1902*, Cambridge 1964 ed., 137 and Joseph Landon, *School Management*, 9th ed. London 1896, 145.
3. Wesleyan Education Committee: Register of Students, preserved at Westminster College, Oxford. A later entry in the Register notes that by the end of 1857, 172 men and 105 women (i.e. 277 students in all) had been trained at the new Westminster College.
4. Adamson, *English Education*, 117.
5. Leonard Naylor, *Culham Church of England Training College for Schoolmasters 1853–1953*, Oxford n.d. c.1953, 4 and 12.
6. Henry Hughes, 'Reminiscences of Summertown Normal School or Training College' in *The Culham Club Magazine*, No. 1 (June 1894), 6.
7. Typescript History of King Alfred's College, Winchester, Vol. I, 1, preserved at the college and *Sixth Report of the Winchester Diocesan Board of Education*, Winchester 1846, 4.
8. Naylor, *Culham Church of England Training College*, 12 and *Sixth Report of the Winchester Diocesan Board of Education*, 7–8. Also Oxford Diocesan Training Institution Pupils' Register from 1840, preserved at Culham College, Oxford.
9. *Third Annual Report of the Church of England Training School, Cheltenham*, Cheltenham 1850, 22–3.
10. Quoted in John Hurt, *Education in Evolution*, London 1971, 120.
11. F. C. Pritchard, *The Story of Westminster College 1851–1951*, London 1951, 19.
12. R. W. Rich, *The Training of Teachers in England and Wales during the Nineteenth Century*, Cambridge 1933, 50 and *Hansard*, 3rd Series, Vol. XXIX, col. 75
13. Minutes of the Committee of Council on Education, 1839–41 at the Public Record Office, Ed.9/1, entries for 1 June, 15 August and 24 September 1839 and 20 February 1840.
14. Rich, *The Training of Teachers*, 64.
15. Quoted in Hurt, *Education in Evolution*, 118.
16. *Minutes of the Committee of Council on Education (England and Wales) for 1845*, Parliamentary Papers 1846, XXXII, Report of the Rev. Henry Moseley on the Battersea Training School, 268.

17. Rich, *The Training of Teachers*, 69.
18. Rich, *The Training of Teachers*, 104.
19. S. J. Curtis and M. E. A. Boultwood, *An Introductory History of English Education Since 1800*, London 1964 ed., 283. And P. H. J. H. Gosden, *How They Were Taught*, Oxford 1969, 208.
20. Rich, *The Training of Teachers*, 75.
21. 'Bonus', 'Recollections of Culham in 1865–66' in *The Culham Club Magazine*, No. 8 (March 1896), 5.
22. Benjamin Bailey, 'A Retrospect' in *The Culhamite*, 7, No. 2 (Nov. 1898), 27.
23. Quoted in Lois Deacon and Terry Coleman, *Providence and Mr. Hardy*, London 1966, 35.
24. Angel L. Lawrence, *St Hild's College 1858–1958*, Darlington n.d. *c.*1958, 26.
25. *Report of the Committee of Council on Education (England and Wales) for 1882–83*, Parliamentary Papers 1883, XXV, Report by the Rev. Canon Warburton on Training Colleges for Schoolmistresses : section on Brighton.
26. Lawrence, *St Hild's College*, 39.
27. Lawrence, *St Hild's College*, 36.
28. Letter dated 17 May 1858, preserved at St Paul's College, Cheltenham and also Cheltenham Church of England Training College Minute Book 1845–64, entries 12 November and 10 December 1863 and 11 February 1864 for other complaints concerning the diet. The Minute Book is preserved at St Paul's College also.
29. *Minutes of the Committee of Council on Education (England and Wales) for 1854–55*, Parliamentary Papers 1854–55, XLII, 340.
30. *Royal Commission on Popular Education—Answers to the Circular of Questions*, Parliamentary Papers 1861, XXI, Pt V, 256.
31. *Royal Commission on Popular Education—Answers to the Circular*, 231.
32. The Rev. Derwent Coleridge, *The Teachers of the People*, London 1862 pamphlet, 27, 28, and 34.
33. A. Shakoor, 'The Training of Teachers in England and Wales, 1900–1939', Leicester University Ph.D. thesis 1964, 72–73. D. H. J. Zebedee, *Lincoln Diocesan Training College 1862–1962*, Lincoln 1962, 49.
34. T. J. Macnamara, 'Training College Student Days' in *New Liberal Review*, 6, No. 32, (Sept. 1903), 227–8.
35. *Minutes of the Committee of Council on Education (England and Wales) for 1845*, Report by the Rev. Henry Moseley on

the Chester Diocesan Training School, 233–4.

36. Hurt, *Education in Evolution*, 98–9. Rich, *The Training of Teachers*, 132.

37. Hurt, *Education in Evolution*, 100.

38. Hurt, *Education in Evolution*, 107–9.

39. *Speech by the Rt Hon. Robert Lowe M.P. on Moving the Education Estimate in Committee of Supply—July 11 1861*, London 1861 pamphlet, 8–9.

40. See the Revised Code for 1863 in *Report of the Committee of Council on Education (England and Wales) for 1863–64* in Parliamentary Papers 1864, XLV.

41. *Hansard*, 3rd Series, Vol. CLXV, 1862, cols. 213, 219–20.

42. Naylor, *Culham Church of England Training College*, 46.

43. *Report of the Committee of Council on Education (England and Wales) for 1864*, Parliamentary Papers 1865, Vol. XLII, 319.

44. Pritchard, *The Story of Westminster College*, 41 and G. F. Bartle, *A History of Borough Road College*, London 1976, 31.

45. Annual Reports of Cheltenham Church of England Training College and entries in the College Minute Books for 4 December 1862, 9 February 1863 and 30 November 1869.

46. Rich, *The Training of Teachers*, 188.

47. Zebedee, *Lincoln Diocesan Training College*, 24.

48. See Winchester Diocesan College Students' Register 1840–72 at the College.

49. Cheltenham Church of England Training College Minute Book 1845–64, entry for 8 October 1863.

50. *Royal Commission on the Working of the Elementary Education Acts (England and Wales): Returns from Training Colleges*, Parliamentary Papers 1888, XXXVI, section on Ripon College.

51. *Report of the Board of Education (England and Wales) for 1912–13*, Parliamentary Papers 1914, Vol. XXV, 'Historical Survey of the Training of Elementary School Teachers', 39.

52. H. C. Dent, *1870–1970: Century of Growth in English Education*, London 1970, 21.

53. Rev. George Gibb, 'The Supply of Teachers' in *Transactions of the National Association for the Promotion of Social Science*, London 1884, 354.

54. Louisa M. Hubbard, 'Elementary Teaching, a Profession for Ladies' in *Transactions of the National Association for the Promotion of Social Science*, London 1873, 377.

55. *Report of the Board of Education for 1912–13*, Historical Survey, 29.

56. Zebedee, *Lincoln Diocesan Training College*, 54, and Pritchard, *The Story of Westminster College*, 73.
57. Rich, *The Training of Teachers*, 158–159.
58. Dr. T. B. Shepherd, 'A Training College in 1855' in *The Schoolmaster*, 26 August 1955, 262. I am indebted to Mr. Patten of Oxford for this reference.
59. Charles Dickens, *Hard Times*, London : Collins Pocket Classics ed., n.d. 17–18.
60. James Runciman, *Schools and Scholars*, London 1887, 141–142.
61. Runciman, *Schools and Scholars*, 149.
62. *Report of the Board of Education for 1912–13*, Historical Survey, 60.
63. Richard D. Altick, *The English Common Reader*, Chicago 1957, 162.
64. Lawrence, *St Hild's College*, 39.
65. Shepherd, 'A Training College in 1855', 262.
66. Rich, *The Training of Teachers*, 165. Shakoor, *The Training of Teachers*, 81.
67. *Report of the Committee of Council on Education (England and Wales) for 1882–83*, Report by the Rev. Canon Warburton on Training Colleges for Schoolmistresses : section on Brighton.
68. L. Clough, 'College Reminiscences' in *The Westminsterian*, XIII, No. 2 (November 1902). Clough was a student in 1900–02.
69. Charles H. Judd, *The Training of Teachers in England, Scotland and Germany*, United States Bureau of Education Bulletin No. 35, Washington 1914, 33.
70. Rich, *The Training of Teachers*, 193.
71. Anon, 'From Hour to Hour' in *The Westminsterian*, X, No. 3, (December 1899).
72. *Report of the Board of Education for 1912–13*, Historical Survey, 68.
73. *Report of the Board of Education (England and Wales) for 1900–1901*, XIX, 27.
74. Asher Tropp, *The School Teachers*, London 1957, 188. By the beginning of the first World War there were twenty municipal colleges in England and Wales with accommodation for nearly 4,000 students; the building of them was encouraged by the provision of building grants in 1905. P. H. J. H. Gosden, *The Evolution of a Profession*, Oxford 1972, 205.
75. The supplementary teachers were introduced in the Code for 1875, Article 32(c). From an official staffing point of view they were regarded as 'equivalent to a pupil-teacher'.

76. Lee Holcombe, *Victorian Ladies at Work*, Newton Abbot 1973, 36. *Report of the Board of Education for 1900–01*, 26.
77. Judd, *The Training of Teachers*, 55.
78. Thomas Alexander and Beryl Parker, *The New Education in the German Republic*, London 1930, 3–4 and 327.
79. Frederick W. Roman, *The Industrial and Commercial Schools of the United States and Germany*, New York and London 1915, 30. Dr Roman's comment related to the general school system and not merely to industrial or commercial schools. The publication of the book during the first World War may also have soured Dr Roman's viewpoint.
80. Holcombe, *Victorian Ladies at Work*, 34 and Judd, *The Training of Teachers*, 63. Alexander and Parker, *The New Education*, 322, noted that even in the late 1920s, 'seventy-five per cent of the elementary school teachers of Germany arc men and in rural schools women are rarely found'.
81. Shakoor, *The Training of Teachers*, 74–6.
82. Dent, *1870–1970*, 21–2.

Chapter 5
THE DAILY ROUND
(pp. 115–150)

1. Marion Johnson, *Derbyshire Village Schools in the Nineteenth Century*, Newton Abbot 1970, 21.
2. Diana McClatchey, *Oxfordshire Clergy 1777–1869*, Oxford 1960, 142–3.
3. McClatchey, *Oxfordshire Clergy*, 142.
4. *Report of an Educational Conference of Parochial Clergy and Schoolmasters in the Diocese of Oxford*, Oxford 1856, 23.
5. South Stoke parish records at Christ Church library, MS.Estates 81.214, letter dated 14 May 1858.
6. Quoted in Gillian Sutherland, *Policy-Making in Elementary Education, 1870–1895*, Oxford 1973, 112.
7. See correspondence, etc. in the Lee Papers at Buckinghamshire Record Office, D/LE/H3/39 and D/LE/H3/40. Also James J. Sheahan, *History and Topography of Buckinghamshire*, London 1862, section on Stone.
8. *Second Report of the Royal Commission on the Employment of Children, Young Persons and Women in Agriculture*, Parliamentary Papers 1868–69, XIII, Evidence, 124.
9. The Hon. Edward Stanhope, for example, noted in the later 1860s that in Lincolnshire it was fairly common for the girls to be 'required to help the schoolmistress in cleaning out the rooms.' *First Report of the Royal Commission on the Employ-*

ment of Children, Young Persons and Women in Agriculture, Parliamentary Papers 1867–68, XVII, 85.

10. Eric E. Rich, *The Education Act 1870,* London 1970, 40.
11. Richard D. Altick, *The English Common Reader,* Chicago 1967, 154.
12. J. M. Goldstrom, *The Social Content of Education 1808–1870,* Irish University Press, Shannon 1972, 25 and 28.
13. Quoted in Goldstrom, *The Social Content of Education,* 170.
14. See W. & R. Chambers, *Fourth National Reading Book,* London 1874.
15. Ellingham School Log Book at Hampshire Record Office, HCJ.
16. Mapledurham School Log Book preserved at the school.
17. William Plomer ed., *Kilvert's Diary,* London 1964 paperback ed., 269.
18. Roger R. Sellman, *Devon Village Schools in the Nineteenth Century,* Newton Abbot 1967, 29. For the comment on Helmingham school see George Ewart Evans, *Where Beards Wag All,* London 1970, 122.
19. J. Lawson, *Primary Education in East Yorkshire 1560–1902,* East Yorkshire History Society 1959, 24.
20. Sir Henry George, *Old Memories,* London 1923, 31–2.
21. *The Countryman,* 81, No. 4 (Winter 1976–77), 141.
22. Benson parish records at Christ Church library, MS.Estates 60:327, 331, 337, 345, 350 and 431.
23. Harry Chester, *Hints on the Building and Management of Schools,* London 1860 pamphlet, 13.
24. E. M. Sneyd-Kynnersley, *H.M.I.—Some Passages in the Life of One of H.M. Inspectors of Schools,* London 1908, 60.
25. Parish school files at the Public Record Office : ED.2/210 for the Herefordshire schools and Ed.2/457 for that in Westmorland.
26. Johnson, *Derbyshire Village Schools,* 84.
27. Quoted in Rex C. Russell, *A History of Schools and Education in Lindsey, Lincolnshire, 1800–1902,* Part I, Lindsey County Council Education Committee 1965, 14.
28. *Final Report of the Commissioners appointed to inquire into the Elementary Education Acts (England and Wales),* Parliamentary Papers 1888, XXXV, 11.
29. *Royal Commission on Popular Education (England),* Parliamentary Papers 1861 XXI, Pt I, 595. Wiltshire had one scholar to 7.8 of total population and Westmorland 1 to 7.9 as compared to Lancashire's 1 to 13.3.
30. Goldstrom, *The Social Content of Education,* 170.
31. *The School and the Teacher,* November 1861, 315.

32. *Report of the Board of Education (England and Wales) for 1910–11*, Parliamentary Papers 1912–13, XXI, Survey of the Curriculum of the Public Elementary School, 9–11.

33. Sutherland, *Policy-Making in Elementary Education*, 198.

34. See Article 101(f) of the Day School Code of 1897 in *Report of the Committee of Council on Education (England and Wales)*, Parliamentary Papers 1897, XXVI. Henceforward the grant was to be calculated for 'specific' subjects 'on the amount of time devoted to the subject' and the number of children studying it.

35. Mary Sturt, *The Education of the People*, London 1967, 402.

36. E. Holmes, *What Is and What Might be*, London 1911, 103–4.

37. *Report of the Committee of Council on Education (England and Wales) for 1876–77*, Parliamentary Papers 1877, XXIX, 504.

38. Nancy Ball, *Her Majesty's Inspectorate*, Birmingham 1963, 223.

39. Weston-on-Avon School Log Book is now preserved at Warwickshire Record Office.

40. H. L. V. Fletcher, *Portrait of the Wye Valley*, London 1968, 56.

41. Fletcher, *Portrait of the Wye Valley*, 55.

42. Russell, *A History of Schools and Education in Lindsey*, Part IV, 1967, 56.

43. W. H. Pullinger to F. S. Marvin, H.M.I. in MS.Eng.lett.e.107 at the Bodleian Library, letter dated 30 November 1892.

44. Great Bardfield British School Log Book at Essex Record Office, E/ML/101/1.

45. Claydon School Log Book at Oxfordshire Record Office, T/SL.16/i.

46. Quoted in *Teachers World*, 23 April 1976, 25.

47. M. K. Ashby, *Joseph Ashby of Tysoe, 1859–1919*, Cambridge 1961, 18.

48. A. J. Swinburne, *Memoirs of a School Inspector*, Saxmundham 1912, 226.

49. Swinburne, *Memoirs of a School Inspector*, 77.

50. Swinburne, *Memoirs of a School Inspector*, 37.

51. T. King, HMI, to F. S. Marvin, HMI, in MS.Eng.lett.c258, letters dated 6 March, 14 March, 19 March and 14 October 1894, for example.

52. Quoted in Pamela Horn, *The Victorian Country Child*, Kineton 1974, 133. In 1895 it was estimated that 61.6 per cent of all elementary schools in England and Wales were Church of England ones—as opposed to 24.2 per cent connected with school boards and 6.2 per cent with the British and Foreign School Society. But in Lincolnshire, church schools at that date comprised 71.7 per cent of the total.

53. Sturt, *The Education of the People*, 308.
54. Sturt, *The Education of the People*, 311.
55. T. King, HMI, to F. S. Marvin, HMI, in MS.Eng.lett.c.258, letter dated 27 March 1894.
56. Horn, *The Victorian Country Child*, 58–9.
57. Claydon School Log Book, entries for 26–30 March 1883 and 31 October 1885.
58. T. McKeown and R. G. Record, 'Reasons for the Decline of Mortality in England and Wales during the Nineteenth Century' in *Essays in Social History*, ed. M. W. Flinn and T. C. Smout, Oxford 1974, 229–231, discuss changing mortality for these diseases and note the declining virulence of scarlet fever from the 1870s.
59. Diary of Albert Brett at Dorset Record Office, D.255/1.
60. *Report of the Committee of Council on Education (England and Wales)*, Parliamentary Papers 1898, XXII, 186 and 244.
61. See Minutes of the Special Committee on Rural and Half Time Schools preserved in the Library of the National Union of Teachers in London—meeting on 17 December, 1887.
62. See report at the Public Record Office, Ed.10/11.
63. Yetminster School Log Book is at Dorset Record Office, S.89/2/1.
64. Puncknowle School Log Book is at Dorset Record Office, S.125/2, entry for 9 January 1872 notes that there was 'very bad attendance, several children being kept at home to do the network.'
65. Horn, *The Victorian Country Child*, 37 and *Second Report of the Royal Commission on the Employment of Children etc. in Agriculture, Evidence*, 277.
66. Horn, *The Victorian Country Child*, 65.
67. Swinburne, *Memoirs of a School Inspector*, 78.
68. 'A Parochial District Visitor', *The Schoolmaster Abroad: An Educational Tract*, London n.d. c. 1875 pamphlet, in the Bodleian Library, 24. The author sternly observed : 'People little know the amount of beating that often goes on in their own parish schools, to say nothing of what is far worse than regular systematic punishment, namely, hasty blows given by an angry master.'
69. Joseph Landon, *School Management*, London 9th ed., 1896, 312–313. The book was first published in 1883.
70. Flora Thompson, *Lark Rise to Candleford*, Oxford 1963 ed., 198–200.
71. Diary of Albert Brett, entry 6 October 1864.
72. Calculated from the 1861 and 1901 *Censuses of Population*

(England and Wales), Parliamentary Papers 1863, LIII, Part I and 1903, LXXXIV, respectively.

73. Fletcher, *Portrait of the Wye Valley*, 54.
74. Sellman, *Devon Village Schools*, 140–141.
75. Fletcher, *Portrait of the Wye Valley*, 54.
76. G. Swinford, *History of Filkins* (manuscript c.1958) at Bodleian Library, MS.Top.Oxon.d.475.
77. Paul Thompson, 'The War with Adults' in *Oral History*, 3, No. 2 (Autumn 1975), 33.
78. Reminiscences of Charles Slater of Barley near Royston at Museum of English Rural Life, Reading, D.71/8, 2–3.
79. Johnson, *Derbyshire Village Schools*, 134.
80. Papers on Littlemore School, 1838–1947 at the Bodleian Library. No catalogue number as yet.
81. Ashby, *Joseph Ashby of Tysoe*, 17–18.
82. Sybil Marshall, *Fenland Chronicle*, Cambridge 1967, 183.
83. F. Storr ed., *The Life and Remains of the Rev. R. H. Quick*, Cambridge 1899, 135–6.
84. Sellman, *Devon Village Schools*, 134.
85. Sellman, *Devon Village Schools*, 136.
86. Austrey School Log Book is at Warwickshire Record Office, entry 7 February 1894.
87. Fred Kitchen, *Brother to the Ox*, London 1963 paperback ed., 10–11.
88. Reminiscences of Old People at Essex Record Office, T/Z 25/176.
89. Sellman, *Devon Village Schools*, 145.
90. Thompson, *Lark Rise to Candleford*, 36, 201–2, 429–30.
91. Henry Winn (1816–1914), 'Some reasons for the Depopulation of Lincs. Villages in the 19th century' in *Lincolnshire Historian*, No. 6 (Autumn 1950), 234–5.
92. Altick, *The English Common Reader*, 171.
93. Altick, *The English Common Reader*, 171–2. E. G. West, *Education and the State*, London 2nd ed., 1970, 135, considers that Professor Altick 'seems to be claiming too much' for the 1870 Education Act, but he himself appears to underestimate the role of that legislation in stimulating *voluntary* schools to improve their standards. Countless voluntary schools became comparatively efficient institutions only because without this they would not have obtained government recognition and the communities in which they operated would then have had to adopt the much-disliked school board.
94. *Final Report of the Commissioners appointed to inquire into the Elementary Education Acts*, 18 and 48.

Chapter 6
LIFE AT THE SCHOOL HOUSE
(pp. 151–176)

1. Calculated from a Report of the Oxfordshire Education Committee on Elementary Schools and School Staffs on 1 March 1904 : Council Schools, at Oxfordshire Record Office CER/I/1. For the national estimate of 'residences free of rent' see *Report of the Board of Education (England and Wales) for 1900–1901*, Parliamentary Papers 1901, XIX, 28.
2. John Hurt, *Education in Evolution*, London 1971, 70–1.
3. Henry W. Bellairs, *The Church and the School, or Hints on Clerical Life*, London 1868, 112.
4. Copies of Letters Selected from Old Letter Books 1847–1858 at the Public Record Office, Ed.9/12, 54.
5. James A. Dewey, 'An Examination of the Role of Church and State in the Development of Elementary Education in North Staffordshire between 1870 and 1903', Keele University Ph.D. thesis 1971, 263.
6. Gerrards Cross National School Managers' Minute Book 1879–1952 at Buckinghamshire Record Office, E/MB/83/1, entries for 19 November 1879 and 7 March 1896.
7. Bix School Board Minute Books at Oxfordshire Record Office T/SM/2/i & ii.
8. *Twenty-fourth Annual Report of the National Union of Teachers*, London 1894: T. J. Macnamara, 'The Village Schoolmistress', lxxxvi–lxxxvii.
9. Rural and Small Schools Committee Minute Book, Vol. 1, preserved at the Library of the National Union of Teachers, 6.
10. Letter from the Rev. H. Williams, vicar of Affpuddle, to the squire, 16 November 1898, at Dorset Record Office, D29/R22.
11. Macnamara, 'The Village Schoolmistress', lxxxvii.
12. Sun Insurance Records at the Guildhall Library, London, entries for 20 January 1843 MS.11,937,286 and 11 September 1861 MS.11,937,512, respectively.
13. 'A Practical Housekeeper', *How a Schoolmistress May Live Upon Seventy Pounds a Year*, London pamphlet n.d. (1887 according to British Library catalogue), 3–4.
14. Minutes of the meetings of the Feoffees of Sir William Borlase Bluecoat School, Great Marlow, at Buckinghamshire Record Office, meeting on 20 April 1876.
15. Quoted in Pamela Horn, *The Victorian Country Child*, Kineton 1974, 34.
16. Secretary's Minute Book 1847–71 at Public Record Office, Ed.9/4, 312.

17. Cublington Mixed School Log Book at Buckinghamshire Record Office, E/LB.58/1.
18. Charlotte Brontë, *Jane Eyre*, Thomas Nelson & Son, London ed., n.d., 436.
19. Flora Thompson, *Lark Rise to Candleford*, Oxford 1963 ed., 212.
20. Quoted in Asher Tropp, *The School Teachers*, London 1957, 60.
21. Letters of Miss Rose A. Knowles of Thorpe Malsor to her mother, at Northamptonshire Record Office, YZ.5541. In a letter written in August 1888, informing her mother that the engagement had been broken off, Miss Knowles added bitterly, 'so perhaps you will be satisfied now'. Hurt, *Education in Evolution*, 140–1 for HMI Cook's comment.
22. See entry in Puncknowle School Log Book at Dorset Record Office, S.125/2, dated 12 August 1864 and correspondence relating to Miss Burroughs at the Record Office. The unexpectedness of the resignation and the difficulty of finding a successor meant that the return of pupils to the school after the harvest holidays had to be postponed from 11 September to 10 October.
23. Bellairs, *The Church and the School*, 120–1.
24. Quoted in Hurt, *Education in Evolution*, 118.
25. Reminiscences of Mr Knight of Sidbury, Devon, in correspondence with the author, May 1976.
26. Correspondence on Wheatley Schools preserved at Bodleian Library, MS.D.D.Par.c.13.
27. The diary of Mr Hart is in the possession of Mr J. Hawkins of Pitstone, who has kindly permitted the author to use it.
28. *Nineteenth Report of the Lincolnshire Committee of the Board of Education for the Diocese of Lincoln*, Lincoln 1859, 6.
29. George Eliot, *Adam Bede*, London Everyman's Library 1906, ed., 225–30.
30. *Jackson's Oxford Journal*, 29 September 1877.
31. *Jackson's Oxford Journal*, 8 May 1897.
32. Mrs F. A. Bowkett in an interview with the author, 29 March 1977.
33. *Jackson's Oxford Journal*, 14 January 1871.
34. Information provided by Mr Barrett's grandson, Mr J. E. Lazenby of Little Barrington, February 1977.
35. Secretary's Minute Book 1848–71 at Public Record Office, Ed. 9/4.
36. Secretary's Minute Book 1889–1900 at Public Record Office, Ed.9/5.

37. The diaries of William Wright are preserved at Lincoln reference library.
38. For details of Nathaniel Sparks and his relationship to Thomas Hardy see L. Deacon and T. Coleman, *Providence and Mr. Hardy*, London 1968, 31 and 33. Diary of Albert Brett at Dorset Record Office, D.255.
39. William Plomer ed., *Kilvert's Diary*, London paperback ed. 1964, 151–2.
40. Autobiography of J. D. Jones of Ruthin, 1827–1870, preserved in typescript at Borough Road College, London. From October 1851 to June 1866 he was head of Ruthin British School, and then ran a private school of his own at Ruthin until his death in 1870.
41. Anonymous, *A Schoolmaster's Difficulties Abroad and at Home*, London 1853, 135–8.
42. Register of Students at Culham College, 1853–1859, preserved at the college.
43. *The School and the Teacher*, September 1861, 248–9.
44. Peter Gordon, *The Victorian School Manager*, London 1974, 45–6.
45. Register of Students at Culham College, 1866–74.
46. Entry in Culham College Discipline Register, preserved at the college.
47. *Syllabus of Lessons on 'Temperance' for Scholars attending Public Elementary Schools*, Board of Education pamphlet, London 1909, 4 and 7. The pamphlet is in the Bodleian Library.
48. Register of Students at Culham College, 1874–79.
49. Second proof copy of the Memorandum at the Public Record Office, Ed.22/1.
50. Letter from P. A. Barnett to Kekewich, dated 12 January 1891 at Public Record Office, Ed.22/1.
51. *The Schoolmaster*, 22 October 1881.
52. *The Schoolmaster*, 19 August 1893.
53. James Cross, 'The Teacher in his Home' in *Report of the Annual Meeting of the Oxford Diocesan Association of Schoolmasters for 1861*, Oxford 1861, 6–7.
54. Thomas Hardy, *Jude the Obscure*, London paperback St Martin's Library ed. 1957, 167–8.
55. For a discussion of Marton see Philip Collins, *Dickens and Education*, London 1965 paperback ed., 120–3.
56. *The School and the Teacher*, July 1854. J. W. and Anne Tibble ed., *The Prose of John Clare*, London 1951, 33.

Chapter 7
TENURE PROBLEMS AND OLD AGE
(pp. 177–202)

1. *Report of the Royal Commission on Popular Education (England)*, Parliamentary Papers 1861, XXI, Pt I, 163.
2. *Annual Report of the National Union of Teachers for 1894*, London 1894, xxxii.
3. *Supplement* to *The Schoolmaster*, 21 April 1900. For annual membership figures of the National Union of Teachers see Donna F. Thompson, *Professional Solidarity Among the Teachers of England*, New York 1927, 325.
4. Earl of Radnor's MSS. : Correspondence on the appointment of masters at Coleshill, at Berkshire Record Office, D/EPb.C.69.
5. Earl of Radnor's MSS : Correspondence on the appointment of master at Coleshill in 1853, D/EPb.C.57—letter from the Rev. John Guthrie, vicar of Calne, dated 28 April 1853.
6. Earl of Radnor's MSS. : Correspondence on the appointment of masters at Coleshill, D/EPb.C.69, letter dated 30th August 1856.
7. Earl of Radnor's MSS. : Correspondence on the appointment of master at Coleshill in 1853, D/EPb.C.57—letter dated 13 April 1853.
8. Letters of Miss Rose A. Knowles of Thorpe Malsor at Northamptonshire Record Office, YZ.5541—letter dated 27 June 1888.
9. Letters of Miss Rose A. Knowles, YZ.5541—letter dated 14 July 1888.
10. Bix School Board Minute Book at Oxfordshire Record Office, T/SM.2/ii. This head's successor was appointed on 18 July, at a salary of £55 per annum, plus half the school grant, as opposed to the £28 10s. plus the school pence (valued at £21 10s. per annum) paid to the original mistress.
11. Roger R. Sellman, *Devon Village Schools in the Nineteenth Century*, Newton Abbot 1967, 110.
12. R. L. Greenall ed., *Naseby: A Parish History*, Department of Adult Education, University of Leicester 1974, 38.
13. Gerrards Cross National School Managers' Minute Book, 1879–1952 at Buckinghamshire Record Office, E/MB/83/1. The vicar was one of the school managers.
14. Minutes of the meetings of the Feoffees of Sir William Borlase Bluecoat School at Buckinghamshire Record Office : meeting on 13 October 1879.
15. Copies of Letters Selected from Old Letter Books 1847–1858 at the Public Record Office, Ed.9/12, 183.

16. *Report of the Committee of Council on Education (England and Wales) for 1889–90*, Parliamentary Papers 1890, XXVIII.
17. *The Schoolmaster*, 1 February 1879.
18. *The Schoolmaster*, 25 January 1879.
19. New Code for 1871 in *Report of the Committee of Council on Education*, Parliamentary Papers 1871, XXII, Article 59.
20. *The Schoolmaster*, 1 February 1879, letter from Assistant Inspector Thomas Eley.
21. Brinkley Endowed School: Report of vestry meeting held at the church on 25 March 1871, at Cambridgeshire Record Office, P16/12.
22. Finchampstead Church of England School Managers' Minute Book at Berkshire Record Office, C/EM.31/1. The original head had been appointed when the new school was opened on 1 January 1872. He had also received a gratuity of £2 a year for acting as secretary to the management committee.
23. Quoted in J. C. G. Lawson, *The Impact of the 1902 Education Act on the Church of England Schools of the Yateley Area*, University of Reading M.Ed. thesis 1975, 21.
24. Lawson, *The Impact of the 1902 Education Act*, 22.
25. Wheatley Schools correspondence at the Bodleian Library, MSS.D.D.Par.Wheatley c.13, letters dated 20 and 23 August 1880.
26. Information supplied by Mr J. E. Lazenby of Little Barrington, Mr Barrett's grandson, in correspondence with the author, February 1977. Mr Barrett worked at Great Barrington from 1883 to 1925.
27. Register of students at Culham College for 1866–74, at the college.
28. Letter from Canon Ridgway, principal of Culham, dated 16 November 1868 at the college, 0306.
29. Quoted in Pamela Horn, 'Grounds for Dismissal' in *Teachers World*, 23 April 1976, 12.
30. *The Schoolmaster*, 8 October and 26 November, 1892 and 11 February 1893.
31. B. Edwards, *The Burston School Strike*, London 1974, 15–16 and 143.
32. Quoted in James A. Dewey, 'An Examination of the Role of Church and State in the Development of Elementary Education in North Staffordshire between 1870 and 1903', Keele University Ph.D. thesis 1971, 190–4. See also *Supplement* to *The Schoolmaster*, 21 April 1900.
33. Dewey, *An Examination of the Role of Church and State*, 261–2.

34. Dewey, *An Examination of the Role of Church and State*, 262.
35. Report on Rural Schools produced by Rural and Small Schools Committee at National Union of Teachers' library, London— meeting 2 June 1899.
36. *The Times*, 18 April 1900.
37. Tenure Committee Minutes, Vol. 1, 1898–1902 contains several examples of membership being withdrawn from teachers who had ignored an NUT boycott. On 20 May 1898, for example, permission was refused to the secretary of the New Forest Association to admit as a member of that local association a master who had been excluded 'owing to his action in connection with the case of Mr Martin of Margam'. See Minute books at NUT headquarters.
38. Tenure Committee Minutes, Vol. 1—meetings on 18 March and 20 May 1898.
39. Quoted in P. H. J. H. Gosden, *The Evolution of a Profession*, Oxford 1972, 154–5.
40. *The Times*, 1 April 1893.
41. Tenure Committee Minutes, Vol. 1, at NUT headquarters.
42. *Supplement* to *The Schoolmaster*, 21 April 1900.
43. *Hampshire County Council: Reports of Education Committee Proceedings 1903–4*, 94 and 135.
44. File on Teachers' political activities, Ed.24.412, correspondence March and April 1910 at Public Record Office.
45. G. R. Barrell, *Legal Cases for Teachers*, London 1970, 69–72.
46. *Minutes of the Committee of Council on Education (England and Wales)*, December 1846, Parliamentary Papers 1847, XLV, 6.
47. Gosden, *The Evolution of a Profession*, 132.
48. Gosden, *The Evolution of a Profession*, 133.
49. *Annual Report of the National Union of Elementary Teachers for 1872*, London 1872, 33.
50. Diary of John Horrocks (b.1820) at Wigan Record Office, entries for 31 December 1863 and 31 December 1865.
51. *Report of the Committee of Council on Education (England and Wales) for 1861*, Parliamentary Papers 1861, XLIX, Report of the Rev. F. Watkins, HMI, 45.
52. *Select Committee on Elementary Schools (Certificated Teachers)* Parliamentary Papers 1872, IX, evidence of William Lawson, interviewed on 20 June 1872, Q.35.
53. New Code for 1890 in *Report of the Committee of Council on Education (England and Wales)*, Parliamentary Papers 1890, XXVIII, 141.
54. *Report from the Select Committee on Elementary Education*

(Teachers' Superannuation), Parliamentary Papers 1892, XII, Evidence of Ernest Gray, interviewed on 15 March 1892, Q.28 and of George Kekewich, interviewed on 1 April 1892, Q.1799.

55. Gosden, *The Evolution of a Profession*, 135.
56. W. R. Barker, *The Superannuation of Teachers in England and Wales*, London 1926, 22; and *Elementary School Teachers (Superannuation) Act 1898, 61 & 62 Vict.*
57. Gosden, *The Evolution of a Profession*, 135.
58. *Elementary School Teachers (Superannuation) Act*, S.2.
59. Register of students at Culham college, 1853–59.
60. Register of students at Culham college, 1853–59.

Chapter 8
BREAD AND BUTTER ISSUES
(pp. 203–230)

1. *Forty-first Annual Report of the British and Foreign School Society*, London 1846, 3–4.
2. Sir George Kekewich, *The Education Department and After*, London 1920, 11.
3. *Royal Commission on Popular Education (England)*, Parliamentary Papers 1861, XXI, Pt I, 159—view of Mr Snell, schoolmaster of East Coker, Yeovil, Somerset.
4. Malcolm Seaborne and Sir Gyles Isham, *A Victorian Schoolmaster: John James Graves (1832–1903)*, Northamptonshire Record Society pamphlet 1967, 11.
5. James Runciman, *Schools and Scholars*, London 1887, 20.
6. Quoted in P. H. J. H. Gosden, *The Evolution of a Profession*, Oxford 1972, 3.
7. Quoted in *The School and the Teacher*, September 1855, 162.
8. *Minutes of the Committee of Council on Education (England and Wales) 1854–55*, Parliamentary Papers 1854–55, XLII, Report by the Rev. M. Mitchell, HMI, on the Eastern Counties, 478.
9. *The School and the Teacher*, October 1855. In its article on 'Discontented Teachers' the journal concluded : 'It is as much in the nature of the case that the teacher should aspire to "something higher," as that the lawyer's clerk should dream of the woolsack, the subaltern of the marshal's "baton," the village curate of episcopal lawn, or the inspector of the haven of a canonry.'
10. Peter Gordon, *The Victorian School Manager*, London 1974, 47.

11. J. R. Blakiston, *The Teacher: Hints on School Management*, London 1879, vi.
12. See entries in Mr Wright's diary at Lincoln Reference Library.
13. Minute Book of Bedhampton School Board at Hampshire Record Office, HCJ, entry 3 April 1875.
14. Asher Tropp, *The School Teachers*, London 1957, 119. For details of the increase in the numbers of HMIs see Gillian Sutherland, *Policy-Making in Elementary Education, 1870–1895*, Oxford 1973, 55.
15. Quoted in Tropp, *The School Teachers*, 41. Tropp also notes that Farnham himself was eventually forced to seek promotion elsewhere, being appointed in 1859 headmaster of the Bombay Education Society's School, Byculla, Bombay.
16. *The School and the Teacher*, August 1861, 197–8.
17. *Royal Commission on Popular Education*, XXI, Pt I, 160.
18. Runciman, *Schools and Scholars*, 265.
19. *Annual Report of the National Union of Elementary Teachers for 1873*, London 1873, 11.
20. *Annual Report of the National Union of Elementary Teachers for 1874*, London 1874, 14.
21. B. Pattison, 'Matthew Arnold' in *Pioneers of English Education*, ed. A. V. Judges, London 1952, 195; Sutherland, *Policy-Making in Elementary Education*, 58–60.
22. File on School Inspectors at Public Record Office, T1/7568B/20733, file 18504/75.
23. Sutherland, *Policy-Making in Elementary Education*, 75 and John Hurt, *Education in Evolution*, London 1971, 42.
24. Tropp, *The School Teachers*, 119.
25. F. A. Spencer, *An Inspector's Testament*, London 1938, 89–91.
26. *Hansard*, 4th Series, Vol. III, col. 1649. The Question was raised by Henry J. Wilson, M.P. for a West Riding constituency on 29 April 1892.
27. J. Hall of Nottingham to F. S. Marvin, 24 January 1892 in Marvin papers at the Bodleian Library, MS.Eng.lett.d.252.
28. W. H. Pullinger to F. S. Marvin, 25 January 1892 in Marvin papers at the Bodleian Library, MS.Eng.lett.d. 252.
29. Sutherland, *Policy-Making in Elementary Education*, 79 and Frederic Harrison to F. S. Marvin, MS.Eng.lett.d.248, letters dated 2 and 22 July 1889 and MS.Eng.lett.e.105, letter dated 4 August 1889.
30. Tropp, *The School Teachers*, 120.
31. T. G. Rooper to F. S. Marvin in Marvin papers, MS.Eng.lett.d. 252, 25 February 1892.

32. Tropp, *The School Teachers*, 213.
33. Quoted in E. J. R. Eaglesham, *The Foundations of Twentieth Century Education in England*, London 1976, 105–6.
34. For an account of the controversy see Eaglesham, *The Foundations of Twentieth Century Education*, 104–8 and Tropp, *The School Teachers*, 199–203.
35. *The School and the Teacher*, August 1861, 198–9.
36. Quoted in Tropp, *The School Teachers*, 18.
37. For details of the Peterborough figures see *Royal Commission Appointed to Inquire into the Working of the Elementary Education Acts (England and Wales): Training College Returns*, Parliamentary Papers 1888, XXXVI, 69. The Westminster College figures have been calculated from the Register of Students at the College.
38. David Lockwood, *The Blackcoated Worker*, London 1958, 30. See also Gregory Anderson, *Victorian Clerks*, Manchester 1976, 20–5.
39. See letter to the Earl of Radnor, dated 18 April 1853, in the Earl of Radnor's MSS. at Berkshire Record Office, D/EPb.c.57.
40. Crockford's *Clerical Directory*, London 1865 and 1891 editions and death certificate at the office of the Registrar-General of Births, Deaths and Marriages. *The Church Rambler*, 1876; information kindly provided by the Rev. W. A. Matthews, the present vicar of Winsley, April 1977.
41. Students' records preserved at Culham College: Register of Students 1860–1866.
42. Herbert Hodge, 'The Teacher Problem' in *Fortnightly Review*, May 1899, 855–61 *passim*.
43. Quoted in Tropp, *The School Teachers*, 147.
44. C. F. G. Masterman, *The Condition of England*, London 1909, 84.
45. Minutes of the Committee of Council on Education 1839–41 at Public Record Office, Ed.9/1, meeting 4 January 1840.
46. *Minutes of the Committee of Council on Education (England and Wales) for 1841–42*, Parliamentary Papers 1842, XXXIII, 26.
47. Winchester diocesan training college: Students' Register 1840–1872 preserved at King Alfred's College, Winchester.
48. *Report of the Royal Commission on Popular Education (England)*, XXI, Pt I, 641.
49. *Report of the Royal Commission on Popular Education (England)*, XXI, Pt I, 161.
50. Henry W. Bellairs, *The Church and the School*, London 1868, 121.

51. *Report of the Committee of Council on Education for 1890–91*, Parliamentary Papers 1890–91, XXVII, xxvi.
52. Advertisements selected at random from *The Schoolmaster* 14 June and 20 September 1873.
53. *Final Report of the Commission on the Elementary Education Acts*, 1888, XXV, 82.
54. Tropp, *The School Teachers*, 133.
55. Tenure Committee Minutes at the National Union of Teachers headquarters, meetings 16 September 1898, 4 January and 21 July 1899.
56. Letters of Miss Rose A. Knowles at Northamptonshire Record Office, YZ.5541.
57. Miss Rose A. Knowles to her mother, undated letter of *c.* 20 August 1888.
58. Gosden, *The Evolution of a Profession*, 22 and 25 and Roger R. Sellman, *Devon Village Schools in the Nineteenth Century*, Newton Abbot, 1967, 149. The Oxfordshire figures were calculated from Filed Report of Oxfordshire Education Committee, 1 March 1904, CER/I/1 at Oxfordshire Record Office.
59. Gosden, *The Evolution of a Profession*, 27.
60. Herefordshire Teachers' Strike, 1914: Secretary's Private Correspondence at the Public Record Office, Ed.24/1768.
61. Herefordshire Teachers' Strike, Ed.24/1770—letter dated 23 January 1914.
62. Herefordshire Teachers' Strike, Ed.24/1770—letter dated 7 February 1914 to Col. Decie, the chairman of Herefordshire local education authority's special salaries committee.
63. Herefordshire Teachers' Strike, Ed.24/1770—letter dated 24 February 1914 to Col. Decie.
64. *Annual Report of the National Union of Teachers for 1914*, London 1914, xxxv.
65. *Daily News*, 5 February 1914.
66. Letter at Public Record Office, Ed.24/1768, letter dated 4 February 1914 and *Hereford Times*, 7 February 1914.
67. Quoted in *The Schoolmaster*, 28 February 1914. This journal gave extensive coverage to the Herefordshire dispute—naturally from the NUT viewpoint.

Chapter 9
COMBINATION AND TRADE UNIONISM
(pp. 231–251)

1. M. G. Jones, *The Charity School Movement*, Cambridge 1938, 109. Joan Simon, *Education and Society in Tudor England*,

Cambridge 1967, 25, mentions discussion groups among some London teachers in the fifteenth century.

2. *The Address and Resolutions of the Society of Schoolmasters*, London 1798 pamphlet, 4, preserved at the Bodleian Library.

3. Asher Tropp, *The School Teachers*, London 1957, 45.

4. Copies of Letters Selected from Old Letter Books 1847–58 at the Public Record Office, Ed.9/12—letter dated 17 March 1848 from J. P. Kay Shuttleworth to Mr W. J. Mantle of Portsea.

5. Tropp, *The School Teachers*, 45–46.

6. *Report of an Educational Conference of Parochial Clergy and Schoolmasters in the Diocese of Oxford*, Oxford 1856 pamphlet, 3, preserved at the Bodleian Library.

7. Hampshire Church Schoolmasters' Association Minute Book 1854–62, HW/49/Bx.2/DR1, at Hampshire Record Office.

8. J. Lawson, *Primary Education in East Yorkshire 1560–1902*, East Yorkshire Local History Society 1959, 24.

9. *The School and the Teacher*, April 1854.

10. *Minutes of the Committee of Council on Education (England and Wales) for 1854–55*, Parliamentary Papers 1854–55, XLII, Report by the Rev. J. J. Blandford, HMI, on the East Midland Counties, 495.

11. Copies of Letters Selected from Old Letter Books 1847–58 at the Public Record Office, Ed.9/12—letter dated 19 February 1852, from R. R. W. Lingen. See also John Leese, *Personalities and Power in English Education*, Leeds 1950, 60.

12. Tropp, *The School Teachers*, 49–50.

13. *The School and the Teacher*, February 1854.

14. J. T. Rathbone, writing on the 'History of the Association of Church Schoolmasters' in *The School and the Teacher*, February 1854.

15. *The School and the Teacher*, February 1854.

16. Tropp, *The School Teachers*, 56–7.

17. Tropp, *The School Teachers*, 52.

18. *The School and the Teacher*, August 1855.

19. Malcolm Seaborne and Sir Gyles Isham, *A Victorian Schoolmaster: John James Graves (1832–1903)*, Northamptonshire Record Society 1967, 7.

20. Tropp, *The School Teachers*, 53.

21. *The School and the Teacher*, October 1861.

22. *The School and the Teacher*, November 1861.

23. *The School and the Teacher*, December 1861.

24. *The Schoolmaster*, 30 July 1892.

25. Tropp, *The School Teachers*, 100 and J. W. Adamson, *English*

Education 1789–1902, Cambridge 1964, 477–9.

26. Tropp, *The School Teachers*, 109.
27. Quoted in Seaborne and Isham, *A Victorian Schoolmaster*, 34–5.
28. Tropp, *The School Teachers*, 113.
29. See *Annual Report of the National Union of Elementary Teachers for 1874–75*, London 1875, 26 and *Annual Report for 1875–76*, London 1876, list of 'Objects of the Union'.
30. Quoted in P. H. J. H. Gosden, *The Evolution of a Profession*, Oxford 1972, 4.
31. R. Bourne and Brian MacArthur, *The Struggle for Education 1870–1970*, London n.d. (c.1970), 31–2. And Donna F. Thompson, *Professional Solidarity Among the Teachers of England*, New York 1927, 325.
32. *The Culhamite*, September 1890, 15–16.
33. Tropp, *The School Teachers*, 116.
34. Lee Holcombe, *Victorian Ladies at Work*, Newton Abbot 1973, 66.
35. *Supplement* to *The Schoolmaster*, 21 April 1900 and *Annual Report of the National Union of Teachers*, London 1900, xxxiv.
36. Calculated from the *Annual Report of the National Union of Teachers for 1894*, London 1894.
37. Rural and Small Schools Committee Minute Book at the National Union of Teachers library—meeting 21 July 1899.
38. *The Schoolmaster*, 25 January 1890, from James Kelly, master of Fittleworth National School, Pulborough, Sussex, in a letter proposing himself as a candidate for the Executive Committee.
39. Sir George W. Kekewich, *The Education Department and After*, London 1920, 62–6 for a discussion of these developments.
40. Thompson, *Professional Solidarity*, 87.
41. *The Schoolmaster*, 20 January 1872.
42. Tropp, *The School Teachers*, 140.
43. Quoted in *The Schoolmaster*, 31 August 1895.

Chapter 10
THE TURN OF THE CENTURY
(pp. 252–273)

1. Quoted in John Leese, *Personalities and Power in English Education*, Leeds 1950, 129.
2. Leese, *Personalities and Power*, 242.
3. Rex C. Russell, *A History of Schools and Education in Lindsey, Lincolnshire*, Pt 4, Lindsey County Council Education Committee 1967, 53.

4. Thomas Nelson & Sons, *Highroads of Literature*, Book 6, London 1914.

5. *Report of the Board of Education for 1900–1901*, Parliamentary Papers 1901, XIX, Mr Fitzmaurice's General Report for 1900 on the North Central Division, 59.

6. *General Reports of H.M. Inspectors on Elementary Schools for the Year 1902*, Parliamentary Papers 1903, XXI, Report on Schools in the Eastern Division, 99.

7. Reminiscences of F. W. Brocklehurst of Sheldon, Derbyshire, at the Museum of English Rural Life, Reading, D.72/1/1, 2.

8. Francis W. Steer, ed., *The Memoirs of Gaius Carley*, Chichester 1964, 4.

9. Roger R. Sellman, *Devon Village Schools in the Nineteenth Century*, Newton Abbot 1967, 139.

10. Gillian Sutherland, *Policy-Making in Elementary Education, 1870–1895*, Oxford 1973, 330–1.

11. *Report of the Board of Education for 1900–1901*, Parliamentary Papers 1901, XIX, 15.

12. Circular on *The Curriculum of the Rural School*, No. 435. The circular recommended that : 'The teacher should as occasion offers take the children out of doors for school walks at the various seasons of the year, and give simple lessons on the spot about animals in the fields and farmyards, about ploughing and sowing, about fruit trees and forest trees, about birds, insects and flowers, and other objects of interest.'

13. Bromsberrow School Log Book at Gloucestershire Record Office, S.62.

14. John Weathers, *The Practical School Garden*, London 1912, 1. Among the schools where this text book was used was Burford Boys' School, Oxfordshire.

15. Thomas F. Plowman, *Fifty Years of a Showman's Life*, London 1919, 164.

16. Plowman, *Fifty Years of a Showman's Life*, 122–3.

17. Patrick Keane, 'An English County and Education : Somerset, 1889–1902' in *English Historical Review*, 88, (April 1973), 298–9.

18. *General Reports of H.M. Inspectors on Elementary Schools for the Year 1902*, 79.

19. Records of Marnhull Roman Catholic School, Dorset, at the Public Record Office, Ed.21/4186, report dated 8 September 1914.

20. *Report of the Board of Education for 1900–1901*, 54.

21. *Report of the Board of Education for 1900–1901*, 57.

22. *Report of the Board of Education for 1899–1900*, 162.

23. Quoted in M. L. Smith, *A Brief History of Schools in Witham*, Typescript at Essex Record Office 1965, quoting from a school log entry at the Witham National Boys' School on 3 November 1905. L. Andrews, 'The School Meals Service' in *British Journal of Educational Studies*, XX, No. 1 (1972), 74.

24. Sutherland, *Policy-Making in Elementary Education*, 330.

25. S. Leff and Vera Leff, *The School Health Service*, London 1959, 28. The authors note: 'Before the end of the nineteenth century, even backward Russia had six school doctors to supervise the elementary schools in Moscow'. See also *The School Health Service*, H.M.S.O. London 1975, 5.

26. Bentley B. Gilbert, *The Evolution of National Insurance in Great Britain*, London 1966, 95–8.

27. Sir John Gorst to Miss Edith Deverell (later Mrs Sidney Marvin)—letter dated 3 June 1904, in Marvin papers at the Bodleian Library, MS.Eng.lett.c.257. Miss Deverell was one of the women inspectors employed by the Board of Education.

28. Gilbert, *The Evolution of National Insurance*, 111–13.

29. *Report on the Working of the Education (Provision of Meals) Act 1906 up to 31 March 1909*, Parliamentary Papers 1910, XXIII, 14 and 34.

30. A. Platts and G. H. Hainton, *Education in Gloucestershire: A Short History*, Gloucestershire County Council 1954, 91.

31. *Annual Report for 1912 of the Chief Medical Officer of the Board of Education*, Parliamentary Papers 1914, XXV, 27.

32. *Annual Report for 1912 of the Chief Medical Officer of the Board of Education*, 31.

33. *Annual Report for 1908 of the Chief Medical Officer of the Board of Education*, Parliamentary Papers 1910, XXIII, 165–6.

34. *Oxfordshire County Council Education Committee: Medical Advisers' Report for 1909*, 2. For an account of the 'head cleaning' campaign see *Report* for 1910, 3.

35. Frances A. Bowkett, 'Reading and Writing Made Interesting', n.d. typescript in the possession of Mrs Bowkett, 4. And interview with Mrs Bowkett on 29 March 1977.

36. H. C. Dent, *1870–1970: Century of Growth in English Education*, London 1970, 69.

37. Old People's Reminiscences at Essex Record Office, T/Z 25/216.

38. Burford Boys' School Punishment Book at Oxfordshire Record Office, T/SP.8.

39. Ivinghoe School Log Book, vol. 2, at Buckinghamshire Record Office, E/LB/16/2, entries for 19 October and 4 November 1903.

40. Peter Gordon, *The Victorian School Manager*, London 1974, 213–37 for a discussion of the Voluntary Schools Act. A. Shakoor, *The Training of Teachers in England and Wales, 1900–1939*, Leicester University Ph.D. thesis, 1964, 116.
41. Eric Eaglesham, 'Implementing the Education Act of 1902' in *British Journal of Educational Studies*, X, no. 2, (May 1962), 162–75.
42. Brian Simon, *Education and the Labour Movement 1870–1920*, London 1965, 141.
43. *General Reports of H.M. Inspectors on Elementary Schools for the Year 1902*, 69.
44. *Return for England and Wales on Elementary Schools (Children Working for Wages)*, Parliamentary Papers 1899, LXXV, 17–21.
45. *Report of the Board of Education for 1900–1901*, 7.
46. *Report of the Board of Education for 1899–1900*, 267. For a description of the importance of shooting parties see, for example, G. E. Mingay, *Rural Life in Victorian England*, London 1977, 37–9.
47. Denis Tye, ed., *Boughton Monchelsea School*, privately printed n.d. *c.*1970.
48. Elmdon School Log Book at Warwickshire Record Office, CR.36–22.
49. *General Reports of H.M. Inspectors on Elementary Schools for the Year 1902*, 106.
50. *Report of the Board of Education for 1899–1900*, 230.
51. *Report of the Board of Education for 1899–1900*, 163–4.
52. Interview with Mrs F. A. Bowkett on 29 March 1977.
53. E. N. Bennett, *Problems of Village Life*, London 1914, 97 and Pamela Horn, *Labouring Life in the Victorian Countryside*, Dublin 1976, 240.
54. S. J. Hurwitz, *State Intervention in Great Britain, 1914–1919*, New York 1949, 214.
55. Fred Kitchen, *Brother to the Ox*, London 1963 paperback ed., 21.
56. E. J. R. Eaglesham, *The Foundations of Twentieth Century Education in England*, London 1972, 40.
57. Kenneth Lindsay, *Social Progress and Educational Waste*, London 1926, 142.
58. Lindsay, *Social Progress*, 134 and 136–7.
59. Lindsay, *Social Progress*, 20.
60. Gerald Bernbaum, *Social Change and the Schools, 1918–1944*, London 1967, 92–93.
61. W. P. Baker, *The English Village*, Oxford 1953, 142–3. J.

Synge, 'The Selective Function and British Rural Education' in *British Journal of Educational Studies*, XXIII, No. 2 (1975), 144.

62. Richard Bourne and Brian MacArthur, *The Struggle for Education 1870–1970*, London 1970, 47.
63. Sellman, *Devon Village Schools in the Nineteenth Century*, 152.
64. H. Rider Haggard, *Rural England*, Vol. II, London 1902, 114.
65. C. F. G. Masterman, *The Condition of England*, London 1909, 190.
66. Platts and Hainton, *Education in Gloucestershire*, 83 and 107.
67. Sellman, *Devon Village Schools in the Nineteenth Century*, 154 and 159.

Bibliography

MANUSCRIPT COLLECTIONS

Aldermaston school records at Berkshire Record Office.

Bampton National School Rules, Oxfordshire, at the Bodleian Library, Oxford.

Begbroke parish records, Oxfordshire, at the Bodleian Library, Oxford.

Borough Road College—correspondence for the 1830s and 1840s, at the College in London.

Frances A. Bowkett, 'Reading and Writing Made Interesting', n.d., typescript in the possession of Mrs Bowkett of Banbury.

Albert Brett, diary of, at Dorset Record Office.

Bristol : Students' entrance book for the diocesan training college at Fishponds, at the College of St Matthias, Bristol.

Burrough Green Charity School, Cambridgeshire, Notice and Admonition to John Charville, master, at Cambridge Record Office.

Cheltenham Church of England Training College Minute Books, etc. at St Paul's College, Cheltenham.

Christ Church Estate and Parish Records at the Library, Christ Church, Oxford.

Culham College students' registers, etc. and records of the Oxford Training Institution from 1840, at Culham College, Oxford.

Education, Copies of Letters Selected from Old Letter Books, 1847–58, of the Committee of Council, at the Public Record Office.

Education, Minutes of the Committee of Council on, 1839–41, at the Public Record Office.

Education, Parish School Files at the Public Record Office.

Education, Secretary to the Committee of Council on : Minute Books 1847–71 and 1889–1900 at the Public Record Office.

Annie Figg's Copy Book for 1893, kindly lent by her niece, Mrs M. Francis of Sutton Courtenay, Oxfordshire.

Finchampstead School, Berkshire, miscellaneous documents, at Berkshire Record Office.

Fremantle Papers at Buckinghamshire Record Office.

Hampshire Church Schoolmasters' Association Minute Book 1854–62 at Hampshire Record Office.

Alfred Hart, diary of, in the possession of Mr J. Hawkins of Pitstone, Buckinghamshire.

Herefordshire Teachers' Strike : Secretary to the Board of Education's Private Correspondence File on, and General Files on, at the Public Record Office.

John Horrocks, diary of, at Wigan Record Office.

J. D. Jones, Autobiography of (1827–70) at Borough Road College, London.

Miss R. A. Knowles of Thorpe Malsor, Northamptonshire, letters of, at Northamptonshire Record Office.

J. E. Lazenby of Little Barrington, Oxfordshire, in correspondence with the author, 1977.

Lee Papers at Buckinghamshire Record Office.

Littlemore parish records, Oxfordshire, at the Bodleian Library, Oxford.

Marvin Papers at the Bodleian Library, Oxford.

G. N. Maynard, 'Recollections of Whittleford School and Schoolmasters in the Eighteenth and Nineteenth Centuries' in Maynard MSS. at Cambridge Record Office.

National Society records, at the Society headquarters in London.

National Society records at Northamptonshire Record Office.

National Union of Teachers : Minutes of the Special Committee on Rural and Half Time Schools, 1887; Minutes of the Tenure Committee from 1898–1902; Minutes of the Rural and Small Schools Committee from 1899. All at the Union headquarters in London.

Oxford Diocese, Clergy Visitation Returns at the Bodleian Library, Oxford.

Oxfordshire Elementary Schools, Returns of, at Oxfordshire Record Office, from 1903.

Population Census, 1841–71, at the Public Record Office.

Pupil-Teachers' Report Books and Notes of Lessons at Buckinghamshire Record Office.

Earl of Radnor's MSS : Correspondence concerning Coleshill school, at Berkshire Record Office.

Bishop Randolph's notes on the formation of the National Society, at the Bodleian Library.

Reminiscences of Charles Slater of Barley, at the Museum of the Museum of English Rural Life, Reading.

Reminiscences of Mr Thomas Hall (b.1817) of Farnborough, with the Misses Hall of Stratford-upon-Avon.

Reminiscences of Mr Henry Knight of Sidbury, in correspondence with the author, 1976.

Reminiscences of Old People at Essex Record Office.

Reminiscences of Mr F. W. Brocklehurst of Sheldon, Derbyshire, at the Museum of English Rural Life, Reading.

School Inspectors, Treasury Files on for 1870s, at Public Record Office.

School log books, school board minute books and managers' minute books at various county record offices : location indicated in footnotes.

M. L. Smith, 'A Brief History of Schools in Witham', typescript at Essex Record Office, 1965.

Sun Insurance Records at the Guildhall Library, London.

G. Swinford, *History of Filkins*, manuscript c.1958, at the Bodleian Library, Oxford.

Teachers' Political Activities, file on, at Public Record Office (relating to c.1910).

Wesleyan Education Committee : Register of Students, at Westminster College, Oxford.

Westminster College Students' registers, at the College, now in Oxford.

Wheatley parish papers, Oxfordshire, at the Bodleian Library, Oxford.

Thomas White of Fordington, Dorset, Apprenticeship Indenture and Teaching Certificate, at Dorset Record Office.

Wilberforce Papers at the Bodleian Library, Oxford.

Winchester diocesan training college, Students' registers and typescript history of the college, at King Alfred's College, Winchester.

William Wright, diaries of, at Lincoln reference library.

OFFICIAL PUBLICATIONS
(Parliamentary Papers = P.P.)

Agriculture, First and Second Reports of the Royal Commission on the Employment of Children, Young Persons and Women in, P.P. 1867–8 XVII; 1868–9, XIII.

Children's Employment Commission, Second Report of, P.P. 1843, XIV.

Children's Employment Commission, Sixth Report, P.P. 1867, XVI.

Curriculum of the Rural School, Board of Education circular, April 1900.

Education, Report of the Select Committee on the State of, P.P. 1834, IX.

Education Enquiry: Abstract of the Answers and Returns, P.P. 1835 XLI–XLIII.

Education in England and Wales, Select Committee on P.P. 1835, VII.

Education in Wales, Report of the Commissioners of Inquiry into the State of, P.P. 1847, XXVII.

Education, Report of the Royal Commission on the State of Popular Education in England (the Newcastle Commission), P.P. 1861, XXI, Pts 1–5.

Education, Select Committee on, P.P. 1866, VII.

Education, Minutes of the Committee of the Privy Council on, 1839–58.

Education, Reports of the Committee of the Privy Council on, 1859–99.

Education, Reports of the Board of, 1900 et seq.

Education, Board of, Annual Reports of the Chief Medical Officer of, for 1908 and 1912, P.P. 1910, XXIII and 1914, XXV.

Education (Provision of Meals) Act 1906, Report on the Working of, up to 31 March 1909, P.P. 1910, XXIII.

Elementary Education Acts (England and Wales), Final Report of the Royal Commission appointed to Inquire into, (Cross Commission), P.P. 1888, XXXV, and Returns from Training Colleges, P.P. 1888, XXXVI.

Elementary Education (Teachers' Superannuation), Reports of the Select Committee on, P.P. 1892, XII.

Elementary Schools (Certificated Teachers), Select Committee Report and Minutes of Evidence on, P.P. 1872, IX.

Factories, Report of Robert Baker, Inspector of, for the Six Months ending 30 April 1871, P.P. 1871, XIV.

How to Become a Teacher in a Public Elementary School: Board of Education Pamphlet, 1907.

Pupil-Teacher System, Report of the Departmental Committee on and Minutes of Evidence, P.P. 1898, XXVI.

Return for England and Wales on Elementary Schools (Children Working for Wages) P.P. 1899, LXXV.

School Health Service: Department of Education and Science pamphlet, 1975.

Suggestions for the Consideration of Teachers and Others Concerned in the Work of Public Elementary Schools: Board of Education pamphlet, 1912 ed.

Syllabus of Lessons on 'Temperance' for Scholars attending Public Elementary Schools: Board of Education pamphlet, 1909.

Hansard's Parliamentary Debates.

NEWSPAPERS AND JOURNALS
The Countryman
The Culhamite
Culham Club Magazine
Daily News
Economist
Hereford Times
Jackson's Oxford Journal
Oxford Times
School and the Teacher
School Board Chronicle
School Guardian
Schoolmaster
Teachers World
The Times
The Westminsterian

PERIODICAL ARTICLES

L. Andrews, 'The School Meals Service' in *British Journal of Educational Studies*, XX, No. 1 (1972).

Sister Joan Bland, 'The Impact of Government on English Catholic Education, 1870–1902' in *Catholic Historical Review*, LXII, No. 1 (Jan. 1976).

David Cressy, 'Levels of Illiteracy in England, 1530–1730' in *Historical Journal*, 20, No. 2 (March 1977).

F. Crampton, 'The Old and the New Schoolmaster' in *The School and the Teacher*, VII (1861).

Eric Eaglesham, 'Implementing the Education Act of 1902' in *British Journal of Educational Studies*, X, No. 2 (1962).

Rev. George Gibb, 'The Supply of Teachers' in *Transactions of the National Association for the Promotion of Social Science* (1884).

J. J. Higginson, 'Dame Schools' in *British Journal of Educational Studies*, XXII, No. 2 (1974).

Herbert Hodge, 'The Teacher Problem' in *Fortnightly Review* (May 1899).

Pamela Horn, 'The Agricultural Children Act of 1873' in *History of Education Journal*, 3, (1974).

Pamela Horn, 'Child Workers in the Pillow Lace and Straw Plait Trades of Victorian Buckinghamshire and Bedfordshire' in *Historical Journal*, XVII, Pt 4 (1974).

Louisa M. Hubbard, 'Elementary Teaching, a Profession for Ladies' in *Transactions of the National Association for the Promotion of Social Science* (1873).

Richard Johnson, 'Educational Policy and Social Control in Early Victorian England', in *Past and Present*, 49 (Nov. 1970).

Patrick Keane, 'An English County and Education : Somerset, 1889–1902' in *English Historical Review*, 88 (April 1973).

D. P. Leinster-Mackay, 'Dame Schools : A need for Review' in *British Journal of Educational Studies*, XXIV, No. 1 (1976).

T. J. Macnamara, 'Training College Days' in *New Liberal Review*, 6, No. 32 (Sept. 1903).

T. J. Macnamara, 'Joints in Our Educational Armour' in *Fortnightly Review* (June 1899).

Lady Evelyn Rayleigh, 'The Pupil Teacher in Rural Schools' in *National Review* (Dec. 1899).

Roger Smith, 'Education, Society and Literacy : Nottinghamshire in the Mid-Nineteenth Century' in *University of Birmingham Historical Journal*, XII, No. 1 (1969).

Lawrence Stone, 'The Educational Revolution in England 1560–1640' in *Past and Present*, 28 (July 1964).

Lawrence Stone, 'Literacy and Education in England, 1640–1900' in *Past and Present*, 42 (Feb. 1969).

J. Synge, 'The Selective Function and British Rural Education' in *British Journal of Educational Studies*, XXIII, No. 2 (1975).

Paul Thompson, 'The War with Adults' in *Oral History*, 3, No. 2 (Autumn 1975).

Henry Winn (1816–1914), 'Some reasons for the Depopulation of Lincs. Villages in the 19th century' in *Lincolnshire Historian*, No. 6 (Autumn 1950).

PRINTED BOOKS AND PAMPHLETS
(excluding novels)

John W. Adamson, *English Education 1789–1902*, Cambridge 1964 ed.

Address and Resolutions of the Society of Schoolmasters, London 1798.

Donald H. Akeson, *The Irish Education Experiment*, London 1970 .

Thomas Alexander and Beryl Parker, *The New Education in the German Republic*, London 1930.

Richard D. Altick, *The English Common Reader*, Chicago 1957.

Gregory Anderson, *Victorian Clerks*, Manchester 1976.

Anonymous, *A Schoolmaster's Difficulties Abroad and at Home*, London 1853.

W. H. G. Armytage, *Four Hundred Years of English Education*, Cambridge 1964.

M. K. Ashby, *Joseph Ashby of Tysoe, 1859–1919*, Cambridge 1961.
M

Norman Atkinson, *Irish Education*, Dublin 1969.

W. P. Baker, *The English Village*, Oxford 1953.

W. R. Baker, *The Superannuation of Teachers in England and Wales*, London 1926.

Nancy Ball, *Her Majesty's Inspectorate*, Birmingham 1963.

H. C. Barnard, *A History of English Education from 1760*, London 1961 ed.

G. R. Barrell, *Legal Cases for Teachers*, London 1970.

G. F. Bartle, *A History of Borough Road College*, London 1976.

G. A. Beck, ed., *The English Catholics, 1850–1950*, London 1950.

Rev. Andrew Bell, *Mutual Tuition and Moral Discipline*, 7th ed., London 1823.

Henry W. Bellairs, *The Church and the School, or Hints on Clerical Life*, London 1868.

E. N. Bennett, *Problems of Village Life*, London n.d. *c.*1913.

Gerald Bernbaum, *Social Change and the Schools 1918–1944*, London 1967.

Angela Black, *Guide to Educational Records in the County Record Office, Cambridge*, Cambridgeshire and Isle of Ely County Council 1972.

J. R. Blakiston, *The Teacher: Hints on School Management*, London 1879.

John Bossy, *The English Catholic Community, 1570–1850*, London 1975.

R. Bourne and Brian MacArthur, *The Struggle for Education 1870–1970*, London n.d. *c.*1970.

British and Foreign School Society, Annual Reports of.

William Brown, *A Narrative of the Life and Adventures of*, York 1829.

M. St Clare Byrne, *Elizabethan Life in Town and Country*, 7th ed., London 1957.

W. & R. Chambers, *Fourth National Reading Book*, London 1874.

Cheltenham Church of England Training School, Annual Reports of.

Harry Chester, *Hints on the Building and Management of Schools*, London 1860.

R. D. Coates, *Teachers' Unions and Interest Group Politics*, Cambridge 1972.

The Rev. Derwent Coleridge, *The Teachers of the People*, London 1862.

Philip Collins, *Dickens and Education*, London paperback ed. 1965.

Thomas Cooper, *Life of*, Leicester 1971 ed.

Crockford's *Clerical Directories*, London 1865 and 1891 eds.

Rev. J. Curtis, *Topographical History of the County of Leicester*, London 1831.

S. J. Curtis, *History of Education in Great Britain*, 7th ed., London 1967.

S. J. Curtis and M. E. A. Boultwood, *An Introductory History of English Education Since 1800*, London 1964.

Lois Deacon and Terry Coleman, *Providence and Mr Hardy*, London 1966.

J. W. Docking, *Victorian Schools and Scholars*, Coventry and North Warwickshire History Pamphlets, No. 3, 1967.

A. H. Dodd, *Life in Elizabethan England*, London 1961.

E. J. R. Eaglesham, *The Foundations of Twentieth Century Education in England*, London 1967.

B. Edwards, *The Burston School Strike*, London 1974.

George Ewart Evans, *Where Beards Wag All*, London 1970.

H. L. V. Fletcher, *Portrait of the Wye Valley*, London 1968.

M. W. Flinn and T. C. Smout, ed., *Essays in Social History*, Oxford 1974.

Charles Freeman, *Pillow Lace in the East Midlands*, Luton Museum and Art Gallery 1958.

Clifford B. Freeman, *Mary Simpson of Boynton Vicarage: Teacher of Ploughboys*, East Yorkshire Local History Society 1972.

Sir Henry George, *Old Memories*, London 1923.

Bentley B. Gilbert, *The Evolution of National Insurance in Great Britain*, London 1966.

J. M. Goldstrom, *The Social Content of Education 1808–1870*, Shannon 1972.

Peter Gordon, *The Victorian School Manager*, London 1974.

P. H. J. H. Gosden, *How They Were Taught*, Oxford 1969.

P. H. J. H. Gosden, *The Evolution of a Profession*, Oxford 1972.

R. L. Greenall, ed., *Naseby: A Parish History*, Department of Adult Education, University of Leicester 1974.

H. Rider Haggard, *Rural England*, London 1902.

Mary A. Hamilton, *Margaret Bondfield*, London 1924.

Hampshire County Council : Reports of Education Committee Proceedings, 1903–4.

Christopher Hill, *The Century of Revolution 1603–1714*, London 1961.

Lee Holcombe, *Victorian Ladies at Work*, Newton Abbot 1973.

E. Holmes, *What Is and What Might Be*, London 1911.

Pamela Horn, *Labouring Life in the Victorian Countryside*, Dublin 1976.

Pamela Horn, *The Victorian Country Child*, Kineton 1974.

Theodore Huebener, *The Schools in West Germany*, New York 1962.

John Hurt, *Education in Evolution*, London 1971.

S. J. Hurwitz, *State Intervention in Great Britain 1914–1919*, New York 1949.

Brian Inglis, *The Story of Ireland*, 2nd ed., London 1965.

Marion Johnson, *Derbyshire Village Schools in the Nineteenth Century*, Newton Abbot 1970.

Rev. James Johnston, *Our Educational Policy in India*, 2nd ed., Edinburgh 1880.

Lance G. E. Jones, *The Training of Teachers in England and Wales*, Oxford 1924.

M. G. Jones, *The Charity School Movement*, Cambridge 1938.

M. G. Jones, *Hannah More*, Cambridge 1952.

Charles H. Judd, *The Training of Teachers in England, Scotland and Germany*, United States Bureau of Education Bulletin, No. 35, Washington 1914.

A. V. Judges, ed., *Pioneers of English Education*, London 1952.

The Rev. H. A. Lloyd Jukes, ed., *Articles of Enquiry Addressed to the Clergy of the Diocese of Oxford at the Primary Visitation of Dr. Thomas Secker, 1738*, Oxfordshire Record Society 1957.

Sir J. Kay Shuttleworth, *Memorandum on Popular Education*, London 1868.

Sir J. Kay Shuttleworth, *The School in its Relations to the State, the Church and the Congregation*, London 1847.

Sir J. Kay Shuttleworth, *Public Education as Affected by the Minutes of the Committee of Privy Council from 1846 to 1852*, London 1853.

Sir George W. Kekewich, *The Education Department and After*, London 1920.

Fred Kitchen, *Brother to the Ox*, London 1963 paperback ed.

Joseph Lancaster, *The British System of Education*, London 1810.

Joseph Landon, *School Management*, 9 ed., London 1896.

Angel Lawrence, *St. Hild's College, 1858–1958*, Darlington n.d. *c.*1958.

John Lawson, *Mediaeval Education and the Reformation*, London 1967.

John Lawson, *Primary Education in East Yorkshire, 1560–1902*, East Yorkshire Local History Society 1959.

John Lawson and Harold Silver, *A Social History of Education in England*, London 1974.

John Leese, *Personalities and Power in English Education*, Leeds 1950.

S. and Vera Leff, *The School Health Service*, London 1959.

Lincolnshire Committee of the Board of Education for the Diocese of Lincoln, *Nineteenth Report*, Lincoln 1859.

Kenneth Lindsay, *Social Progress and Education Waste*, London 1926.

David Lockwood, *The Blackcoated Worker*, London 1958.

Rt Hon. Robert Lowe, *Speech on Moving the Education Estimate in Committee of Supply*, London 1861.

Diana McClatchey, *Oxfordshire Clergy 1777–1869*, Oxford 1960.

J. Stuart Maclure, ed., *Educational Documents: England and Wales 1816–1968*, London 1972 ed.

Bernard Mandeville, *The Fable of the Bees*, London 1970 paperback ed.

Sybil Marshall, *Fenland Chronicle*, Cambridge 1967.

William Marshall, *The Review and Abstract of the County Reports to the Board of Agriculture*, Vols. 4 and 5, York, 1818.

C. F. G. Masterman, *The Condition of England*, London 1909.

G. E. Mingay, *Rural Life in Victorian England*, London 1977.

James Murphy, *Church, State and Schools in Britain, 1800–1970*, London 1971.

National Society, Annual Reports of, from 1812.

National Union of Teachers, Annual Reports of, from 1871.

Leonard Naylor, *Culham Church of England Training College for Schoolmasters 1853–1953*, Oxford n.d. *c.*1953.

Oxford Diocesan Association of Schoolmasters, Report of, Oxford 1861.

Oxford Diocesan Board of Education, Annual Reports of, from 1840.

Oxford Diocese, *Report of an Educational Conference of Parochial Clergy and Schoolmasters in the*, Oxford 1856.

'Parochial District Visitor', *The Schoolmaster Abroad: An Educational Tract*, London n.d. *c.*1875.

A. Platts and G. H. Hainton, *Education in Gloucestershire: A Short History*, Gloucestershire County Council 1954.

William Plomer, ed., *Kilvert's Diary*, London 1964 paperback ed.

Thomas F. Plowman, *Fifty Years of a Showman's Life*, London 1919.

'Practical Housekeeper', *How a Schoolmistress May Live Upon Seventy Pounds a Year*, London n.d. *c.*1887.

F. C. Pritchard, *The Story of Westminster College, 1851–1951*, London 1951.

Edward Rainsberry, *Through the Lych Gate*, Kineton 1969.

William Reitzel, ed., *The Autobiography of William Cobbett*, London 1967 paperback ed.

Eric E. Rich, *The Education Act 1870*, London 1970.

R. W. Rich, *The Training of Teachers in England and Wales during the Nineteenth Century*, Cambridge 1933.

Rev. Sanderson Robins, *The Church Schoolmaster*, London 1850.

Rev. Sanderson Robins, *A Lecture Delivered Before the Church Schoolmasters' Association*, London 1858.

Derek Robson, *Some Aspects of Education in Cheshire in the Eighteenth Century*, Manchester : The Chetham Society 3rd Series, XIII 1966.

Frederick W. Roman, *The Industrial and Commercial Schools of the United States and Germany*, New York 1915.

N. Rowley, *Education in Essex c.1710–1910*, Chelmsford 1974.

James Runciman, *Schools and Scholars*, London 1887.

Rex C. Russell, *A History of Schools and Education in Lindsey, Lincolnshire 1800–1902*, Parts 1–4, Lindsey County Council Education Committee 1965–1967.

David Salmon, ed., *The Practical Parts of Lancaster's Improvements and Bell's Experiment*, Cambridge 1932.

James Saunders, *Practical Hints for Pupil Teachers on Class Management*, Wolverhampton 1877.

Malcolm Seaborne and Sir Gyles Isham, *A Victorian Schoolmaster: John James Graves (1832–1903)*, Northamptonshire Record Society 1967.

Roger R. Sellman, *Devon Village Schools in the Nineteenth Century*, Newton Abbot 1967.

James J. Sheahan, *History and Topography of Buckinghamshire*, London 1862.

Pamela and Harold Silver, *The Education of the Poor*, London 1974.

Brian Simon, ed., *Education in Leicestershire 1540–1940*, Leicester 1968.

Brian Simon, *Education and the Labour Movement 1870–1920*, London 1965.

Joan Simon, *Education and Society in Tudor England*, Cambridge 1967.

Mary Smith, *Schoolmistress and Nonconformist, Autobiography of*, London 1892.

E. M. Sneyd-Kynnersley, *H.M.I.—Some Passages in the Life of One of H.M. Inspectors of Schools*, London 1908.

Richard A. Soloway, *Prelates and People*, London 1969.

P. F. Speed, *Learning and Teaching in Victorian Times: An Elementary School in 1888*, London 1964.

Francis W. Steer, ed., *The Memoirs of Gaius Carley*, Chichester 1964.

Gilbert Stone, *A History of Labour*, London 1921.

Lawrence Stone, ed., *The University in Society*, Vol. I, Princeton 1974.

F. Storr, ed., *The Life and Remains of the Rev. R. H. Quick*, Cambridge 1899.

Mary Sturt, *The Education of the People*, London 1967.

Gillian Sutherland, *Policy-Making in Elementary Education 1870–1895*, Oxford 1973.

Gillian Sutherland, *Elementary Education in the Nineteenth Century*, Historical Association Pamphlet G.76, 1971.

Gillian Sutherland, ed., *Matthew Arnold on Education*, London 1973.

A. J. Swinburne, *Memoirs of a School Inspector*, Saxmundham 1912.

Arthur J. Taylor, *Laissez-faire and State Intervention in Nineteenth-Century Britain*, London 1972.

William Taylor, *Society and the Education of Teachers*, London 1969.

Joan Thirsk, ed., *Land, Church and People*, Agricultural History Review Supplement 18, 1970.

Donna F. Thompson, *Professional Solidarity Among the Teachers of England*, New York 1927.

Flora Thompson, *Lark Rise to Candleford*, Oxford 1963 ed.

Flora Thompson, *Still Glides the Stream*, Oxford 1966 ed.

J. W. and Anne Tibble, ed., *The Prose of John Clare*, London 1951.

Asher Tropp, *The School Teachers*, London 1957.

Denis Tye, ed., *Boughton Monchelsea School*, privately printed n.d. c.1970.

John Weathers, *The Practical School Garden*, London 1912.

Fred. Aug. Wendeborn, *A View of England*, London 1791.

E. G. West, *Education and the State*, 2nd ed., London 1970.

E. G. West, *Education and the Industrial Revolution*, London 1975.

Winchester Diocesan Board of Education, *Sixth Report of*, Winchester 1846.

D. H. J. Zebedee, *Lincoln Diocesan Training College 1862–1962*, Lincoln 1962.

THESES

James A. Dewey, *An Examination of the Role of Church and State in the Development of Elementary Education in North Staffordshire Between 1870 and 1903*, Keele University Ph.D. 1971.

J. P. Dodd, *Rural Education in Shropshire in the Nineteenth Century*, Birmingham University M.A. 1958.

W. F. E. Gibbs, *The Development of Elementary Education in*

Dorset from the early Nineteenth Century to 1870, Southampton University M.A. 1960.

J. C. G. Lawson, *The Impact of the 1902 Education Act on the Church of England Schools in the Yateley Area*, Reading University M.Ed., 1975.

A. Shakoor, *The Training of Teachers in England and Wales 1900–1939*, University of Leicester Ph.D. 1964.

NOVELS

Charlotte Brontë, *Jane Eyre*, Thomas Nelson & Son, London ed. n.d.

Charles Dickens, *Hard Times*, London : Collins Pocket Classics ed. n.d.

George Eliot, *Adam Bede*, London Everyman's Library ed. 1906.

Thomas Hardy, *Jude the Obscure*, London 1957 paperback ed.

Thomas Hardy, *Under the Greenwood Tree*, London Papermac ed. 1968.

Thomas Hardy, *An Indiscretion in the Life of an Heiress*, London 1976.

Index